Race Man

Race Man

The Rise and Fall of the "Fighting Editor," John Mitchell Jr.

ANN FIELD ALEXANDER

University of Virginia Press

Charlottesville and London

UNIVERSITY OF VIRGINIA PRESS
© 2002 by the Rector and Visitors of the University of Virginia
All rights reserved
Printed in the United States of America on acid-free paper

First published 2002

1 3 5 7 9 8 6 4 2

LIBRARY OF CONGRESS CATALOGING-IN-PUBLICATION DATA
Alexander, Ann Field, 1946–
  Race Man : the rise and fall of the "fighting editor," John Mitchell Jr. / Ann Field Alexander.
      p. cm.
  ISBN 0-8139-2116-3 (cloth : alk. paper)
   1. Mitchell, John, 1863–1929. 2. African Americans—Biography. 3. African American
political activists—Biography. 4. African American politicians—Virginia—Richmond—
Biography. 5. Newspaper editors—Virginia—Richmond—Biography. 6. African American
newspapers—Virginia—Richmond—History. 7. African Americans—Civil rights—
Virginia—Richmond—History. 8. Civil rights movements—Virginia—Richmond—
History. 9. Richmond (Va.)—Race relations. 10. Richmond (Va.)—Biography. I. Title.
   E185.97.M64 A44 2002
   975.5'45100496073'0092—dc21

                                                                    2002002854

To the memory of
Ruth Webb Field
(1917–2001)

Contents

List of Illustrations

Preface

On June 6, 1996, the Richmond Chapter of the Society of Professional Journalists presented the George Mason Award to John Mitchell Jr., the editor of the *Richmond Planet*, in recognition of his contributions to freedom of the press. The ceremonies took place in a hotel in downtown Richmond, and a series of speakers rose to pay tribute to a man known to his contemporaries as the "Fighting Editor." They told of Mitchell's fearless crusade against mob violence in the 1880s and 1890s, his visits to jails and courthouses in rural Virginia, his defense of condemned prisoners, and his five-year term as president of the national Afro-American Press Association. Mitchell, born to slave parents in 1863, edited and published the *Planet* for forty-five years. He produced his first issue in 1884 not long after graduating from Richmond Normal and High School; he wrote his last editorial the week before he died in 1929 at the age of sixty-six.

What many in the hotel dining room may not have realized was that journalism was only one of Mitchell's many interests. A man of abundant energy, he placed himself at the center of nearly every public dispute of his day. He served for eight years (1888–96) on the Richmond city council as a representative of the predominantly black Jackson Ward. At a time when few black southerners held elective office, he lobbied for his constituents and persuaded the city to construct new black schools and an armory for the black militia. After disfranchisement ended his political career, he played a leading role in the economic revival that made Jackson Ward a center of black capitalism in the early twentieth century. In 1902 he founded the Mechanics' Savings Bank of Richmond, and for nearly twenty years he was the only African American to attend the annual meetings of the American Bankers Association. Although his editorials grew more circumspect in the twentieth century, he never made peace with segregation or disfranchisement. In 1904 he led a boycott of Richmond's newly segregated streetcars, in 1911 he protested the city's residential

segregation ordinance, and in 1921 he ran for governor of Virginia on what
whites termed a "lily-black" ticket. No matter what the issue, he always presented himself as a "race man," one of those public figures who promoted the
interests of African Americans on every front.

Biographers are notorious for identifying with their subjects, and as I listened to the accolades in 1996, I could not help but think how pleased the
Planet editor would have been by this belated recognition. In 1929, the year of
his death, African Americans entered white hotels in the South only as servants, and white journalists took scant notice of what black editors said or did.
The high point of the evening for me, however, was the chance to have dinner
with members of the Mitchell family. Although the *Planet* editor never married, his younger brother married and had children, and their children came
to the ceremonies. Tom Mitchell, the editor's grandnephew, had already given
me a four-hour walking tour of Jackson Ward, and now I had a chance to
meet some of his siblings. Their quick wit, ready laughter, and zest for life reminded me of *Planet* editorials. Although this book is not an authorized biography, I am grateful to family members who offered encouragement and
shared stories about their famous uncle.

The joke in my family is that I have worked on this project for as long as
John Mitchell edited the *Planet*. Although not precisely true, the charge is
closer to being true than I like to admit. I first came across Mitchell in the fall
of 1966 as a very young first-semester graduate student in history at Duke University. While retrieving a microfilm reel of the white *Richmond Dispatch*, I
happened upon a nearby reel of the *Richmond Planet*. Having grown up in the
segregated white South, I was only vaguely aware of the existence of black
newspapers and was both surprised and intrigued by what I saw. Mitchell's
crusade against lynching, his fight for civil rights, and his defiant approach to
race relations seemed oddly contemporary at a time when talk of black power
was making national headlines. Furthermore, like most white southerners of
my generation, I was woefully ignorant of life behind the veil of segregation.
As I made my way through reels of microfilm, I was introduced to a world that
seemed foreign and yet somehow familiar and commonplace. I read about
weddings and funerals, church suppers, high school commencements, fraternal meetings, dinner parties, and election campaigns. I soon realized that
everything about southern history looked different if one viewed events from
Mitchell's vantage point in Jackson Ward, rather than from Monument Avenue or Capitol Square.

Although the conventional wisdom at the time was that there were too few
sources for such a biography, I discovered that this was a misconception. In

the decades after the Civil War, black southerners produced an outpouring of books, magazines, and newspapers in which they pressed their campaign for full citizenship. If Mitchell was virtually unknown to white historians, he was something of a hero to his black contemporaries. I also discovered that no matter how invisible African Americans might be in the private manuscript collections of white politicians, they were far from invisible in public records. Throughout his career Mitchell paid taxes, bought and sold property, petitioned mayors and governors, testified in courtrooms, and defended himself against law suits. In the Richmond city hall, I found large boxes of unexamined records. I am grateful to Robert F. Durden, who supervised my dissertation at Duke and encouraged me to pursue this topic, and to August Meier, who read the dissertation and urged me to publish it.

By the time I finished my dissertation, the job market had soured, and I left the academic world in the early 1970s to raise a family and pursue other interests. My dissertation notes went into the attic. When I returned to college teaching in the fall of 1989 as a member of the faculty of Mary Baldwin College, I was surprised to discover that my dissertation was still being cited and that historians were talking about Mitchell, lynching, and the *Richmond Planet*. Although at first I was reluctant to resurrect an old topic, I finally resolved to catch up on the secondary literature, pursue some loose ends, and publish the biography.

By the 1990s the historical landscape had changed significantly, and it is perhaps helpful to indicate how this book differs from the earlier dissertation. In the first place, by the 1990s Booker T. Washington no longer loomed quite so large on the southern scene. As a graduate student I had tried to position Mitchell along a continuum that stretched from Washington to the more radical W. E. B. Du Bois, but I was never able to pin down his place precisely, and with good reason. Like most black southerners, Mitchell learned to improvise, and he pushed against the boundaries of discrimination whenever he saw an opening. The old dichotomy of protest and accommodation no longer seemed quite so helpful.

A second change was the new emphasis on gender. I am still baffled as to how years ago I could have discussed Mitchell's "manly protest" without seeing gender implications, but such is the case. Certainly no one writing at the end of the twentieth century would make this mistake. A generation of historians have explored the role of women in the African-American community and deepened our understanding of both gender and race. The stress in this book, however, is on black masculinity and the ways in which Mitchell projected manliness, as a newspaper editor, politician, and fraternal leader.

When writing my dissertation I stopped abruptly in 1905, even though Mitchell lived until 1929. Partly this was because the dissertation was already long enough, but there were other problems. Although I found it easy to sympathize with the courageous editor who battled lynching and ran for public office, I was much less comfortable with the middle-aged Mitchell, a well-to-do banker who owned a Stanley Steamer automobile and urged *Planet* readers to comport themselves with dignity and behave as ladies and gentlemen. Only gradually did I come to understand that his conservative inclinations were as revealing as his militancy and that they were part of the same essential picture. Mitchell saw himself as a Virginia gentleman, one of the "better sort" who deserved to be treated with respect.

The final problem with Mitchell's story, at least as I originally conceived it, was its unhappy ending. A year after he ran for governor in 1921, his bank failed, and he was convicted of fraud and sentenced to three years in the state penitentiary. The conviction was overturned on technicalities, but he spent his last years in poverty and died in some disgrace. I realized I had to make sense of his final decade. In the process I discovered the significance of the progressive "reforms" that opened the way for state regulation of black businesses in the early twentieth century. I am grateful to the State Corporation Commission in Richmond for granting me permission to use the records of the banking division. What I discovered helped me place his problems in a new and broader perspective.

While working on this book, I received three summer grants that supported my research: a Mellon Research Fellowship from the Virginia Historical Society, a Mednick Fellowship from the Virginia Foundation for Independent Colleges, and a grant from the Virginia Foundation for the Humanities and Public Policy. I am also grateful to Mary Baldwin College for the Karl H. and Patricia Menk Award in support of a yearlong sabbatical.

An earlier version of chapter 1 appeared as "Between Two Worlds: John Mitchell's Richmond Childhood," in *Virginia Cavalcade* 40 (Winter 1991): 120–31. © 1991 by The Library of Virginia. Used by permission. An earlier version of chapter 7 appeared as "No Officers, No Fight: The Sixth Virginia Volunteers in the Spanish-American War," in *Virginia Cavalcade* 47 (Autumn 1998): 178–91. © 1998 by The Library of Virginia. Used by permission.

Over the course of the past decade, family, friends, and fellow historians have read and critiqued the manuscript. August Meier resumed our conversation in 1990 as if days rather than decades had passed since we last talked; he reread the manuscript and offered his famously helpful suggestions. Others responded to my plea to a read a chapter or two, or perhaps the entire manuscript. Rather than try to rank their contributions in order of importance, I will list these readers alphabetically, with gratitude: Paul Beers, Fitzhugh Brundage, Roger Cunningham, Willard B. Gatewood, Susan Blair Green, Robert Grotjohn, Kenneth W. Keller, John Kern, Gregg Kimball, John T. Kneebone, Suzanne Lebsock, and Brent Tarter. My apologies to anyone I have forgotten. Although Elsa Barkley Brown did not read the manuscript and probably will disagree with some of my conclusions, I benefited from several spirited lunchtime discussions about Mitchell and gender. She taught me to look at old sources in new ways. At the University Press of Virginia, Richard K. Holway pushed me to make this a better book, while an anonymous reader asked perceptive and wise questions. I only wish I could have answered them all. Friends in Christiansburg volunteered their expertise in areas other than history. Nelson W. Ridinger and the late Charles E. Straub educated me about the challenges of running a small bank; the late Rod Crowgey used everyday language to explain complicated legal proceedings; Michael Piersol answered questions about life insurance; and Mike Payne explained the meaning of medical symptoms and death certificates.

In the Richmond area, librarians, archivists, and other professionals made my work easier. I wish to thank Charles Bethea of the Black History Museum and Cultural Center, Teresa Roane of the Valentine Richmond History Center, Bryan Green of the Virginia Historical Society, Tyler Potterfield with the city of Richmond, and Lucious Edwards of Virginia State University in Petersburg. Celia Suggs of the Maggie Walker National Historic Site accompanied me not once—but twice—to visit Mitchell's grave at Evergreen Cemetery. Dr. Francis Foster of Richmond, a retired dentist who knows more about African-American history than most historians, was amazingly helpful. He shared his knowledge of black Richmond, retrieved photographs, and took me to nursing homes to interview elderly residents who remembered Mitchell. He also reminded me, time and again, that what I was doing was important.

The staff at the Library of Virginia could not have been more supportive, and I am grateful to Sandy Treadway, Sara Bearss, Julie Campbell, Gregg Kimball, Kip Campbell, Errol Somay, and Elizabeth Gushee. Minor Weisiger retrieved every document that I asked for but also directed me to important sources that I did not know existed; my research is much fuller in several places because of his expertise. Brent Tarter and John Kneebone expressed interest in this project for more than a decade. They read and critiqued chapters and fragments of chapters, which I submitted to them out of order and in various states of readiness. They took me to lunch, laughed at my jokes, asked tough questions, and made my trips to Richmond much more fun.

It is customary to thank one's spouse "without whom this book could never have been written." In the case of Michael Van Cleave Alexander, my husband of more than thirty years, I can be unusually specific. In June 1981, near the end of an exhausting move into a new house, I suggested that we toss out my old dissertation notes that were moldering in the attic. He dismissed this idea as folly and personally carried the boxes to the waiting truck. For this, and countless acts of kindness and love, I am grateful. Time and again he set aside his own scholarly work to read and reflect upon mine.

Watching our sons grow up was always more interesting than writing history, and Mike and Peter Alexander are partly responsible for this book being such a "mature" work of scholarship. They are now accomplished, handsome young men, and I am enormously proud of them both. My aunt, Dr. Bailey Webb, gave me a place to live while I was in graduate school and continued to ask about the book long after others had forgotten it. Finally, I owe a profound debt of gratitude to my parents, Art and Ruth Field. This book is dedicated to the memory of my mother, who died April 17, 2001, and who would have enjoyed distributing copies to all her friends.

Race Man

CHAPTER ONE

The Making of a "Colored Gentleman"

As a child John Mitchell worked as a servant in the home of James Lyons, a white attorney who had owned his parents before the Civil War. During the 1870s Lyons lived in one of Richmond's finest houses, a Greek Revival mansion on Grace Street about three blocks west of Capitol Square. One morning Mitchell answered the doorbell and discovered a black man standing before him. The man asked to speak to Lyons, so Mitchell ran to fetch his employer. When he told Lyons that a "colored gentleman" was waiting to see him, Lyons grew agitated. There was no such thing as a "colored gentleman," he told the boy. The title of gentleman was reserved for white men only. Years later when he was editor of the *Richmond Planet*, Mitchell remembered the rebuke and recalled why he had identified the visitor as a "colored gentleman." His mother had taught him that he himself would grow up to be a gentleman, he said. She had "different ideas from . . . the 'blue blood' on that score." He described this encounter with Lyons as a pivotal event of his childhood, one of those moments when obscure matters became clear.[1]

Mitchell's image of himself as a boy and his assumptions about what sort of adult he would become were molded by the circumstances of his childhood. He was born on July 11, 1863, at Laburnum, the suburban estate of James Lyons in Henrico County on the northern outskirts of Richmond. His parents were house servants. His father, John Mitchell Sr., was Lyons's coachman, while his mother, Rebecca Mitchell, worked as a seamstress. Little is known of their background, save that Rebecca had once belonged to the Pollards, a family living in nearby Hanover County, but was purchased by Lyons sometime before the Civil War. Lyons thought she was born in 1836 and her husband John in 1841, but they assumed themselves closer to the same age, both born about 1835. Probably neither was certain of a birthday. Rebecca Mitchell gave birth to seven children, but only two survived infancy. The first to live was named for his father and called Johnny. A second son, Thomas William Mitchell, or Tom, was born on March 9, 1868.[2]

As an adult John Mitchell Jr. liked to remind white Richmonders that he had been "born at Laburnum." It was a way of connecting himself to the Old South and to images of wealth and power. The big house at Laburnum might easily have served as the setting for an antebellum novel. It had a broad veranda, tall white columns, and a wide expanse of lawn. Shade trees surrounded the house, and beyond the lawn were gardens, orchards, stables, and outbuildings. John S. Wise, the son of Governor Henry A. Wise, visited Laburnum often as a child, and he remembered the estate as richly appointed, with furniture imported from Europe, massive silver, shelves lined with books, elaborate carriages, thoroughbred horses, and legions of servants. Varina Davis, the wife of Jefferson Davis, attended parties at Laburnum during the Civil War, and she thought "a finer example of a high-bred Virginia household could not have been found." The 160-acre estate was about a mile and a half beyond the Richmond city limits, just off the Brook Turnpike, the main road leading north toward Washington, D.C.[3]

James Lyons, the master of Laburnum, was himself the epitome of the Virginia gentleman. Born in Hanover County in 1801, he was the son of a physician and the grandson of a superior court judge. After attending the College of William and Mary, he set up a law practice in Richmond and entered politics, winning election to the General Assembly in 1840 as a Whig, but he was best known as a friend and host to politicians. Among his guests during the antebellum years were Henry Clay, Daniel Webster, and various members of the French and English nobility. Descriptions of Lyons are so effusive as to border on caricature. According to contemporaries he was "the handsomest man of his day." He had flawless manners and carried himself with the "conscious air of a superior and a leader." He was much in demand as a public speaker and had "great presence and marked personal beauty."[4]

Lyons was also habitually in debt, a matter of no small importance to slaves who feared the breakup of families that could result from white extravagance. Fortunately for his finances, he married well. His wife, Imogene Penn Lyons, was from a wealthy New Orleans family whose money helped support their lavish lifestyle. According to the 1860 census, he owned twenty-seven slaves, ten of whom were children. He did some farming at Laburnum, growing wheat and corn and raising livestock. Like other members of his social class, he assumed that his slaves were privileged men and women. In 1861 he described slavery as a "blessing" and quoted with approval the English philosopher Edmund Burke: "Slaves are often much attached to their masters. . . . It is sometimes as hard to persuade slaves to be free as it is to compel free men to be slaves."[5]

Lyons was an ardent secessionist, and with the outbreak of the Civil War, he opened his home to Confederate officials. A neighbor recalled meeting Jefferson Davis and members of his staff and cabinet at Laburnum, as well as many of the leading Confederate generals. When former president John Tyler died in 1862, Lyons was elected to the Confederate Congress to take his vacant seat. The Southern cause must have seemed invincible to John and Rebecca Mitchell, at least during the first years of the war. In October 1862 their master made an impassioned speech in the Confederate Congress attacking Lincoln's proposed Emancipation Proclamation, calling it "the most inhuman and atrocious . . . [proclamation] that was ever issued by any man or power professing to be civilized." He fulminated against this attempt "to incite servile insurrection against us" and proposed draconian measures against slaves who revolted.[6]

By the time Johnny Mitchell was born, in July 1863, the effects of the war were beginning to show at Laburnum. Almost within sight of the house were earthen fortifications built to protect the Confederate capital from Union troops. On three occasions Lyons was required to send a male slave to labor on the defenses. Deserting soldiers and runaway slaves roamed the nearby woods, causing him to worry about his family's safety. A few days before the boy's birth, he reported to the police that someone had broken into his stable and stolen several harnesses. On the occasion of Dahlgren's raid on Richmond, on March 1, 1864, shells landed on his lawn. Although no damage was done, Lyons rushed to the War Department to report that the enemy was bombarding his house.[7]

In March 1864 Lyons learned the possible consequences of slave infidelity. Early that year one of his house servants, William, aged seventeen, the younger brother of John Mitchell Sr., escaped. Lyons was aggravated by the loss of William, but much of his ire was soon directed against Wilson, a mulatto who belonged to a neighbor. Wilson was married to one of Lyons's slaves and lived at Laburnum with his wife and children. Lyons at first believed him "an honest, worthy Negro" and was glad to have him about, but after William disappeared his opinion of him changed. Wilson admitted that he knew where William was hiding but would not reveal his whereabouts. Lyons then concluded that Wilson's character was "very bad." He blamed him for a series of thefts at Laburnum and accused him of inciting his slaves to escape. Unable to punish a neighbor's bondsman, he had the police arrest Wilson on the charge of "conniving at the escape from his owner of William, the property of James Lyons."[8]

At a hearing in the mayor's court in Richmond on February 28, 1864, Lyons laid out his charges against Wilson. Losing his temper, he warned that "if the negro . . . ever put his foot upon his plantation again he would administer to him his breakfast or dinner in the shape of a load of buckshot." Wilson was remanded to the hustings court for trial, but the judge found insufficient evidence to proceed and on the afternoon of March 15 ordered his release from jail.[9]

That night shortly after midnight someone set fire to a large pile of wood shavings that had been scattered beneath the foundations of the house at Laburnum. Wilson was the presumed arsonist, although no proof of his guilt was offered. The flames spread quickly, eating their way into the first floor before being detected. According to newspaper accounts, "Every room in the house was filled with smoke before anyone was aroused." Lyons and his wife "on awakening . . . had barely time to escape in their night dresses." Their grown daughter was nearly overcome by smoke as she stumbled out. Trying to save whatever he could, Lyons returned to the burning building, suffered a bad fall, and knocked out several teeth. The family sounded alarms and roused the slaves, but there was no way to extinguish the fire.[10]

Mary Chesnut, the Civil War diarist, told of her visit to Laburnum several days later: "Mrs. [Jefferson] Davis took me to drive with her. We went to Laburnum to inquire of the Lyons's welfare since the fire. It was really pitiful. Only a few days before, we had been there . . . and found them all taking tea under those beautiful shade trees. And now—smoke and ashes—nothing more." Chesnut said they did not get out of the carriage because crowds of people were already there. "They lost everything," she said. "Library filled with books and papers—&c. &c. Even Mrs. Lyons's diamonds." She assumed the fire was the work of an arsonist: "A few weeks before, they accused a Negro of theft." Also lost to the flames was a wooden tenement where slaves lived.[11] Johnny Mitchell was less than a year old, but surely he later heard stories of the fire and thus learned firsthand that not all slaves were loyal and trustworthy during the Civil War.

After the fire Lyons moved his family into a cottage on the property that had escaped the flames. Scarcely a month later Imogene Lyons wrote a friend that "you would really be surprised to see how bright & comfortable the old cottage looks." She acknowledged that Laburnum would never be the same, but she said the family remained cheerful and had even managed to entertain Jefferson and Varina Davis for dinner. In a rare surviving reference to one of her slaves, she noted that she had saved "two old silks" from the fire and Rebecca had washed them in "potatoe water" and had made them into "quite decent" dresses.[12]

A year later Union troops entered Richmond, and the city surrendered. From behind the barred windows of Lumpkin's slave jail came this song:

> Slavery chains done broke at last!
> Broke at last! Broke at last!
> Slavery chains done broke at last!
> Gonna praise God till I die!

Not long afterward Johnny Mitchell, still a toddler, saw Union troops for the first time and being too young to understand their purpose was terrified. The changes also unsettled James Lyons. At a public meeting in August 1865, he made a statement some observers thought unwise. He said the Yankees had destroyed slavery and he "wished to God" they would take all the black people as well.[13]

As so often happened, Lyons gradually grew accustomed to the new order, and his fortunes rebounded. After the war his father-in-law purchased for them an elegant town house, the Stanard house on Grace Street. The three-story Greek Revival mansion, built in 1839, had enormous rooms with frescoed ceilings and hand-carved mantels of Italian marble. The house was so large that after Lyons's death it served as headquarters for an exclusive men's club for white Richmonders. "When two years of age," the *Planet* editor later wrote, "I was brought to Richmond and lived at the residence of Attorney James Lyons, which place is now known as the Westmoreland Club."[14]

As the son of domestic servants, Johnny Mitchell observed on Grace Street a style of life that would have dazzled all but a few whites. One of his earliest memories was of the 1867 visit of Jefferson Davis, who had come back to Richmond for his treason trial and retained Lyons as one of his attorneys. Unmindful of greater issues, the four-year-old Mitchell was preoccupied with stories that Davis had a glass eye. As he grew older, the boy was put to work. He learned to greet guests at the door, pour their wine, and wait on them at the dinner table. When he was ten years old, he became Lyons's carriage boy. In what was surely an autobiographical note, he reminded whites of the ease with which domestic servants learned the ways of the white aristocracy: "The father as a butler or coachman, and the mother as a nurse or chambermaid, became acquainted with all the rules of polite society."[15]

It would be interesting to know what Mitchell actually thought of his former master. He seldom mentioned Lyons and then only to affirm that he had indeed worked as a servant for the famous attorney. He did once call him a "typical Southerner," probably not a compliment. But the two must have come to know each other well. As a teenager Mitchell often drove the aging attorney out to the Laburnum estate. When the weather was mild, Lyons liked to spend his mornings at Laburnum, tending his garden and puttering about the grounds before returning to his law office for an afternoon of work. On the way back and forth from Laburnum, he read legal papers. The former slave and former master must have occasionally chatted, perhaps at times discussing the fire that destroyed the original house. That Lyons had an influence on the child seems a safe enough assumption, and while it may be true that no man is a hero to his valet, this aristocratic old gentleman, who so impressed white Virginians, left his mark on John Mitchell. Like his former master, Mitchell was long remembered for his distinguished appearance, his courtly manners, and his aristocratic bearing.[16]

The first tangible evidence of Mitchell's existence, aside from census data, comes from 1873, when at the age of nine he deposited some of his earnings in the Richmond branch of the Freedman's Savings Bank. The bank was chartered by Congress in 1865 to encourage thrift among ex-slaves. In Richmond children as young as six made their way to the office on Tenth Street to make deposits. The clerk inscribed his name as "Johney Mitchell," an unorthodox spelling that someone corrected to read Johnny Mitchell. He gave his birthplace as the "Turnpike Road" (a reference to Laburnum) and his residence at "6th and Gray [Grace] Sts" (the home of James Lyons). He reported the names of his father, mother, and four-year-old brother Thomas. His occupation was to "work for Mr. Lyon[s]." The bank clerk left space at the bottom of the application form for him to make his mark, but he wrote his name in careful script and spelled it correctly: "Johnny Mitchell." Finally, under "complexion" appear words that surprise: he was "very light."[17]

Northern visitors to Richmond sometimes referred to Mitchell as a mulatto, but his skin was dark enough to cause no confusion about his race. His features revealed his African descent, and he always kept his hair shaved close to his head. As he later joked in a *Planet* editorial, "We wouldn't be white if we could, and we couldn't if we would." Shades of skin color were difficult for whites to describe, however, and almost invariably they saw color through a filter of class. At the age of nine he may have volunteered (helpfully) that he was very light, or perhaps a clerk saw before him a handsome, well-dressed child with money in his pocket and judged him lighter than he was.[18]

As an adult Mitchell liked to watch black children at play, and he reasoned that their exuberance and self-confidence came from having never known slavery. He felt certain that the next generation would grow up without the psychological shackles that restricted some older blacks. He once described an imaginary child at play. Perhaps he was thinking of himself as a boy, or at least of how he remembered himself. "How black he is!" he wrote. "See how he struts up and down the street. Hear his merry laugh! . . . Watch him scamper away! Does he know he is inferior to white people? Of course not."[19] Obviously other influences were contributing to his self-confidence beyond what he learned from James Lyons.

Mitchell always gave his mother credit for much of his success, and she served as an essential counterbalance to the white attorney. Lyons thought carriage boys had no need for an education, but when Johnny was quite young, she taught him to read and write. She drilled him in the "a-b abs, e-b ebs, and other monosyllabic beginnings." How she had learned to read in such formal fashion is unclear, but Mitchell was convinced that slave literacy on rural plantations was much higher than whites imagined: "The slave child, being a boon companion to the white one, learned when the lessons were to be studied." He was at first an indifferent student, preferring play to study, but whenever his attention wandered too far from his studies, he could expect "the full force of her hand on his young face to give him a better appreciation of his lessons." She was also fastidious about his appearance. Sometimes she pulled a fine-toothed comb through his hair with such enthusiasm that he screamed out in protest.[20]

Rebecca Mitchell remained a strong influence on her son until 1913 when she died after her long cotton skirt caught fire from a woodstove in her kitchen. She was nearly eighty years old at the time of her death, and the white press reported the sad demise of an "old mammy." A decade later the United Daughters of the Confederacy proposed erecting a monument to honor the antebellum black mammy, an idea that both intrigued and bemused the *Planet* editor. He said that many white southerners seemed confused in their recollections. According to him black mammies were often not black but light-skinned; they were not servile in demeanor but proud, dignified, and forthright; they were not the recipients of white culture but its purveyors, imposing order and discipline on entire households; they were firm with their white charges but even more resolute "in teaching the same lessons" to their own children. Reading between the lines, one can guess he was remembering his mother. He erected a monument of an angel at her grave and included an inscription, "A Son's Tribute," that suggests that Rebecca Mitchell was a woman of strong character and moral rectitude. It is an oddly stern inscription for a gravestone and focuses more on the survivor than on the deceased: "She

Hated Deceit and Despised Hypocrisy. Her Christian Training and Upright Conduct Made Me All That I Am and All That I Hope to Be."[21]

The role that the boy's father played in the life of the family is less clear, although there are indications that John Mitchell Sr. had as forceful a personality as his wife. In the aftermath of the Civil War, he had an altercation with Lyons that ruptured their relationship and resulted in the two men facing off in a Richmond courtroom. The affair was reminiscent of Lyons's earlier conflict with Wilson, although the outcome from Lyons's perspective was happier.

The episode began on the night of December 7, 1865, when someone broke into Lyons's stable and stole a pair of horses. Several days later word reached Richmond that the prize horses, valued at $500 each, had been offered for sale in Petersburg. Lyons's kinsman, Judge William Henry Lyons, decided to investigate and set out in pursuit. He spent the day in Petersburg and after persistent questioning discovered the horses in the possession of a black man, Albert Wallace. He had Wallace arrested and taken into custody and arranged for the return of the animals to Richmond. He reached home late that evening "well satisfied with his exploit in the detective line."[22]

James Lyons was glad to have his horses back but was sure the theft was part of a larger plot. He had seven men arrested, including John Mitchell Sr. and John's younger brother William, both of whom he had seen near the stable on the night of the theft. Their trial took place on December 27, 1865, in the provost court, established in Richmond during the military phase of Reconstruction to handle cases involving ex-slaves. The provost court usually dealt with minor infractions, which were resolved quickly, but the hearing of the "seven negroes charged with stealing Mr. Lyons's horses" took nearly all day. A reporter for the *Dispatch* believed the defendants guilty but noted that in gathering evidence it had been necessary, as he so carefully phrased it, "to inflict an amount of corporal punishment upon one of the seven."[23]

The next day John and Thomas Mitchell were acquitted and released. What happened to the other defendants is unknown, but the Mitchell brothers were clearly furious at their former master. Unwilling to let the matter rest, they filed suit against Lyons, charging him with false imprisonment. They protested that they had been confined to the city jail for twenty-three days for no cause. Lyons was ordered to appear before the Freedmen's Bureau court, but General Alfred H. Terry, military commander of the Department of Virginia, intervened and asked that the suit be dropped. Describing the Mitchells' complaint as "vexatious and malicious," Terry contended that Lyons had not acted improperly and that his suspicions were reasonable. The brothers then appealed to General Orlando Brown of the Freedmen's Bureau, but Brown declined to become involved, and the matter evidently died.[24] One fact is obvious: less than a year after the war, John Mitchell Sr. had shed all vestiges of servility and was prepared to confront his former master—one of the state's leading lawyers—in the courtroom. The *Planet* editor may have owed his success to his mother, but he seems to have inherited at least some of his courage and pluck from his father.

According to the 1870 census, John Mitchell Sr. was not living with his wife and two sons, and probably he never worked for Lyons after the horse-stealing incident. The 1880 census again listed him with his family, but this time his occupation is described as railroad hand. By then the Mitchells had moved out of Lyons's home and were living in a tenement on North Adams Street, in a building shared by eight black families. White Richmonders were sometimes puzzled by their servants' preference for separate housing. "Before the war millions of negroes slept under the same roof with the whites," wrote one perplexed Richmonder. "Now a house-girl getting $6.00 a month will give $1.50 of it for an attic-room away from an employer."[25]

The senior John Mitchell left Richmond sometime after 1880 to work for the railroads in Illinois, but he remained in touch with his children. The *Planet* editor visited him in Chicago on at least three occasions during the 1890s. In 1893, for example, father and son toured the Columbian Exposition and attended Buffalo Bill's Wild West Show.[26] Although Mitchell seldom spoke of his absent father, at least in print, he paid him a lifelong tribute: he always signed him name "John Mitchell Jr." and thus affirmed his connection to the Laburnum coachman.

Family influences help explain Mitchell's transformation from carriage boy to "Fighting Editor." Nearly as significant were events taking place outside the home. During Reconstruction the black community was in ferment as former slaves tested the meaning of freedom. They crowded into schools and churches, cast their first votes at the ballot box, negotiated labor contracts, and marched in Emancipation Day parades. It was a time of rapid and exhilarating social change. Mitchell was always attracted to the wealth and power of Grace Street, but the pull of the black community proved much stronger.[27]

Of all the institutions that influenced him, probably the most important was the First African Baptist Church, where he worshiped as a child. The church was founded not long after the American Revolution. At first white and black Baptists met in the same building, but when the white members erected a new church in 1841, they permitted the much larger black congregation to purchase the old building on Broad Street. Richmond was the home of a well-to-do free black community, and the members of First African—slave and free—enjoyed considerable autonomy. They elected their own deacons, conducted church trials, and disciplined wayward members."[28]

The church's minister after 1841 was Robert Ryland, a white Baptist appointed by the mother church. Ryland never challenged slavery outright but was sympathetic to the needs of his congregation, at least by the standards of his day. "I treat the colored people from the pulpit," he wrote, "exactly as I would a white congregation, i.e., with the greatest possible respect." He gave only oral instruction and thus abided by the letter of the law, but in one matter he violated its spirit. Because of memories of Nat Turner, blacks were not allowed to preach in church. "As a sort of recompense for this slight," he called on the deacons "to *pray* several times at each religious service."[29]

After Emancipation, Ryland resigned his position on the assumption that the congregation would prefer a black minister. In 1867 Rev. James H. Holmes became pastor. A former slave and longtime member of First African, Holmes had been separated from his wife and two children in 1848 and sold south to New Orleans. Returned to Richmond in 1852 by another master, he went to work in the tobacco factories and purchased his freedom in 1862 by paying his master $1,800 in Confederate currency. After the war he attended Richmond Theological Seminary (later Virginia Union University) but regretted that he was never able to "slip off and go north to college." An energetic pastor and respected community leader, he served the church—known after the war as First Church—until his death in 1900.[30]

For a boy who spent much of his time taking orders from James Lyons, First Church was no doubt an inspiring place. The congregation was the largest in Richmond, black or white. Indeed, during the 1870s it was reputed to be the largest Protestant church in the United States. The members prided themselves on the church's size and on the decorum of the services. According to one visitor, the only difference between First Church and the city's white Baptist churches was that the black congregation sang the hymns with unusual fervor and then during the last hymn members began shaking hands and continued to sing as they left the building. Another visitor was moved by the spiritual intensity of the preaching and the powerful use of language. He said he heard at First Church "some of the finest word paintings that ever fell from human lips." Known as a silk-stocking church, First Church was too large to be truly exclusive, but among its members were many of the city's most prominent black families.[31]

While sitting in the pews of First Church, Mitchell heard the familiar stories from the Bible. As *Planet* editor he alluded to Daniel, Moses, Joshua, and Job as if they were friends. He took his faith seriously and derived from Scripture the sure conviction that God would one day "wipe away the tears from our eyes." He quoted from the Old Testament more often than from the New and almost never from the Epistles of St. Paul, where there were admonitions about servants obeying their masters. Like other members of First Church, he was not immune to the attractions of a more emotional form of worship. As one member explained, "When a revival was in full sway the bars were let down and no one was restricted as to manner of expression." During one such revival, in June 1878, the fourteen-year-old Mitchell professed religion and was baptized by Holmes. He said that cold chills ran through his frame as he heard the moans of the suffering Christians, the "appeals made to Daniel's God," and the complaints sent up to the throne of Grace.[32]

Another Baptist minister who had an influence on Mitchell was Anthony Binga Jr., the son of a black abolitionist who was born and educated in Canada. Binga at first hoped to become a physician but was converted to Christianity and came to Richmond in 1870 to work among the freed people. He opened a private school, which Mitchell attended during the term 1871–72. Black parents who could afford private schools for their children often chose them over public schools because they thought them academically stronger and they wanted their children to study with black teachers.[33]

A year later Binga moved to neighboring Manchester, where he began a long tenure as pastor of that town's First Baptist Church and also served as an elementary school principal. After his departure Mitchell enrolled at Navy Hill School, one of the city's four public schools for black children and the one parents generally considered the best. Navy Hill was the only public school in Richmond that employed black teachers. The school was housed in two large frame buildings at the corner of Sixth and Duval Streets. The principal was Mary Elizabeth Knowles, a white woman from Worcester, Massachusetts, who claimed abolitionist descent. Her father had spoken out strongly against slavery, and after the war she left her family and friends to come south to teach. She presided over nearly four hundred students and a faculty of nine black teachers at Navy Hill. The "exemplary conduct" of Ann F. Smith, Mitchell's teacher when he was eleven years old, "elicited the warmest praise . . . from all the school officials of the city." His teacher the next year was O. M. Steward, the founder in 1877 of the city's first black newspaper, the *Virginia Star*. Mitchell did well at Navy Hill, winning prizes each June for scholarship and attendance.[34]

When he was thirteen Mitchell graduated from Navy Hill and was admitted to the Richmond Normal and High School, a school founded by the Freedmen's Bureau in 1867 to train black teachers. The principal was Ralza M.

Manly, a white Methodist clergyman from Vermont who served during the Civil War as chaplain of the 1st U.S. Colored Cavalry. While stationed at Fort Monroe, Manly established schools for illiterate soldiers, who he insisted should be treated not as children but as "*men* and the best specimens of the colored race." After the war he was named superintendent of education for the Freedmen's Bureau in Virginia. He had a hand in establishing schools throughout the state but always pinned his greatest hopes on Richmond Normal. The school would educate teachers for the public schools and in the process "elevate the aspirations of the colored youth of the city."[35]

Manly determined to make the school a showplace and with money supplied by the Freedmen's Bureau bought a lot on Twelfth Street in downtown Richmond on a hill overlooking Shockoe ravine. When completed in 1867, the two-story brick building with a bell tower was the city's most imposing schoolhouse. Manly installed the best modern school furniture, set up a science laboratory, and assembled a library of more than five hundred books. The teachers, whose salaries were paid by northern missionary societies, were white women recruited from the North. They taught Latin, German, French, algebra, science, history, geography, cartography, music, and government. They also taught "non-sectarian" religion, by which they meant the Ten Commandments, Lord's Prayer, and Apostles' Creed. Like northern teachers throughout the South, they ascribed to a strict Victorian code of conduct and stressed the importance of service.[36]

White Richmonders were at first suspicious of this New England enclave, where former slaves could be found conjugating Latin verbs and solving algebraic equations. They were startled to see "well-nigh grown negro men and women hastening through the streets, carrying great packages of books." But white fears sometimes subsided in the face of the students' accomplishments. When the school graduated its first class in 1873, the *Richmond Dispatch,* no friend of the black race, conceded that there was "no colored school of higher grade than this in the State, and we venture to assert that there is no school where more pains are taken with instruction than this." When northern money began to grow scarce in the mid-1870s, Manly persuaded the city to accept the building as a gift and incorporate Richmond Normal into the public school system. Although the school was never again adequately funded, Richmond at least had a public high school for black youths at a time when most southern cities did not.[37]

Mitchell attended Richmond Normal for five years, from 1876 until his graduation in 1881. He had a quick and retentive mind and finished his first year with top honors, winning a silver medal for having the highest scholastic record in a class of thirty students. The next year at the age of fourteen he was accepted into the preparatory division. Admission requirements included "the ability to write a fair hand, to read and spell with tolerable fluency, to pass a good examination in the whole of geography and in the primary grammar, and to be found thoroughly proficient in arithmetic." Again that year he excelled, winning a medal for scholarship and another for a map he drew of Africa. By his final year he had accumulated quite a collection of medals, including several for elocution. His talents as an artist, however, caused the most comment. With ordinary lead pencils he drew maps and pictures that were said to resemble steel engravings. During the Christmas holidays of his senior year, he labored over a special map of Virginia, which he decorated with an elaborate border and historical illustrations.[38]

At Richmond Normal, Mitchell received a classical education patterned on the New England model. He learned French and Latin, acquired an appreciation for history, and mastered the rudiments of science. He was never apologetic about his lack of a college degree, understanding that he was better educated than most Virginians of his day. At class reunions he and other graduates gathered to acknowledge their debt to the school. At one reunion D. Webster Davis read a poem in which he recalled the nervousness he felt when asked to recite:

> As I stand up here reading I'm quaking with fear,
> For I think 'tis Miss Stratton, whose footsteps I hear;
> Or dear Mr. Manly, or sainted Miss Knowles,
> Come tripping behind me and ready to scold.

Davis remembered with affection Miss Stratton, Miss Patterson, Miss Hadley, and Mr. Manly: "They were my ideals of what men and women should be."[39]

Another graduate, Wendell P. Dabney, the son of caterer John Dabney and a member of the class of 1883, remembered most vividly the "battles fought between the white boys of Central School and the black boys of the Normal." The white high school was only a block away, in the former Confederate White House. Dabney was convinced that there was no racial enmity between the students, that the fistfights and rock throwing took place in a spirit of fun, but school officials were not so sure: "The afternoon scraps . . . were eagerly looked forward to until finally the school authorities made a law that the colored pupils should use one side of the street, the whites the other." Dabney believed that these adolescent battles had important consequences: "In Richmond white boys and colored boys had played together and fought together and therefore knew what each other would do."[40]

The first surviving photograph of Mitchell was taken not long after he graduated from Richmond Normal. It shows a handsome young man, impeccably dressed in a new suit, staring solemnly into the camera. This was a formal portrait, and there was no hint of a smile. He was by this time nearly full grown, over 5'10", lean and physically fit, although his face was still boyish. Friends would later notice that he walked proudly, with a "sort of free arrogance and independence." The camera missed his most distinctive feature: he had "flashing eyes" that could light up with laughter or turn cold and harsh.[41]

On the night of June 14, 1881, a crowd gathered at the Second Baptist Church to watch the graduation exercises of Richmond Normal. They applauded proudly as Mitchell, a few weeks short of his eighteenth birthday, delivered the valedictory address. He had won top honors every year since his earliest days at Navy Hill. When his speech was over, A. M. Keiley, the white master of ceremonies and a former mayor of the city, awarded him a special gold medal for his map of Virginia, telling the audience it was the "best production ever executed by any pupil, white or black, in the State."[42] One would like to imagine that James and Imogene Lyons attended the ceremonies, but they probably spent the evening at home. James Lyons, now eighty years old and in ill health, had sold their town house to the Westmoreland Club and retired with his wife to the cottage at Laburnum.

When Mitchell read the account of his graduation on the front page of the *Dispatch*, he must have understood that he had been an exceptionally fortunate young man. Spared the poverty of the sharecropper's cabin, he had grown up amid the wealth of Grace Street. As a domestic servant he learned "all the rules of polite society," and he was never intimidated by well-to-do whites. As a child he was also nurtured and protected by adults who took seriously the promise of Reconstruction. James H. Holmes, Anthony Binga Jr., Ralza M. Manly, Elizabeth Knowles, and O. M. Steward, among others, contributed to his self-confidence and enlarged his horizons. From his mother, Rebecca Mitchell, he learned there were no barriers he could not surmount. His father's influence is harder to document, but in those endless admonitions in the *Planet* about making a "manly" protest, one can probably hear an echo of his father's voice. In yet another important way he had been fortunate. Had he been born twenty years earlier, he might easily have spent his eighteenth birthday as a slave, driving a carriage around his master's plantation. But the fire that destroyed the house at Laburnum opened a new era, and John Mitchell Jr. was in truth a "colored gentleman."

CHAPTER TWO

"Colored Teachers for Colored Schools"

After his graduation from Richmond Normal in 1881, Mitchell taught for three years in the public schools of Virginia. These were important, formative years. His coming of age coincided with a period of intense political activity, and as a teacher he found himself at the center of disputes that altered the course of Virginia politics and changed the way blacks and whites viewed race relations. It was also a period of rapid development for him personally. He lived away from home for the first time, supervised his first classroom, and wrote his first newspaper column. By the time his career as a teacher was over, he had emerged as an ambitious and highly articulate young man, someone to be reckoned with in the black community.

Mitchell's decision to become a teacher probably came easily. He had taught in a model classroom at Richmond Normal and had absorbed from Elizabeth Knowles and R. M. Manly the idea that education was the lever that would up-lift the race. Teaching was also a relatively well-paid profession given the lack of other employment opportunities. Richmond teachers—black and white—earned $42 a month in 1881, at a time when live-in servants had to settle for as little as a dollar or two a week.[1]

When he applied for a teaching position, however, he became embroiled in a controversy that festered in Richmond for decades and perplexed outside observers. "In one or two Southern cities," wrote George Washington Cable in 1884, "the teachers in the colored public schools must be white. In certain others they must be colored; and in still others they may be either." When Mitchell graduated from high school, Richmond belonged in this last category. Although black teachers were assigned to Navy Hill School, the teachers in the other black grammar schools (Valley, Baker, and Leigh) were white, as were all the principals, and only whites were allowed teach at Richmond Normal, a school run by the city for the express purpose of training teachers. "There was no stigma attached to the whites teaching in the Negro schools," explained a later historian. On the contrary, white teachers showed a stubborn devotion to the schools of both races. By the time Mitchell graduated, Richmond had 14 black teachers and 129 white teachers; of the 129 whites, 35 taught in black schools.[2]

The whites who taught in Richmond's black schools were by the 1880s seldom the "Yankee schoolmarms" who had been so familiar during Reconstruction, although a few New Englanders like Manly and Knowles remained. More often they were native-born whites eager for work. Some of them were ineffectual in the classroom and "had not the best interests of the race at heart." A poem by O. M. Steward poked fun at one white teacher, an especially unpopular man who taught at Baker School:

> I am a white man of the whites.
> My scholars they are black.
> I don't believe in civil rights,
> But money I do lack.
>
> I tried my luck for Central School,
> But I could not succeed.
> They said they did not want a fool
> To teach white boys to read.

Black parents worried that even the best white teachers stifled the ambitions of their children, while the worst were lazy and incompetent.[3]

In contrast, the black men and women who taught at Navy Hill were a superbly gifted group, reflecting in part the lack of other employment options. Several were on the thresholds of truly distinguished careers. James H. Hayes, for example, would study law at Howard University and graduate first in his class in 1885. An accomplished orator, he was one of the few southern blacks in the twentieth century to challenge the accommodationist philosophy of Booker T. Washington. Another teacher, James Hugo Johnston Sr., left Navy Hill in 1887 to assume the presidency of Virginia Normal and Collegiate Institute in Petersburg (later Virginia State University), a position he held until his death in 1914. Daniel Barclay Williams also joined the Petersburg faculty in the 1880s. He had attended Brown University and could read French, German, Hebrew, Latin, and Greek. D. Webster Davis published several volumes of poetry, and after his death in 1913, four public schools in Virginia were named in his honor. Rosa Dixon Bowser would play a leading role in the women's club movement, and the reading circles she established in the mid-1880s became the nucleus of the Virginia State Teachers Association. This vast array of talent explains why black parents considered Navy Hill the strongest of the city schools. On its faculty were the black community's best and brightest young people.[4]

While Mitchell was still a student at Richmond Normal, black parents throughout Virginia began to demand that teachers of their own race be hired in the schools. The movement reflected growing racial confidence and a desire on the part of parents to assume greater control of their children's education. Parents wanted their sons and daughters to "receive a liberal education and know they are the equals of all other people." In Petersburg students boycotted the schools rather than be taught by whites, and in Farmville, in Southside Virginia, parents kept their children at home. "Our people have 'race pride,'" wrote one father, "and will not be proscribed by these Bourbons." In Fredericksburg parents petitioned the school board to appoint teachers who would treat their children with respect, mingle freely with them in the churches, speak to them on the sidewalks, and not assume themselves superior.[5]

The demand for black teachers also found expression in Richmond. In July 1880 a group of taxpayers petitioned the school board to assign black teachers to all black schools. They buttressed their plea with statistics taken from published school reports. According to the board's own records, the attendance rates at Navy Hill were the highest in all Richmond, whether black or white. Attendance records were a key indicator of parental support at a time when attendance was voluntary. Navy Hill's scholastic records were better than those at Leigh, Baker, and Valley Schools, where whites held teaching positions, and surpassed those at several white schools. The figures proved, the petitioners said, that black teachers were more effective than whites when working with black children. Anticipating a familiar argument, they protested that it was unfair to say that qualified applicants were unavailable. Ninety-two students had graduated from Richmond Normal since its founding, and only six had found jobs in the city schools. Most were forced to seek positions in remote rural counties where salaries were low and conditions harsh.[6]

The school board rejected the petition on the grounds that it would be unjust to dismiss white teachers who had proved acceptable. Economic considerations probably influenced its decision, as well as a desire to maintain white control of black education. "It is not pleasant," wrote the *Dispatch* some years later, "for white ladies to be crowded out of the seats in the public parks and in the street cars by colored teachers clothed in 'purple and fine linen' bought . . . with money which might more properly have gone in the pockets of white young ladies."[7]

Because no vacancies developed at Navy Hill, Mitchell found himself still unemployed. Like other graduates of Richmond Normal, he was forced to look beyond Richmond for a job. Eventually he found a teaching position in Fredericksburg, the Civil War battlefield town about fifty miles north of the capital. The town had a population of 3,151 whites and 1,859 blacks. It had one black school, Fredericksburg Colored School, which had three teachers and more than two hundred pupils. The frame building was badly crowded, and children had to be turned away for lack of room, but the school was more progressive than the one-room schoolhouses of the countryside. It was a modern graded school and remained open ten months a year. Salaries, however, were low. Mitchell would earn $22 a month in Fredericksburg, about half of what he would have made in Richmond. He was assigned to Grade No. 2 of the Colored School.[8]

The head teacher at Fredericksburg Colored School was Sophia L. Hatch, a white woman from Ohio who had previously taught in nearby Caroline County. A veteran teacher, she was in her fifties when she arrived in Fredericksburg in 1880. She at first refused the position because the salary was so poor but consented to teach after unnamed friends promised to supplement her earnings. She told the school board that her aim was to upgrade the curriculum and raise academic standards.[9]

The third teacher was Marietta L. Chiles, a young woman whom Mitchell already knew and with whom he would have a long and complicated relationship. A member of a prominent Richmond family, Chiles was born in January 1862, the daughter of Richard Chiles, the servant who in April 1865 carried the message to Jefferson Davis, attending Sunday church services at St. Paul's, that it was time to abandon the Confederate capital. After the war Richard Chiles worked in the tobacco factories while his wife Martha kept house. Something in the family inspired excellence. One son graduated from the University of Michigan and practiced law in Kentucky; another edited a newspaper; another had a long career in the Richmond post office; nearly every member of the next generation entered the professions. Marietta Chiles was a gifted student who graduated from Richmond Normal in 1880 with highest honors. She was hired by the Fredericksburg school board several weeks before Mitchell arrived and may have helped him win his position.[10]

In Fredericksburg, Mitchell rented a room at Shepherd Brown's boarding-house where he paid eight dollars a month for room and board. He lived frugally that first year and saved almost half his salary, which he carried home to his mother. Fredericksburg probably seemed a sleepy town, at least compared to the state capital. He attended the local Baptist church and on weekends hiked across Civil War battlefields for exercise.[11]

Fredericksburg may have been tranquil, but apparently the atmosphere in his classroom was not. He had over fifty students in average daily attendance, and as a novice teacher—he was only eighteen—he struggled to prepare lessons and maintain order in a classroom crowded with high-spirited children. His room was on the second floor of the building, directly above Sophia Hatch's, and she soon complained to him that the loud noises overhead interfered with her teaching and distracted her pupils from their work. She conveyed her discontent to E. M. Crutchfield, the superintendent of schools, who visited the school and agreed that the situation was not "progressing" as one would hope with a new teacher. In December, Crutchfield recommended to the school board that Mitchell be dismissed and a replacement found.[12]

With his job on the line, Mitchell faced the school board on the night of December 15, 1881. The minutes of the meeting give an early glimpse into his character. Standing before the board, he made a lengthy statement. If his position was restored, he promised to maintain better discipline and rather brashly insisted that his "influence & authority" not be "further impaired by the interference of the H.T. [head teacher]." He implied that the cause of the trouble was Sophia Hatch. After he left the room, the board discussed the matter "in all its aspects." Either Mitchell was exceptionally persuasive in presenting his case, or the board had its own reasons for doubting Hatch's assessment. They directed the superintendent to restore Mitchell to his position and to inform the head teacher that she should not interfere with the conduct of the other classes in the building.[13]

After Christmas troubles flared again, and this time Hatch came before the board herself. Unwilling to entrust her case to Crutchfield, she presented charges against Mitchell in a written document that she read aloud to the board. She insisted that discipline remained lax in his classroom and that he showed "a positive & determined unwillingness to co-operate" with her during recess and at the opening and closing of school. She accused him of "incivility." After Hatch read her statement, Mitchell was given a chance to respond. Speaking more briefly this time, he said that in no instance since his reinstatement had he "failed to obey the Head Teacher, cooperate with her, or treat her with the respect due her." He professed dismay at her unhappiness and said that nothing could have surprised him more than to discover new charges against him. He asked that specific examples of his misdeeds be given.

According to the minutes, "The Board allowed quite a free colloquy between Miss Hatch and Mr. Mitchell." [14]

After the two teachers left the room, board members asked Crutchfield to sort out the trouble. He replied that he had made several visits to the school and was convinced that Mitchell's pupils were in truth better behaved than in the past. He speculated that the real problem was not poor discipline but that the noise "complained of as disorder" was inevitable because the two-story wooden building was so poorly constructed. Mitchell's classroom on the second floor was "neither lathed & plastered nor ceiled," and every sound his pupils made reverberated through the building. [15]

The rest of the term proceeded smoothly for Mitchell, or at least no more complaints reached the school board. As for Hatch, every sound from above must have annoyed her beyond measure, and she did not apply for reappointment the next fall. When school began in September 1882, Marietta Chiles became head teacher, and another black youth took the third position. [16]

Mitchell's name came before the school board only once the following year, on September 13, 1882, when he and Chiles presented a petition "praying for an increase [in their salaries] stating it was too little for them, considering they had to leave their homes etc. and two months of the year had nothing etc etc etc." After some discussion the board agreed to raise teachers' pay from $22 to $25 a month. [17] In these encounters Mitchell was quick to assert his rights, prone to find himself in the midst of controversy, and persuasive in presenting his viewpoint, the same traits he would show as editor of the *Planet.*

Mitchell might have remained in Fredericksburg indefinitely had it not been for shifts in political power that were taking place in the state government. The upheavals of the Readjuster era help explain the self-confidence he displayed in his encounters with the school board and provide the backdrop for his return to Richmond. Across Virginia black voters seized upon divisions among whites as a way of advancing their own agenda and influencing public policy. [18]

The issue that caused the conflict was the question of the state debt, and from it the two emerging factions, the Funders and the Readjusters, derived their names. In 1871 the General Assembly decided that Virginia had no choice but to honor its antebellum debts, even though they were incurred long before the Civil War in a largely futile attempt to build canals and railroads. The state owed more than forty million dollars to various bondholders, the majority of whom lived outside the Commonwealth. Virginia had been the battleground for much of the war, and after the depression of 1873, it had difficulty even with paying current interest. In desperation the General Assembly began to siphon off funds from public services. The amount of money given to public schools declined from $483,000 in 1876 to $195,000 in 1878. In 1879 rural schools throughout Virginia began to close. In an often quoted phrase, Funder John Daniel insisted it would be "better to burn the schools" than repudiate the debt.

In the summer of 1879, General William Mahone, the Confederate hero of the Battle of the Crater and a railroad entrepreneur, bolted the Democratic Party, appealed to black voters for support, and led his followers to victory in the state legislative elections. He promised to scale back the debt (or readjust it) and save public education. In 1881 the Readjusters elected their own governor, William E. Cameron of Petersburg, and sent Mahone to the U.S. Senate.

Once in power, the Readjusters pumped money back into the schools, and children who had been turned away in the past were able to matriculate. They enacted other reforms designed to please black voters, whose support they needed. Conceding that it was only fair to have "colored teachers in all colored schools," they increased the number of black teachers in the state from 415 in 1879 to 1,588 in 1884. Black enrollment in the schools soared, going from 36,000 to 91,000. They mandated equal pay for black and white teachers and thus refused to leave this important matter to the goodwill of local authorities. They required school board members and superintendents to take an oath pledging to "recognize and accept the civil and political equality of all men before the law." They founded the state's first publicly supported black college, Virginia Normal and Collegiate Institute in Petersburg, and appointed an all-black board of trustees. John Mercer Langston, an ex-slave and former abolitionist, became the school's first president. Black voters in Virginia had felt little obligation to pay an antebellum debt acquired by their former masters. Mahone's decision in 1884 to lead the Readjusters into the Republican Party only cemented the alliance.[19]

In Richmond black parents for years had lobbied for more black teachers, and they saw the Readjuster victory as an opportunity to have the matter settled. As one Richmonder explained, "While it was probably not quite time to have mixed schools in Richmond, it was only right to have colored teachers for colored schools." When members of the all-white Democratic school board failed to take the new oath of office, Governor Cameron removed them and appointed Readjusters to take their places. John S. Wise, himself a Readjuster, later called this "the worst political mistake that could have been made," and certainly Cameron's action was unpopular with many whites. When the governor revealed that two of his school board appointees were black, Democratic anger intensified. The *Dispatch* warned that black men would roam freely through white schools, discipline and spank white children, hire and examine white female teachers, and preside at commencement ceremonies. Knowing how much the issue would damage the Readjusters, anti-Mahone forces began to churn out literature predicting "mixed schools, mixed marriages, and miscegenation." According to one black Richmonder, the white folks were "just tearing the hair of their heads, because these two gentlemen have the privilege, at their own sweet wills, to question their white teachers." [20]

The two blacks appointed to the school board were Richard G. Forrester and R. A. Paul. Forrester was of free descent and so light-skinned he probably could have passed for white. He owned a house on College Street near First Church and worked in the post office. In the 1870s he was regularly elected to the city council as a Republican from the predominantly black Jackson Ward, and yet according to the *State* he "never presumed to push himself forward or become obnoxious by officiousness." When his wife died in 1883, a large number of white people attended the funeral. [21]

R. A. Paul, however, was not nearly so acceptable to whites, and he exhibited a new, more assertive style of leadership that Mitchell would embrace. Born to literate slaves in Nelson County in 1846, he came to Richmond after emancipation, worked as a waiter, and was elected captain of the State Guard, an all-black unit of the Virginia militia. Paul's efforts on behalf of the Readjusters led to his appointment in 1882 as doorkeeper and messenger to Governor Cameron. "He is a very impudent and forward negro," said the *State*, "who pushes himself everywhere and by his officiousness and persistent demand for recognition has rendered himself very offensive and annoying." According to one story, when he was first assigned to the governor's office, "he answered readily to the name of 'Paul,' or 'John,' or 'Richard,' or whatever his name might be . . . but it was not long before he began to 'stand upon his dignity,' and when addressed after that manner declined to respond, telling all requiring his services that he was 'Captain Paul.'" [22]

The new Readjuster school board quickly made changes. Three Navy Hill teachers—James H. Hayes, James H. Johnston, and Albert V. Norrell—were promoted to principalships, which meant that their salaries nearly doubled. Although whites were allowed to keep their jobs at Richmond Normal, blacks were given teaching positions at all of the black grammar schools, necessitating the dismissal of some thirty white incumbents. The headline in the *Dispatch* read, "How the School Board Knife Works." [23] Among those benefiting from the school board's knife were Mitchell and Chiles, who in the summer of 1883 came home from Fredericksburg to teach in Richmond.

When the new school year began, Chiles filled a fifth-grade vacancy at Baker School, taking a position she would hold for nearly forty years. Mitchell was assigned to Valley School, where James H. Hayes was principal. Valley School had sixteen teachers and over eight hundred pupils. The three-story brick building had been erected in 1816 as a white charity school, and its location was unfortunate, for it was across the street from the city jail, in the Shockoe ravine near a creek filled with sewage. On warm days when the windows were open, students could hear the curses of jail inmates and smell odors from the creek. Despite problems with the building, Mitchell found teaching in Richmond more to his liking. Twice during the year he made presentations at citywide teachers' meetings that were held on Saturday mornings. His first talk was on the use of blackboard drawings in the classroom. In the spring he delivered a second paper, on a subject Sophia Hatch would have approved of, "How to Teach Children Morals and Manners."[24]

His life outside the classroom was also more satisfactory. He rented an upstairs room in a boardinghouse at 222 East Broad Street where several graduates of Richmond Normal lived. On the ground floor was a book and stationery shop operated by Reuben Thomas Hill, an enterprising youth from Caroline County. R. T. Hill was an early proponent of self-help. "If we wish to be clerks, tellers and cashiers in banks," he wrote in 1883, "we must create such institutions. . . . Friends, we must be the builders of our fortunes." His bookstore was reputedly the first to be operated in the South by an ex-slave, and it functioned as a gathering place for the men and women of Mitchell's generation. They came to the store to socialize and browse among the books, magazines, and newspapers. By the 1880s nearly every American city of any consequence had a black-owned weekly, and Hill offered for sale such papers as the *Virginia Star,* the *Petersburg Lancet,* and the *New York Globe.*[25]

Not long after his return to Richmond, Mitchell was invited to write the "Old Dominion" column for the *Globe.* Founded by T. Thomas Fortune, the *New York Globe* was the nation's most influential black newspaper. Fortune was attracted to the economic ideas of Henry George and in an 1884 book predicted that the future conflict in the South would not be "racial or political in character, but between capital on the one hand and labor on the other." These ideas resonated well in Richmond, where the Knights of Labor were making inroads and where some Readjusters envisioned a similar alliance. Fortune was also a militant defender of civil and political rights and spoke out strongly on race issues.[26]

Fortune recruited correspondents from across the country to write for the *Globe.* He paid his writers no salary, but aspiring journalists were glad to see their prose in print and performed the service as a "labor of love and duty." One of the *Globe* correspondents in 1883 was the sixteen-year-old "Willie Du Bois" of Great Barrington, Massachusetts. Fortune asked his columnists to report the news matter-of-factly and let him write the editorials, but the injunction was difficult to enforce. He knew that many of his writers expressed their views as freely as the editor. Mitchell probably received his chance to write for the *Globe* through his friendship with "Reub," the previous correspondent, who was better known as R. T. Hill.[27]

Mitchell's first column appeared on September 22, 1883. He took the pen name "More" and described a public hanging that he had witnessed in Henrico County. A black woman, Barbara Miller, had been found guilty of conspiring with her lover to kill her husband. The case had caused a sensation in Richmond, and the twenty-year-old Mitchell chose his words carefully and worked hard to build suspense as he described the execution:

> She [Barbara Miller] kissed those around her and proceeded to take up her death march. She passed out to the gallows with a slow but firm step. Sheriff Southward read the death warrant. The ministers bade her good bye. The sheriff placed the manacles on her wrists, and strapped her feet. The rope was adjusted, and the black cap drawn down. . . . The bar which supported the trap door was pulled back, and the body shot through the opening. . . . A heart rending scream rang through the air. It was her mother. . . . The body hung about twenty-three minutes, when the doctors pronounced her dead.[28]

Evidently his writing pleased Fortune, for he moved the "Old Dominion" column to the front page.

Like other *Globe* columnists Mitchell was tempted to editorialize, and his views reflected the heady optimism of the Readjuster period. When a Democratic delegate to the General Assembly proposed a bill requiring teachers to remain neutral in politics, he responded angrily: "It is undoubtedly a slash at the colored male teachers who have had the manliness to speak their sentiments. Let them apply muzzles." He was upset when black teachers were directed to the gallery of the Richmond Theatre. "Prate not to us about social equality," he said. "We want none of it. We want those God-given rights which no man has a right to take away, and until we get them we intend to keep, if necessary, this whole nation in a ferment." He showed an early gift for invective, calling the editor of the *Richmond Dispatch* a "Rip Van Winkle slave-holder" who slept through the Civil War and woke up breathing "hatred of the black man." He described black southerners as oppressed but resilient. Using words and ideas that would become commonplace in the *Planet,* he wrote: "There is a determination to take what comes, die when we must and go down contending for those God-given rights that no man has a right to take away."[29]

Other columns were less partisan, although all conveyed confidence and race pride. As a teacher he was part of a close-knit group of young men and women who were ambitious for the race and saw no limits to what they could accomplish. Having grown up in the shadow of slavery, they felt keenly their own freedom, and although many would be compelled at some point in their lives to work in domestic service, their values and aspirations were distinctly middle-class.

In January 1884 Mitchell and his male friends organized a Chautauqua Literary and Scientific Circle, using the curriculum and materials provided by the national organization. The group had twenty-seven members, and Mitchell served as president. These young men met once a week at R. T. Hill's bookstore to consider a wide assortment of topics. They debated scientific questions ("Do we receive all of our heat either directly or indirectly from the sun?") and history ("Was Alexander a greater general than Napoleon?"). They discussed the tariff and staged a mock Congress with Mitchell presiding as the senior senator from Ohio. They read William Haikie's best-selling book on fitness, *How to Get Strong and How to Stay So* (1879). When former abolitionist Wendell Phillips died, they called a special meeting to commemorate his memory. Their energy seemed boundless, and no topic was too challenging or time-consuming. During the course of the year, each member was expected "to tell the story of . . . one of Shakespeare's plays and to give extracts from the same." Self-help groups of this sort were common in late nineteenth-century America, but they had special meaning for black youths who saw self-improvement as a means of advancing the race.[30]

Another group Mitchell joined, the Acme Literary Association, had a broader focus, although the membership rolls of the two groups overlapped. The Acmes pledged to "consider questions of vital importance . . . so that the masses . . . may be drawn out to be entertained, enlightened and instructed thereby." The Acmes held their meetings in churches, invited the public to attend, and welcomed women as members. Lectures were given on topics such as "The Relative Condition of the Colored Man, North and South," "The Political Outlook of the Negro," and "What Is the Future Destiny of the Negro Race in America?" A special project was a lending library that John W. Cromwell, then a teacher at Navy Hill, assembled in the 1870s. When Mitchell joined the group, the Acmes' librarian was Mary Woolfolk, a teacher who opened her home on Friday evenings to those who wished to borrow books.[31]

Mitchell was also active at First Church where he taught Sunday school and was involved in fund-raising work for African missions. He participated in debating societies and helped judge the oratorical contests at the 1884 graduation exercises at Richmond Theological Institute. When a banquet was held honoring Amos A. Dodson, a black member of the House of Delegates who was moving to Tennessee, he was one of the featured speakers, taking as his topic "Liberty" and the "denial of this God-given principle to the down-trodden races of the earth." Amid these activities he somehow found time to pursue his interest in art. He finished a pen-and-ink portrait of Chester A. Arthur and drew more illustrated maps. "The map of Yorktown with the historical pictures surrounding, drawn by John Mitchell Jr., may be seen at R. T. Hill and Co.'s book store," he told *Globe* readers. His life, in short, was a whirl of activity. He wrote of baseball and croquet, dinner parties and formal dances, masquerades, picnics, garden parties, and railroad excursions.[32]

He also attended to his personal life, although in this regard he was much less forthcoming. At some point during this period, probably while still in Fredericksburg, perhaps even earlier, he and Marietta Chiles began a courtship. On the surface it was an ideal match. Chiles was from a good family, and the two teachers had much in common. They belonged to many of the same organizations, and both attended First Church. Furthermore, they had spent two years together in Fredericksburg, and it is easy to imagine them commiserating after school about homesickness, Sophia Hatch, and unruly pupils. When they continued to keep company after their return to Richmond, onlookers naturally assumed they would marry.

Mitchell never married, however, nor did Chiles, and by all accounts he was the reluctant suitor. Their friendship spanned the decades. Well into the twentieth century they could be seen together at dinners and parties or riding through the streets in Mitchell's automobile. Although they never lived together, this was not a clandestine affair, and onlookers assumed it was consummated. He bought her expensive jewelry and escorted her to public functions. When he became grand chancellor of the Virginia Knights of Pythias in the 1890s, she took over leadership of the female affiliate, the Courts of Calanthe. Their romance was so public that it inspired endless gossip and much speculation as to why they never married. According to one story Mitchell was too self-centered to marry, too preoccupied with his own liberties and the rights of the race to care about the rights of Marietta Chiles. According to another story he promised her he would marry her once his mother died and then "forgot" his promise. Another version said he was too stubborn to marry Chiles but too afraid of her protective brothers to marry anyone else.[33]

The pressures on men to marry were powerful in late Victorian America—
it was the proper, manly thing to do—but significant numbers of young men
also defied convention and remained single. Indeed, one historian has called
this the "Age of the Bachelor." Like many bachelors Mitchell deflected questions about his marital status by telling jokes. "Every man should marry," he
said, because it was "good to be acquainted with trouble." Perhaps he never
married because he doubted his ability to remain faithful. In later years there
were rumors of other liaisons and illegitimate children.[34]

Another female teacher played an important role in his life, although here
too the relationship was complicated. Maggie Lena Mitchell, better known by
her married name of Maggie Walker, was born in Richmond in 1867. She attended the public schools and after graduating from Richmond Normal in
1883 taught at Valley School with Mitchell. In the twentieth century they became friendly competitors as journalists and business leaders. They may also
have been cousins of a sort. Walker's mother, Elizabeth Draper, had worked as
a cook in the home of Elizabeth Van Lew, the celebrated Union spy, and according to family tradition Walker's father was Eccles Cuthbert, a northern
abolitionist. Elizabeth Draper later married William Mitchell, a hotel waiter,
and the young Maggie took her stepfather's name. William Mitchell, who died
in 1876, was probably the younger brother of John Mitchell Sr. Walker and
Mitchell worked closely together as adults, but neither talked openly about any
family connection, perhaps because the relationship was difficult to explain.[35]

During the 1880s most white Richmonders seemed entirely oblivious to the
world in which Maggie Walker, Marietta Chiles, and John Mitchell moved.
Probably most would have been startled to learn that in a Broad Street bookstore black youths gathered to debate the tariff and recite Shakespeare, or that
a young teacher was writing weekly columns for a New York newspaper.
When T. Thomas Fortune visited Richmond in 1883, he found a level of so-
phistication in the former Confederate capital that surprised him. "The tone
of society here is agreeable, rich, without affectation," he wrote. "Most of the
ladies sing and play on the piano, and quiet elegance is a feature of the homes
I have visited."[36] Within this world Mitchell was beginning to make his mark.
Although barely out of his teens, he was already exhibiting qualities that
would serve him well as *Planet* editor: he had an independent spirit, was not
afraid to speak his mind, and enjoyed being in the public eye.

CHAPTER THREE

Founding the *Planet*

In the fall of 1883, shortly after he began writing for the *Globe,* Mitchell reported that a group of black Richmonders were planning to publish a weekly newspaper. The first issue would go on sale in December, and the founders hoped to make the *Richmond Planet* "the liveliest paper ever published in this city." On December 10 he noted that many schoolteachers had come to town to witness the appearance of "a new *Planet.*" By mid-January the journal had become, according to his enthusiastic reports, the most popular newspaper in the city.[1] Thus he described the founding of the paper he himself would edit and publish for nearly forty-five years.

The original editor of the *Planet* was not Mitchell but Edwin Archer Randolph, a black lawyer born in Amelia County in 1850 of free parentage. As a young man Randolph worked as a driver for Dr. James B. McCaw, a well-to-do white physician who lived across from James Lyons on Grace Street. Mitchell and Randolph may have known each other during the 1870s when both worked as drivers for neighboring white families, although Randolph was more than a decade older. Randolph left Richmond in the mid-1870s for Washington, D.C., where he attended Wayland Seminary, and in 1878 he entered the Yale Law School. After his graduation from Yale, he returned to Richmond, established a law practice, and was elected to the board of aldermen.[2]

Working with Randolph on the *Planet* were three assistant editors, all well educated and light-skinned. George W. Lewis was a lawyer trained at Howard University; Edward R. Carter, a graduate of Richmond Normal, worked in the post office; and James E. Merriweather taught at Navy Hill. The paper had a staff of eight reporters, among them James H. Hayes, James H. Johnston, and Albert V. Norrell, the three teachers promoted to principalships by the Readjusters. R. T. Hill was the *Planet's* business manager. Like most black newspapers of the period, the *Planet* was four pages long and appeared weekly. The first page was devoted to news, the second to editorials, and the third and fourth pages contained advertisements and miscellaneous articles. The printing of the paper was contracted to the white firm of Johns & Goolsby.[3]

The *Planet* was founded during a time of rapid expansion in American journalism, which helps explain the ease with which these men launched the venture. The number of weekly newspapers in the United States actually trebled between 1870 and 1890. The reasons were partly technological. As paper mills converted from rag paper to wood pulp, the price of paper plummeted, dropping from twelve cents a pound in the 1870s to under three cents by the 1890s. Ink was cheap, and the federal government in effect subsidized the newspaper industry by permitting publishers to mail their newspapers from their local post office at a bulk rate. Improvements in printing techniques lowered the cost of printing presses and reduced the time required for typesetting, and manufacturers were eager to sell their latest equipment on the installment plan. By 1880 it was said that no other business required such a modest outlay of capital as journalism. Throughout the South ex-slaves resolved to publish their own newspapers and provide some alternative to the prejudicial coverage of the white dailies. The average weekly paper, black or white, was a small undertaking. Two-thirds of the nation's weeklies reported a circulation of less than a thousand, and like the *Planet* many of these papers contracted out their printing.[4]

If it was a simple matter to found a weekly paper, it was much more difficult to sustain one, particularly in the black community where illiteracy was high and few families had much disposable income. "To those who are outside of a newspaper office," wrote one black journalist, "it may seem very easy to send out a paper every week, . . . but it is indeed a trying task." Richmond's *Virginia Star*, founded in 1877 by O. M. Steward, was the state's oldest and best-established black newspaper. Steward published it almost single-handedly while working other jobs on the side. When a reader complained to him of typographical errors, he responded that he had little time for proofreading. He served as the paper's "editor, manager, solicitor, mailing clerk, compositor, proofreader, office boy, and general supervisor." Even the strongest black newspapers, such as the *New York Globe* and *Washington Bee*, suffered from chronic financial difficulties.[5]

The *Planet* survived its infancy in large part because of the support it received during its first year from an organization called the Independent League. Founded in the fall of 1883 and headed by D. Webster Davis, the Independent League in many ways resembled the Acme Literary Association, as its purpose was to "foster enterprises and encourage literary culture." The league's special project, however, was the subsidizing of the *Planet*, and its name probably was a shield to protect its founders from political reprisals. Members were asked to pay monthly dues of two dollars, plus an initiation fee of three dollars, all of which would be "added to the receipts of the said newspaper." Thirty men from Richmond, including R. A. Paul, R. T. Hill, Mitchell, and nearly all the male teachers in the schools, signed up as charter members. Women were not invited to participate, a circumstance that Maggie Walker probably remembered in 1902 when she founded her own newspaper, the *St. Luke Herald*.[6]

Although the *Planet's* beginnings were auspicious, its first year was filled with an unusual amount of strife and turmoil. Political upheavals were again impinging on the lives of the men and women of Mitchell's generation. In November 1883 the Readjusters suffered a disastrous setback at the polls. The reasons were complex, but at the heart of the matter was race. Democrats charged that Mahone had surrendered the public schools to black trustees and had placed black men in authority over white women. When a well-publicized and suspiciously well-timed "race riot" broke out in Danville only a few days before the election, Democratic victory was assured. In the tense aftermath of the election, Mitchell warned that blacks should be prepared to take up arms in self-defense. "We are indeed an oppressed people," he wrote, "and often wonder what benefit is the Federal government to us anyhow." He was certain that fewer would have died in Danville had more black men been armed.[7]

When the new legislature convened in 1884, the Democrats enacted the Anderson-McCormick elections law, a complicated set of provisions that masqueraded as a reform but placed the election machinery firmly in their own hands. The General Assembly also ruled that the "places of all [school] trustees now in office . . . be and become vacant on the expiration of thirty days." This second act, which removed school boards throughout Virginia, was designed to reverse the situation in Richmond, where Governor Cameron's appointments had infuriated whites. As the legislature explained, in some cities school boards had been "appointed under the law by other than the local authorities." The act went into effect on March 4, 1884, and two weeks later the city council met and on the authority of the General Assembly replaced the Readjusters with Democrats. A worried Mitchell voiced the concerns of black Richmond in the *Globe:* "The community has been much stirred up over a report that certain members of the present [Democratic] school board are in favor of ousting the colored principals and teachers and putting white persons in their places."[8]

As it turned out, Mitchell's concerns were justified. The all-white board gave the positions formerly held by Hayes, Johnston, and Norrell to white men. The Democrats apparently reasoned that if blacks were going to teach in the public schools, then whites must be there to supervise them and collect the higher salaries. Not until 1933—half a century later—did Richmond again have a black principal, long after most southern communities had turned over the management of black schools to black administrators. The school board did not stop here, wrote Mitchell, "but descended so low as to oust every male teacher appointed by the Readjuster board but one." Marietta Chiles, Maggie Walker, and the other female teachers held on to their positions, but eleven men involved in founding the *Planet* were fired, including Mitchell.[9]

The dismissal of the teachers did little to inspire confidence in the newspaper's future. D. B. Williams, who taught at Navy Hill and was one of the few male teachers to survive the purge, had written a series of articles for the *Planet*. He declined to contribute anything more on the grounds that he could not afford to be identified with the paper's editorial policy. The Independent League languished. In the fall of 1884, many of its members left Richmond to take charge of schools in rural districts. James H. Hayes, who had served as principal of Valley School, moved to Washington, where he enrolled in the law department at Howard University.[10] Mitchell also looked beyond Richmond for employment, although by now he was too ambitious to be content teaching school in the hinterlands.

During the summer of 1884, Mitchell traveled by train to Washington, D.C., to seek an apprenticeship in the Bureau of Printing and Engraving. Every government position was considered a political appointment, and it required finesse and inveigling to win one. He took to Washington a portfolio of maps and drawings as well as endorsements from leading politicians, including Senator Mahone. "See his drawings," wrote Mahone. "They will interest you. There is talent here that ought to be encouraged." In Washington he met Frederick Douglass, who also agreed to write a letter. On one memorable summer evening, Mitchell and the great abolitionist played croquet on the lawn of Douglass's home at Anacostia. "I have no fear," wrote Douglass, "but that young Mitchell will make his way and be a credit to our race." Senator John A. Logan of Ohio and former senator B. K. Bruce of Mississippi also contributed letters.[11]

Mitchell failed to win the apprenticeship, but probably because of political decisions having little bearing on his talents. The disappointment rankled. "His mind inclined to the artistic," wrote an admirer, and "would have, had its bent been given full play, achieved for him fame in the artistic world."[12] He came home to Richmond and found other work but never said publicly what he did. In all likelihood he returned to domestic service.

As for the *Planet,* its future remained imperiled. In December 1884 Randolph resigned the editorship and moved temporarily to Washington, leaving behind a list of delinquent subscribers and a printer's bill for $104.51. It seemed certain that the paper had failed when an emergency meeting of the Independent League was called to discuss its problems. Eleven men attended, including Mitchell, D. Webster Davis, R. T. Hill, and a number of teachers who had lost their jobs. They resolved to form a new organization, the Planet Publishing Company, and purchase a second-hand cylinder press that had been offered for sale in Petersburg. At some point during the meeting, Mitchell volunteered to relinquish his *Globe* column to Marietta Chiles's brother R. J. Chiles and take sole responsibility for the *Planet.* The members elected him editor and manager, after which Hill turned over to him all the ledgers and records.[13]

The meeting was scarcely over before Mitchell set out on a tour of the state to introduce himself to subscribers and drum up support. George W. Bragg, the editor of the *Petersburg Lancet,* reported his visit on December 13: "There is some attraction in this city for the young editor of the *Planet.*" Mitchell must have made a strong first impression. Only twenty-one years old, he was handsome, articulate, and self-assured. As he later explained, "I win over the colored people by coming in personal contact with them and bringing them over to my way of thinking." With the assistance of friends, he installed the press in his room at 222 East Broad. John Merriweather, who later became a physician but was then working for a white printing firm, helped him set the type for the first *Planet* issue printed on its own press. Mitchell needed little equipment to publish a four-page weekly: a hand-cranked press, "a few cases of type . . . one or two galleys, a proof press, a supply of ink, a bundle of ready print paper, a roller towel and wash pin."[14]

The earliest surviving *Planet* clipping dates from January 31, 1885, barely a month after he became editor. The article tells the story of First African, from its antebellum origins to the construction in the 1870s of a new brick church on College Street. Mitchell almost surely wrote the unsigned article, though a reporter may have helped. He described how during the Civil War slave worshipers prayed for the success of Union troops: "Worn down by the cares of life, crushed and bruised by the lash of the master's whip, [they] sought divine aid and consolation by an appeal to the almighty." The article contained triumphant flourishes. "Changes have taken place," said the *Planet.* "A generation has nearly passed away [since the war] and we stand at the dawning of a new era, the beginning of a new age. . . . Black and white all alike. What a change!"[15]

No nearly complete file of the *Planet* exists until 1890, but other scattered quotations attest to Mitchell's high spirits and identify him as the same writer who the previous year had submitted columns to the *Globe*. His experiences with the Democratic school board had not dampened his enthusiasm for politics or quieted his voice. If anything, losing his teaching position freed him from restraints, and the *Planet* was fervently Republican. In April 1885 T. Thomas Fortune printed this sample of the *Planet's* prose: "We shall march to the charge with the word 'Republicanism' emblazoned on our banners, defiant in defeat and marching proudly to the front when bearing the laurels of victory." The older and more sophisticated Fortune, who was losing confidence in the Republican Party, chided his former correspondent: "That's all very nice, Mr. Mitchell, but don't get excited." Three years later Mitchell was again extolling the Republicans, this time in a convoluted metaphor in which the Republican Party appears as a ship and Mahone as its captain. His prose was florid: "The old ship is on the sea of dissension while the lightning of desire for office plays around it and the thunder of discordant opinions shake the heavens."[16]

Mitchell's devotion to the Republicans was fairly routine at a time when most blacks agreed with Frederick Douglass that the Republican Party was the deck and all else the sea. More noteworthy in the long run was his crusade against lynching and his militant, unforgiving approach to race relations. "We regret the necessity," he wrote in the *Planet*, "but if the government will not stop this killing of colored men, we must stop it ourselves." His opposition to mob violence and his eagerness to fly in the face of southern prejudices won him something of a national reputation. In 1887 the white *New York World* described him as "one of the most daring and vigorous negro editors," and added, "The fact that he is a negro, and lives in Richmond, does not prevent him from being courageous, almost to a fault." Other white journalists labeled the *Planet* an incendiary paper, and even black editors were sometimes startled by his vehemence. "The young editor of the *Richmond Planet* is in such dead earnest," said Fortune, "that he sometimes grows hysterical."[17]

Mitchell's militancy won him considerable fame and assured the success of the paper. He articulated the aspirations of his generation in ways that made readers want to subscribe, and he used the lynching issue to give his editorials focus. John W. Cromwell, the editor of the *People's Advocate* of Washington, was probably right when he said that "no newspaper in the United States started by a colored man has ever had *only* a mercenary desire." Mitchell hoped to make a living as a journalist, but he knew that his paper served as the "mouthpiece for the groans and woes of a suffering people."[18]

His early years as editor are bound to have been difficult. He spent much of 1885 in his bedroom sorting through unpaid bills. He later recalled how he lived in an attic and for nearly eight months "received not a penny's pay in salary." After delivering sacks of newspapers to the post office on Saturday mornings, he found himself gazing "only on a fifty-cent piece." He liked to romanticize his lowly beginnings, but there is no reason to question his Horatio Alger account. Nearly every black journalist reported the same hand-to-mouth existence. The stockholders in the Planet Publishing Company gradually lost interest in the enterprise, fearing the *Planet* would never return a profit, and he was left to put out the paper alone.[19]

The turning point seems to have come in 1888 when he purchased a new electric press on the installment plan for $600 and moved the *Planet* out of the boardinghouse on Broad Street. The *Planet*'s new headquarters were in the Swan Tavern, a long frame building with a rambling front porch at 814 East Broad not far from the Capitol. Built in the 1770s, the tavern had an illustrious history (Thomas Jefferson and Edgar Allan Poe had slept there), but by the 1880s it was dilapidated and needed paint. He rented a room or two in the basement, just below street level, and shared the building with an assortment of businesses: a Chinese laundry, a tailor's shop, a scouring and dyeing establishment, and a hatter's shop. Aside from Mitchell, the only black men in the building were lawyers—James H. Hayes and E. A. Randolph. Eventually they were joined by attorneys George W. Lewis and Giles B. Jackson and real estate agent B. F. Turner.[20]

The *Planet* office was never especially prepossessing from the outside, but a journalist who visited Richmond in 1890 was surprised to find "five colored young men at work in the job department, and the colored foreman of the establishment running off the *Planet* on Mr. Mitchell's own electric press." The *Planet*'s emblem was a strong, muscular arm with a clenched fist that held lightning bolts, suggesting power and modern electricity. "Office lighted and machinery propelled by electricity," explained the caption. In 1892 he rented more space and acquired more equipment: an elevator, a telephone, and a new Campbell rotary press valued at $3,000. A special *Planet* issue in 1895 described his office, which was decorated in late Victorian fashion. He had an oak rolltop desk for himself, a standing double desk for clerks, a Remington typewriter, nickel cuspidors, and shelves lined with books. Lace curtains at the windows and patterned wallpaper added to the impression that he had arrived.[21]

Just how Mitchell managed to sustain the *Planet* at a time when so many other newspapers failed is a difficult question to answer. His contemporaries lauded his "power to manage," and certainly his boundless energy and keen intelligence helped. He threw himself into the enterprise, worked long hours, and was willing to go into debt to make improvements to his printing establishment. He also never neglected the business side of the enterprise. He knew that no matter how eloquent his editorials, he had to find some way to make money if he hoped to survive as a journalist.[22]

During the late nineteenth century, publishers of weekly newspapers commonly relied on job printing to help finance their papers, and certainly this was true in Mitchell's case. After he purchased his electric press in 1888, he aggressively sought printing contracts, and all sorts of materials began to bear the *Planet* imprint: pamphlets and small books, stationery, invitations, church bulletins, insurance forms, and the bylaws, constitutions, and minutes of various organizations. Richmond was the home of dozens of beneficial and fraternal organizations, and many of them turned to the Planet Publishing Company for job printing. When T. Thomas Fortune visited Richmond in 1891, he described the job printing department as a paying business and thought it remarkable that a black editor could actually make a living from his trade.[23]

Northern editors also thought it noteworthy that Mitchell relied on an all-black staff. After his brother Thomas graduated from Richmond Normal in 1886, Mitchell put him in charge of the job printing department. Tom Mitchell was said to have a sunny disposition, and much of the success of the venture probably was due to his efforts. As early as 1885 J. C. Farley, a black photographer, prepared cuts for the *Planet,* while Thomas M. Crump, an 1887 graduate of Richmond Normal and one of Mitchell's closest friends, kept the books and managed the paperwork. For several years Benjamin P. Vandervall, the son of a city councilman, was circulation manager.[24]

Another source of income for Mitchell may well have been the Republican Party. During the late nineteenth century, journalists often maintained close ties with political candidates. Indeed, some newspapers flourished during campaigns only to cease publication once the election was over. The negotiations between editors and politicians were seldom publicized, but scraps of evidence suggest that Mahone routinely paid small stipends to those who supported him. In 1883, for example, he sent a list of names and addresses to O. M. Steward, who agreed to mail the *Virginia Star* regularly to targeted voters, many of whom were Baptist preachers. Mahone undoubtedly paid Steward for his trouble, and in 1884 the journalist received an important political plum, an appointment as a gauger in the U.S. Custom House in Richmond. Other black editors solicited Mahone, including W. Calvin Chase of the *Washington Bee,* who reminded the senator of the "column after column in our paper the *Bee* supporting your cause." Like other newspapermen swamped with bills and "in a tight place," Chase begged Mahone to send him some money.[25]

The *Planet* was ardently Republican, suggesting that it too was the recipient of funds. In 1888 readers received the *Planet* wrapped in campaign literature promoting the presidential prospects of John Sherman, the Republican senator from Ohio who had Mahone's backing. There were rumors the next year that Mitchell aspired to become recorder of deeds for the District of Columbia, a lucrative position usually reserved for a nationally known politician. He never won a political appointment, but until the turn of the century he was active in party affairs. It was perfectly legitimate, he later said, for "Afro-American journalists to receive money from the Republican campaign managers, as long as it did not bring with it a sacrifice of principle."[26]

The *Planet* was further supported by revenues from advertising and subscriptions. Advertising became more important in the 1890s as a black entrepreneurial class emerged in Richmond that offered services to the black community rather than to whites. The *Planet* was soon sprinkled with pleas for support from locally owned black-operated businesses. Much of the advertising was of an indirect sort with the line dividing news from advertising less distinct that it usually is today. On the front page of the *Planet,* for example, Mitchell would tell the story of a newly founded insurance company; on the editorial page he would urge his readers to support the venture; and on the back page he would place the actual paid advertisement. He also agreed to promote without cost those enterprises that gave their job printing to the Planet Publishing Company. Conversely, those who took their printing elsewhere were required to pay small fees for articles.[27]

Finally, Mitchell depended upon revenues from subscriptions to finance his newspaper. A year's subscription cost $1.50. The *Planet's* readership grew slowly—the earliest records show 1,200 subscribers—but by 1896 the actual sworn circulation had reached 6,400, a more than respectable figure for a weekly newspaper. He used various promotional devices to entice readers to subscribe and tried to expand his readership beyond the small, highly educated elite. He offered premiums to new subscribers and gave away portraits of Lincoln, biblical illustrations, history books, and sheet music.[28]

Mitchell was sometimes frustrated that so many who read his newspaper never subscribed. Old and worn-out copies of the *Planet* were passed from family to family, and in lunchrooms and barbershops customers read aloud the latest issue. Fraternal lodges, beneficial societies, and Sunday school classes routinely bought one subscription and circulated the paper among their members. "Do you subscribe to the *PLANET* or do you borrow it?" he asked his readers in an ill-tempered moment. He once estimated that a third of his subscribers were delinquent: "You'll spend $1.50 in frolic, and yet be unwilling to give that amount to a struggling race defender in order that he may send you his paper for one year." Sometimes his pleas grew frantic, and according to a story told by R. T. Hill, on occasion he was forced to hound subscribers personally in order to pay his bills. "I will go to Danville," he was quoted as saying, "and collect from my subscribers, and I think I can pull through." As late as 1894 he complained of a flat pocketbook and a stack of bills. Despite the appearance of prosperity that he cultivated, he was far from well-to-do until after 1900 when he ventured into banking, insurance, and real estate.[29]

Although the *Planet*'s circulation remained small compared to that of Richmond's white dailies, its impact may have been as far-flung. The *Planet* was never really a local newspaper. Like Fortune before him, Mitchell recruited correspondents to report the news from distant cities, serve as agents, and sell subscriptions. Letters addressed to the *Planet* came from every region of the country, and one of his promotional devices indirectly revealed something about its circulation. For several months in 1891, he printed ballots for a voting contest to determine the most popular preacher. Clergy from northern cities such as New York and Philadelphia received significant blocks of votes, as did preachers from communities as far south as Vicksburg, Mississippi. When Mitchell ran into Frederick Douglass in Washington in 1891, the race leader congratulated him on his success as a journalist and observed, "You have indeed nationalized yourself."[30]

There are other hints that the *Planet* was more widely read than one might at first suspect. In 1891 Albion W. Tourgée, a white novelist and civil rights attorney, wrote to Mitchell from New York and said he had "received the *Planet* now and then" and had been "familiar with its character since its first issue." Tourgée went on to say that "from what I hear from the friends of liberty in England, I think the *Planet* is better known there than any paper edited by a colored man in this country." Edward W. Blyden of Liberia wrote that he occasionally saw the *Planet* in Africa. Although the evidence is circumstantial, it is possible that northern Republicans provided the *Planet* with financial assistance and in other ways encouraged its dissemination. One of the leading foes of lynching was Senator William E. Chandler of New Hampshire. On occasion Chandler paid small subsidies to Magnus Robinson, the editor of the *Alexandria Weekly*

Leader, so that Robinson could publicize lynchings. Whether Chandler helped Mitchell is unknown, but certainly he read the *Planet,* for in 1888 he inserted a list of lynchings compiled by Mitchell into the *Congressional Record.*[31]

Mitchell's success with the *Planet* won him laurels from his fellow editors and led to his prominence in the Colored Press Association, a national organization of black journalists founded in the 1870s. He attended his first meeting in Atlantic City in 1886 and was named to the committee on "Southern Outrages." The next year in Louisville he delivered a speech on "Labor and Capital—Their Relation." He was elected vice-president in 1890 and assumed the presidency after the death of William J. Simmons. He held the position for five years and injected new vigor into an organization that was struggling to define its mission.[32]

Mitchell envisioned the annual meetings as forums where black journalists could discuss matters of practical interest while coordinating broader efforts on behalf of the race. Over fifty editors attended the 1891 meeting in Cincinnati, and under his leadership they changed the name of the organization to the Afro-American Press Association. The 1891 program reflected his dual concern with protest and business success. The editors attended sessions on "How to Make Afro-American Journals Pay" and "The Necessity of Syndicating Our Own News," but they also endorsed a number of resolutions that were frankly political, such as one that deplored the U.S. Senate's failure to pass the Lodge federal elections bill of 1890, which would have ensured federal supervision of southern elections. Another resolution said that the organization's central mission was "to maintain the just rights of the race." At the 1892 meeting in Philadelphia, he surprised his fellow editors with his militancy and warned that if the race failed to win its rights with the ballot, it would resort to the bullet. In 1893 he was again elected president, outpolling his principal opponent for the job, Fortune himself.[33]

Although Mitchell had indeed "nationalized" himself, he was involved in a series of legal battles at home in Richmond that nearly undermined his position as editor. In his haste to promote the *Planet,* he inadvertently left himself open to legal assault. Although known as "Mr. Planet," he was not at first the legal owner of the newspaper. The *Planet* was instead owned by the Planet Publishing Company, a joint-stock venture chartered by the chancery court in 1884 at the time the Independent League disbanded. In 1891 a number of stockholders, led by R. A. Paul, James H. Hayes, and E. A. Randolph, complained to the chancery court that the *Planet* was now a "very considerable source of profit." Together they had raised the money to buy the original equipment and therefore should have received a return on their investment.

Nothing was owned in Mitchell's name, and yet he refused to let them see the books. He had "purchased at various times in the name of the Planet Publishing Company . . . printing presses, type, fireproof safe and other articles, without consulting your orators." They asked that the partnership be settled and a receiver appointed.[34]

This particular case dragged on for months, and other suits were instituted against Mitchell, some for failing to pay his debts. He retained control of his paper until his death in 1929, but in 1892 Paul, Hayes, and Randolph won an important case against him. The *Planet* went into receivership and was offered for sale at public auction. Mitchell canvassed the state to raise money to save the paper and on the day of the auction outbid his rivals, buying the *Planet* back for $1,625.[35] His quarrels with the original *Planet* founders were a preview of other wrangles and feuds in years to come. Despite his gracious manners he could be feisty and boastful in his dealings with others, and he was by nature more combative than conciliatory. Sophia Hatch was not the only one to accuse him of incivility.

Although the founders probably exaggerated when they spoke of the *Planet*'s handsome profits, their eagerness to regain control suggests that it was no longer a drain on Mitchell's resources, and through its pages he was making a name for himself throughout the country. His prominence in Richmond became clear in October 1890 when he served as chief marshal of an Emancipation Day celebration held in the Virginia capital. Many black Richmonders saw the celebration as their answer to the festivities that had occurred earlier that year, when the equestrian statue of Robert E. Lee was unveiled on Monument Avenue. Black militia units and representatives of more than forty fraternal orders marched in a parade that stretched for two miles through the downtown streets. W. Calvin Chase of the *Washington Bee* came to Richmond for the parade, and he thought "Mr. Mitchell looked as if he was governor of Virginia." He wore a fashionable "light colored slouch-hat, black suit with cream colored sash, and was mounted on an iron grey horse." Years later, after he had grown more cynical about racial progress, Mitchell said that personal publicity of this sort was about all any black editor ever got "out of the publication of a race journal."[36]

As Mitchell well knew, however, the black press has always done more than ensure the livelihood of editors. To quote sociologist Gunnar Myrdal, it has served as the "safety-valve for the boiling Negro protest." In a personal sense the *Planet* may have served as Mitchell's safety valve. During a period of tense and troubled race relations, he was compelled to respond in print, week after week, to events occurring around him. Like other editors he made endless pleas for self-help, urging subscribers to save money, venture into business, and support black-run enterprises. "If we are downtrodden and oppressed," he wrote, "let us work, accumulate as much money as we can and buy land." These were familiar words of uplift repeated like a litany in black newspapers across the United States. But he did not stop with this appeal: "In the meantime, let others be assigned to howl, yes howl loudly, until the American people hear our cries." Mitchell considered it his special mission "to howl, yes howl loudly." In the process he won a reputation as the "Fighting Negro Editor," a man who would "walk into the jaws of death to serve his race." [37]

CHAPTER FOUR

"Lynch Law Must Go!"

In his early years as editor, Mitchell designed an advertisement to entice readers to subscribe. "Have You Seen the *Planet*!" read the headline. "It is a journal published in the interest of colored people every Saturday at Richmond, Va." Beneath the banner was a picture of the strong arm of the *Planet*. The ad continued:

> Do you want to see what the Colored People are doing? Read the *Planet*.
> Do you want to know what Colored People think? Read the *Planet*. Do
> you want to know how many Colored People are hung to trees without
> due process of law? Read the *Planet*. Do you want to know how Colored
> People are progressing? Read the *Planet*. Do you want to know what Colored People are demanding? Read the *Planet*. . . . Do you want to know
> how to get the paper? Send $1.50 to JOHN MITCHELL JR., 814 E. Broad
> Street, Richmond, Virginia.[1]

Mitchell's advertisement highlighted the appeal of the black press. Subscribers to race journals could read news of their own communities, stories of everyday events that enriched their lives and yet were ignored or misrepresented in the white press. In black-owned newspapers people of color were portrayed as dignified, resourceful, enterprising and quick to protest injustice. In 1884 southern novelist George Washington Cable observed, "If anyone can think the Freeman does not feel the indignities thus heaped upon him, let him take up any paper printed for colored men's patronage."[2]

Mitchell's initial fame as a journalist came from his attacks on lynching and his efforts on behalf of black prisoners. Each week he ran in the *Planet* a drawing of a lynching, a grisly cartoon that showed a black man hanging from a tree. The caption read, "Shall this barbarity continue until the God of retribution marshals his strength against the barbarians?" Beneath the drawing was a list of lynching victims. He documented the violence that was sweeping the post-Reconstruction South and wrote fearless editorials in protest. He urged blacks to take responsibility for their own defense. "If the government cannot stop the killing of black men," he said, "we must stop it ourselves." He made the "incendiary" proposal that black males purchase rifles and be prepared to fire on lynch mobs in order to protect themselves and their families. "The best remedy for a lyncher or a cursed mid-night rider," he wrote, "is a 16-shot Winchester rifle in the hands of a dead-shot Negro who has nerve enough to pull the trigger." [3]

Mitchell's crusade against lynching involved him in a series of incidents that enhanced his reputation as a "Fighting Editor" and assured the success of the *Planet*. One of the most famous occurred little more than a year after he took over the newspaper. In May 1886 Richard Walker, a black man accused of attempted rape, was taken from jail and lynched by a mob of whites near Drake's Branch in Charlotte County, Virginia. Although the white press in Richmond dismissed the lynching in a back-page paragraph, Mitchell wrote a furious editorial for the *Planet*. The next week he received an anonymous letter from Southside Virginia that said, "If you poke that infernal head of yours in this county long enough for us to do it we will hang you higher than he was hung." On the outside of the envelope was a crude drawing of a skull and crossbones. Instead of ignoring the threat, Mitchell printed the letter in the *Planet* and answered with a quotation from Shakespeare: "There are no terrors, Cassius, in your threats, for I am armed so strong in honesty that they pass me by like the idle winds, which I respect not." He then traveled by train to Charlotte County wearing Smith & Wesson revolvers. He walked five miles from the train station to the scene of the lynching, toured the neighborhood, and visited the jail from which the man had been kidnapped. "The cowardly letter writer was nowhere in evidence," he chortled. At a time when blacks were being lynched on much flimsier pretexts, his trip to Charlotte County at the age of twenty-two was a daring act that earned him accolades from his readers. [4]

As a recent historian has pointed out, Mitchell's visit to Southside Virginia required courage but was also in keeping "with nineteenth century traditions of grandstanding newspapermen." [5] A later incident from the 1880s, the Simon Walker case, reveals even more clearly the way in which Mitchell combined journalism and protest. He used sensational stories to build up the *Planet*'s circulation while at the same time taking advantage of his position as editor to champion black causes.

The Simon Walker case began on May 1, 1889, when Mary Ann Quill, a twelve-year-old white girl from Ettrick, a settlement in Chesterfield County on the outskirts of Petersburg, took a shortcut home through the woods after a trip into town to sell eggs. Ettrick was the site of the state's publicly supported black college, Virginia Normal and Collegiate Institute. While away from the road, Quill was accosted by a black youth who allegedly pushed her to the ground and raped her at knifepoint. When she reached home she told her story to family and friends, who grew furious at the sight of her torn clothing and talked of a lynching.[6]

Two days later authorities arrested Simon S. Walker, a fifteen-year-old black youth who had no connection to the college. Walker was taken to the Petersburg jail for safekeeping and early on the morning of May 14 was escorted under heavy guard to Chesterfield Courthouse, where his trial took place quickly and without incident. Walker did not testify in his own behalf; he appeared listless and "paid no special attention to what was going on." The jury at first was unable to reach a verdict but after being sequestered overnight found him guilty of rape and asked for the death penalty. Judge W. J. Clopton of the county court sentenced Walker to be "hanged from the neck until he be dead" at Chesterfield Courthouse on August 30.[7]

The Simon Walker case contained all the elements of high drama, but white dailies made only passing mention of the trial. Mitchell said later he knew nothing of the matter until the week before the scheduled execution when he saw a brief notice in a white paper. Though he had no information about the crime, he was convinced it would be a "disgrace to the commonwealth" to execute a fifteen-year-old boy no matter what his offense. "It was not a case of race or color," he said, "it was one of humanity." Determined to stop the execution, he appealed to Democratic governor Fitzhugh Lee (the nephew of General Robert E. Lee) for a reprieve. As it happened, Lee was vacationing in the Virginia mountains to escape the summer heat. Mitchell, showing the sort of initiative that would become his trademark, rode the train 250 miles to Dagger's Spring, a resort west of Roanoke, where he found Lee and persuaded him to grant Walker a thirty-day stay of execution. Lee signed the papers, and the hanging was rescheduled for September 27.[8]

As the date for the execution neared a second time, Mitchell met again with Lee, this time at the Executive Mansion, but the conference was not entirely cordial. He sensed that the governor found his forward manner irritating. As he explained in the *Planet,* he decided to "apparently drop out" and work behind the scenes to furnish the "sinews of war." He met in Petersburg with E. S. Robinson, the white lawyer who had been appointed by the court to defend Walker. Robinson agreed to resume work on the case, and Mitchell promised to pay his fees out of his own pocket if necessary. Mitchell also persuaded black attorneys James H. Hayes and Giles B. Jackson to help. Unfortunately, Governor Lee was again out of the city, this time vacationing at Natural Bridge, but he arrived back in the capital on the evening before the scheduled execution. After conferring with Robinson and Hayes at the Executive Mansion, Lee signed a second stay of execution, this one for two weeks. The two lawyers rushed across Broad Street to the *Planet* office, arriving with the official papers around 10:00 P.M.[9]

Next ensued the sort of swashbuckling adventure that Mitchell relished and that sold copies of the *Planet*. The last train having left for Chesterfield, he was forced to find some way to deliver the papers to the sheriff before dawn, or Walker would hang. He borrowed a horse from Dr. Robert E. Jones, an Alabama-born physician who had come to Richmond from the University of Michigan. Jones was the "first colored physician to drive around in his own buggy," and according to the *Planet* "no one would presume he was colored by the style in which he lives."[10] Jones volunteered his horse but was reluctant to lend his expensive carriage because of the bad condition of the road to Chesterfield. Mitchell then woke Henry Cook, a merchant friend, who offered his sturdier buggy. Cook's son John agreed to accompany the *Planet* editor on his journey. It was nearly midnight when Mitchell and John Cook crossed the James River by Mayo's Bridge and began the sixteen-mile trip to Chesterfield Courthouse. The unpaved road was deep in mud, and there was a light rain. After many adventures along the way, they arrived at the jail just as dawn was breaking.

By the time they reached Chesterfield Courthouse, Mitchell was cold, wet, and disheveled, and he approached the sheriff with considerable misgivings. Across a field he could see the gallows that had been erected for Walker's execution. Armed white men guarded the jail because of rumors that blacks in the neighborhood might try to free him by force. He greeted the sheriff "laughingly," an odd demeanor given the gravity of the situation but one his readers surely understood. A ready laugh could sometimes placate hostile whites. He also reached out to shake the sheriff's hand—a more assertive gesture—and explained his purpose. He said he became involved in the case only because Walker was so young. The sheriff examined the papers and agreed to stop the execution.

Mitchell next accompanied the sheriff to Walker's cell, where he met the prisoner for the first time. He described the jailhouse scene to the *Planet*'s readers in a passage with all the pathos of a sentimental novel. Walker was dressed in faded jeans and was barefoot, with one ankle chained to the stone floor. His chubby face was "the picture of sadness." Mitchell advised him to pray, to look to the Savior ("the mother of the motherless and the father of the fatherless"), and "to conduct himself as to merit the respect of those around him." He told the boy: "I'll go to Richmond and fight for you until the last moment. If I win you will see me again. If I lose, you will see me no more." According to the *Planet*, "These words were delivered in a tremulous voice. When Editor Mitchell looked up Jailer Cheatham was wiping tears from his eyes while the noble-hearted Sheriff was trying to conceal his emotions. It was a touching scene." Mitchell illustrated the story with sketches of the jail, the gallows, the rope, the hood that would be placed over Walker's head when he was hanged, and his intended coffin. His drawings gave the story immediacy.[11]

During the next two weeks, Mitchell persisted in his efforts on Walker's behalf. He spoke at churches to raise money for lawyers' fees and circulated petitions that he wrote out in his own hand. Among those who signed the petitions were some of the original *Planet* founders, including R. A. Paul, E. A. Randolph, D. Webster Davis, George W. Lewis, and James E. Merriweather. On October 4 Mitchell arranged for nine black ministers to ride in carriages to Chesterfield Courthouse, where Anthony Binga of Manchester and James H. Holmes of Richmond pleaded with Judge Clopton on the boy's behalf. On their return the clergy met with Fitzhugh Lee at the Executive Mansion. Pastors from black churches in Lynchburg, Petersburg, Danville, and Hampton also wrote the governor and asked him to commute the sentence, reminding him that it was always better to err on the side of mercy. James H. Hayes circulated more petitions and acquired the signatures of the faculty and staff at Virginia Normal and Collegiate Institute. Throughout the state blacks rallied to the cause of Simon Walker.[12]

While Mitchell and Hayes coordinated black support, attorney E. S. Robinson worked among whites. Although he failed to win a new trial for his client, he persuaded ten of the twelve original jurors to sign a petition asking Lee to commute the sentence to a prison term. He even secured the signatures of Mary Ann Quill's mother, her grandparents, and her aunt and uncle, a sure sign that public opinion was shifting. Robinson said he worked with such fervor because his own son was the same age and he had come to sympathize with the boy. Privately he raised questions about the girl's character and tried to shift the blame to her. Mary Ann Quill's family had come to Chesterfield County from the North three years before. Robinson told Lee that she was not "as careful & particular as she might have been" and was "in the habit of associating with colored boys." The Quills were "northern People & very ignorant," said another letter writer. Hearing that Quill's reliability was in question, Judge Clopton took umbrage. He described her as from a poor family but "simple and modest in her demeanor" and above average in intelligence. Black petitioners prudently made no mention of her virtue, choosing instead to stress Walker's immaturity and stories of his impoverished background.[13]

On October 9 Mitchell met again with Lee, who was obviously troubled by this case, which involved, as he put it, a "very young and weak-minded" boy and a girl who was reputed to be "bad generally." The governor confessed to Mitchell that he had made an impromptu trip that morning to Chesterfield Courthouse to question Walker in person so he could judge his guilt for himself. He thought the prisoner gave a "reasonable" account of what happened. Much encouraged, Mitchell responded that Lee's visit to the jail was "a grand act on the part of a grander man."[14]

Insisting that he needed still more time to study the matter, Lee signed a third reprieve. Probably he was trying to postpone a final decision until after the November election. William Mahone was running for governor in 1889 in a desperate attempt at a political comeback, and Lee had no wish to appear soft on the race issue during the final weeks of a campaign that was described as "hot-red-hot." Although some whites in Chesterfield sympathized with Simon Walker, others were angry at what they regarded as outside meddling in their affairs. They resented Lee's reluctance to abide by the court's decision and promised a lynching if Walker was not executed. "We know it to be a fact," one anonymous letter writer told the governor, "that the negroes of Richmond led by one John Mitchell are exciting the negroes of our county to an alarming degree. . . . Now we do not intend that the negroes of Richmond shall say in any way what shall be done in our county." Another writer described Walker as a "charcoal monster." Finally, on November 7, 1889, with the election over and Democrat Philip W. McKinney of Farmville the winner by a landslide, Lee commuted Walker's sentence to twenty years in the penitentiary. Although the sentence seems harsh by modern standards, it was considered by Walker's defenders to be a victory.[15]

In a *Planet* article headlined "Truth Stranger than Fiction," Mitchell described the final episode in the Simon Walker case, a denouement which suggests that much in southern race relations remained unpredictable. Lee once more waited until the last possible moment to sign the papers, and Mitchell once more made a midnight ride to Chesterfield Courthouse in a borrowed buggy. Fearing that whites might carry out their threats to lynch Walker, he roused the sheriff at his home in "the dead of the night" and proposed that they take the prisoner to Richmond under cover of darkness. The sheriff agreed, and he and Mitchell set out for the capital with Walker, without bothering to handcuff him or restrain him in any way. The November night was cold, and for a time the sheriff jogged alongside the buggy to keep warm. Mitchell carried with him a small arsenal of guns, a fact that surprised the white official but did not seem to alarm him. Mitchell and the "noble-hearted" sheriff had obviously established a rapport of sorts. Arriving in Richmond at dawn, they toured the city briefly, giving Walker his first glimpse of the capital, and then went to the *Planet* office, where Mitchell introduced Walker to an awestruck staff. "I am a thousand times obliged for what you all done for me," said the prisoner. They next stopped at J. C. Farley's gallery where photographs were taken for broadsides and a pamphlet that Mitchell published about the case. Only then did the sheriff deliver Walker to the state penitentiary.[16]

Walker disappeared behind prison walls, but in the years to come Mitchell's admirers often recounted his story. *Planet* readers responded to this saga because of their sympathy for the boy but also because they respected Mitchell's courage. In the Simon Walker case, he exhibited the sort of bravery they could appreciate. He was fearless but never foolhardy or reckless in his dealings with white officials; he was unfailingly polite to those in authority but never servile; he moved with confidence among governors, lawyers, judges, and sheriffs; and he shrugged off threats of a lynching. Mitchell saved Walker's life, but he also salvaged the self-respect of countless blacks who read the story and learned how the race had rallied to support one of its own. "It's a grand thing to be on the side of the oppressed," he told his readers. "It gives you something for which to fight." He presented an image of courage that was forthright and masculine. "Stand up like men!" he said. "Don't cringe and cower. Demand your rights with manly dignity, and all will be well." [17]

For Mitchell journalism meant both words and action, and the Simon Walker case set the pattern for *Planet* protests during the 1890s. He publicized cases that whites ignored and interceded personally on behalf of those who had fallen victim to a judicial system that was far from color-blind. Attacks on legal injustice were standard fare in the black press, but no other editor took it upon himself to champion the cause of prisoners in such direct and personal fashion. In the process he was often flamboyant and self-promoting, but most readers seemed to understand that he was displaying in the public arena the sort of behavior he hoped they would emulate in their private lives. He urged blacks to give up the mannerisms of slavery—the shuffling gait and downcast eyes that had served them well during the years of bondage—and

assume the erect posture of free people. At an 1888 meeting of the Colored
Press Association, he spoke on "Southern Outrages." Ida B. Wells of Memphis, herself a leading crusader against lynch law, wrote that she was profoundly moved by his "burning words and earnest delivery." She concluded
her tribute to him by saying, "May his life be spared to continue the great work
he has set for himself. May his personal bravery and courage be an incentive
to others!"[18]

During the early 1890s racial violence reached its peak in the South, as a
black man died at the hands of a lynch mob on the average of every two days.
Increasingly lynchings became public spectacles, accompanied by torture,
mutilation of bodies, and human bonfires. Mitchell filled the pages of the
Planet with eyewitness accounts and reported lynchings that failed to reach the
white press. Fearing that this epidemic of violence would break the spirits of
black men, he hammered away at the necessity of self-defense. "The best way
to secure protection in the South," he wrote, "is to own a repeating rifle and a
shot-gun and to know how and when to use it." He was convinced that there
would be fewer lynchings if every white mob was compelled "to carry back one
or more of its members as a silent testimonial to the unerring aim of some Negro." Lynchings were intended to keep black men in their place and strip them
of their manhood. Mitchell reclaimed manliness with defiant prose and his
masthead featuring a strong, muscular arm with powerful electric flashes. "We
believe in praying to God," he boasted, "while leaning upon your rifle."[19]

Mitchell was careful to advocate only self-defense, and he also urged readers to cultivate good manners and be "polite and obliging" in their everyday
encounters with whites. In nearly every issue he extolled the middle-class virtues of thrift, sobriety, respectability, hard work, and clean living. There was
always something a bit jarring about the way he mixed pleas for politeness
with exhortations to buy rifles, but for him there was no real contradiction.
He saw good manners and manliness as part of the same essential picture. A
gentleman was never servile or sycophantic; a gentleman never cringed or
cowered or brooked an insult; a gentleman was a man of honor; he insisted
upon his rights in a "manly, respectful way." This mixture of advice evidently
made sense to his readers, many of whom had learned similar lessons from
their parents. The historian Carter G. Woodson told how his father, an illiterate farmer in Southside Virginia, "taught his children to be polite to everybody but to insist always on recognition as human beings; and if necessary to
fight to the limit for it."[20]

Knowing that endless accounts of lynching's horrors were likely to demor-
alize his readers, Mitchell focused on incidents that demonstrated black initia-

tive and resolve. In 1893 he followed closely the case of Isaac Jenkins, a farm laborer from Nansemond County in eastern Virginia who was accused of burning barns and poisoning horses. Because no evidence could be found against him, Suffolk authorities arrested him on the trumped-up charge of selling liquor without a license. Jenkins had allegedly shared a flask with friends while on an excursion. After his arrest he was abducted from the sheriff by a mob of whites who beat him senseless, shot him twice, and hanged him. Miraculously, he survived. Apparently the rope slipped as he was being lynched, and at a critical moment his feet touched the ground. He regained consciousness several hours later and somehow loosened the rope from around his neck though his hands were tied. He dropped down from the tree and headed home, stopping only to ask a neighbor to pour cold water over his wounds. Worried that whites might pursue him if they discovered his "corpse" missing, he spent the night in the woods wrapped in a blanket.[21]

The next morning Jenkins walked thirteen miles to Norfolk to find a physician. There he was arrested, indicted on new charges of arson and poisoning horses, and again jailed. Authorities made no move to arrest his assailants, although their identities were well known, and instead concentrated on preparing a case against him. Mitchell was horrified that those who lynched Jenkins remained at large while their victim was incarcerated. Unwilling to rely on white accounts of the affair, he rode the train to Norfolk to interview this survivor of a lynching. He found Jenkins in jail, in physical torment because of a badly infected bullet wound and understandably despondent at the prospect of having to stand trial in Nansemond County. "It is natural, Mr. Mitchell, for a man who has been through what I have to feel uneasy," he said. Unnerved by the sight of the rope burns about Jenkins's neck, Mitchell wrote one of his fiercest editorials. "Every pain that shoots through the frame of this defenseless man will be recorded against you in heaven," he told the lynchers. "Every prayer he sends up will have an answer and . . . you, gentleman, must answer for your sins." As in the Simon Walker case, he raised money for lawyers' fees and illustrated *Planet* stories with sketches he drew himself. In May 1894, nearly a year after the aborted lynching, Jenkins was tried, acquitted, and released from jail. Mitchell arranged for him to make a speaking tour of Richmond churches, where collections were taken on his behalf. As they made the round of churches, congregations responded with hymns and prayers of thanksgiving. Soon after, Jenkins moved to New Jersey.[22]

For Mitchell the Isaac Jenkins case demonstrated the ability of blacks to withstand the worst. There was something inspirational about the story of a black man who physically removed the noose from around his own neck.

The Jenkins case also highlighted the refusal of white officials to take the lynching threat seriously. "Where is Gov. McKinney?" Mitchell asked in exasperation as Jenkins languished in jail.[23] Despite his admiration for Jenkins, he knew that acts of heroism could not in themselves end lynch law. The lynching threat would disappear only when white officials decided that it was in their interest to uphold the law and when those who joined lynch mobs risked jail sentences and public disgrace. In *Planet* editorials he tried to reason with white southerners; he lectured them on their civic responsibilities, quoted Scripture to them, appealed to their sense of fair play, and pleaded with them to uphold the law. Because so few whites actually read the *Planet,* he was forced to intercede personally with those in a position to help. He lobbied lawyers, prosecutors, judges, and other court officials. He also appealed directly to Virginia's Democratic governors, men who were uniquely positioned to speak out against lynch law and influence public opinion. His success depended to a large extent on the personalities of those involved.

During his term as chief executive (1886–90), Democrat Fitzhugh Lee proved willing on occasion to intervene on behalf of black prisoners, as in the Simon Walker case, but he showed little appreciation for the underlying issues. He was silent on the subject of lynching. His successor (1890–1894), Philip W. McKinney, was even less responsive to Mitchell's entreaties. A lawyer from Farmville in Southside Virginia, McKinney brought to Richmond the racial assumptions of the Black Belt and a reputation for lassitude. One of his few initiatives as governor was to urge—unsuccessfully—that the General Assembly segregate the state's trains. He condemned lynchings in such roundabout language and with so many equivocations that his criticisms sounded like praise for white mobs. At least twenty-two black Virginians were lynched during his four years in office, and Mitchell feared that the state was adopting the ways of the Deep South. Nearly every week he excoriated McKinney for his listless response to the lynching menace. His editorials ended with the refrain, "Lynch law must go!"[24]

McKinney's successor as governor (1894–1898) was Charles T. O'Ferrall, a lawyer and former judge from the Shenandoah Valley who proved more willing to wield power and was more sensitive to the black plight. Like McKinney, O'Ferrall was an archconservative. A former Confederate officer and a member of the Grover Cleveland wing of the Democratic Party, he held conventional views on most subjects and was an ardent foe of Populism, labor unions, and free silver. He sent the militia to the coalfields to suppress strikes and angered party regulars in 1896 by refusing to support William Jennings

Bryan. But he had no stomach for mob violence and was offended by the notion that anyone—white or black, rich or poor—would receive less than a fair hearing in a court of law. In an age of deteriorating race relations, he somehow seized upon the idea that the law must be color-blind, even if the rest of society was not.[25]

An event that occurred in Southwest Virginia shortly before O'Ferrall took office set the stage for his antilynching campaign and encouraged a firmer stance by state officials. In September 1893 a mob of whites in the railroad town of Roanoke surrounded the jail and threatened to lynch Thomas Smith, an unemployed black laborer accused of beating and robbing a white woman. The city's mayor, Henry S. Trout, suspected that Smith was innocent and called out the Roanoke Light Infantry Blues to protect him. When the mob stormed the jail, the militia opened fire. By the time the shooting ended, dozens of whites were injured, some critically, and eight in the crowd had been killed. Horrified by the loss of life, the militia dispersed, and a night of rioting followed, during which marauding whites ransacked buildings, looted, and threatened to lynch the mayor. Trout was shot in the foot and fled to Richmond by train. Smith was left to the mercy of the mob.[26]

Next followed one of those saturnalias of violence that made lynching such a hideous spectacle. With the coming of dawn, whites hanged Smith from a tree at an urban intersection, making him the scapegoat for the economic troubles that had befallen the city. They fired bullets into his corpse and hung a sign on his mangled body that identified him as "Mayor Trout's Friend." They then built a pyre and set his body on fire. Thousands of Roanokers came to watch as Smith's corpse burned: "Everyone that went seemed to wish to contribute something to the blaze by throwing a twig or chip on it."[27]

Across Virginia, whites who had been uneasy all along about lynch law read the news from Roanoke with consternation. This was not the Virginia way. The eight white deaths, the destruction of property, the treatment accorded Trout, and the savagery of the mob unsettled lynching's staunchest defenders. Outgoing governor McKinney was inspired to speak out in defense of the militia, and in his final address to the legislature, he condemned mob violence in language that was at last clear enough for all to understand: "Let us profit from this terrible lesson and learn in all cases to respect the authorities and obey the law." White clergy took to their pulpits to plead for law and order, while white editors warned of the dangers of anarchy. The Roanoke riot showed how a lynching could wound an entire community.[28]

Mitchell deplored the violence but speculated that the calamity in Roanoke might "be productive of much good." Such was the case. Taking advantage of the changing public mood, O'Ferrall managed during his four years as governor to reduce the number of lynchings in the state to a fraction of what they had been in the past. He called out the militia on at least a dozen occasions to protect blacks in danger and bombarded mayors, sheriffs, and police chiefs with telegrams demanding that they protect their prisoners. "Act with caution but firmness and preserve the peace and uphold the law at all hazards," he wired one sheriff. Refusing to rely on the local militia, he almost always sent in troops from neighboring towns, thus sparing soldiers the ignominy of aiming rifles at friends. When the Charlottesville and Harrisonburg militia arrived in Staunton in April 1894, after Lawrence Spiller was accused of murdering a fourteen-year-old white girl, "the presence of the troops had the effect of subdueing and overaweing the turbulent element," wrote the captain. Noting how quickly the crowd dispersed, the *Richmond Dispatch* observed that the "memory of the riot at Roanoke is still fresh in the recollection of the people of Virginia." [29]

During O'Ferrall's first two years in office, no lynchings were reported in the state, a remarkable achievement given Virginia's recent history and the level of violence reported elsewhere in the South. "The rule of Judge Lynch is broken in Virginia," rejoiced Mitchell. "Gov. O'Ferrall did it." The governor's perfect record was marred during the second half of his term when two blacks and one white died at the hands of lynch mobs. The lynching O'Ferrall most regretted was that of Joseph McCoy in Alexandria across the river from the nation's capital on April 23, 1897. "It seems most singular to me," he wired local officials afterward, "that in Alexandria with Police Force and strong military company and hours notice such a thing should occur. Where rests the blame?" He eventually concluded that city officials were themselves at fault. Knowing how difficult it was to convict lynchers in courtrooms, he proposed to the General Assembly a series of legislative deterrents (none of which was enacted), including fines of up to $10,000 on any county or city in which a lynching took place. "Lynchings cannot be too severely reprobated," he told the legislature. "No argument can excuse them, no circumstances can justify them in Virginia." [30]

In countless editorials Mitchell praised O'Ferrall's campaign against lynch law and his willingness to send in the militia to protect prisoners. He was convinced that the governor had "done more to check the spread of lawlessness in this state than any other Chief Executive since the war." He drew a front-page cartoon to portray new forces at work. The cartoon showed a familiar lynching scene, with white men preparing to hang a black victim from a tree, but in the distance appeared row upon row of white men carrying rifles. The approaching whites held high a banner that read, "LAW AND ORDER." "Colored men's prayers are answered," explained Mitchell. "Liberal-minded white men are coming to the rescue."[31]

Mitchell felt certain that his campaign against racial violence helped educate O'Ferrall about lynching's impact. He arranged to have the *Planet* delivered every Friday evening to the Executive Mansion. On one occasion, after the two men conferred about a pardon, O'Ferrall thanked him for the *Planet*. "I read it every week," he said, and added with a smile, "I read what you say about me too." Although O'Ferrall shared fully in many of the prejudices of his day, he always greeted Mitchell courteously, shaking his hand, a small gesture that was much appreciated. According to the *Planet* editor, the governor had "Chesterfieldian manners."[32]

Mitchell extolled O'Ferrall's "manifest love of fair play," but he knew that preventing a lynching was only the first step on the road to legal justice, and he pushed the governor to move beyond law and order to the more complex issue of fairness in the courts. Like other observers of the southern scene, the *Planet* editor worried about what happened in courtrooms after the militia arrived. Sometimes the wheels of justice moved with remarkable speed. Even though the militia's arrival preventing the Staunton mob from lynching murder suspect Lawrence Spiller, he was arrested, tried, convicted, and executed within sixty-four hours of the girl's death. When crimes were heinous, hysteria could override the evidence. When Henry Robinson was tried for rape in Berryville in 1895, the militia surrounded the courthouse to prevent a lynching, but Robinson was found guilty and sentenced to fourteen years in the penitentiary despite a well-documented alibi. Mitchell hoped that O'Ferrall would pardon Robinson, but the governor declined. He apparently reasoned that if he second-guessed judges and juries, he would undermine his own antilynching campaign. Eventually he was forced to respond to this problem of legal lynchings, but in the beginning he held back.[33]

O'Ferrall did use his pardoning power to even the scales of justice in less controversial cases. He released sick and elderly blacks from the penitentiary on humanitarian grounds and reduced sentences when the evidence seemed weak or the punishment out of proportion to the offense. As Mitchell noted, often his pardons called attention to underlying inequities in the judicial system. One of his first acts as governor was to commute from eight years to eight months the sentence of Nelson Shores, a twelve-year-old black youth from Richmond convicted of grand larceny. Shores had driven a horse and buggy into the countryside and left it by the road. Because the Virginia Industrial

School for Boys, established at Laurel in 1891, refused to admit black children, O'Ferrall felt he had no choice but to send the boy to prison. "White boys go to the reformatory," protested Mitchell; "colored ones to jail." Black children as young as eight were sometimes incarcerated. By the end of the decade, black lawyer John H. Smythe, a graduate of Howard University and a former minister to Liberia, was spearheading a move to build a reformatory in Hanover County in an effort to save youths like Nelson Shores and Simon Walker from the penitentiary.[34]

A wildly disproportionate number of inmates in the penitentiary were black, a statistic that whites cited as evidence of black criminality and Mitchell used as proof of an unfair judicial system. Between 1870 and 1902 the penitentiary received 2,671 white and 9,692 black prisoners. The disparity was worst among women: 85 out of the 90 women prisoners in 1896 were black. Mitchell was convinced that white judges and juries simply did not think it mattered what happened to black defendants. Judges assumed that the race was given to crime and happily warehoused blacks in the penitentiary. White juries made capricious and arbitrary decisions. He cited case after case in which black defendants received harsher sentences than whites for the same offense when tried in the same courtroom. For example, a white woman stole a cow in Henrico County (a second offense) and was sentenced to one month in jail and fined $5; a black man stole a calf and was sentenced to five years in the penitentiary. Or again, a white man in East Radford was fined $10 for killing a black man; a black man robbed a white man and was hanged. Cases such as these caused Mitchell "anguish of the heart," he said. They nerved him to write as if his pen was "dipped in vitriol."[35]

In 1895 Mitchell championed the cause of Richard Brown, a black Richmonder whose story attracted attention perhaps because it was so ordinary. Brown, aged thirty-four, an illiterate laborer with a wife and child, drove a delivery cart for Charles H. Page, a Richmond coal merchant. One week Page deducted $2.00 from Brown's wages to pay a fine imposed by the city for operating the cart without a license. Brown only made $3.33 a week, and he protested mightily this reduction in his pay. He said he could not support his wife and child on $1.33 and it was not his fault that Page had neglected to register the cart. Losing his temper, he threatened to take the money by force. Page relinquished the two dollars but the next day had his deliveryman arrested on the charge of highway robbery. At a hustings court trial on January 14, 1895, a jury of ten whites and two blacks found Brown guilty and sentenced him to five years in the state penitentiary.[36]

When Mitchell read about the case, he was incredulous. Only the month before, a policeman was convicted in the hustings court of shooting a black man while off-duty and was fined $25. Now Brown was sentenced to five years in the penitentiary for threatening to take from his employer money that rightfully belonged to him. Mitchell met with Judge S. B. Witt of the hustings court to discuss the case. Witt conceded that the sentence was excessive and explained that he had worked out a more charitable settlement. Once the trial was over, he dismissed the charge of highway robbery on a technicality, in return for which Brown pleaded guilty to a new charge of assault and battery. The judge then sentenced Brown to twelve months in the city jail.[37]

Mitchell was not comforted by this compromise, nor was Brown, who protested that he never struck Page: "I did not assault and batter Mr. Charles H. Page, and he does not claim that I did." Once more black leaders came to the aid of an obscure defendant. Rev. James H. Holmes, Dr. Robert E. Jones, and other professional men gathered at the *Planet* office on a snowy February morning to discuss strategy. They signed petitions, wrote letters, and conferred with the commonwealth's attorney. Eventually they found themselves in the office of the governor. O'Ferrall listened closely to their story and promised to do what he could to help. As they left, he shook their hands.[38]

The petitioners professed to be much pleased with their meeting with O'Ferrall, but days passed, and then weeks, with no word of a pardon. Mitchell kept up the pressure on the governor, whose secretary apologized that they were behind in their paperwork. Brown dictated a second letter, which Mitchell transcribed and delivered to the governor. "I beg your excellency to grant me pardon," said the prisoner. "I have never been in jail before, am a hard working man, and have not knowingly committed any crime." He reminded O'Ferrall that he was the sole support of his wife and child. Unable to entice the pardon from O'Ferrall, Mitchell appealed to an unlikely source for help—Charles H. Page. The coal merchant conceded, none too graciously but in writing, that the "boy" had probably learned his lesson. With Page mollified, Judge Witt and the commonwealth's attorney signed petitions asking for his release. On April 25 the governor processed the papers, and Brown walked out of jail. Mitchell had again engineered a triumph, but he had expended much time and energy to bend the judicial system, even in a case as straightforward as this one.[39]

Mitchell's efforts on Brown's behalf won the attention of Lewis Harvie Blair, a white Richmond merchant and philanthropist who in 1889 published *The Prosperity of the South Dependent upon the Elevation of the Negro*. Blair advocated full civil and political rights for black Americans, a nearly unheard-of stance for a white southerner during this period. Although he adopted a cynical air in his writings and argued that good race relations meant good business, he was more softhearted than he liked to let on. When the Richmond school board in 1893 purchased sets of the *Encyclopedia Britannica* for white schools, he delivered identical sets to black schools as Christmas presents. He praised Mitchell's efforts on behalf of Richard Brown and offered to contribute $100 annually toward a legal fund to assist impoverished black defendants. "Keep up your good work," he told Mitchell, "but be temperate however hard it may be to be temperate in view of the gross legalized injustice done to your race." He urged him "to make special effort to get what you say read by white people and copied by white people." Mitchell was heartened by Blair's response, seeing in it confirmation of his belief that white southerners could be persuaded to speak out against injustice.[40]

During 1895 and 1896 Mitchell was preoccupied with a series of trials that for the first time brought him widespread attention in the white press. The cases involved Mary Barnes, her daughter Pokey Barnes, and Mary Abernathy, three black women from Lunenburg County who were accused of the murder of Lucy Pollard, a white woman. The only evidence against them came from Solomon Marable, a twenty-two-year-old black farm laborer who was himself implicated in the crime and who continually changed his story. Racial tensions in rural Southside Virginia were inflamed by the murder, and at the request of the sheriff, O'Ferrall sent the militia from Richmond to prevent a lynching. According to a reporter for the *Dispatch*, "There has not been such excitement since the war."[41]

Though the women were illiterate, they were given no legal counsel, a circumstance that nearly everyone acknowledged was unfortunate. During the trials Mary Barnes and Mary Abernathy appeared stunned, but the younger and more assertive Pokey Barnes put together her own defense. She called witnesses, conducted cross-examinations, and addressed the jury. "You mens of the jury," she said, "please believe my witnesses, who have not lied, and don't believe Solomon, who done lied to you all." When her star witness crumbled under cross-examination, she protested that "you lawyers done took my witnesses from me for you alls use." It was a truly pathetic scene, as some whites realized. Mary Barnes was convicted of second-degree murder and sentenced to ten years in the penitentiary. Mary Abernathy, Solomon Marable, and Pokey Barnes were sentenced to be hanged. Members of the Richmond militia listened to the testimony, and they returned home with stories of how the women would surely have been acquitted had they had a lawyer.[42]

Through the *Planet*, Mitchell raised money to appeal the convictions. He eventually collected over a thousand dollars, some from sympathetic whites such as Lewis Harvie Blair but much of it from blacks who responded to his appeals for help. Churches, lodges, and mutual-aid societies made pledges to the defense fund. Rosa D. Bowser founded the Richmond Women's League, and with Marietta Chiles as secretary, they managed to raise $690. With the money Mitchell hired three prominent white attorneys to represent the prisoners: George D. Wise was a former congressman, A. B. Guigon had served on the Richmond city council, and Henry W. Flournoy was a former judge of the corporation court in Danville. Ignoring threats on his life but taking the precaution of wearing revolvers, Mitchell made investigative trips to Lunenburg. According to a story that circulated in Richmond for years, at one point during the affair he was eating lunch at a restaurant in Lunenburg when a friend burst through the door to warn him that a white man was "coming down the street flourishing a revolver and threatening to kill him." Mitchell stood up to confront him, but the white man was "so awed by Mitchell's coolness and bravery that he . . . turned and walked away."[43]

The legal proceedings dragged on for months, and eventually the governor, the General Assembly, the Virginia Supreme Court, a series of lower courts, and a host of minor characters were involved. The affair dominated the front pages of the white press and the *Planet* for more than a year. Although O'Ferrall in the past had been reluctant to intercede in cases such as this, the helplessness of the women apparently moved him. As Mitchell observed, "To hang a woman . . . is bad enough," but to hang an innocent woman "was too fearful a thing to contemplate." Mary Abernathy was pregnant, which made her seem especially vulnerable. At one point O'Ferrall refused to let the prisoners return to Lunenburg for trial unless they had a proper military escort. "As you well know," O'Ferrall explained to the Lunenburg judge, "one of the women is about to be confined; all are in mortal terror, and overwhelmed with fear of being lynched if returned to your county jail." He tried to convince the General Assembly to let him send in the militia without the approval of local officials, but the delegates balked. The conflict became a struggle of epic proportions: between O'Ferrall and local officials, between the urban capital and the rural countryside, between different notions of justice.[44]

One of the attorneys for the women, Henry W. Flournoy, revealed how broadly he viewed the cases when he pleaded for a new trial before a circuit court judge. "We know there is a growing and perplexing question in this country," he said. "It is the Negro question. One way to settle it, the best and the right way to settle it[,] is for the white people to do justice to them even though the heavens fall." Mitchell for years had urged black men to make a manly protest. He hoped now that "the white man's conscience will . . .

be touched and that the female portion of his being will be . . . aroused to demand justice for us." He wrung every ounce of sentiment out of the story: "Poor MARY ABERNATHY! Brave-hearted POKEY BARNES! Pitiful MARY BARNES!"[45]

The white attorneys won their case before the Virginia Supreme Court, and new trials began in Lunenburg in February 1896. Local farmers, townspeople, and reporters descended upon the Lunenburg courthouse, at a crossroads miles away from railroad tracks and telegraph lines, in a section of the state dominated by tobacco fields. The people arrived "in buggies, in wagons, on horseback, on muleback, and on foot, white and colored." Fearing that the women would not receive a fair trial in Lunenburg, defense lawyers requested and received a change of venue, and the trials were moved to Farmville in nearby Prince Edward County. Again the courtroom was crowded, with blacks seated on one side of the room and whites on the other. Making the most of his ties to the defendants, Mitchell filled the *Planet* with exclusive interviews with the prisoners and their families. He later admitted he sold more copies of the *Planet* during the Lunenburg trials than at any other time in the paper's history. Even the white press acknowledged his central role in the affair.[46]

On May 5, 1896, the prosecution conceded that it had no case against Pokey Barnes, and charges against her were dropped. When she was released from jail and left for the capital, Mitchell led several hundred blacks to the Richmond train station to meet her. Men and women stood in line to shake her hand, and crowds filled the sidewalks as she made a triumphant carriage tour of the city. Mitchell found her a place to live and bought her fashionable clothing. Photographs suggest a startling transformation: she emerged from her ordeal a glamorous young woman staring confidently into the camera. On the Sunday after her release, she began the customary round of churches to thank those who had contributed to her defense fund. She proved to be an effective speaker despite her lack of education. She was "Pokey Barnes, C. S.," she told cheering crowds—"Pokey Barnes, Common Sense."[47]

In September the prosecution admitted it had no case against Mary Abernathy, and she was released from jail and came to Richmond. Solomon Marable meanwhile was convicted and executed. His last words were a request that his personal effects be given to Mitchell to deliver to his wife. Responding to a long-standing grievance in the black community, the *Planet* editor made certain his body did not go to medical students for autopsy but received proper burial. On Christmas Eve 1896 O'Ferrall pardoned the last of the defendants, Mary Barnes, who had been serving a ten-year term in the penitentiary. The governor said that "every mandate of justice and dictate of conscience" demanded her release.[48]

The freeing of the Lunenburg women marked the culmination of an important epoch in Mitchell's life. He came away from the trials with an enhanced reputation for courage and new confidence in his ability to mold events. W. Calvin Chase of the *Washington Bee* praised his achievement: "No man or set of men, no church or organization will ever be to the Southern colored people what Mr. Mitchell is to the people who are oppressed in the South." Nearly every black editor condemned racial violence, but Mitchell dramatized the issue in ways that caught the attention of his readers. Through words and action he proclaimed that the race would not be intimidated by the lynching menace. He advertised himself as the people's defender. Years later he marveled at his youthful enthusiasm. He had believed he could serve as a one-person NAACP, he said: "I was in my prime then, full of vigor and determination, and it was in dealing with cases like these that my record was made."[49]

CHAPTER FIVE

A Manly Protest

On Friday afternoons, as Mitchell and his staff prepared the *Planet* for delivery to the post office, he must have felt an occasional twinge of apprehension. In the racially charged atmosphere of the 1890s, it was all too possible that his newspaper might fall into the wrong hands and arouse white fury. He told a story once about a white Richmonder who accidentally purchased the *Planet* from "a little colored boy with a bundle of papers under his arm." The man assumed he was buying a white daily and realized his mistake only after he had made his purchase. He was not happy with the *Planet*. He thought the "damned thing was not fit to read and wondered why the city allowed such damn stuff to be peddled on the streets."[1] Mitchell was more amused than frightened by the incident, but the story called attention to the public nature of his protest. The *Planet* was never an underground publication. It was sold on street corners, mailed each weekend to the city's white editors, and delivered on Friday evenings to the Executive Mansion. At a time when a defiant look or failure to remove one's hat could incite a lynching, it was easy enough to imagine a white mob gathering outside the *Planet* office.

Black journalists throughout the United States understood that there was no sure protection from an angry mob. In 1892 Mitchell's friend and contemporary Ida B. Wells was harried out of Memphis after she protested the lynching of three black men whose only crime appears to have been their success in the grocery business. Her suggestion that white women on occasion invited sexual advances from black males inflamed public opinion against her.[2] In 1898, at the close of a bitter political campaign, whites in Wilmington, North Carolina, torched the newspaper office of journalist Alexander Manly and ran him out of town. What followed in Wilmington was more a pogrom than a riot. During a night of terror more than a dozen blacks were killed, and scores of families lost their homes as fires swept black neighborhoods. Mitchell was unsettled by the ferocity of the violence in Wilmington. "A colored man down here is in the same predicament as were the early settlers on the frontier with the Indians," he wrote in the aftermath. "He knows not the day nor the hour when the howling white mobs will be having a song and dance in his front yard." He also knew that powerful forms of intimidation short of violence could be used to silence a journalist. Near the end of his life he observed, a bit wearily, that any black editor who thought he could say what he pleased in his newspaper and the white folks would never bother to read it was living in a "fool's paradise."[3]

Mitchell edited the *Planet* primarily for black readers, and whether white folks read his newspaper was never his primary concern. As he explained in advertisements, the *Planet* was a journal published by blacks and "in the interest of colored people." Even so, he could never entirely forget his potential white audience. He always hoped that a well-reasoned argument or a perfectly crafted editorial might soften the heart of a white Virginian or change the direction of a public debate. He liked to believe that his newspaper made a difference in the larger community. He was also aware that what he said in the *Planet* could be used against him.

Mitchell worried that the race lacked manliness. What bothered him most about the Wilmington riot, for example, was not the white brutality and loss of life, though that "surpassed comprehension," or the failure of state and federal authorities to protect black citizens, which he also deplored, but the image of black men as helpless victims of white aggression. News reports from Wilmington described families fleeing to the woods in pell-mell retreat. He was convinced that stories of this sort encouraged white violence and made lynchings more likely. He said that had he been in Wilmington, he would have stayed in town to protect his newspaper regardless of the consequences: "When we buy presses and pay for them we will make our bed in our office. Lawless mobs must face bullets and editorial citizens of color must have their guns loaded." He projected an image that was brave and courageous and would make a white assailant think twice before attacking the *Planet* office. "If a black mob went to a white editor's residence to destroy his property and take his life, what would he do?" he asked. "You do exactly what he would do and you will come near acting properly."[4]

A central challenge of Mitchell's career was how to make a manly protest without placing his life in jeopardy and without alienating those few white southerners like O'Ferrall and Blair who seemed sympathetic to the race's plight. For Mitchell, manhood was always more than a gender concept. Like others of his generation, he believed a man became "manly" by virtue of his relations with other men, not because of the ways in which he was different from women. In other words, manliness meant more than being macho or virile. A popular dictionary in 1890 defined *manliness* as "possessing the proper characteristics of a man; independent in spirit or bearing; strong, brave, large-minded, etc." From Mitchell's perspective, these words had special meaning: a man was mature, not a child or a "boy"; he was civilized, not savage or bestial; he was a freeman, not a slave. To his mind, manliness was the prerogative of a gentleman and signified honor. He knew that many white southerners assumed black men could never be gentlemen, just as they believed black women were incapable of being ladies.[5]

In the *Planet,* Mitchell urged male readers to cast off all traces of servility and comport themselves in manly fashion. Typical bits of advice that appeared regularly on his editorial page included: "Never let us sacrifice manhood or jeopardize our self-respect in order to succeed." "White men admire manhood and respect those of us who respect themselves." "It is unmanly to shirk trouble; meet it squarely." "Respect white men, but do not grovel. Hold your heads up. Be men!"[6] Mitchell believed that true manhood was best expressed through respectable, middle-class behavior, and yet he was prepared to defend himself physically. In 1896, after an acquaintance struck him during a quarrel, he was quick to respond and quick to publish the results on the front page of the *Planet:* "Editor Mitchell returned blow after blow, striking his cowardly assailant repeatedly in the face and forcing him to retreat."[7]

Mitchell felt certain he could make overtures to white southerners in a manly fashion, an assumption that would be sorely tested in the years to come. His interactions with O'Ferrall demonstrate the difficulties he faced. No southern governor was more opposed to lynching or more sensitive to black aspirations, and yet even this most "liberal-minded" and "open-hearted" of white men was unwilling—or unable—to challenge racism in any fundamental way or to envision any significant alteration in southern life and customs. Two of Mitchell's interactions with the governor are revealing for what they say about race relations during the 1890s.

The first of these encounters occurred in September 1894 when the Afro-American Press Association held its annual meeting in Richmond. Mitchell had served as president of the organization since 1890, but this was the first time the editors had come to Virginia. He was pleased to be hosting the event and looked forward to giving tours of the *Planet* office. The guest of honor would be Ida B. Wells, probably the best-known antilynching crusader in America. Mitchell and Wells had been friends since the 1880s and had similar backgrounds. Both were born to slave parents during the Civil War and taught school before becoming journalists. After being forced out of Memphis in 1892, Wells moved to New York and joined the staff of T. Thomas Fortune's *New York Age*. She published a book about lynching (*Southern Horrors: Lynch Law in All Its Phases*) and in 1894 traveled to Great Britain and helped found the British Anti-Lynching Society. Mitchell knew that Wells's appearance at the meeting would energize the gathering. She was a fearless speaker who championed self-defense and boasted of carrying a pistol. Hers was a "manly" protest, though Mitchell avoided that conundrum. Mitchell also invited O'Ferrall, the nation's leading antilynching governor, to address the opening session and welcome the journalists to Virginia.[8]

The event did not proceed as Mitchell had hoped. Early in September, O'Ferrall received a telegram from the *New York World* asking his opinion of a projected tour of the South by investigators from the British Anti-Lynching Society. O'Ferrall was obviously miffed: "Things have come to a pretty pass in this country when we are to have a lot of English moralists sticking their noses into our internal affairs." He reminded the *New York World* that he had called out the militia on at least a dozen occasions to protect prisoners from white mobs. British investigators had no reason to visit Virginia, he said. The very idea was "the quintessence of brass and impudence."[9]

Two days later, as black leaders arrived in Richmond for the press association meeting, O'Ferrall announced that he would not address the convention unless the journalists repudiated Wells, something he must have known they would never do. He evidently felt he had to put some distance between himself and black activists. In a statement issued to the press, he advised the editors to focus on combating crime and rape in their own neighborhoods and let him lead the battle against lynching.[10]

Mitchell responded to O'Ferrall with a letter written on behalf of the Afro-American Press Association. The tone of the letter was polite and courteous, as befitting correspondence with a governor, yet he was unapologetic about the central issues. Avoiding any references to Wells's assertive personality, he said it was "the principle for which she contends that inspires confidence and regard, and touches a responsive chord in our hearts." He explained that Wells had toured England in defense of liberty just as Frederick Douglass, Wendell Phillips, and Henry Ward Beecher had gone to Great Britain in support of emancipation. He compared her to the Hungarian patriot Louis Kossuth and the Irish nationalist Charles Stewart Parnell. He reminded O'Ferrall that black editors were invariably held to a double standard. If white men were tortured and hanged by black mobs, "every Southern white man and woman would rise in open indignation and rebellion against such atrocities, and they would be right." Black editors could not muffle their protests or rely on others to defend the victims of violence: "We cannot stand idly by and see our race hung without judge or jury by a lawless mob." Editors in the South felt a special responsibility to speak for those who could not speak for themselves.[11]

Mitchell's response to O'Ferrall was straightforward, without the posturing and double-talk that became almost obligatory in the early twentieth-century South. He was convinced that "liberal-minded" white southerners did not demand elaborate displays of obsequiousness, just as they did not expect their domestic servants to cringe and grovel. They appreciated competence and candor. As it turned out, his assessment of what white southerners appreciated was far too optimistic, but for the time being he remained unrepentant. "If race agitation . . . does the race harm," he said, "then the race will have to stand it." He genuinely believed that in the long run accommodation would work against the race: "Cringing has never settled any great question. Cowardice has never served to do otherwise than to awaken contempt."[12]

As for the press association meeting, it proved to be a disappointment. At the last moment Wells failed to appear, and the sessions were marked by some bickering among the editors as they debated the association's purpose. Mitchell declined to run for election, and the organization entered a moribund period. Not until the founding of the NAACP in 1910 did a national organization emerge that embraced the rhetoric of protest and united blacks and whites against lynching. Although the press association's troubles predated the Richmond meeting, Mitchell's difficulties in putting together a program in 1894 were symptomatic of the profound challenges facing black journalists. It was not clear how to awaken the conscience of white America, or what role the press could play in advancing the race's agenda, or how to join forces with "liberal-minded" whites who preferred to keep them at arm's length.[13]

Mitchell had another encounter with O'Ferrall that demonstrated how hard it was for black activists and white southerners to find common ground. In March 1895 a committee from the Massachusetts legislature passed through Virginia on a tour of the mills and factories of the New South. While in Richmond the legislators were scheduled to have lunch at the Executive Mansion. Once they arrived, O'Ferrall discovered that among the visitors was Robert Teamoh, a black journalist from Boston who was a member of the Massachusetts legislature. With Teamoh was Mitchell, who joined the group at some point, although it was never clear who issued the invitation. As the biracial delegation filed into his parlor, O'Ferrall made a decision he may have regretted later. "Rather than have it heralded over the North that the Governor of Virginia . . . had insulted the whole committee," he decided to conceal his surprise and, in his own words, "get through the disagreeable thing as soon as possible." After an exchange of pleasantries, he ushered the men into the dining room for lunch.[14]

Some years later Teamoh recalled the event: "John Mitchell was sent for, . . . I shall never forget, and we all went to the Governor's Mansion. His Excellency's valet . . . took my overcoat and hung it upon the rack and smiled as he did so. That I remember." According to the *Planet* the meal proceeded smoothly. "Both [Mr. and Mrs. O'Ferrall] were complying with the strict rules of etiquette, and in no case did they display any sign they regarded it unusual the colored officials being present." Mitchell noted that the governor's wife did not dine with the guests or shake hands, but O'Ferrall was a gracious host who shook hands with everyone. Mitchell said he was not surprised by the courtesy, understanding that it was "simply the state of Virginia acting through its official head and was in no wise a private or social affair tendered by an individual." He acted as if he routinely dined with governors, but he must have known the significance of the occasion. According to Teamoh, when the group sat down to lunch, the *Planet* editor leaned over to him and whispered, "There will be the devil to pay after this affair is over." [15]

There was indeed the devil to pay. The prohibition against "eating with Negroes" was one of the white South's strongest taboos. The *Dispatch* got wind of the incident and in an editorial revealed the "meanness, treachery and ingratitude displayed by Teamoh and Mitchell in presenting themselves at the Governor's lunch table." The *Dispatch* speculated that Teamoh received his "despicable inspiration" from Mitchell. O'Ferrall responded with a statement in which he protested the press's misrepresentation of the event. "I received the visitors from Massachusetts in an official capacity and I only did what anyone else would have done in my position," he said. "While I knew that I was to receive a committee from the Legislature of Massachusetts, I was not aware until the last moment whom this delegation consisted of." O'Ferrall added that he was "greatly surprised and embarrassed, but I concealed my embarrassment as much as possible." Warming to the subject, he said that the white delegates conveyed to him privately "their mortification on being burdened with the negro." [16]

To O'Ferrall's own mortification the controversy refused to die. Southern Populists, led by Marion Butler of North Carolina and Tom Watson of Georgia, seized upon the incident as an excuse for attacking the conservative governor. Watson, who could play the race card when it suited his purposes, charged that O'Ferrall dined at the same table with a black man "just as natural as if he was a human being." Populists in North Carolina, themselves reeling from attacks made on them for adjourning the legislature on the occasion of Frederick Douglass's death, heaped ridicule upon the "aristocratic governor" from the "aristocratic Democratic state." The *Progressive Farmer* of Raleigh poked fun at O'Ferrall's increasingly labored explanations: "He says he didn't know there was a colored brother with the committee until the carriages arrived at his door, etc. etc. But you notice he didn't tell the colored men to stay outside. He didn't tell them not to enter his parlor; he didn't say, 'Nigger, don't you go with us to the dining room.' In fact, he didn't say a word until three days after the occurrence." Francis W. Darling, the chairman of the delegation, meanwhile challenged the governor's veracity. Darling claimed that O'Ferrall knew all along who was coming to lunch and treated the black men with "utmost consideration." He saw no evidence that anyone was mortified. In the weeks that followed, other disagreements surfaced, such as arguments over whether the meal was a formal luncheon or merely light refreshments. The debate was a preview of the controversy that erupted in 1904 when Booker T. Washington dined at the White House.[17]

In an era so racially sensitive that a biracial lunch could cause such furor, it was perhaps inevitable that Mitchell learned to moderate the tone of his protest. With the passage of time, he grew more temperate in his use of language and less likely to swagger and boast. After the turn of the century, he espoused many of the ideas about self-help and business success that have come to be identified with Booker T. Washington. That he grew more cautious in the twentieth century should come as no surprise; nearly every black editor in the South did the same thing. That he remained so forthright throughout the 1890s was remarkable, given the dangers he faced. He was probably right that his brandishing of Smith & Wesson revolvers afforded him a measure of protection, while his "steely" resolve and proud demeanor made it less likely he would be bullied. Moreover, by the 1890s he had come up with a number of editorial devices that enabled him to make a strong protest in the *Planet* while avoiding the fates that overtook Alex Manly and Ida Wells.

In the first place Mitchell never under any circumstances cast aspersions on white women. This was what got both Manly and Wells in trouble. Wells suggested in 1892 that what whites assumed to be rape was sometimes consensual intercourse. Manly was more explicit, asserting that white women on occasion seduced, romanced, and loved black men. "Every negro lynched is called a Big Burly Black Brute," he wrote in the *Wilmington Record*, "when, in fact, many of those [lynched] . . . had white men for their fathers, and were not only not black and burly, but were sufficiently attractive for white girls of culture and refinement to fall in love with them, as is very well known to all."[18] Nothing was more likely to arouse white fury than statements such as this, and Mitchell never made them. In the Simon Walker case, for example, whites might speculate that Mary Ann Quill was a willing accomplice in the sexual encounter, but he said nothing that reflected poorly upon her or impugned her virtue. In *Planet* editorials he advised male readers to treat all women with courtesy. "We must respect our women in order that others may respect them," he wrote.[19] Only rarely did he acknowledge that his readers might themselves be women, and despite his admiration for Ida Wells, he never specifically explored what a "womanly" protest might be.

In truth, Mitchell's views on women were not much different from those of most white males of his time and place. Like his white contemporaries he usually referred to the softer virtues as "she." Mercy, justice, kindness, pity, and compassion were female attributes, while strength, courage, bravery, and independence were male. He thought the black race was insufficiently manly—too kind, too generous, too spiritual, too nurturing, too quick to forgive; in other words, too feminine—while the white race was excessively manly and in desperate need of feminizing influences. He drew one cartoon in which a white woman representing "Justice" guarded the state penitentiary to prevent the entrance of an innocent prisoner. In another a fair-skinned, ladylike angel hovered over a black man who knelt in prayer in the wake of lynchings.[20] But usually white women made only the briefest appearances in the *Planet*, as when Jane O'Ferrall greeted her guests in the parlor, chatted for a few moments, and then withdrew, leaving the lunch and the discord to the men.

Mitchell's refusal to entangle white women in the race issue did not mean he was oblivious to issues of sexuality. On the contrary, the vigor with which he attacked male sexual transgressions made his silence on the subject of women more noticeable. He was certain that miscegenation had not ended with slavery and that "white men who talk against social equality practice it." According to the *Planet* white men patronized black houses of prostitution, kept black concubines, and seduced and assaulted domestics: "They yell about Negro supremacy and the effort of the colored man to secure social equality, and yet those same howling hypocrites live upon a plane of absolute equality with Negro women whose houses they furnish and whose illegitimate children they educate." The hypocrisy of this "mixing" infuriated him. He suggested that a law be passed making it a felony for a white man to keep a black mistress: "Some of our friends think such a law would depopulate certain portions of this and other communities, while others are of the opinion that the exodus of white men from the State to escape the rigors of the law would leave the colored men in possession." He thought "Jim Crow beds" were more essential to racial harmony than "Jim Crow cars." He never suggested, however, even in jest, that black men should feel free to reciprocate and cross the color line themselves or that white women might welcome their advances. To have made such a proposition, in the context of the times, would have been the height of folly.[21]

Mitchell's shielding of white women from racial discussions was one device he used to protect himself from retaliation. Another was the way he combined militant pleas for self-defense with more conventional praise of middle-class virtues. He did this in the context of manliness, and in nearly every issue he admonished black men to behave like gentlemen. He could be priggish in his defense of good manners and extravagant in his praise of whites who exhibited "Chesterfieldian manners." He exhorted parents to teach their children to be polite, respect their elders, save money, go to school, mind their manners. He thought it important that "no man, be he white or black, show himself to be more of a gentleman than ourselves." Respectability was an issue that in Mitchell's case always cut both ways. On the one hand, his assumption that he was a gentleman—the peer of James Lyons—was an affront to southern mores; on the other hand, so much emphasis on minding one's manners inevitably undercut the radicalism of his protest.[22]

Mitchell also used humor to soften the thrust of his editorials, although in this respect the effect was usually to enliven them. Rather than attack racial prejudice head on, he liked to poke fun at whites and expose their frailties by indirection. He could put an unexpected twist on the most ordinary observations about southern race relations and thereby make whites appear foolish, as in the following example: "The colored man is in everything. You can't keep him out and the Southern white folks like him. If they want a man to wait on them they get a Negro. If they want a shave, they get a Negro. If they want a bootblack, they get a Negro. If they want a man to curse, they get a Negro, and if they want a man to hang and burn, they get a Negro. Strange people, are these Southern white folks."[23] He often connected unrelated events in surprising ways. When the bubonic plague broke out in India, he offered to sign a petition asking that the mayor of Richmond be sent to Calcutta as the American representative at twice his usual salary. He noted that the mayor was already suffering "from a severe attack of Negrophobia, sometimes known as racial epizooty."[24]

Mitchell's ironic comments were safer, probably, than frontal assaults on white racists, and certainly they were easier on his readers. The writer James

Weldon Johnson once observed that many black journalists seemed weighed down by the race problem. He found their editorials depressing—too ponderous, too much in earnest, too relentlessly bleak: "If the mass of Negroes took their present and future as seriously as do the most of their leaders, the race would be in no mental condition to sustain the terrible pressure which it undergoes; it would sink of its own weight." Partly in reaction, Mitchell stressed race resiliency and the fundamental irrelevancy of much that went on in the white community. He thought any race that had withstood "250 years of galling slavery, four years of bitter war and thirty years of so-called liberty" was not likely to "die or get out of breath" because of the malevolent doings of southern racists.[25]

Mitchell made other distinctions in his editorials that were commonplace in the black press and served to temper his militancy. He championed self-defense but not retaliation or aggression. He insisted that not all white people were adversaries and lavished praise on "liberal-minded" white southerners, even though he must have known that they seldom lived up to his expectations. "A Southern white man is one of the best of friends and one of the worst of enemies," he explained. Or again, with more bite: "Colored men, give the friendly white people all the praise you can and give the unfriendly ones all the devil you can handle." He steadfastly protested against racial injustice but never suggested that blacks lacked responsibility for what happened to them or were in any way absolved from making their best effort. "We are responsible for some of the things from which we suffer," he wrote. "We can improve our condition if we will. . . . It is no use to stop and complain. Keep on working."[26] These self-help admonitions grew trite and hackneyed with the passage of time, but at their best they offered readers a way out of the terrible morass of deteriorating race relations and gave them power over their own lives. Finally, when discussing segregation and civil rights, he made the familiar distinction between public civil rights and "private social ones."

Having grown up in the upper South and in a large city, Mitchell was accustomed to a measure of flexibility in race relations, although the extent of this flexibility and its significance have occasioned much historical debate. In 1882 a white visitor to Richmond observed that "there was a universal disposition on the part of the white people to avoid difficulty and conflict with the colored people respecting their civil rights, and the negroes were, in general not disposed to contend for them." By the time Mitchell took over the *Planet* in 1884, the churches, schools, theaters, hotels, and restaurants in Richmond were segregated, at least in most instances, but until the twentieth century blacks sat where they pleased in streetcars, trains, and public parks. There were no Jim Crow laws in Virginia, save for regulations regarding separate schools.[27]

An incident reported in the *Planet* in 1890 revealed both the pervasive nature of segregation and the lingering uncertainty about where to draw the color line. On a summer evening in June 1890, Dr. Joseph E. Jones, a member of the faculty at Richmond Theological Seminary, attended a revival service conducted by a visiting white evangelist. Jones, a former slave who was light-skinned, arrived early at the tent meeting and chose one of the better seats. An usher asked him to move. "You will find colored people over there," he said. Jones replied: "I am not hunting for Colored People. I came here to hear the Word of God preached, and prefer sitting here." When the usher summoned a policeman, the professor refused to move. "Am I at all disorderly?" he asked the police officer. "Am I disturbing religious worship?" Fearing an altercation, the manager of the event decided it would be prudent on this occasion to bend the color line, at least slightly. He apologized to Jones for the inconvenience, shook his hand, and found him another chair: "While not placing it in the apartment arranged for Colored people, yet [he] sat it near there." After a few minutes in this new location, Jones decided that the compromise was not good enough and left.[28] The positioning of a chair "near" the "Colored people" was obviously a minor concession, as Jones himself realized, and yet even this small negotiating space would soon disappear. In the twentieth century a curtain dropped between the races, leaving scant room for mediation or breaches in the color line.

As customs hardened and states to the south enacted Jim Crow legislation, Mitchell defended the full civil rights of black Americans in forthright terms: "We are opposed to any man, be he white or black, Democrat or Republican, who will not recognize our rights as citizens and accord to us all the rights and privileges of every other citizen. To ask more would be unreasonable; to accept less, out of the question." He dismissed as "legal quibbling" the idea that separate facilities could in fact be equal and decried the Supreme Court's 1896 decision in *Plessy v. Ferguson* that upheld segregation in public transportation. Segregation was humiliating because it asked the race "to display a badge of inferiority upon all occasions." Self-respecting whites would not be flattered if they were roped off at public meetings or forced to ride in a separate section on trains as if suffering from smallpox. Furthermore, segregation was a serious inconvenience to the black traveler, forcing him to "carry his provisions with him." He insisted that the "public hotels, bars, etc., should be made to accommodate all classes of citizens."[29]

In his attacks on Jim Crow, Mitchell explained over and over the vast difference between civil and social rights. He assured whites that "I do not intrude myself where I have not been invited," and he said he had no ambition to attend private parties in white homes. He had attended the luncheon at the Executive Mansion only because it was a public, civic event. The rules regarding public accommodations were different from those governing private parties: "A man who opens a place of business becomes a public servant and he cannot discriminate against those whose servant he is, save upon the grounds of public decency, safety, etc., but not on account of color. . . . Prices alone should govern the accommodations, and when any white man or black man places a bar to a man's privilege and declares that he shall not come over it, simply on account of color, it will not be tolerated by a free and independent people. . . . We demand no 'social equality.' We insist upon our civil rights."[30] He was also quick to point out inconsistencies in the segregationist position: "When you really want an absolute isolation from the race practice it at home and in your private affairs and our people may be more liable to believe in your sincerity."[31]

Occasionally Mitchell protested segregation in more direct ways. While traveling by train through Kentucky in 1893, for example, he blithely ignored Jim Crow signs and sat among whites, pretending he did not understand the state's customs. He challenged segregation under more difficult circumstances in 1899 when he made a train trip to Jacksonville, Florida. He said that until he reached Atlanta he had no trouble, but after transferring to the Central of Georgia line, he saw a partitioned area set apart for black people. Because he had purchased a Pullman ticket in Richmond, he took a berth in the sleeper. The white conductor who discovered him there was aghast: "Don't you know it is against the laws of Georgia for you to ride in a car with white people?" Mitchell replied that he was an interstate passenger and not subject to Georgia's local restrictions. The conductor ordered him to vacate the sleeper, but he refused. Finally the conductor stalked off after warning, "You will certainly have trouble if you stay in here, and it will be at your own risk." As the train moved through south Georgia, Mitchell heard strange noises outside his compartment and had trouble falling asleep, but he arrived safely in Jacksonville the following morning. He stepped off the train into the Florida sunshine feeling quite pleased with himself. He remembered the incident fondly in later years: "We felt that our time had come and had made up our minds as to how we would 'cross the river.'"[32]

Mitchell's determination to make a manly protest, no matter what the consequences, was in part a reflection of his personality. Possessing a fiery temperament, he was first inclined to be combative and stand his ground rather than accommodate. Residing in the Virginia capital also afforded him a measure of protection. If race relations were never as friendly in Richmond as whites sometimes liked to pretend, the city exhibited at least a veneer of civility and a reluctance to exercise power in the most brutal, violent fashion. Furthermore, in Richmond hundreds of black men continued to vote, a circumstance that altered the public discourse in significant ways. When a white detractor once dismissed Mitchell as a "would-be-self-appointed leader," he answered proudly that he was in truth a public official and a duly elected member of the city council.[33] As long as he remained successful in electoral politics, he would find the courage to protest boldly, without the equivocations and servility he found so distasteful.

CHAPTER SIX

The Politics of Jackson Ward

In many respects Mitchell was a natural candidate for a career in politics. He had a fine speaking voice at a time when politicians were expected to entertain the voters with extravagant displays of oratory. His first important speech was made in 1888 at the state Republican convention in Petersburg when he was twenty-five. "He exhausted his venom before the audience," reported the Democratic *Dispatch*. He cataloged the "horrors of Democratic rule" and charged that the Democratic Party was composed of "broken-down aristocrats, who speak of the blood that courses through their veins, who forget that the war is over, and who are only allowed to live as a manifestation of divine mercy." To a group of Republicans who were bolting the convention, for reasons having nothing to do with him, he replied grandly, "Fare thee well, and if forever, still forever, fare thee well." The *Dispatch* called it a bitter speech, but a reporter for the more friendly *Richmond Whig* acknowledged that "he talks well." After he lectured in New York on Henry Grady's New South, those in attendance concluded that he spoke "at times after the fashion of evangelist Sam Jones, being forcible and pleasing in style." [1]

Mitchell also enjoyed the rough-and-tumble of city politics. Despite his polished manners and Grace Street upbringing, he was not at all reluctant to rub shoulders with ordinary folk or spend an evening politicking in a saloon. As a young man he threw himself into party work at the precinct level and acquired the skills needed by a local politician. He learned to negotiate and bargain. In April 1888 a white Republican complained to Senator Mahone that at a citywide meeting the *Planet* editor "voted first one way and then another . . . and was expecting honors from both sides." [2] He also took full advantage of his ownership of the *Planet*. He promoted his campaigns in front-page articles and used the *Planet* press to print broadsides and other political literature.

Mitchell brought to politics more than his share of talents, but he arrived at a time when black officeholders were becoming increasingly rare in Virginia.

After the collapse of the Readjuster movement in 1883, the Democratic Party in Virginia consolidated its control, and the number of blacks elected to office in the state decreased steadily from year to year. "There are 8 colored men in the legislature," wrote Mitchell in 1888. "We wish there were 50." By 1891 no blacks and only three Republicans sat in the General Assembly. Fraud was made easy for the Democrats by the Anderson-McCormick Elections Act of 1884, which gave election officials considerable leeway in how they counted the ballots. As one Democrat admitted, the act was written "so that the officers of election, if so inclined, could stuff the ballot boxes and cause them to make any returns that were desired." [3]

In defiance of trends throughout Virginia, Mitchell served on the Richmond city council for eight years, from 1888 until 1896. He was first elected to the common council, the thirty-member lower house of Richmond's large and unwieldy bicameral city council. He was young when he took office—not quite twenty-five—and he arrived at his first meeting outwardly self-confident and eager to begin the business at hand. Showing an independent spirit from the start, he cast the lone dissenting vote against a measure expanding the all-white police force on the grounds that blacks should be hired as patrolmen. [4] In 1890 he won a seat on the more powerful eighteen-member board of aldermen. As an alderman he spoke up often in debates and introduced dozens of resolutions that he wrote out in his own hand and submitted to the council clerk. The right to vote was "the badge of the freedman," he told *Planet* readers. To his mind there was no question more important than "Shall the Negro be allowed to vote?" [5]

Mitchell was able to win elective office not because white Richmonders were unusually tolerant but because of racial gerrymandering. When the last federal troops left the city at the end of Reconstruction, whites discovered that they had an uncertain hold on city government. Although they made up more than 60 percent of the population, they had the barest numerical advantage in each of the city's five wards—Clay, Jefferson, Madison, Marshall, and Monroe. Blacks lived in nearly every section of the city during the postwar period, but their largest settlements were on the northern outskirts of town, where black neighborhoods spilled out into Henrico County, and on low-lying, undesirable land such as that bordering Shockoe ravine. In 1871 the General Assembly approved a redistricting plan that created a sixth ward, Jackson Ward, to take into account postemancipation realities. The new ward was oddly shaped, with boundaries that twisted and meandered in the area north of Broad Street. Included within the ward were as many ex-slaves as authorities could possibly squeeze into one political subdivision. [6]

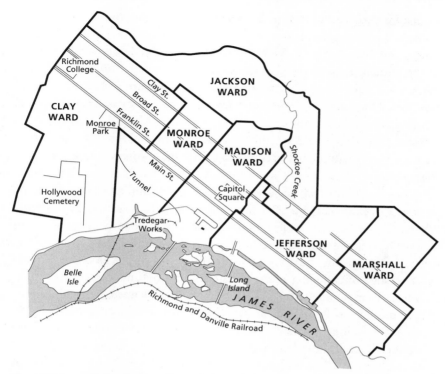

Map of Richmond showing ward boundaries, 1890s

In one sense racial gerrymandering worked to the disadvantage of black voters, and certainly that was the intention. By the 1890 census blacks made up just under 40 percent of Richmond's population and yet were dispersed in such a way as to be outnumbered in five of the six wards. To make matters more unfair, Jackson Ward was a huge, densely populated ward, with nearly twice as many voters as the affluent Madison Ward, thus undermining the notion of equal representation. The only larger ward was Clay Ward, in the rapidly expanding white suburbs to the west. If gerrymandering weakened black influence, however, it also meant a reprieve for Mitchell and other aspiring black politicians. In Jackson Ward blacks were in such a large majority that they could hardly be shut out of the electoral process. As the *Richmond State* explained in 1883, black officeholders became a "political necessity" once the city "penned up the mass of colored voters."[7]

Between 1871 and 1896 thirty-one blacks, all Republicans, were elected to the council from Jackson Ward. The ward sent three representatives to the board of aldermen for staggered four-year terms and five to the common council for two-year terms. The black councilmen came from a mix of back-grounds, but among them were lawyers (E. A. Randolph and James H. Hayes), a physician (Dr. Robert E. Jones), artisans, barbers, factory workers, mer-chants, and businessmen. A majority appear to have been mulattoes, and sev-eral, such as Edward R. Carter and Henry Moore, were so light they could have passed for white. With perhaps a few exceptions, they were of high social standing, literate, and economically independent.[8]

Because the Republican organization was strong and vibrant, the Demo-crats made only halfhearted attempts to recruit black voters in Jackson Ward. "Blessed are the Jim Crow Democrats," joked Mitchell, "for they shall ride in Jim Crow cars." Instead, the Democrats sought to limit the impact of the black vote by means of fraud. Their favorite tactic was the simple one of delay. When the polls opened on election day, black and white voters were placed in separate lines at the four precincts in Jackson Ward and allowed to vote alter-nately. As soon as the short line of white voters was empty, elections officials began to stall, often taking an inordinate amount of time to ask the simplest questions. Democratic Party workers meanwhile challenged the qualifications of each black voter for as long as half an hour. When the polls closed in the evening, the waiting voters (sometimes as many as six hundred) were sent home. As O'Ferrall conceded, "In this way the sun set upon the heads of many a colored voter who had for hours been standing in line with his uncast ballot in hand."[9]

After the 1888 congressional election, James C. Smith, a barber from Jack-son Ward, described how the delaying technique worked in practice:

> In one instance a man came in by the name of Harris, about 50 years old. He was asked if he was 21 by challenger, what year he was born in, where his mother lived, and if the last freshet had washed the dung off his house. The objection was made to this man's voting on count of his residence; the judge sent some men with him to see if he lived where he said he lived. They came back and said it was all right. There was some question then about his voting, and this supervisor, Kolbe, said he be damned to hell if he would vote, and said he'd sit on the ballot-box first.

Democrats conceded that there had been delays but protested that it was a "well-known fact that negroes are hard to identify and that it requires perfect acquaintance and long familiarity to distinguish one from another." In the 1888 election there was good evidence that the length of time needed to iden-tify voters depended on how well the Democratic candidate for Congress, George D. Wise, was faring in other parts of the district. After 465 voters from

Jackson Ward testified before federal commissioners of fraud and harassment at the polls, the House of Representatives refused to seat Wise and instead gave his place in Congress to the Republican challenger, Edmund Waddill Jr. That same year John Mercer Langston of Petersburg became Virginia's first black congressman when he contested his defeat in the heavily black fourth congressional district.[10]

The threat of fraud, rather than intimidating black voters, seemed to inspire Mitchell and other Republican leaders to greater efforts. On the night before an election, they gathered in the darkened streets to prepare for the coming contest. After the gubernatorial election of 1889, the *Dispatch* described the scene in Jackson Ward on election eve: "The negro population . . . slept very little Monday night. They began to gather around the voting-places before midnight, and in the early hours of the morning fires were kindled in the streets. . . . By 3 o'clock the colored population, men and women, had turned out in large numbers." Bands of "patriotic women" served sandwiches and hot coffee, while entire families took to the streets. The *Planet* described a similar scene before the 1892 presidential election: "As early as 12:00 Monday night, these devoted Republicans were standing, waiting for the dawn. Some procured chairs, benches, etc., and patiently waited, while others cracked jokes, discussed the situation, and condemned the unscrupulous white men who made this course necessary."[11]

Once the polls closed voters gathered at party headquarters to await the returns. After Mahone's defeat in 1889, the crowd quietly dispersed, but victories brought massive celebrations. After winning the 1892 council election, Mitchell rode through the streets in a horse-drawn buggy decorated with flags and Chinese lanterns. According to the *Planet,* Robinson's Brass Band headed the procession. "Then came the carriages with some of the successful candidates. Four stalwart colored men carried torches on each side of [Mitchell's] buggy. The line bristled with torches and transparencies. . . . Fully three thousand people were in the procession. A number of little boys with drums, about ninety in all, were marching through the streets." Clearly the residents of Jackson Ward enjoyed their participation in city politics.[12]

The two races may have wrangled on election day, but they seem to have been on much better terms once they reached the council chamber. Mitchell said that whites on the council almost always treated him with courtesy, and he was pleased that he was identified in council minutes as "Mr. Mitchell" without racial identifiers or first-name references. Another Jackson Ward councilman, Edward R. Carter, later insisted that the atmosphere was "very amicable." Much of the business that came before the council was of a routine administrative nature, with no racial overtones, and the two races inevitably found themselves in agreement on many issues. Although Mitchell took an active part in debates, he learned early on that there was no point in needlessly antagonizing the Democratic majority. He sometimes abstained when an awkward matter arose, as in 1890 when the council deeded the White House of the Confederacy to the Confederate Memorial Literary Society for a museum. In 1893 he dutifully voted yes to a measure for which he had little sympathy when the council appropriated $4,000 to bring the body of Jefferson Davis back to Richmond for burial in Hollywood Cemetery.[13]

The most controversial issue to face the council during Mitchell's tenure was municipal reform. On the eve of the Progressive Era, the city government was the focus of a number of investigations sponsored by "good government" leagues. The corruption in Richmond was on a relatively petty scale, but many citizens rightly suspected that the city was poorly managed and that the council dispensed contracts, franchises, and other favors for a price. According to the *Dispatch*, "It is seldom that one hears a kind word spoken of the average councilman." On the contrary, "he is the object of constant criticism and the target of many idle and malicious shafts." Mitchell nearly always voted with the reformers, which may indicate that Republicans were being denied their fair share of the spoils. Certainly it seems significant that the charge of corruption was never leveled against him or any of the other councilmen from Jackson Ward, especially when one recalls how often during Reconstruction black officeholders in the South were accused of profiting from their positions.[14]

White Richmonders tolerated their black councilmen with little fuss and often overlooked them partly because the delegation from Jackson Ward possessed so little real political power. Whenever any issue of importance arose, fifteen Democrats on the board of aldermen could easily outvote three Republicans. It was always possible, of course, that whites might disagree on a controversial issue and allow blacks to assume the balance of power. Something of this sort happened in 1886 when the Knights of Labor won control of the council by combining forces with Republicans from Jackson Ward. By the time Mitchell reached the council chamber in 1888, however, the labor movement had lost momentum, and whites seemed determined never to allow a breach in their ranks. When contentious issues arose, they often went into caucus, occasionally going so far as to ask the Republicans to leave the council chamber so they could deliberate in comfort.[15]

While hardly holding the balance of power, Jackson Ward councilmen did manage to secure some concessions. In 1891 Mitchell made a strong appeal for $20,000 for school buildings for blacks, an appropriation that was eventually granted and led to the construction of a new brick building to replace the tumbledown Navy Hill School. Three years later he persuaded the council to construct an armory for the black militia. The First Battalion Armory had been on the agenda for more than a decade but was not fully funded until 1894 and then only after Mitchell and Major Joseph B. Johnson, who commanded the First Battalion, hired a carriage and called on the councilmen individually to make the case. The council unanimously overrode the veto of Mayor Richard M. Taylor, who thought it "unnecessary, unwise, and against public policy to maintain colored soldiers in this city." The First Battalion Armory turned out to be much smaller than the Howitzers Armory, erected in 1895 for white soldiers, but it was still an impressive brick building, a castlelike structure with corner towers and terra-cotta and stone trim.[16]

Construction projects usually had a fair chance of success, perhaps because they permitted some boondoggling. Mitchell also lobbied for better streets in black neighborhoods, more lighting, more free coal for the city's poor, and a night school for black children. In the time-honored fashion of local politicians, he smoothed the way when constituents negotiated with city officials. For example, in 1890 he assisted Rev. William Troy, the pastor of Sharon Baptist Church, in his efforts to receive a refund after he overpaid his property tax.[17]

Other controversies proved more troublesome. Throughout his years on the council, Mitchell sought to reverse an 1887 decision that only "native whites" could be employed on construction projects. When the new city hall opened in 1894, city officials boasted that the massive neo-Gothic building was constructed entirely with white day labor, although they acknowledged that this was one reason it cost so much more than projected and took so long to build. By the 1890s blacks were denied even the most menial positions. According to Mitchell, less than 3 percent of the city's payroll went to blacks. He described how a man who cleaned the council chamber lost his job. "But a head loomed up," he said. "A white man desired to wash spittoons." He pleaded with the councilmen "as Virginians, as Richmonders, as patriotic citizens, as Christians" to give black men their share of employment. "Labor cannot afford to make war upon labor," he told the Democrats. He supported "retrenchment and reform" partly because the reformers advocated giving construction contracts to the lowest bidder, even if that meant black laborers shared in the city's largess. The Powhatan Club, an organization of Democratic stalwarts, meanwhile campaigned to have black teachers fired so that whites could draw their salaries, a retrograde move that the school board resisted.[18]

On at least one occasion Mitchell prevailed in the matter of city hiring. In

February 1895 the all-white Bricklayers Union complained that the white contractor in charge of building the First Battalion Armory had sublet the brickwork to Armstead Walker, a black contractor. Mitchell appeared before the building committee to plead Walker's cause. Walker was an expert brick mason, a graduate of Richmond Normal, and the husband of Maggie Walker, who was already well known for her work with the Independent Order of St. Luke. Desperate to make the case for Walker, Mitchell included in his presentation a sentimental appeal that seemed to sway the committee: "Mr. Mitchell referred to the good feeling existing between the white and colored people of the city, spoke of the care taken of white children by colored nurses today and in sympathetic tones told of the labors of the old black mammies during the late war and the colored men who remained at home." After listening to this oration, the committee decided to allow Walker to finish the brickwork.[19]

Another frustrating issue for Mitchell, surely the most discouraging of all, involved the location of a garbage incinerator that the city decided to build in 1891. Until the 1890s Richmond disposed of waste matter in primitive ways, primarily by hauling trash to the countryside. The health department, alarmed by the threat of epidemics and the growing mountains of trash, proposed in 1890 that the city build an incinerator to burn waste products. A committee traveled north to study waste disposal plants and came home convinced that an incinerator was the best solution for an inland city unable to dump its garbage into the ocean. The committee confidently assured the council that a crematory would be no more objectionable than "any ordinary factory, as the gases which are evolved are likewise consumed."[20]

In April 1891 the council agreed to build the crematory on Buchanan Street, on vacant land along the railroad tracks on the east side of Shockoe Creek. Three months later more than a hundred whites who lived in the vicinity crowded the council chamber to demand that construction stop. Surprised by the outcry, the councilmen bowed to political pressure and agreed to find a less offensive location. "The city council should be very careful in selecting a [new] site," cautioned the *Dispatch*. Even if burning garbage produced no odors, the hauling of refuse was bound to be objectionable to those who lived nearby. In the weeks that followed, various sites were proposed, but each provoked citizen wrath. At one point Mayor Taylor, weary of the controversy, made the facetious suggestion that the city build the crematory in Monroe Park, in the midst of an affluent white neighborhood, a suggestion designed to underscore the council's predicament: no one wanted to live next door to a garbage furnace. Members of the health committee finally came up with their own proposal: the city should erect the crematory in a black residential neighborhood in Jackson Ward on St. Paul Street between Bacon and Orange in the area known as ' Postletown.[21]

For weeks Mitchell held off a decision by the force of his oratory and by appeals to conscience: "We beg you, for God's sake, not to put that garbage furnace among us." He pleaded with the councilmen to find another location and made impassioned speeches, sometimes talking with such emotion that no one interrupted him even when he spoke much longer than his allotted ten minutes. "The speaker quoted Scripture quite freely" and was "really very forcible," admitted the *Dispatch* on one occasion. In the end his rhetoric was no match for political exigencies. On September 17, 1891, the council approved the St. Paul location by a vote of twelve to six. Three white Democrats joined the three Republicans in opposing the Jackson Ward site.[22]

Construction began once more on the furnace, this time in a black neighborhood, and by 1892 a barnlike structure with an eighty-five-foot-high brick chimney had risen on the property. On a wintry February morning, city officials gathered to light the fires and test the incinerator. By noon the furnace was hot enough to receive a sample load of garbage, a stomach-turning mix of household trash, butcher-shop trimmings, fish, spoiled meats, and animal carcasses. As the refuse burned, white officials professed to be enormously pleased with the results. They could detect almost no odor and thought the fumes barely visible.[23]

Two months later, as the weather warmed and the garbage sample gave way to wagonloads of trash, the situation deteriorated. In April 1892 Mitchell introduced the first in a series of protests against the crematory. He asked the health committee to investigate the "nauseating smells" emanating from the furnace. On May 9 he requested that the crematory suspend the burning of "fetid animal matter." On June 13 he pleaded for an end to the cremation of animal carcasses and human excrement. In August he changed tactics and asked the city to hire three appraisers "to ascertain the relative decrease in the valuation of real estate in the neighborhood of the present crematory." Although officials tried to put a good face on the matter, something was clearly wrong. In a private letter to the health committee, the builder confessed he was "chagrined and disappointed in the operation of the crematory."[24]

In an effort to make the furnace less offensive, the city engineer tinkered with the machinery and raised the smokestack twenty-five feet to release "objectionable gases and smoke" at a higher altitude. No remodeling, however, could make the crematory a community asset. Mule-drawn garbage carts entered Jackson Ward from every section of the city, and in summer, when garbage arrived faster than the incinerator could burn it, rotting piles of trash rose on the premises. Probably nothing better illustrated black political vulnerability during this period than the building of the crematory on St. Paul Street. In 1895 Mitchell was still introducing resolutions against the furnace.[25]

Mitchell's failure to protect his constituents from the crematory underscored his weakness as a councilman. He was often outvoted in matters relating to Jackson Ward; he was never appointed to the most influential committees, such as finance or buildings and grounds; and he failed to persuade the council to hire blacks to many city positions. But he was at least able to present the grievances of the black community publicly and with a degree of dignity; he was at least present at the bargaining table when decisions were made. After the turn of the century, the informal give-and-take of the council chamber would be sorely missed. Biracial meetings of any sort became rare in Richmond, and blacks had to rely entirely on backdoor appeals and hat-in-hand supplications.[26]

Mitchell knew that the voters of Jackson Ward needed outside help if they were to retain a political base, and he was determined to hold on to his council seat. In February 1889 he led a delegation of black journalists to Indianapolis to meet with Benjamin Harrison, the Republican president-elect. Mitchell pleaded with Harrison to do something to protect the freedom of the ballot in the southern states. He specifically asked that he appoint an attorney general with the power to investigate election frauds. According to the *New York Times,* the journalists were given a scant fifteen minutes of Harrison's time: "The General made no speech to them of any kind—good, bad or indifferent, pleasant or cross." Years later Mitchell recalled his meeting with Harrison. "We received instructions to look pleasant and to announce that we have been well received," he said. "As a matter of fact, President Harrison received us about as coldly as an iceberg. . . . As a matter of fact, all of our delegation were 'boiling over with indignation.'"[27]

The next year Congress turned down the Lodge federal elections bill, which would have ensured federal supervision of southern elections. Mitchell insisted that "we have no time to suck our thumbs and grieve over what Congress failed to do," but he understood the broad implications of the bill's defeat. In 1891 Judge Robert W. Hughes of the U.S. circuit court in Richmond dismissed the "Jackson Ward Cases," a series of grand jury indictments brought against Democrats for conspiring to defraud in the 1888 congressional election. In dismissing the cases the judge, himself a Republican, ruled it was not a federal crime to prohibit someone from voting, even in a federal election; instead, the matter came under the jurisdiction of state and local courts only.[28] Then in 1894 the Virginia General Assembly passed the Walton Act, a measure that disfranchised thousands of black Virginians and set the stage for Mitchell's defeat.

The Walton Act was advertised as a move toward honest elections because it provided for a secret (or Australian) ballot and required that all voting take place within the polling booth. The real purpose was to transform the ballot itself into a literacy test. According to the Walton Act, ballots were to be printed by the local electoral boards and not by the respective political parties. The custom had been for party workers to distribute marked ballots to waiting voters. Now voters had to mark their own ballots, which they were not allowed to see until they entered the polling booth. No symbols or names were permitted on the ballots to show party affiliation. The method of choosing candidates was itself odd. A ballot was properly marked only if straight lines were drawn at least three-fourths the way through the names of those candidates for whom the voter meant not to vote. If illiterates desired assistance, they could receive it from a constable appointed by the electoral board. The electoral boards in turn were named by the Democratic General Assembly.[29]

The Walton Act almost always worked to the advantage of the majority party, just as the General Assembly had hoped. Often the constables, themselves Democrats, refused to assist illiterate voters or provided assistance that resulted in miscast votes. Ballots were thrown out for frivolous reasons: because the lines drawn by the voters were too long, too short, too crooked, or too faint. To make matters still more complicated, some local boards began to print a bewildering assortment of ballots for each election. In Richmond the names of the candidates were arranged helter-skelter, thus making it impossible for an illiterate voter to memorize the position of his candidate's name on the ballot. Spurious names were added to create confusion. For example, the name "John Mitchell" mysteriously appeared on the ballot during the 1896 congressional election even though the *Planet* editor was not a candidate. Voters were given only two-and-a-half minutes in the polling booth, no matter how confusing the list of names. According to Mitchell, the Walton Act was "one of the most outrageous measures ever enacted by any state for the disfranchisement of the colored man."[30]

The Walton Act provided the Democrats with the means to win an election in Jackson Ward if they chose to execute fraud on so grand a scale. In the council chamber, meanwhile, race relations were not as amicable as when Mitchell first arrived. In May 1895 tempers flared after a joint meeting of the two chambers was called to choose a superintendent of gasworks, an appointment that was controversial because of a long tradition of corruption in that department; a former superintendent had gone to jail. When Mitchell arrived at city hall, he was told that the Democrats had gone into caucus and that the meeting would be delayed. When the meeting was called into session an hour later, he rose to speak. In an angry outburst he said he had come to city hall fully prepared to cooperate, but he could not endorse a decision he had no part in making. He nominated a Republican for the position, a white man who was easily defeated by the partisan vote of 40 to 8. Several months later a similar incident occurred, although this time Mitchell grew tired of waiting and left the council chamber in protest. Tensions among whites were evidently contributing to the breakdown in race relations. Caucuses were necessary, said the *Dispatch*, "to prevent combinations with the members from Jackson Ward."[31]

By the 1890s another factor endangered Mitchell's seat on the council. Despite much talk heard in the city about the "solid Negro vote," the black electorate in Jackson Ward was itself divided. On election day two slates of Republican candidates invariably opposed the Democratic ticket. The more powerful of the factions, and the one to which Mitchell belonged, was called the Whiskey Ring. The other faction, the Post Office Gang, was led by James H. Hayes.

Mitchell's faction was called the Whiskey Ring because of his alliance with James Bahen, an Irish saloonkeeper from Jackson Ward who was first elected to the board of aldermen in 1886. Born in Ireland in 1845, Bahen had worked as a teamster for the Union army during the Civil War, and after the war he and his mother operated a grocery and liquor store in Jackson Ward. To the rear of the store was a drinking room—a proverbial smoke-filled room—where politicians gathered. Edward R. Carter later explained one secret of Bahen's success: "Mr. Bahen used to run a grocery and bar at 1st and Baker Streets. We used to take our constituents there and feed them and set up a keg of beer and some sandwiches and get them in good trim. They we'd go into a political meeting and get our slate elected without any trouble." The Mitchell-Bahen alliance proved to be an unusually effective political combination. Mitchell was the more visible of the two men, speaking up often in the council chamber, but Bahen worked well behind the scenes. He was "the man everyone had to see about their requests," and he could also appeal to the ward's white voters. Jackson Ward was predominantly black, but there was a significant white minority, making up about one-fifth of the population.[32]

As one might imagine, Bahen's influence did not go unchallenged. Just as white Richmonders had good-government leagues, so too did the voters of Jackson Ward. The most celebrated of the reformers was James H. Hayes, the

Howard-trained lawyer who helped found the *Planet* in 1883. Elected to the common council in 1886, Hayes chafed under Bahen's domination and resented the way the white saloonkeeper tried to control ward politics. Hayes and Mitchell had much in common, which may explain why they clashed so often: both were fiery orators and "brainy" race defenders.

In 1890 Hayes bolted the Republican Party and supported an independent, all-black slate of candidates in the council elections. The reform ticket included several of the most respected men in Jackson Ward, among them Joseph E. Farrar, a contractor who had served on the council during the Readjuster era. Mitchell's ticket, on the other hand, included Bahen and M. T. Page, another white saloonkeeper who had a somewhat unsavory reputation. Mitchell conceded that the reformers hoped to replace the "white rum-keepers" with respectable black men. The fight began with a "cry against James Bahen, the Republican leader who had virtually controlled politics in Jackson Ward." Mitchell and Bahen won handily in 1890, however, which suggests that the Whiskey Ring retained a firm grip on ward politics. In 1892 Hayes put forward another reform slate and founded his own newspaper, the *Southern News*, to promote his cause. Again Mitchell and Bahen easily defeated the insurgents.[33]

Although Hayes proclaimed himself the reform candidate, the question of which faction was actually truer to the race was more complicated. Generally the working-class whites of Jackson Ward supported Mitchell and Bahen. Mitchell welcomed their votes and pleaded for a rebirth of the working-class coalition that had taken over the council in 1886. "The time for the poor whites and poor blacks to clasp hands has not yet passed," he said at a political rally in 1890. He was proud that Bahen had always been identified with "the laboring class of people." In truth, it was never clear in Jackson Ward exactly where virtue resided. Hayes supported an all-black ticket in council elections but allied himself with the faction within the state Republican organization that was less sympathetic to black aspirations and more interested in the distribution of federal patronage. The prominence of government employees among his supporters, many of whom lived outside the ward, gave his faction the label Post Office Gang.[34]

In many ways factionalism in Jackson Ward, despite all the sound and fury, was little more than a sign that the body politic was healthy. Voters of all persuasions took part in politics, and no one ever won a seat on the council by default. After the 1894 council elections, voters marched in parades that lasted until after midnight. "The torches were lighted and the transparencies brought out," said the *Planet*. Cheering crowds lined the streets, and a band played "Rally 'round the Flag, Boys."[35] Rather than being apathetic, the voters of Jackson Ward (and their wives and children) seemed consumed by politics. The ward was small enough that candidates knew each other well, and nearly every issue that divided the black community found its way onto the political battlefield. Campaigning was carried on in barbershops and saloons, on porch stoops, in lodge meetings, and in churches. Quarrels took on a life of their own until finally, in the end, probably no one remembered for sure exactly why Hayes and Mitchell disliked each other so much.

During the spring of 1896, the layers of controversy grew increasingly complex. Dr. Joseph E. Jones and Dr. Daniel N. Vassar, two highly respected members of the faculty at Richmond Theological Seminary, campaigned against "rum-keepers." They were also on opposite sides from Mitchell in a controversy that was dividing the Virginia Baptist State Convention: Jones and Vassar urged closer cooperation with northern white Baptists; Mitchell advocated a more independent course. Similarly, much of the conflict that spring reflected a threatened schism within the United Order of True Reformers, the community's largest and most influential mutual-aid society.[36] Even the Lunenburg trials entered the controversy. When Pokey Barnes was released from jail three weeks before the election, Mitchell took her on carriage rides and attended church services with her. One white reporter thought she was "aiding Mitchell materially in his canvass for votes," but another surmised that some voters resented the way he used her to advertise his candidacy. None of these issues seemed trivial or in any way unrelated to politics. "The [Republican] war is become more bitter every day," noticed a white observer. "Meetings are held nightly and each one stirs up bad feelings."[37]

In the end factionalism proved to be a risky indulgence for black voters. As early as 1890 Mitchell warned that the Democratic Party hoped to exploit divisions within Jackson Ward and "announce to the country that a split was in progress among the Republicans themselves" so that the Democrats could carry the ward. At a time when fraud was commonplace, a divided black electorate offered abundant opportunities for chicanery. In 1892 the city Democratic chairman reported that he had received "time and time again propositions by which the vote should be thrown in favor of the Democrats." He thought each side was willing to sell the other out.[38] White Republicans from the state organization also invaded the ward, seeking allies in the squabbles that were plaguing the party during Mahone's last years, adding to the political confusion.

A united electorate in Jackson Ward might have better withstood Democratic challenges, but probably not. The key factor in Mitchell's 1896 defeat was Democratic fraud—abetted by the Walton Act. The *Richmond Times* described the familiar scene in Jackson Ward on election day, May 21, 1896: "The negroes formed in line at the different precincts yesterday morning and waited with great patience and praiseworthy perseverance while the procession wound its way with tortoise-like pace to the mecca of their desire—the ballot-box. Those well up to the front succeeded in voting, but when the sun went down upon the city, the hindmost ones were still there, eyeing with wistful eyes the small bits of paper with which they had hoped to pave the way of . . . colored brethren to power." Election officials described the counting of ballots as a tedious job and conceded that they threw out hundreds of ballots because they were "improperly" marked. No black candidate won election anywhere in the city, but Bahen somehow survived the Democratic sweep, a circumstance that prompted charges of collusion. "To say that the colored people of Jackson Ward are angry," said Mitchell, "is expressing it mildly." He headlined the story the "Jackson Ward Robbery" and called the results "nothing more nor less than a farce."[39]

Mitchell attended his last council meeting on June 8, 1896, as a lame-duck councilman. The business that evening was routine, and the Democrats readily consented to his proposal that black soldiers be excused from paying rent for the First Battalion Armory. As the meeting was about to close, he stood before the council to introduce a final measure, a courtesy resolution praising the contributions of William M. Turpin, a white lawyer from Jefferson Ward who served as the board's presiding officer. He thanked Turpin for his years of service to the board, his "fearless advocacy" of all measures, his fidelity to duty, and his "uniform courtesy in dealing with members of this body." He asked that a copy of his tribute be given to Turpin. Just why Mitchell chose to honor the white councilman is unclear. He may have felt genuine regard for Turpin, who was one of the few Democrats to side with him on the crematory issue; perhaps he wanted to remind his Democratic foes that he, at least, was a gentleman and man of honor; or perhaps he hoped that someone would rise to thank him for his eight years of service to the council. If he expected praise, he was disappointed. His resolution commending Turpin was the final action of the evening—and his last act as a city official.[40]

When the new board assembled on July 1 for an organizational meeting, the clerk submitted a letter from Mitchell contesting his defeat and claiming his old council seat. He seemed incapable of leaving without one final protest. The account in the minutes is brief. A Democrat proposed that the communication from Mitchell be tabled. Henry J. Moore, a partner in the construction firm of Farrar & Moore and the sole surviving black councilman (elected in 1894 to a four-year term), moved that Mitchell's letter be referred to a special investigative committee. Moore's motion failed. Before adjourning, the aldermen attended to one final piece of business, adding to the sense that black councilmen were anachronisms. They accepted the invitation of the United Confederate Veterans to participate in ceremonies surrounding the laying of the cornerstone of Jefferson Davis's monument in Hollywood Cemetery.[41]

In the presidential election on November 3, 1896, Jackson Ward voters turned out in force to vote for William McKinley. By daybreak over five hundred voters stood in line at each of the four polling places, refusing to believe they had been ousted from politics. As the sun rose women arrived "carrying breakfast to their husbands, brothers, sons, etc." According to the *Planet,* the presence of the women cheered the voters, "especially when they saw those smiling cups of coffee and hot biscuits." The men waited patiently all day, standing in line until dusk, but many never reached the polling booth, and there was grumbling as election officials stalled for time. Once the polls closed Republican Party workers made their own private tally to compare with official returns. According to Mitchell, the extent of the fraud was unprecedented: 2,300 Republican ballots were thrown out during the course of the count. "It is only a very short time before the people of Jackson Ward will refuse to submit to the outrageous robbery which is visited upon them at every election," he warned. "If the time has come that we must be placed in jail for demanding our rights, the sooner we get there the better."[42]

When Mitchell walked out of the council chamber on July 1, 1896, he could not have known that he would never again hold public office or that half a century would pass before another black Richmonder won election to the city council. As the years went by, he found new outlets for his energy and came to terms, at least somewhat, with a Jim Crow South that had no place for black officeholders. The refusal of the courts to intervene and the apathy among Republicans in the North made it clear he had little to gain by brooding over rights denied or making symbolic protests. But the wounds never entirely healed. He understood that more was lost in the 1896 election than a chance to lobby for streets and sewers. Gone was any sense that black Richmonders were citizens of the first rank or legitimate participants in the affairs of the city. Henceforth he would appear before civic bodies as a supplicant, trying under excruciatingly difficult circumstances to make his voice heard and to win for the black community a small share of what whites were dispensing.

CHAPTER SEVEN

"No Officers, No Fight!"

After Mitchell's defeat in the council election of 1896, his editorials grew more somber. The exuberant good spirits that had marked his earlier protests gave way to more guarded assessments of the race's prospects, marked by occasional touches of melancholy and real bitterness. He felt confident that as long as the Reconstruction amendments remained a part of the U.S. Constitution, black voters would someday regain the franchise, but he no longer had much faith in the good intentions of state or federal officials. Nowhere was his disillusionment more evident than in his response to the Spanish-American War.

When war with Spain threatened in the spring of 1898, some black journalists saw the conflict as an opportunity for the race. They reasoned that valor on the battlefield and a conspicuous show of patriotism would call attention to the race's plight and halt the erosion of political and civil rights. Mitchell, on the other hand, was more skeptical. He said that his study of American history suggested that whenever black troops fought bravely in battle, the battles were forgotten. When black soldiers were defeated, the battles were "speedily remembered." Reminding readers that he had risked his life many times in his crusade against lynching, he said he had no need to demonstrate his bravery or prove his manhood in a war against Spain. If the federal government failed to protect his right to vote and hold public office, then why should he fight to protect the federal government?[1]

He also challenged the fundamental assumptions of America's expansionist foreign policy. He termed the war a "war of conquest" and speculated that "colored Cubans" would be no better off under an American administration than under Spanish rule. If humanitarian issues were at stake, he suggested that some foreign nation investigate conditions in Mississippi, Louisiana, or Texas. They would discover that "in the South today exists a system of oppression as barbarous as that which is alleged to exist in Cuba." He urged white soldiers to take up the cause of freeing Cuba: "White men, rally 'round the flag! Die for your country! . . . Join the army. Endure the mosquitoes and the hot weather! Face the Spanish bullets and the machetes!"[2]

Usually white journalists ignored Mitchell's editorials, but in May 1898 the *Washington Post* took exception to what it described as a particularly "stupid and ignorant outburst." Mitchell was pleased to be noticed and in a perverse way enjoyed sparring with the white editor. The *Post* editor said that no one cared "three straws" whether blacks enlisted in the army. Mitchell answered that "if no one cares three straws," he was going to stay home. The *Post* warned that "noisy complainants" like Mitchell did not represent the race. Mitchell wondered if the white editor really imagined that the *Washington Post* represented the race. When the *Post* suggested that blacks were to blame for their woes, he answered with a long sardonic passage that revealed his sense of history and his resentment of white interpretations of the American past:

> We are to blame for the Dutch steamer's bringing our forefathers to this country and landing them at Jamestown. . . .
>
> We are to blame for the two hundred and fifty years of slavery which the white folks inflicted upon us.
>
> We are to blame for taking a part in the War of Independence and dying at Bunker Hill.
>
> We are to blame for being with Commodore Perry on Lake Erie during the War of 1812.
>
> We are to blame for being with the white folks of this country in the Mexican War.
>
> We are to blame for helping to save the government in the late Civil War, and sending tens of thousands of the best able-bodied men we had to a carnage of death. . . .
>
> "Poor, mortals, we!" "Damned if we do, and damned if we don't." Will our trials never end?

He warned that at the beginning of every war, blacks hoped that valor in battle would win them respect and yet it never happened.[3]

Mitchell's apprehensions about the war were not shared by the soldiers of the First Battalion who occupied the armory on Leigh Street. The First Battalion had its origins in militia units founded by black Richmonders during Reconstruction. Benjamin Scott, a plasterer, organized a company of soldiers on his own initiative not long after the end of the war. According to a white physician, Scott liked to "array himself in a brilliant uniform and drill his company for hours in some of the best white residential sections for pure devilishness." By 1866 the Navy Hill "Irrepressibles" were said to number more than two hundred members, and they protected black neighborhoods from gangs of marauding white youths. As one might imagine, the appearance of black men carrying rifles made some whites uneasy. As the *Richmond Times* asked in 1866, "Who do the negroes expect or propose going to war with?"[4]

In 1871 the General Assembly authorized the formation of separate white and black militia units under state auspices. The soldiers received no pay except when called into service and were expected to provide their own uniforms, but the state provided ammunition and equipment. These militia units proved popular among black Virginians. The soldiers marched in parades, decorated the graves of the Union dead, participated in sham battles, and traveled to the countryside for target practice. As one officer from Petersburg conceded, drill night had its "frolic" side. Before the evening drills began, the men competed in "boxing competitions, wrestling matches, jumping contests, indoor target practices, indian club swinging and dumb bell handling." Women congregated at the armory to watch the parades and help with fund-raising. They "would stage concerts, conduct lawn parties, participate in many occasions in which funds were being raised for the boys."[5]

According to state law, members of the militia elected their own officers, who in turn received commissions from the governor. At the time of the Spanish-American War, the commanding officer of the First Battalion was Major Joseph B. Johnson of Manchester. Born free in Amelia County in 1847, Johnson had worked since the Civil War as a mechanic at the Tredegar Iron Works. He first came to prominence in the 1880s as an organizer for the Knights of Labor, and he was secretary-treasurer of the Galilean Fishermen's Relief Association, a flourishing mutual-aid society. Major Johnson was handsome in uniform, "a man of fine physique, tall, erect, and of good voice." Like other officers in the state militia, he saw the Spanish-American War as an opportunity for his soldiers to take part in a great national adventure and prove their mettle.[6]

Once it became apparent that black soldiers were determined to enlist, Mitchell shifted his focus to the question of black officers. During the late nineteenth century, only a handful of blacks served as commissioned officers in the regular army. Most black soldiers served in segregated units under white commanders, just as they had during the Civil War; usually they were stationed in remote areas of the West far from centers of population. Mitchell protested that the time had come for black officers to take their place at the head of black troops. "If we are to be subjected to the insult of the separation," he said, "let us enjoy the privilege of being officered by men of our own selection."[7]

Mitchell felt even more strongly about the issue of black officers for volunteer units. The Spanish-American War was fought by two categories of soldiers, those who joined the regular army and those who enlisted in state-run militias. The most famous militia unit during the war was Theodore Roosevelt's Rough Riders. Prospective soldiers usually preferred the militias (or National Guard) because discipline was believed to be easier and they could serve alongside friends and neighbors and under commanders of their own choosing. Mitchell insisted that black Virginians deserved the same rights in the volunteer militia as white soldiers. When rumors spread that the First Battalion would be mustered in without their officers, he coined the slogan "No officers, no fight!" The phrase was picked up by black editors across the United States.[8]

At the first hint of war with Spain, Major Johnson volunteered his men to Governor J. Hoge Tyler "as presently officered." In other words, his soldiers would join the war effort but only if their officers received commissions. His offer placed the Democratic governor in a difficult position. Although most whites were glad for blacks to enlist, few were comfortable with the notion of black officers. The *Richmond Dispatch* thought their use in wartime a "dangerous experiment" and worried that they would panic at the first sound of gunfire. The *Richmond Times* was concerned about the social implications. What would happen if a white officer came upon a black officer who outranked him? Would the white officer be expected to salute first? Joseph Button, the clerk of the Virginia Senate, believed the idea folly and warned Tyler against flouting white sensibilities: "For God's sake do not take such a step, for I verily believe it will cast a cloud over your entire administration." Scores of whites meanwhile wrote the governor pleading for the well-paying commissions. Their letters would not have reassured Mitchell. "I have a facility for handling men of this color and . . . have worked them on the railroads," wrote one applicant. Another prospective officer promised the governor he would have no trouble "controlling and managing these laborers—as I know thoroughly the racial characteristics, etc. etc."[9]

When the first call for soldiers came in April 1898, Tyler sidestepped the controversy and mustered in white militia units only. The white volunteers were accepted with their own officers, although in accordance with congressional guidelines Tyler commissioned an officer from the regular army to serve with each regiment and prepare the men for battle. In May, Congress issued a second call for troops, and black Virginians again clamored to serve. "What to do with the negro troops is a perplexing problem," confessed Tyler, who seemed genuinely unsure of how to proceed. For days he mulled the matter over and at times obfuscated his position. He implied that he was under pressure from Washington to appoint black officers, although this was apparently untrue. He spoke vaguely about unexplained difficulties and hidden complications.[10]

In early June, Tyler announced his decision: he was calling up eight companies of black soldiers with their own elected officers. In defending an action that was unpopular with many whites, he fell back on the Fourteenth Amendment, an unlikely refuge for a southern governor. "I could do nothing else than allow the negro officers to retain their commissions," he told a disgruntled correspondent. He went on to explain the historical context for his decision: "Our state legislature authorized the formation of these colored battalions years ago. The officers are efficient, and have drilled their men well, and have them under good discipline." He said that removing them would mean "discriminating against them in violation of the laws of my state, of the United States, and in violation of my oath, and it would have been manifestly a disposition to be unfair and unjust to these officers simply on account of their color." He conceded that had he been forming new units, he might have chosen a different course, but he could not in good conscience take the shoulder stripes from those who had served the state faithfully for years.[11] Letters from black Virginians poured into Tyler's office congratulating him on his "manly" defense of racial justice. Nearly every letter specifically mentioned the *Planet,* suggesting that Mitchell had something to do with the letter-writing campaign.[12]

The First Battalion celebrated Tyler's announcement with drumrolls and a parade through Jackson Ward. In July the soldiers underwent physicals and prepared to embark for Camp Corbin, a training camp about ten miles from Richmond near the Civil War battlefield of Seven Pines. The soldiers were mustered in as part of the Sixth Virginia Volunteers, an all-black regiment made up of two battalions of four companies each. At full strength each company had 106 men. The First Battalion was commanded by Major Joseph B. Johnson of Manchester. The Second was led by Major William H. Johnson, a graduate of Hampton Institute and a principal in the Petersburg schools. Like their white counterparts these volunteers believed themselves superior to the "riffraff" of the regular army. A Richmond soldier maintained that the Sixth Virginia was made up of skilled laborers and professionals, "men who moved in the higher walks of life."[13]

Career officers in the War Department viewed such claims skeptically and worried that state-organized militia units, regardless of race, were little more than social clubs. They encouraged governors to commission an officer from the regular army—a professional soldier—to accompany each regiment and bring the men up to standard.[14] The officer Tyler chose for the Sixth Virginia Volunteers was Lieutenant Colonel Richard C. Croxton, a thirty-four-year-old West Point graduate whose father was a judge and former congressman from eastern Virginia. The *Dispatch* described Croxton as a "West Pointer, a

Virginian, and a gentleman." Although Mitchell was unhappy about Crox-ton's appointment, his protests were not terribly frantic as Tyler had appointed West Point graduates to white regiments as well.[15]

Probably any white Virginian would have had trouble commanding an all-black regiment, but Croxton proved to be a poor choice for a position requiring sensitivity and tact. Despite surface charm and good looks, he had a mercurial temperament that often proved his undoing. He had performed poorly at West Point, graduating seventy-first in a class of seventy-seven. "Mr. Croxton is a young man who thinks he knows it all," complained a superior officer in 1891. Other evaluations over the course of his career reiterated concerns about his psychological makeup: "Col. Croxton is a difficult man to get along with. Is of a critical disposition. Is not a well balanced man. . . . I would not care to have him under my command. Could not trust his judgement." Black officers eventually used much the same language to describe him. They thought him "peevish, fretful, and irascible by nature."[16]

To make matters worse, Croxton was in poor health by 1898. Originally slated to command a white regiment, he was too sick to report for duty. It was partly by happenstance that he ended up with the Sixth Virginia Volunteers. The press failed to name his illness, but medical records indicate that he had contracted gonorrhea. During his months with the Sixth Virginia, he had reasons for feeling out of sorts. He was easily fatigued and found it painful to mount a horse. His medical problems probably explain the appearance in the Sixth Virginia of a second white officer, Dr. Allen J. Black, a physician from Tyler's hometown of East Radford.[17]

Like most black journalists Mitchell could not afford to employ a full-time correspondent to report the news of the war but relied instead on letters from soldiers. In early July he arranged for an officer from the First Battalion to serve as special *Planet* correspondent. The officer, who used the pseudonym "Ham," composed vivid accounts of life at Camp Corbin. His identity is uncertain, but internal evidence suggests that he was Captain Benjamin A. Graves, a teacher at Valley School and one of Mitchell's closest friends. At first Ham reported only peace and quiet within the Sixth Virginia Volunteers. "The men seem to be perfectly contented and spend their leisure moments in playing cards, baseball and writing letters home," he wrote. He thought the new recruits were learning quickly and moved together like clockwork. Zachary Fields, a private from Norfolk, wrote home to his wife Nettie complaining only of boredom and homesickness, the traditional laments of servicemen: "My Dear Darling you must not greave about me. My being heare is for your good[.] give my love to the children[.] tell them to write to me . . . for you are all I have to think a bout."[18]

The men of the Sixth Virginia were always glad to receive news from home. "A few *Planets* were brought down to camp Sunday and were warmly welcomed," wrote Ham, who noted that "the editorials are freely commented upon." During the brief and popular Spanish-American War, no attempts were made to censor the press, and Mitchell's antiwar editorials circulated freely among the soldiers. Although Croxton complained privately about the illiteracy of his troops, he did not encourage newspaper reading. His General Order No. 18, issued from Camp Corbin on September 2, said that "the practice on the part of enlisted men of begging newspapers at the trains must be stopped at once." [19]

The Sixth Virginia Volunteers had barely settled into camp when the war ended, thus precluding battlefield glory. A black regiment from the regular army won fame at San Juan Hill, an event that inspired pride among black Americans. "You hear the negroes all over town bragging about it," complained one white Richmonder. The men of the Sixth Virginia had enlisted for two-year stints, and speculation began that they would be sent to Cuba as part of the occupying forces. On September 12 the soldiers embarked by train for Camp Poland on the outskirts of Knoxville, Tennessee. According to the *Dispatch,* "Hundreds of colored people crowded around the trains at the Chesapeake and Ohio station to bid the men good-by." [20]

When the soldiers reached Knoxville, they were for the first time encamped in the vicinity of white troops, and Croxton cautioned them to be careful and stay away from white soldiers. Not long after they arrived, fighting broke out between a white regiment, the First Georgia, and an all-black regiment from North Carolina. For nearly an hour the two regiments fired at each other, evidently shooting without much conviction because no one was injured. "The North Carolina & Georgia Soldiers had a scrumarge," explained Zach Fields to his wife. "They called us to gather & gave us balls[.] We thought it would be an offul time for a few moments[.] No one was hurt[.] love you told me not to run a way[.] dear I am not thinking about that." [21]

Within two weeks a battle of another sort had broken out at Camp Poland, one with more lasting consequences. The relationship between Croxton and his officers deteriorated once they reached Knoxville, and on October 1 the white colonel asked that a military board be summoned to examine the qualifications of nine officers of the Second Battalion, including Major William H. Johnson of Petersburg, the school principal. Croxton charged that the officers "could not learn" and that their ineptitude hampered the regiment. In requesting this hearing he was within his rights, as the mechanism was established by Congress in April 1898 to enable the army to rid itself of state-appointed officers who proved incompetent. Just why Croxton chose to challenge the Petersburg officers while leaving those from Richmond in place was never clear. He later told a presidential commission that he simply concluded early on that there should be "one battalion officered by white men and one by negroes."[22]

The examination was scheduled for the morning of October 3, but half an hour before the hearing was to begin, the black officers submitted their resignations to the War Department. In a letter addressed to Mitchell and published in the *Planet*, Major William H. Johnson explained why he refused to defend himself. He said that conversations emanating from Croxton's tent that morning convinced him that this was a case of "trot them out and knock them down." Furthermore, his experiences with the Sixth Virginia had been far from pleasant. When mistakes occurred, he was summoned to Croxton's tent and subjected to "a tirade of execrations and oaths." Croxton's curses were profane and very loud. Johnson decided that a major's pay was poor recompense for these indignities and so resigned. Mitchell headlined the story: "Colored Officers Resign . . . Refused to Submit to Humiliation . . . A Bungling Effort to Do by Unfair Means What Could Not Be Accomplished Otherwise."[23]

When Governor Tyler learned of the resignations, he reminded Croxton that promotions were to come from the rank and file, but the white officer insisted it would be an injustice to promote black soldiers because they "would prove their inefficiency and would suffer the humiliation afterwards." Tyler was clearly provoked with Croxton, whom he regarded as headstrong and immature, but his commitment to this "dangerous experiment" was weakening. Inundated with white requests for commissions and battered by pleas from influential Democrats on behalf of cousins, brothers, and sons, he at last relented and agreed to appoint white officers. Major Johnson's replacement was Major Charles E. Cabell, a protégé of Senator John W. Daniel.[24]

When Tyler announced the appointment of white officers, Mitchell responded with predictable anger, although he reserved most of his fury for Croxton, whom he accused of duping the well-meaning governor. In a series of maliciously clever editorials, he referred to the ailing officer as the "invalid with the 'swollen head.'" One editorial was entitled, "Lieutenant Colonel Croxton, Sah!" James H. Hayes called a meeting in Jackson Ward to protest the appointments and spent nearly an hour conferring with Tyler. He then headed for Washington to lobby the War Department and President McKinley. Stung by the public outcry, Tyler informed Croxton that "the colored people at home are much inclined to complain that an injustice has been done to them."[25]

For months Mitchell had proclaimed, "No officers, no fight!" and now he saw his slogan take on a life of its own. Seventeen officers from the First Battalion, led by Major Joseph B. Johnson, addressed a letter to the adjutant general in Washington protesting the appointment of white officers and asking that the regiment be mustered out. Captain William A. Hankins of Richmond failed to sign the petition, probably because he aspired to a career in the regular army, and at least a few privates were either indifferent or glad to see their officers go. Zach Fields, who had been disciplined on several occasions by his commanding officer, Captain Edward W. Gould of Norfolk, assured his wife that she should not be alarmed by what she read in the papers: "We will get white officers and we are glad of it." Most soldiers, however, seemed ready to leave the army. "The boys are still loyal to the Stars and Stripes," explained Ham, "but they feel that their days of usefulness are at an end and to a man they want to give up the business and return home to their families and friends." Mitchell said that the appointments had caused waves of indignation across Virginia. Again he repeated, "No officers, no fight!"[26]

The white officers arrived in Knoxville at the end of October only to find the camp in an uproar over their presence. On the morning of November 2, they called out their first commands, but the soldiers appeared sullen and unresponsive: not a single enlisted man moved. After lunch they tried again to issue orders, but the men hooted and hissed. Furious at their intransigence, Croxton reported to his commanding officer that his men had mutinied. High-ranking generals appeared on the scene, but their exhortations and appeals had little effect on the men, who grew even more violent in their denunciations of white officers. The generals then ordered two white regiments to assume positions surrounding the soldiers. Fearing bloodshed if either side began to fire, Major Joseph Johnson at last rose to speak. Reminding the soldiers of their sworn duty to obey their officers, he asked them to submit their grievances through proper military channels. When Croxton promised to forward their complaints to Governor Tyler, the men agreed to end their protest. Peace and quiet returned to the Sixth Virginia, although resentments simmered below the surface.[27]

Two weeks later, to the surprise of nearly everyone, the white officers resigned. In letters addressed to the War Department, they maintained that their positions were untenable. They said that the enlisted men pretended obedience but in reality mocked their efforts and laughed at them behind their backs. According to Captain George H. Bentley of Roanoke, "A silent force was at work, inspiring the men to careless & unwilling compliance with my orders." Captain Robert LeMasurier of Richmond complained in a private letter to Tyler that no white officer could hope to succeed with the Sixth

Virginia: "The men are constantly receiving letters from home goading them on to mischief; this, combined with the flaming articles published in the negro newspapers and the conduct of their own officers, has resulted in making our positions very uncomfortable." In the *Planet*, Mitchell made no apology for the "mutiny" or for the more subtle resistance his "flaming articles" inspired. He said that the Sixth Virginia had made the "most heroic stand ever taken by any colored regiment."[28]

The secretary of war refused to accept the white resignations on the not unreasonable assumption that a new set of officers would only make matters worse, and the regiment was ordered to prepare for departure to Camp Haskell in Macon, Georgia. The news that the regiment was leaving for Georgia caused consternation among the soldiers. Ham said that they dreaded moving south "as each step carries us farther from home and friends."[29]

The regiment left Knoxville by train on November 18. The trip to Macon lasted more than twenty hours with several mishaps along the way, and Croxton retired to his tent to convalesce. The soldiers discovered in Georgia a harsher, more repressive version of race relations than they had encountered in east Tennessee. Cotton fields, chain gangs, and Jim Crow streetcars were reminders that they had entered the Deep South. The *Macon Telegraph* reported lynchings nearly every day and told worrisome stories about the Wilmington riot, which had recently taken place in North Carolina. "This state [Georgia] has created a very unfavorable impression in my mind," admitted Ham.[30]

The day after the soldiers arrived in Macon, someone pointed out a persimmon tree, a "hanging tree," where a black man, Will Singleton, reportedly had been lynched nine years before. According to the story Singleton was castrated, and his testicles were displayed in a jar of alcohol in a Macon drugstore. A group of men from the Sixth Virginia decided to take revenge by demolishing the tree. Attacks on the physical symbols of repression were part of a time-honored tradition among black soldiers. During the Civil War, Union troops hacked away at slave pens and whipping posts. The soldiers from Virginia fired rifles at the lynching tree and then chopped it down with axes, gathering splinters as souvenirs to mail home. At a nearby park they tore down a sign prohibiting the entrance of "dogs and niggers." Rumors spread that they intended to kill all the white people of Macon, although apparently the worst that happened was that a few men carrying rifles entered a white restaurant and demanded to be served.[31]

Shortly before dawn the next morning, white officers from army headquarters awakened Major Johnson and informed him the regiment was under arrest. They asked his help in peacefully disarming the men. Always the good soldier, Johnson roused his men and told them they were receiving new rifles and should stack their old Springfields. The men did as they were told. Once they were disarmed, white officers searched their belongings and confiscated pocketknives, razors, and other possible weapons. A white general appeared and "gave the negroes to understand that they must behave or they would all be shot." Tyler confessed to Senator Daniel that he was "perplexed beyond measure about the trouble with the 6th regiment."[32]

In the weeks that followed, Ham wrote long letters to the *Planet* to assure family and friends that the situation at Camp Haskell was not so desperate as the white press would have them believe. Although the soldiers were confined to camp and had no razors, they were not physically constrained and continued to carry out routine duties. "It is a noticeable fact that while under arrest, the boys are cheerful and in good spirits," he told the *Planet*. To ease the boredom the soldiers improvised nightly entertainments and formed singing ensembles. On Saturdays they played baseball and held track meets. They even organized a secret fraternal order, the Grand United Council of Uglies. "Ugliness is a prerequisite to membership, and everything has to be done in an ugly manner," explained Ham. Another anonymous correspondent wrote angrier letters, though he too reported that the men remained reasonably philosophical about what had happened: "After the day's duties are done, at the blazing camp fires, tales are told, songs sung and for the time being all are oblivious to the trouble." Thanksgiving dinner brought pork and beans instead of "turkey and celery," but aside from colds and a few sore throats, everyone was healthy, albeit homesick. Zachary Fields wrote his wife that he would never have left Norfolk had he known he would miss her so much. "I will eat you up when I come home," he warned. "You will have to hide from me to keep me from eating you up."[33]

After twenty days of confinement, the regiment was released from arrest. According to Ham, a cheer rose from Camp Haskell such as had not been heard in Georgia since the end of the Civil War. Mitchell's editorials by this time had grown terse, restrained, and angry. In issue after issue he asked that the regiment be mustered out.[34]

The regiment suffered its first casualty while still in Virginia when Albert McClellan, a private from Danville, was killed by a white police officer while home on furlough.[35] On December 22, 1898, the Sixth Virginia lost a second soldier. Elijah Turner, a thirty-four-year-old private from Richmond, was killed on a Macon streetcar. Race relations had grown tense in Macon with so many soldiers in town, and much of the conflict took place on streetcars. To ease the situation the transit companies attached wooden trailers to the rear of trolleys and designated them for the use of black soldiers. Turner apparently had been drinking and took a seat in a "white" streetcar. When he refused to leave, the conductor shot him.[36]

The next day a coroner's jury ruled Turner's death a justifiable homicide. Word spread that Virginia soldiers would avenge his death by lynching the conductor, although this was apparently just talk. As a precaution Macon police jailed twenty black civilians whose presence in town appeared to them suspicious, and Croxton again restricted the Sixth Virginia to camp. A white officer investigated the shooting for the War Department and concluded that Turner, who had a wife and two children, was at fault "but his offense did not warrant the conductor's killing him." His body was sent home to Richmond for burial.[37]

The army assigned provost guards to patrol the streetcars, but confrontations continued. On Christmas Eve three soldiers from the Sixth Virginia accompanied by "three well dressed colored girls" attempted to board a trolley on the line connecting Macon and Camp Haskell. When the conductor directed them to the trailer, they set out on foot. Their little-noticed protest was a preview of the Richmond streetcar boycott of 1904 that Mitchell would lead.[38]

After Turner's death Croxton tried to maintain discipline but confessed to a friend that it seemed unlikely his soldiers would ever embark for Cuba: "They have either to be kept practically as prisoners, or else they raise thunder." In January 1899 the news came that all had been waiting for: the regiment was being mustered out. Mitchell was delighted, but so too was a writer for the *Richmond Times* who thought it fitting that the soldiers leave the service: "Their career since their enlistment has been a succession of riots and drunken brawls and this seems to be the happiest solution of a much vexed question."[39]

Under ordinary circumstances the soldiers would have been mustered out in Macon, but the War Department feared conflicts between black Virginians and white Georgians. Railroad tracks were laid directly to Camp Haskell so the men could be put on the train without coming into contact with civilians. Each private was given $60 in back pay. When merchants learned that the soldiers were leaving Georgia with pocketfuls of money, they loaded their wares onto wagons and headed for camp. The *Macon Telegraph* lavished last-minute praise on the soldiers in an attempt to loosen purse strings. A soldier from Ohio reported the unexpected result: "The soldiers had been ridiculed so badly by the white people of Macon that they would not buy a cent's worth, and now they [the merchants] blame the war department."[40]

When the train pulled into the C&O station in Richmond, families and friends again thronged the platform, but this was not the triumphant return that many had envisioned. Rather than battlefield glory, the regiment had won the nickname "The Mutinous Sixth." Mitchell had warned that participation in the war was unlikely to turn back the tides of racism, but he could hardly have anticipated the disastrous outcome. In the spring of 1899, Governor Tyler, frustrated by what had happened and unable to envision how black soldiers could possibly serve the Commonwealth in the future, formally reorganized the state militia and abolished black units across Virginia. Without black soldiers there was no need for black armories. During the summer of 1899, the city of Richmond converted the First Battalion Armory on Leigh Street into a public school.[41]

In the aftermath of the war, the men of the Sixth Virginia went their separate ways. Captain Benjamin A. Graves was offered a commission in the regular army, but he turned it down, saying he preferred the poor pay of a schoolteacher. In a comment worthy of the *Planet* editor, he said he would rather work for the uplift of black people at home rather than their annihilation in the Philippines. Years after his death the First Battalion Armory became part of Benjamin A. Graves Junior High School. Private Zachary Fields had had his fill of soldiering and returned to his wife and children in Norfolk. Major Joseph B. Johnson, usually mild mannered, in 1906 became so angry at white Republicans for their contemptuous treatment of black voters that he ran for Congress as an independent candidate, but he lost. Major William H. Johnson of Petersburg became the regiment's unofficial historian. In 1923 he wrote *A History of the Colored Volunteer Infantry of Virginia, 1871–1899*, which he dedicated to those black Virginians who had volunteered to fight against Spain. As for Croxton, his military career proceeded along its unhappy, star-crossed course. After months of treatment in New York for venereal disease, he left for Manila, where he was shot in the head during an off-duty rumble and was blinded in one eye.[42]

For Mitchell, the results of the war were mixed. On the one hand, his aggressive reporting of the troubles of the Sixth Virginia Volunteers won him national acclaim. No black journalist was more forceful in opposing the war or more sensitive to the contradictions inherent in offering uniforms and rifles to men who were in the process of losing their rights as citizens. His slogan "No officers, no fight!" served as a rallying cry for black editors across the United States. But the outcome of the war left him depressed. For thirty years black soldiers had marched in the streets of Richmond, their uniforms and rifles serving as symbols of freedom. In 1898 they found themselves in Macon, Georgia, disarmed, held up to public ridicule, and riding in wooden trailers attached to the rear of streetcars. By any standard it was poor reward for volunteering to serve their country.[43]

CHAPTER EIGHT

Disfranchisement

The loss of his council seat and the disbanding of the militia forced Mitchell to reconsider the efficacy of protest. In the aftermath of the Spanish-American War, his editorials grew less strident and his protests less feverish. This was the period black historians have called the "nadir," that low point when race relations were marked by violence and oppression and white prejudice seemed intractable. Writing in 1903, W. E. B. Du Bois observed that "today the young Negro of the south who would succeed cannot be frank and outspoken, honest and self-assertive, but rather he is daily tempted to be silent and wary, politic and sly; he must flatter and be pleasant, endure petty insults with a smile, shut his eyes to wrong."[1] By temperament something of a scrapper, Mitchell began to rein in his emotions and exercise restraint. Changes in his personal circumstances also contributed to a new sense of caution.

In 1897 Mitchell moved the *Planet* out of the Swan Tavern and into a brick boardinghouse on Fourth Street, just north of Broad. He purchased the building, which he refurbished and painted white. Over the front porch he erected a billboard displaying the strong arm of the *Planet*. His new headquarters were roomier and more substantial than the old *Planet* office and allowed for expansion. He purchased a folding machine that weighed nearly a ton and in 1905 bought a Mergenthaler Linotype machine. New and up-to-date equipment improved the appearance of the *Planet* and enabled him to compete with white firms for job printing. Perhaps inevitably, as he grew older and better established, he seemed less willing to take chances.[2]

He also had new responsibilities at home. In June 1900 his brother suffered a concussion in a bicycle accident. Tom Mitchell lived for two weeks after the accident and was expected to recover but died suddenly on June 15. For the *Planet* editor this was a major loss. The two brothers had always been close. They worked side by side in the *Planet* office, attended the same church, and belonged to the same fraternal lodges. Tom was survived by a widow, Sylvia

Mitchell, who later remarried and moved to New Jersey, and two children, Roscoe, aged twelve, who worked in the *Planet* office after school, and Rebecca, aged eight. Although the children remained on good terms with their mother, Mitchell assumed financial responsibility for their upbringing and became a surrogate parent. In 1904 he purchased the only home he would ever own, a handsome residence at 515 North Third Street. Built in the Italianate style, the attached brick house had wrought-iron railings and good architectural details. Moving into the house with him were his mother Rebecca, who was nearing seventy, and his niece and nephew.[3] By then it was clear to everyone, except perhaps Marietta Chiles, who lived a few blocks away on Leigh Street, that he was unlikely to marry.

As the plight of the race worsened, Mitchell's own financial situation improved in ways that made his retreat on other fronts less depressing. In 1894 he was elected grand chancellor of the Virginia Knights of Pythias, a fraternal order that was licensed to sell life insurance. By the end of the decade, he was making trips out of town nearly every week to open new lodges and sell insurance. With the funds of the Knights of Pythias serving as a core of deposits, he founded the Mechanics' Savings Bank in 1902. Moneymaking helped him salvage his self-respect during a time of troubles. He said that while white folks frittered away their time discussing the race problem, he and other black leaders were working quietly to achieve economic success.[4]

The coming of the twentieth century marked an important turning point for Mitchell as he shifted his attention from politics to business, but the divisions were never neat and tidy. He had enjoyed the prerogatives that came from holding public office, and he knew that without political power the race's economic gains would be difficult to defend. In the spring of 1900, a year after the soldiers' return from Georgia, he ran again for the board of aldermen. Although much has been made of the apathy of the southern black electorate during this period, Mitchell and the voters of Jackson Ward showed a stubborn devotion to politics. On the eve of disfranchisement, they nominated their own slate of candidates for office; they turned out at the polls to vote for them; and once the election was over, they challenged their apparent defeat in the courts.[5]

The campaign to redeem Jackson Ward began on the night of April 17, 1900, when nearly a hundred voters met in closed session to discuss the coming council elections. Present were Mitchell, Hayes, and representatives of the various Republican factions that had battled throughout the decade. Also attending were church and business leaders. No agreement was reached that night, causing the *Dispatch* to observe that "Jackson Ward negroes are so far apart in their political beliefs that it is impossible for them to agree upon anything." When a second meeting was called two weeks later, Republican leaders resolved to forget past quarrels and support a common ticket. The two candidates for the board of aldermen were Mitchell and Benjamin P. Vandervall. A member of a well-to-do family of free descent, Vandervall was the former circulation manager for the *Planet,* the clerk of First Church, and the son of Nelson P. Vandervall, a former councilman. Five blacks also were nominated for the vacant seats on the common council. No white Republicans came to the meeting, and Alderman James Bahen announced that henceforth he would campaign as a Democrat.[6]

Mitchell believed the ward united, but on May 4 the *Richmond Times* reported that the usual multitude of black politicians were aspiring to office in Jackson Ward. Fourteen Republicans were vying for seven open seats. "The [Republican] party seems to be very much split," said the *Times,* and predicted another Democratic victory.[7]

As soon as he saw the article, Mitchell must have known something was wrong. Among the Republican candidates were several friends who had pledged him their support. Other names had obviously been added to cause confusion. John Mitchell and John Mitchell Jr. would both be on the ballot, as would James I. Smith and James Y. Smith, H. E. Jonason and H. F. Jonathan, G. R. Porter and J. R. Porter, and so forth. Because voters were allowed only two-and-a-half minutes in the polling booth, even the most sophisticated voter would have trouble sorting through the list of names. An 1896 amendment to the Walton Act prohibited officials from shuffling the order of candidates from ballot to ballot, but until election morning no one would know for certain the order in which the names would appear, and there would be nothing on the ballot to indicate which candidates belonged to which party.[8]

Mitchell soon learned how the ballot had come to be so overburdened with candidates. According to the story he printed in the *Planet,* the candidates were "nominated" by Henry S. Beck, one of the Democratic candidates for the board of aldermen. Beck allegedly prepared a list of nominees, placed it in an envelope, and paid Royal Racks, "a well known negro about town," fifty cents to deliver the list to the hustings court.[9]

Once he discovered what had happened, Mitchell went to work to clear the ballot of phantom candidates. He made little headway until May 8, when he persuaded William L. Royall, a white attorney and an editorial writer for the *Richmond Times,* to represent the interests of black voters. "I have been employed by a number of colored men in Jackson Ward," said Royall, "and my fee has been paid." Royall was in many ways a surprising choice for this case.

A conservative, pro-business Democrat, he was an avid proponent of disfranchisement. In 1897 he published a history of the Readjuster movement that he subtitled *The Negro's Vicious Influence in Politics*. But Royall was also a champion of honest elections and was never sure which was worse, "a negro government or a white government resting upon stuffed ballot boxes." He took the case in Jackson Ward, he said, because names had been dishonestly added to the ballot to confuse illiterate voters.[10]

Eventually some of the bogus names were removed, although it took considerable legal maneuvering by Royall, who was hampered by the lack of precedent for dealing with the case. No one knew for certain whether the courts or the electoral board had jurisdiction. The state's attorney general, Andrew J. Montague, finally ruled that the electoral board had the right to hear evidence, though he admitted the board was under no obligation to act. To no one's surprise, the all-white board chose to do nothing. Royall then took the case to the city circuit court, where arguments were heard late in the afternoon of May 12. Benjamin Jackson, a former councilman and the manager of the dining room at the Westmoreland Club, appeared before the judge and protested that he was not a candidate and that his signature had been forged. After some deliberation the judge ordered that "the electoral board be enjoined from placing Benjamin Jackson's name on the ballot." The judge also agreed to remove other names if affidavits were delivered to him the following morning by those who wished not to run.[11]

That night Mitchell and several friends, including R. T. Hill, a notary public, worked until dawn to gather the affidavits that would purge names from the ballot. Riding through the darkened streets of Jackson Ward in a "squeaking, overcrowded buggy," they knocked on doors and woke sleeping men in order to gain the necessary signatures. The next morning they presented affidavits to the judge, who issued further restraining orders. Some of the names, such as that of "John Mitchell," remained on the ballot for the oddly logical reason that no John Mitchell could be found to request that his name be stricken.[12]

Election day dawned rainy and disagreeable in Jackson Ward on May 24, 1900, but black voters again crowded around the precincts. "Never before in the history of Jackson Ward," said Mitchell afterward, "have colored men shown a greater tenacity of purpose. . . . All during a steady downpour of rain they stood waiting to vote." Because the ballot was still a confusing jumble of names, no illiterates tried to vote. Republican schools were set up at each precinct, and only those who could sort through the names quickly and accurately were told to go to the polls. According to the *Planet*, "Every man marked his own ballot and did not ask the aid of the judge." The lines moved slowly all day, and only about 500 blacks actually reached the polling booth, a far cry from the previous decade when as many as 2,500 had voted. Many voters "remained in the booth longer than the two-and-a-half minutes," said the *Times*, and therefore lost their votes. Others were still in line, standing in the rain, when the polls closed.[13]

When the votes were counted late that evening, the Democrats appeared to have made a clean sweep of the election. In the contest for the board of alderman, James Bahen and Henry Beck, the two white Democrats, each received nearly 600 votes. The runner-up was James I. Smith, a Democratic incumbent who had been dropped from the ticket to make room for Bahen and ran as an independent. Smith had 172 votes, Vandervall had 145, and Mitchell trailed behind with 138. Although the mysterious "John Mitchell" had received only a handful of votes, the Democrats had won the election by a landslide.[14]

In the *Planet*, Mitchell described the election as another "Jackson Ward Robbery" and protested that on this occasion the Democrats had gone too far. They had thrown out the votes of law-abiding, taxpaying citizens and shamelessly altered the returns to give themselves the victory. Conceding that it was hard "to submit to continuous wrong-doing," he praised the party faithful who remained at the polls in miserable weather and the "noble hearted women who urged the men forward." Royall had watched this election with interest, and he considered the fraud blatant enough to warrant a court challenge.[15]

Royall began to interview voters in Jackson Ward and by June had collected testimony from twenty-one men who were convinced, as he phrased it, that their rights had been "outraged" by fraudulent returns. Among those signing the affidavits were various community leaders, including James H. Holmes, the aging pastor of First Church. Because contested elections were usually resolved by the council itself, Royall was forced to prepare a careful legal argument. The candidates were not contesting the election, he said. Instead, aggrieved voters were appealing to the courts for justice.[16]

When the case was brought before the hustings court on June 18, the courtroom was crowded. Political observers knew this case could serve as a bellwether foretelling the court's attitude toward disfranchisement. In one corner of the room, a group of blacks were huddled together, apparently in prayer. The prestige of the opposing white lawyers also attracted attention to the case. Opposite Royall in the courtroom was George D. Wise, the former Democratic congressman from the third district who had helped defend the Lunenburg women in 1896. After both lawyers presented arguments, Judge S. B. Witt delivered a sixteen-page opinion in which he ruled that the hustings court had no jurisdiction in the case. "The council shall be the judge of its own elections," he said, and the council alone could determine whether fraud had taken place. When the decision was announced, Mitchell reportedly broke down and wept. His brother had died three days before, leaving him psychologically ill equipped to deal with an adverse decision.[17]

That afternoon Royall applied to the Virginia Supreme Court of Appeals for a writ of mandamus in an effort to compel the hustings court to try the case. On July 5, 1900, the Supreme Court heard arguments in the case of *Mitchell v. Witt* but refused to grant the writ. The higher court concurred with the Richmond judge that the city council was the only arbiter of its contested elections. With this decision ended Mitchell's last chance to win back his council seat.[18]

This legal setback was only the prelude, however, to a more far-reaching debacle for Mitchell and the voters of Jackson Ward. On May 24, 1900, the same day of the council elections, Virginians were asked to decide whether to call a constitutional convention, the avowed purpose of which was to disfranchise black voters. "The question is," said the *Dispatch*, "Do we desire to get rid of the negro as a voter, or not? What do the white people say?" Mitchell knew how few black votes would be counted, so he urged *Planet* readers to lobby with whites behind the scenes. He specifically asked domestic servants to plead the race's cause with white women, who in turn would intercede with their voting husbands.[19]

Although the election was closer than many had anticipated, those who wanted a new constitution carried the day. In a state with an estimated 435,000 registered voters, 77,362 voted yes and 60,375 voted no. Delegates were chosen in May 1901, and deliberations began in Richmond the following month. According to Mitchell, to win the campaign candidates stood on every street corner in Virginia and yelled, "Nigger! Nigger! Nigger!" The Virginia convention, unlike earlier disfranchising conventions in Mississippi and South Carolina, was an all-white assemblage.[20]

Once the convention opened Mitchell published a steady stream of editorials about the proceedings and interpreted the issues for readers. He was convinced that much of the conflict within the convention hall reflected sectional differences between the eastern Black Belt and the mountainous west. The "moneyed classes," eager to obscure important economic issues, resorted to the "scarecrow of Negro domination." As for the franchise, it had been "taken away, nullified by fraud, and made a mockery in the streets of the city." Now the thieves had "tired of their vocation" and were trying to find a way to ease their consciences. In *Planet* editorials he defended universal manhood suffrage and maintained that "well-behaved, law abiding, industrious colored people should have the right to vote whether they can read or not."[21]

While Mitchell protested against disfranchisement in the *Planet,* more soft-spoken "colored gentlemen" were sent as emissaries to the white community to plead the race's cause. The leader of this conservative protest was Giles B. Jackson, a black attorney whose presence would be felt in Richmond for years to come. Unlike Mitchell, Jackson was willing to appear servile in exchange for concessions.

Jackson's background helps explain his accommodating approach to race relations. Throughout his life he demonstrated an uncanny ability to win from whites more than they had intended to give. He was born a slave in Goochland County in 1853, moved to Richmond after the war, and after working at several odd jobs took a position as a servant in the household of John Stewart of Brook Hill, the wealthy father-in-law of Joseph Bryan, the editor of the *Richmond Dispatch.* Stewart's wife taught Jackson to read and write. He next won a position in a white law firm. Whether he worked as a clerk or servant is unclear, but attorney William H. Beveridge, a Republican supporter of Mahone, recognized his abilities and schooled him in the law. In 1887, at the age of thirty-four, he was admitted to the Richmond bar. He established a close relationship with Judge John J. Crutchfield of the police court and soon had a thriving practice. Financially he did much better than James H. Hayes, E. A. Randolph, and other black lawyers. One white reporter remembered how "in the old days . . . nine out of ten negroes in trouble got Giles to either get them out or push them further in." He also served as attorney for the True Reformers and in 1907 organized the Negro Exhibit at the Jamestown Exposition.[22]

Jackson was man of clear ability, and his private letters reveal him as candid and articulate. In public, however, he reverted to dialect and played the sycophant. He knew how to be obsequious and could disarm even the most hostile white audience with self-deprecating humor. Some of his stories were obviously suspect, such as the one that explained how Jackson Ward received its name: Ulysses S. Grant was so pleased to find a "white folks' nigger" (as Jackson described himself) that the general named the ward for him. Probably equally fictitious were stories about being Fitzhugh Lee's body servant during the Civil War and of tending Robert E. Lee's horse. Blacks were embarrassed by his anecdotes—he was known as a handkerchief-head—but few doubted his power. As he admitted, whites regarded him "as a kind of bureau of information as to the acts and doings of the colored people of our City and State."[23] For men of Mitchell's temperament, Jackson's influence was bound to be galling.

Not surprisingly, Jackson was drawn to the ideology and methods of

Booker T. Washington. In 1900 he was among three hundred blacks who met in Boston to form the National Negro Business League, an organization that Washington tightly controlled and that reflected his ideas about self-help, racial solidarity, and economic advance. At the Boston meeting Jackson was named vice-president. When he came home to Richmond, he formed a local branch of the Business League but also a Constitutional Rights Association, a shadow organization that had a similar membership and was opposed to the spread of Jim Crow. Like Washington, Jackson was more complicated than he appeared on the surface and was eager to work behind the scenes against racial injustice. In 1900 he cooperated with Washington on a court case involving disfranchisement in Louisiana.[24]

Jackson was just as committed to the ballot in Virginia but saw little to be gained by the angry protests that characterized many *Planet* editorials. He preferred instead the indirect approach. Aware of the pride many whites took in the state's supposedly harmonious race relations, he decided that a visit to Richmond by Booker T. Washington would remind the "better class" of their duty to black Virginians. In his own words, he "prepared a resolution and had the legislature adopt it inviting Dr. Washington to lecture in one of the leading theatres in the City." The resolution pointed out that Washington had done more than anyone else to restore the "harmony between the races" that existed before the Civil War.[25]

Washington spoke at Richmond's Academy of Music on February 11, 1901, with many members of the General Assembly in the audience. According to the *Times*, "Giles was in his glory." Sitting with Washington and Jackson on the platform were a number of black leaders, including John H. Smythe, the president of the Negro Reformatory Association; W. F. Graham, the pastor of Fifth Street Baptist Church; Anthony Binga Jr. of Manchester; D. Webster Davis from the public schools; and Mitchell. In one of those anomalies of southern race relations, these black men, dressed in formal attire, stared out at a sea of white faces. After being introduced by Jackson, Washington made a cautious speech, although at the end he spoke briefly to the legislators about the "state and local problems before you." He would "dare not meddle," but he did want to "take the liberty of adding this, that no question is ever permanently settled until it is settled right, in absolute fairness and justice to all parties concerned." He rested his case with the southern white man and said, "I do not believe that we are going to be disappointed."[26]

The *Dispatch* asserted that Washington's speech "pleased not only the whites, but the better and more intelligent negroes." Mitchell made no editorial comment, breaking his silence only to note the embarrassment of sitting on the platform while blacks were excluded from the main auditorium.

Jackson thought it significant that on this occasion black people were permitted to occupy the balcony.[27]

Washington's speech was only one device Jackson used to influence the convention's outcome. In June the Virginia branch of the Negro Business League published a paper that it mailed to delegates. It was signed by a number of black Richmonders, including Jackson, W. F. Graham, and R. T. Hill. The tone of the paper, said the *Dispatch,* was "dignified, moderate, and conservative." The petitioners made a plea for the suffrage that was direct but hardly rude or demanding: "The negro does ask, however, that since he is taxed, works the roads, is punished for crime, is called upon to defend his country, that he have some humble share in choosing those who shall rule him, especially when he has proven his worthiness by becoming a taxpayer and a reliable citizen." The *Richmond Times* responded favorably to the petition, saying that the race issue was indeed a moral issue and that regarding the suffrage "we must deal justly, in a way becoming the Anglo-Saxon race." [28]

The next month six black men appeared before the suffrage committee of the convention. Among them was D. Webster Davis, Mitchell's old friend who taught at Baker School. A gifted raconteur, Davis made lecture tours in the North, telling stories about plantation life. In his presentation before the suffrage committee, he echoed the conciliatory approach of the Negro Business League. To ingratiate himself with the delegates, Davis began with a joke about a black Virginian who liked a "hot sun and warm hearts." He moved to Maine where the "climate and the people froze him to death." He asked to be cremated so he could get warm once more. When someone opened the furnace door before he was completely incinerated, "the old darkey yelled out, 'Shut the door; I can't stand the [draft]!'" Having mollified his listeners with this story, Davis turned to the suffrage. He said he would not object to a poll tax, property requirement, or literacy test, but he asked that restrictions be applied equally to both races.[29] Black protests had by this time become formulaic: first there was praise for southern whites, then derision of the North, then pleas for fairness.

So long as the constitutional convention was in session, men like Jackson and Davis set the tone for the city's protest. Flattering words seemed more likely to stave off disfranchisement than stirring appeals for racial justice. As the debates in the convention grew increasingly acrimonious, Mitchell sometimes feigned indifference to the whole affair. "The colored people are not worrying themselves about the matter," he wrote in the *Planet.* He quoted with approval the "old colored brother" who said, "They don't bother me none; I can't vote no how." But Mitchell's show of unconcern was in part a front to hide his deepening depression. "We submit," he wrote, "simply because we are powerless to help ourselves." He continued to write his familiar words of advice, although his tone grew defensive, as if he understood that the races had come to a fundamental parting of the ways: "Every colored man should own a shot-gun and a repeating rifle. He should be polite and obliging, yet ready to defend his home and protect his wife and little ones. . . . With white men who are friendly to him, he should be friendly. With those who hate him, he should have no dealing." In editorials he borrowed the phrases he had heard so often at First Church: "We bow to the inevitable and submit our case to that God who neither slumbers nor sleeps but who in his own good time will gather unto himself those who have hindered our progress."[30]

The continuing agitation of the race question took its toll on Mitchell and on other blacks as well. Throughout the time the convention was in session, the white press was filled with stories about the servant problem. Complaints about the unreliability of domestic help were hardly new in white Richmond, but they were repeated with fresh urgency during the period of the convention. The *Dispatch* finally surmised that perhaps black Virginians were "incensed at the disfranchising features of the new constitution." Another white reporter noticed that blacks in his neighborhood had lost their easygoing, happy-go-lucky ways. He thought the average black man appeared sullen, withdrawn, moody, reluctant to talk to white strangers. "He seems to bear a grudge," he said. "He thinks he is being cheated out of his rights." For his part Mitchell advised his readers to ignore the harsh rhetoric. "Everybody is discussing us," he said. "Don't worry. They'll get tired after a while."[31]

There was yet another reason for the somber mood in black Richmond. "The colored people are stirred up," said the *Times,* but "they are protesting not so much about being disfranchised as against losing their schools." By the time the convention opened, whites throughout Virginia had begun to argue for a new method of financing public education: tax revenues should be divided according to race, with taxes paid by whites returned to white schools and taxes paid by blacks returned to black schools. Mitchell was at first taken aback by the audacity of this proposal, which struck at the heart of public education. Would anyone suggest that "only the taxes paid by the poor white people should be expended upon their schools?"[32]

The division of the school tax was a plan with enormous initial appeal among whites because it would mean more money for poorly funded white public schools without the levying of additional taxes. Also, many whites blamed black education for the state's deteriorating race relations. "When they learn to spell cat and dog, they fling away the hoe," complained the

Farmville Herald. The *Dispatch* pronounced black education a failure and blunder, a waste of tax dollars, a needless expense that made "hotbeds of arrogance and aggression" out of black schools. Ideas of this sort were not confined to ill-tempered journalists but were espoused by white educators and moderates. One white Richmonder summarized the views of many when he said he favored "giving the white child all the education possible, and the black child as little as possible."[33]

From the perspective of black Richmond, the division of the school tax would have meant a calamity of untold proportions. Although blacks made up nearly a third of the city's population, they paid less than 2 percent of the taxes on real property. Black Richmonders usually lived in rented houses; few owned expensive commercial property. They paid taxes indirectly, when landlords shifted the tax burden to them through their rents. Had the proposal been enacted and had additional money not been forthcoming, Navy Hill, Baker, Valley, Richmond Normal, and the other black schools would have been forced to shut their doors. It was not clear in 1901 where the limits of oppression lay, and whites were not above using the issue to silence dissent. The *Dispatch* once warned that race relations were strained and that if any unspeakable crime against white women occurred while the convention was in session, black schools throughout Virginia would close. When few blacks turned out to vote in the 1901 gubernatorial election, Democrats speculated that black leaders realized that "a formidable demonstration by them at the polls at this time would be hurtful of their interest in the matter of the division of the school fund."[34]

The black community thus had reason to approach the issue warily. In January 1901 an organization of black clergy from Richmond issued a carefully worded statement that made no mention of the franchise but asked for continued support for black schools. In a predictable passage the pastors reminded whites of slave fidelity during the Civil War: "In the most trying point of your history, when your families were exposed and your fields deserted, this people continued to guard your homes and turn your furrows without reward." They went on to note that "while we are not disposed to awaken unpleasant memories, yet it is but just to say this may be the greatest reason why the negro is lacking in resources to educate himself."[35]

On July 24, 1901, a delegation from the Negro Business League appeared before the convention's education committee to plead for black schools. Among the Richmonders who spoke were W. F. Graham and Giles B. Jackson. They knew that a single false step on their part might cripple black education in Virginia for decades to come, and they spent much of their time trying to placate the committee. Jackson was especially obsequious. He said that "he and others of his race wished to live among Southern white folks." Whenever he went north "white Yankees blackened his boots, shaved him, drove him in a carriage, and waited on him at the table, and he did not like any such foolishness." Graham likewise lavished compliments on the white delegates, although in doing so he appealed cleverly to their better instincts. Black Virginians were superior to blacks from other states, he said, because they had received "generous treatment from the white men" who had set before them "high standards of justice and fairness." The delegation also presented a pamphlet to the committee that dropped the double-talk and argued forthrightly for black education.[36]

Fortunately for the black community, white sentiment about the schools was divided. On reflection, at least some whites agreed with the *Richmond Times* that it would be cruel to end public funding for black education. "It is a mockery," said the *Times*, "for any Christian community to send teachers abroad to educate the heathen [in Africa], and yet fail to do anything for the black man's children at home." Charles T. O'Ferrall came out of political retirement to emphasize the seriousness of the proposal: "After a lapse of some years almost the entire negro population will be unable to read and write. . . . Will we give them a stone when they are begging for bread?" Eventually other state leaders, including Carter Glass and John W. Daniel, spoke out in opposition to the plan, as did William Jennings Bryan. One of the telling arguments they used was that closing black schools would inspire another invasion of "Yankee schoolmarms" and the education of black Virginians would be turned over to "outside dreamers and fanatics." They also worried that dividing the school tax would invite northern scrutiny of the disfranchising features of the state's constitution.[37]

Opponents of black education nonetheless won a significant victory at the convention. According to the new constitution, state funds were to be distributed to the counties for the equal benefit of all children. This first provision reflected no special concern for black schools. Rather, those who lived in predominantly white areas were determined that tax money not be distributed to the counties on the basis of their population, thus giving white children in the more populous Black Belt counties a bigger share. Local tax dollars, on the other hand, which made up the bulk of school funding, could be used by school officials "as in their judgment the public welfare may require." The only requirement was that all schools be kept open four months each winter. Although this was not precisely the disaster that some had feared, the four-months school provision meant that black children in the poorest rural

counties would receive at best a rudimentary education. Mitchell, perhaps recalling his own days as a teacher, wearily observed that many children would
have eight months a year to forget what they had learned in four. By 1910 the
annual amount spent educating each white child in Virginia was $12.84; the
amount spent educating each black child was $5.60.[38]

The suffrage issue proved to be an even thornier problem for the delegates
than the schools. All sorts of proposals were made as to how to disfranchise
black voters without running aground the Fifteenth Amendment, which
specifically prohibited discrimination on the basis of race. Some delegates
were willing to have educated blacks retain the franchise, while others were
committed to an all-white electorate. The debates dragged on for months, and
Mitchell grew tired of the controversy. He quoted one Jackson Ward observer
who laughed at the delegates' difficulties: "Dey want water to run down the
hill, without water running down the hill. Dey want the man to shoot the turkey, without the man shooting the turkey." Mitchell's reputation for militancy
kept him out of the limelight, although he lobbied privately with one Richmond delegate, C. V. Meredith, who had served as city attorney while Mitchell
was on the board of aldermen. Meredith assured him that in the end "respectable Negroes" would retain the franchise.[39]

On May 25, 1902, the delegates agreed on a complicated suffrage article that
effectively disfranchised the vast majority of black Virginians. According to
the new Virginia constitution (which was never submitted to the voters but
was proclaimed by the convention itself), during the period before January 1,
1904, a man could place his name on a permanent list of voters if he could sat-
isfy one of three requirements: he was able to read or understand the state
constitution; he had paid taxes on property worth at least $333; or he was a vet-
eran of either the U.S. or Confederate army or the son of a veteran. Thus the
constitution contained an understanding clause, a property qualification, and
a grandfather clause, all designed as loopholes to incorporate whites into the
electorate while keeping blacks out. After 1904 anyone who wished to register
had to fill out in his own handwriting on a blank sheet of paper "without aid,
suggestions or memorandum" his name, age, date and place of birth, residence, occupation, and other sundry information. Registrars were further
empowered to question prospective voters about their qualifications. When
asked whether this clause might lead to discrimination, delegate Carter Glass
replied: "Discrimination! Why, that is precisely what we propose; that, exactly,
is what this convention was elected for." Finally, all save veterans were required to pay an annual poll tax of $1.50, a significant sum for all but the
wealthiest voters.[40]

On June 20, 1902, the old pollbooks were purged, and a new registration began throughout Virginia. Mitchell described the registration in Jackson Ward as a "howling farce," though he admitted that those with tax receipts had little difficulty placing their names on the books. He registered easily, as did others who owned their homes or businesses. Those who sought to register by way of the understanding clause faced stiffer challenges. Prospective voters were asked all manner of question: What was meant by viva voce? What was a common carrier? What was a representative body? What were the powers of the corporation commission? Whites laughed at blacks' mistakes and traded stories about the foolishness of the answers, but the anecdotes suggest that some rather sophisticated insights into the technical workings of government were required. George St. Julien Stephens, a property owner in Jackson Ward and a member of the Sixth Virginia Volunteers, grew tired of the stories and decided to test the understanding clause, perhaps with an eye to a court challenge. On the day he registered, illiterate whites were asked to explain a passage in the constitution describing how poor schoolchildren could receive free textbooks while he was grilled about the circumstances under which property could escheat to the commonwealth. He answered the questions in rapid-fire fashion and was given more and more difficult passages to interpret. Finally the registrar conceded rather glumly that he did in fact understand the constitution.[41]

A few blacks invoked the grandfather clause and registered as veterans. Captain Benjamin A. Graves and other members of the Sixth Virginia Volunteers presented their discharge papers and were excused from paying the poll tax. Some elderly blacks registered after demonstrating that they had been mustered in to fight for the Confederacy during the closing months of the war. Still others insisted they were the offspring of Confederate veterans and presented their fair complexions as evidence. One light-skinned Negro registered after providing "proof" that his father was an ex-Confederate soldier, a man whose name was a household word. "What could we do?" asked the registrar. "There was the law, and he had the facts." The state's attorney general quickly ruled that illegitimate offspring could not take advantage of the grandfather clause.[42]

Just how many blacks in Jackson Ward tried to register but failed is unknown. In the mountains of southwest Virginia stories circulated for years of the shame felt by illiterate whites who struggled to "understand" their new constitution. Whites assumed blacks felt no shame, but many did, and stayed away from the polls. A few remained at home as a matter of principle, refusing to cooperate with a system designed to exclude them, a form of protest

Mitchell discouraged. Whatever the percentage of failure, the effects on the Jackson Ward electorate were devastating. When the books closed in October 1902, the number of white voters in the ward had dropped from 789 to 468; the number of black voters had fallen from 2,983 to 347. Whites at last had their majority in Jackson Ward. Citywide the black electorate was reduced by 88 percent, from 6,407 to 760. By the time the permanent registration ended the next year, 815 names were inscribed in the city's leather-bound "Register of Colored Voters."[43]

Although an important core of black voters remained, the new constitution meant the end of a political era in Richmond. The grassroots organizations that had nurtured and sustained political activity in Jackson Ward withered. With the outcome of every election known in advance, few could be bothered to go to the polls, and apathy prevailed among both races. In the fall of 1902, a Democratic rally had to be called off because of poor attendance, and the election returns for Jackson Ward read like misprints. In the ward's densely populated second precinct, with its huge black majority, the Republican candidate for Congress in 1902 received 25 votes, the Democratic candidate 16. In the third precinct only 13 Republicans voted. "The non-participation of the negroes was even more noticeable than it was expected to be," wrote a reporter for the *Dispatch*, who seemed nonplussed by the lack of activity.[44]

For thirty years Jackson Ward had stood as a political fortress, but after disfranchisement it was a wasteland, shorn of its voters and serving no real purpose. In 1904 the Virginia General Assembly redistricted the city, and the predominantly black ward was parceled out among its neighbors. Although the term *Jackson Ward* remained a familiar geographical designation in Richmond for decades to come, its political significance was gone.

For Mitchell the period of the constitutional convention was a time of frustration. Accustomed to playing an active role in politics, he found himself powerless to mold events and unable to do much more than document the stripping away of the last vestiges of black political strength. He must have realized that leadership in race relations was shifting to those like Giles B. Jackson who were willing to placate and flatter and who were adept at negotiating from a position of weakness. Unless he was content to remain on the margins, he would have to find some way to advance his views without enraging those white Democrats who controlled the political process. He would have to find his own voice and his own way of promoting his ideas.

Mitchell spent much of his childhood in the home of James Lyons on
Grace Street, later the Westmoreland Club. From *Art Works of Richmond*
(Chicago, 1897), pt. 2. (Photo courtesy of the Valentine Richmond
History Center)

First African Baptist Church as it appeared when Mitchell was a child.
From *Harper's Weekly,* June 27, 1874, drawn by W. L. Sheppard.

Mitchell during his early years as *Planet* editor. From William J. Simmons, *Men of Mark: Eminent, Progressive, and Rising* (Cleveland, 1887).

Mitchell illustrated *Planet* stories with his own drawings. Here he depicted himself as a reporter transcribing the final words of Solomon Marable, a prisoner awaiting execution. From the *Planet,* July 25, 1896. (All photos from the *Planet* courtesy of the Library of Virginia, Richmond, unless otherwise noted)

In this cartoon Mitchell depicted the Virginia militia intervening to prevent a lynching. From the *Planet*, Feb. 23, 1895.

Mitchell's rescue of the fifteen-year-old Simon Walker from the gallows in 1889 won him considerable fame. From the *Planet*, Oct. 24, 1896.

Pokey Barnes after her release from prison in 1896. From the *Planet,* Oct. 24, 1896.

The *Planet* office on
Fourth Street. From the
Planet, June 19, 1897.

The *Planet* mast-
head featuring the
strong arm and the
"electric flashes."
From the *Planet,*
June 19, 1897.

Marietta L. Chiles, Mitchell's longtime friend and a teacher at Baker School. (Courtesy of Lillian Williams Lovett)

First Church at the time of the Baptist schism. (Courtesy, National Park Service, Maggie L. Walker National Historic Site)

Mitchell in his Pythian regalia. (Courtesy of John Thomas Mitchell)

As a banker, Mitchell projected wealth and stability. From A. B. Caldwell, *History of the American Negro, Virginia Edition* (Atlanta, 1921).

Maggie L. Walker mobilized women in support of the St. Lukes. In this photograph she stands to the far right; the boy is probably one of her sons. (Courtesy, National Park Service, Maggie L. Walker National Historic Site)

An architectural rendering of the Mechanics' Savings Bank building, which opened in 1910. From the *Planet*, Oct. 2, 1909. (Microfilm at University of Virginia Library, Charlottesville)

Mitchell beside his bank vault. (Courtesy of the Black History Museum and Cultural Center of Virginia, Richmond)

Mitchell's 1919 purchase of the white Strand Theater on Broad Street was audacious and got him into trouble. (Courtesy of the Valentine Richmond History Center)

When this photograph of black leaders was taken in May 1922, Mitchell knew his bank was likely to fail. He stands front and center; Maggie Walker is to his right. (Courtesy, National Park Service, Maggie L. Walker National Historic Site)

CHAPTER NINE

"Did God Call the Pastor?"

Mitchell's reluctance to cooperate with Giles B. Jackson in his maneuverings against disfranchisement probably came as no surprise to his admirers. His reputation as a firebrand made it unlikely that he would appear before white delegates with hat in hand or entertain them with self-effacing anecdotes. More puzzling, however, was his lukewarm response to the efforts of James H. Hayes to overturn the state constitution in the courts. Once the new constitution was proclaimed in May 1902, Hayes announced his intention to mount a legal challenge to disfranchisement and promised to carry the case as far as the U.S. Supreme Court. Mitchell's refusal to support Hayes was the first sure sign that his career was entering a new phase, that he was no longer willing to place himself on the frontline of black protest.

The origins of the movement to challenge disfranchisement are obscure, but apparently Mitchell was never involved. As early as August 1900 an organization calling itself the Negro Industrial and Agricultural Association met in Charlottesville. The founders agreed to buy farmland, establish an industrial school, and organize a fair. The talk of farms and fairs was probably a smoke screen. The next year the group elected Hayes solicitor and resolved "to have the matter of the disfranchisement of the Negro carried to the Supreme Court." The organizers seemed undeterred by the odds against them: "Some tell us we can do nothing. To them we answer: We have not tried; and that the world will respect us if we try and despise us if we use no effort to win back that which was purchased at greatest cost." Two prominent white Republicans, John S. Wise and Lunsford L. Lewis, also joined the effort.[1]

Mitchell responded to the news of the court challenge with a surprising lack of enthusiasm. Although he had maintained for months that the suffrage article was unconstitutional, he threw cold water on the movement by predicting its ultimate defeat. He reminded *Planet* readers of the Supreme Court's disastrous ruling in *Plessy v. Ferguson* (1896) and its poor record on race since the time of *Dred Scott* (1857). He suggested that there were better ways to spend money. As so often happened when Hayes took the lead in an enterprise, Mitchell found reasons to object.[2]

As it turned out, Mitchell may have underestimated the pent-up resentment among black Virginians. Although the white press railed against Hayes and threatened to close black schools if the constitution was overturned, a white observer noticed that the movement seemed to find great favor among the rank and file. From across Virginia came reports of fund-raising ventures. "The many colored lodges of the county are getting together at various points," wrote a white reporter from Norfolk. In Southside Virginia rallies were held on Thursday evenings, the traditional meeting night for lodges. "We are not absolutely laying down," wrote Hayes to a friend, "but the Negro men, women, and children are putting their dimes together in the fight." Black women fought disfranchisement because they knew how severely their own liberties were eroded when their husbands lost the vote. At a meeting in Richmond, Maggie Walker moved an audience to tears with stirring oratory. She called upon black men "to stand up for their rights, to fight slavery, to live for their children and for hers."[3]

On November 28, 1902, Hayes appeared with John S. Wise in the U.S. circuit court in Richmond, where he spoke fervently in defense of black voters. His presentation must have been impressive, for the hostile *Dispatch* conceded that he elicited from whites "a sympathy and toleration which a colored orator seldom receives." The judge was unmoved, however, and dismissed the two suits, *Jones v. Montague* and *Seldon v. Montague*. The cases were appealed to the Supreme Court but were not heard until April 1904, when they were again dismissed, just as Mitchell had predicted from the start.[4]

Although Mitchell never expressly condemned Hayes for pursuing the court challenge, his gloomy editorials did little to help him. Fellow journalists were puzzled by the subdued tone of the *Planet* and the emptiness of so many editorials. Harry C. Smith of the *Cleveland Gazette,* an old friend who had lauded Mitchell's opposition to the Spanish-American War, wondered why the "*Planet* has not shown its old time vigor along editorial lines." Smith thought it essential that the black press support men like Hayes who "are manly and brave enough to say what we all feel." Other journalists were similarly perplexed. An editor from Arkansas received a copy of the *Planet* and concluded that this "is not the John Mitchell of ten years ago." W. Calvin Chase of the *Washington Bee* tried to prod the "Fighting Editor" into activity. "What has become of John Mitchell?" he asked. "Old boy, let the country hear from you!"[5]

Mitchell's lassitude was the result of a number of factors—his longtime rivalry with Hayes, his preoccupation with his business ventures, his fatigue from fighting so many losing battles, perhaps even a midlife crisis of sorts occasioned by his brother's death. But there was another reason for his silence. Even as Hayes prepared legal briefs, Mitchell was enmeshed in a different political struggle, one that received only passing attention in the white press and yet was as bitter and disruptive as any that took place in Jackson Ward. This was a church conflict, ostensibly involving the question of who should succeed James H. Holmes as pastor at First Church. Holmes's death on November 25, 1900, at the age of seventy-three precipitated a power struggle within the congregation. As so often happened, a quarrel that began within church walls and seemed of trifling significance spilled out into the community in unexpected ways. As the conflict widened, it revealed how deeply suspicious blacks were of all whites, not just those who disfranchised them.

Mitchell got caught up in this quarrel because of his position as a trustee of Virginia Seminary, a black-operated school in Lynchburg that was founded by the Virginia Baptist State Convention in 1886. The school had its origins in tensions between black Baptists and the American Baptist Home Mission Society, an organization of northern whites, many of them former abolitionists, who established schools and colleges in the South after the Civil War. The Home Mission Society founded two schools in Richmond: Richmond Theological Seminary in 1867 and Hartshorn Memorial College for women in 1884. From the very beginning black Baptists in Virginia pushed the Home Mission Society to appoint blacks to faculty positions and give the race a greater voice in school administration. The society responded in the 1870s by sending two gifted students, Daniel N. Vassar and Joseph E. Jones, to Madison College (later Colgate University) in Hamilton, New York. After completing graduate work, they returned to Richmond and joined the faculty. Black clergy were also named to the board of trustees. The society did not move fast enough, however, and by the 1880s black Baptists had begun to lobby for a school owned, operated, and managed by themselves.[6]

In 1886 the all-black Virginia Baptist State Convention purchased six acres of land in the suburbs of Lynchburg and resolved to found its own school, Virginia Seminary. P. F. Morris, the pastor of Court Street Baptist Church in Lynchburg and a graduate of Howard University, was named president. He articulated an educational philosophy that would guide the school for the next century. According to Morris the finest education of black youths had to rest on a foundation of race pride, self-reliance, and "ancestral reverence." Construction began on an ambitious brick building, but money ran out before the first floor was completed. By 1890 only thirty-three students were enrolled, and the school was in debt by $4,400. As one Baptist minister conceded, the unfinished building was "a monument to our financial weakness."[7]

Virginia Seminary took on new life in 1891 when Mitchell was named to the board of trustees and Gregory W. Hayes became president. Hayes, born in 1862 to slave parents in Amelia County, had come to Richmond after the war, and he and Mitchell were classmates at Navy Hill. At the age of eleven or twelve, he was sent north to live with relatives. After serving briefly in the navy, he enrolled at the predominantly white Oberlin College in Ohio, where he made a reputation as a splendid orator and charismatic student leader. He and the Richmond-born Wendell P. Dabney were fellow students at Oberlin, and Dabney told a story about their college experiences that gives insight into Hayes's personality. On one occasion, when scheduled to speak, Hayes handed Dabney an expensive book and said, "When I get through speaking, send that book up to me." When Dabney asked why, Hayes responded: "Because the white speakers generally get tributes of flowers or books. I want them to see that I am just as well thought of as they are. It makes them respect you more."[8]

The dark-skinned Hayes spent seven years at Oberlin, working his way through the preparatory and college departments and taking his M.A. in 1888. After leaving Oberlin he joined the faculty at Virginia Normal in Petersburg, where he taught math for three years. According to one story he was dismissed from his position after the 1891 commencement exercises when he refused to hand out diplomas and walked off stage to protest racist comments in a speech by Governor Philip W. McKinney. Another version says he clashed too often with accommodationist president James H. Johnston.[9]

Hayes brought to Virginia Seminary enormous energy and commitment. He helped the students build a temporary wooden structure to be used for classrooms until the main building could be completed. He hired additional faculty, and by 1894 the school had enrolled four hundred students, male and female, ranging in age from nine to adult. He insisted that boys and girls study the same academic curriculum. Mitchell visited the campus often as a trustee, sometimes riding the train to Lynchburg as frequently as once a month, and he thought the school made remarkable strides given its meager resources. He was heartened that the students responded so well to Hayes's emphasis on race pride, and he liked the boys' band, which played rousing numbers and executed military maneuvers. After one visit to Lynchburg, he wrote, "Oh, if we could only picture the work to you as we saw it last week, exhortations would be unnecessary and appeals for money out of place."[10]

Money of course remained the crux of the problem. Hayes and his students crisscrossed the state, speaking at churches and pleading for contributions, but the amounts given were small. Hayes received nickels and dimes when he needed thousands of dollars, and Mitchell and the trustees had little choice but to turn to the Home Mission Society for help. In 1891 the society agreed to pay Hayes's salary from a special fund set up by John D. Rockefeller. In 1895 the society loaned the school $4,000 to prevent foreclosure on the property. In return for white assistance, Hayes was required to submit monthly financial reports to the Home Mission Society. Mitchell argued that it was sometimes necessary to make compromises in order to gain financial advantage, but he was pleased that the school's principal benefactor was Adolphus Humbles, a well-to-do black contractor from Lynchburg who loaned Hayes $10,000.[11]

Virginia Seminary appeared to have turned a corner when the Home Mission Society in the mid-1890s precipitated a crisis by inaugurating a new approach to its schools. The society owned and operated thirteen black colleges in the South and partially supported fifteen others, many of which like Virginia Seminary were secondary schools administered by black Baptists. Rather than spread its dwindling assets so thinly, the society decided to concentrate its resources on several flagship schools. According to early reports Richmond Theological Seminary would be moved to Atlanta to become part of a complex including Morehouse and Spellman Colleges, an idea that caused dismay throughout Virginia. The society resolved instead to open a consolidated school in Richmond on property acquired on the north side of town. Virginia Union University, scheduled to open in 1899 on a new campus, would combine Richmond Theological Seminary, Hartshorn Memorial College, and Wayland Seminary in Washington. Virginia Seminary in Lynchburg would remain a secondary school.[12]

In 1896 the Virginia Baptist State Convention approved plans for the new university and agreed to raise $15,000 toward its support. Black Baptists also lobbied for an enhanced role in the school's administration. Mitchell thought that Dr. Joseph E. Jones at least should head an academic department at Virginia Union, but whites were given all the supervisory positions. Thomas J. Morgan, the corresponding secretary of the society and a former abolitionist, reiterated the society's commitment to strong academic training and promised to hire the finest faculty regardless of race. He counseled patience in the face of disappointments and urged black leaders to forsake "for the present all personal ambition and race pride," an admonition that was hard to swallow. Rumors meanwhile abounded about the Lynchburg school: that it would become entirely subordinate to the new Virginia Union University, that the college department would be dropped, and that President Hayes would be demoted to principal. Most damaging of all, a prominent white official was heard to say it would be a hundred years before a black man was ready to serve as a college president.[13]

Relations between black Baptists and the society deteriorated, and Hayes grew restive, insisting that he—not the Home Mission Society—was in charge of Virginia Seminary. Malcolm MacVicar, the white president of Virginia Union, was upset by talk of black separatism and worried that the Lynchburg school had become "a hot bed of racism." He professed to feel "sorry for President Hayes . . . sorry for his shortsightedness. . . . He is a race man through and through." Deteriorating race relations made everyone nervous and edgy. Speaking in Boston at a national meeting, one black pastor tried to explain to white church leaders why southern blacks appeared so sensitive: "The terrible race proscription throughout the whole country has caused most of the colored people to look upon all white men with suspicion. [They] are continually reminded that they are Negroes, and as such, unfit for the company of white men." A few months later Mitchell cautioned black Baptists not to be rude to their white benefactors: "They have been kind to us, but . . . we have been crawling for some time and the monotony of the thing is tiresome." A black pastor in Lynchburg was more blunt: "We are tired of being bossed around and now we are going to do our own bossing."[14]

The conflict between Hayes and the society worsened in January 1899 when an anonymous editorial appeared in the *Home Mission Monthly* attacking Hayes. Complaining of the school's mounting debt, the white author placed the blame on several unnamed trustees and on the president, "who delights to call himself a 'race man'; appeals to the race prejudices; is constantly inculcating foolish ideas as to race independence; carries his theory to the absurdity of advocating a 'Negro nation within a nation'—as if such a thing were conceivable." The society found these expressions of black nationalism "folly," "madness," and "very discouraging." Mitchell acknowledged the difficulties but sounded worried. Like most black Baptists he wanted black autonomy and white help.[15]

The final rupture came in May 1899 when the Virginia Baptist State Convention held its annual meeting in Lexington. Normally about 250 Baptists attended the sessions, but on the morning of the convention, 700 supporters of Hayes arrived at the train station in Lexington. They marched to the church with the enthusiasm of an invading army, and the meeting became known as the Battle of Lexington. The convention named three new trustees, all partisans of Hayes, and the reconfigured board severed its ties to the Home Mission Society. Mitchell voted with the separatist majority but still sounded uncertain as to how the school would be financed: "Virginia Seminary will live, if the colored folks say so, and die if it is their decree."[16]

In the weeks that followed, the cooperationists launched a vigorous counterattack, and the middle ground that Mitchell had tried to occupy fell away. A number of the state's most respected clergy, including Anthony Binga Jr. and Joseph E. Jones, published a broadside condemning the "radical, revolutionary, uncivil, illegal and unchristian action" of the Lexington convention. They charged that the separatists had used unsavory political tricks to accomplish their ends, stacking the convention with Hayes's supporters, many of whom were merely "women and girl children." (During the conflict both sides accused the other of relying too heavily on women, who were playing an increasingly important role in church affairs.) Binga and Jones thought it irresponsible to jettison white assistance at a time when the race had so few resources. Hayes's supporters answered that the race's desperate plight made any sacrifice possible except the surrender of race pride. Attacks on Hayes and Virginia Seminary grew increasingly harsh, making reconciliation unlikely. Mitchell finally entered the fray as a separatist, writing spirited editorials in Hayes's defense.[17]

On June 20, 1899, representatives of forty-two churches convened in Richmond to form the General Association of the Colored Baptists of Virginia, a rival association of cooperationists. Although smaller than the Virginia Baptist State Convention, the breakaway association included some of the state's largest and wealthiest urban churches. To Mitchell's dismay his own church joined the General Association.[18]

After Holmes's death on November 25, 1900, the congregation at First Church split into factions as the members began their search for a new pastor. Some supported cooperation with the Home Mission Society, while others, like Mitchell, supported independence. Because the vacant pulpit was one of the most desirable in the South, black Baptists from across the region watched the conflict closely.

The leading contender for the position and the candidate Mitchell favored was Dr. Walter H. Brooks, aged forty-nine, a native Richmonder who had served for nearly two decades as pastor of Nineteenth Street Baptist Church in Washington, D.C. A graduate of Lincoln University in Pennsylvania and holder of several honorary doctorates, Brooks had first come to national prominence in 1889 as one of three black clergy chosen to contribute articles to the *Baptist Teacher*, a publication of the white American Baptist Publication Society. When white southerners protested the inclusion of black-authored lessons, the Publication Society rescinded its offer and published them in a separate tract. The incident contributed to the founding in 1896 of the black-run National Baptist Publishing House in Nashville, Tennessee. Brooks was a leading spokesman for independence and was also a formidable candidate because of his ties to family and friends in Richmond. His wife, Eva Holmes Brooks, was the daughter of James H. Holmes; his sister, Lucy Brooks Lewis, was prominent in Baptist circles and was married to Mitchell's close friend attorney George W. Lewis.[19]

The second candidate, Rev. William Thomas Johnson, a native of Manchester, also had impressive credentials, although he was younger and not quite so well connected. Aged thirty-four, he was a graduate of Richmond Theological Seminary and pastor of the First Baptist Church of Lexington, Virginia. His church had been the host church for the 1899 convention, and during the "Battle of Lexington" he emerged as a leading spokesman for cooperation. A dynamic speaker, Johnson was handsome and articulate. His congregation had flourished during his pastorate and had raised the money to erect a new sanctuary.[20]

Under ordinary circumstances two strong candidates might have proved a blessing, but these were not ordinary times. The committee to select the pastor deadlocked, unable to choose between the separatist Brooks and the co-operationist Johnson. After a series of protracted meetings, the deacons decided to place three names before the congregation. The candidates were Brooks, Johnson, and a last-minute contender, Dr. A. W. Pegues, a faculty member at Shaw University in Raleigh, North Carolina. The election was scheduled for Monday evening, June 3, 1901. Although women ordinarily did not vote at church meetings and never served as deacons, the calling of a pastor was considered of such importance that all were invited to participate.[21]

Nearly six hundred men, women, and children braved a driving rain to attend the meeting on June 3. Mitchell arrived at the church in an agitated frame of mind, upset about reports that some of Johnson's female supporters had campaigned aggressively and had canvassed the black community, going door to door to ensure a large turnout. The meeting began with some skirmishes about parliamentary matters, and from the start Johnson's advocates appeared to have the upper hand. They sat on one side of the church, and whenever Mitchell tried to speak, they hectored him and made their displeasure known. When the votes were counted, Johnson was the winner with 369; Brooks had 181, and Pegues 19.

Mitchell, unaccustomed to defeat, then strode to the front of the church. He declared that the meeting was "a disgrace to the Christian religion" and that during "the stormiest day of politics" he had never been treated so poorly. He thought "the course of certain females . . . disgraceful, but so far [as] he was personally concerned, he believed that 'they knew not what they did.'" Overcoming his outrage, he finally moved that the vote be made unanimous in the interest of church unity.[22]

In the aftermath of the June 3 meeting, the *Planet* was strangely silent. Mitchell at first did not report the results of the vote or even acknowledge that a meeting had taken place. He was clearly furious, and his sense of grievance festered and grew with time. He eventually cast his role in a heroic mode, as if he had been the victim of a lynch mob rather than the loser in a church quarrel. "I saw the same spirit [of lawlessness] in Chesterfield County, when the 16-year-old Simon Walker was on the verge of eternity," he said. He was also embarrassed that he, a veteran of years of campaigning in Jackson Ward and a former councilman, had been outmaneuvered by women who were supposedly inexperienced in politics. He accused Johnson's female supporters of being distracted by gossip about Brooks. One woman admitted that she voted for Johnson because she heard that Brooks on Sunday mornings "wouldn't let the sisters give vent to their feelings. He would stop in his sermons and wait for order." As so often happened, various community conflicts intersected in complex ways. Johnson was a member of the True Reformers, and the quarrels at First Church replicated some of the divisions within that organization. For Mitchell the underlying issue was support for Hayes and Virginia Seminary. Other members of First Church clearly had different agendas.[23]

The *Planet* broke its silence on July 6, 1901, with a front-page article that ran under the headline, "Did God Call the Pastor?" Mitchell described in unflattering detail the lack of decorum at the June meeting and implied that Johnson had won by virtue of the votes of "youngsters and misses" while those who had grown gray serving the church were ignored. He also printed in its entirety a letter from Johnson that made the Lexington pastor appear greedy and supercilious. After expressing gratitude for the call, Johnson told the deacons, "I take for granted that you will AMPLY provide for your Shepherd, although you did not say so in your letter of June 4, 1901." According to the *Planet*, the word *amply* was underlined twice. At the next monthly meeting, Mitchell tried to have the call rescinded, but the congregation confirmed its support of Johnson and agreed to pay him $1,000 a year, the same salary Holmes had received. When Mitchell challenged the amount, female opponents poked fun at his well-known vanity and said, "Don't he look pretty."[24]

The following Sunday, Nelson Williams Jr., a teacher in the public schools, requested that the deacons call a special meeting to consider sanctions against

Mitchell. Williams contended that Mitchell should never have advertised the church's troubles in the *Planet,* that he brought discredit upon the congregation (and by implication the race) by lampooning members on the front page, that his account reflected poorly on "factory people" (or working-class members of the church), and that his printing of Johnson's private letter was unconscionable. Mitchell stayed away from the meeting, but the deacons asked that he appear on August 5 to show cause why he should not be expelled.

The August meeting was essentially a church trial with Mitchell represented by Hezekiah Jonathan, a former councilman from Jackson Ward. During the trial Mitchell's offhand, dismissive manner angered some onlookers; he pretended to be bored. By the time the vote was taken, it was well past midnight, and most members had gone home. Those who remained voted by a margin of 64 to 56 to withdraw from him the right hand of fellowship, which was tantamount to expulsion. The news made the front page of the *Dispatch:* "John Mitchell Jr. Excluded from Church."[25]

Church quarrels are notoriously bitter, and this one proved especially so. Mitchell continued to give the "muddle at First Church" front-page coverage despite not being present at meetings. He boasted that he had been in the newspaper business long enough to find ways to acquire information. On one occasion a *Planet* reporter was discovered lurking outside an open window. He ridiculed several members but reserved his most brutal satire for Nelson Williams, the rather prim teacher who had requested the trial. For years Williams had refused to take communion at First Church because the church used wine instead of grape juice, and according to the *Planet* he inflicted long-winded prayers upon innocent Sunday school children. Williams also had made an important procedural error. Although church protocol required that a request for a special meeting be signed by fifteen members, he had simply inscribed the names in his own hand to the July 7 request. In the *Planet,* Mitchell invariably referred to Williams as "Williams, who forged the names to the application for the meeting," a refrain he repeated often enough to be funny. He mocked Williams's physical appearance, making sport of his gold-rimmed spectacles and his "capacious body" which "looked as though it had passed through the severest processes of a rhinoceros hide tan yard." His attacks on "Educated Hog" grew personal and vituperative, and not so funny. He made jokes about Williams's wide backside and "quivering hindquarters."[26]

Mitchell's abuse of "Hindquarters Williams" ended in March 1902 when the schoolteacher filed suit in law and equity court charging the *Planet* editor with thirty-one counts of libel and asking for $10,000 in damages. Once the suit was filed, Mitchell dropped the personal attacks. As he wryly noted, not many journalists could afford to wear a $10,000 suit. His trial did not take place un-til January 1903, but during the period when Hayes was undertaking his legal assault on disfranchisement, Mitchell was preparing for his own day in court. He must have known that his treatment of Williams had been heavy-handed. He hired as counsel two of Richmond's best-known white attorneys, ex-con-gressman George D. Wise and former city attorney C. V. Meredith. During the fall of 1902, he was in no position to launch bold attacks on disfranchisement. His lawyers, both Democrats, had served as delegates to the constitutional convention.[27]

Meanwhile at First Church business meetings continued to be stormy, and W. T. Johnson, who was installed as pastor in September 1901, must have won-dered why he had ever left Lexington. Quarrels that had once been settled in the polling booths of Jackson Ward were now fought out in church meetings, and no one seemed certain what rules applied. On one occasion a deacon de-clared that "the females were the cause of all the trouble," whereupon a large number of women rose from their pews and left the church. Clearly women (and "girl children") were more assertive in this setting than in municipal pol-itics and refused to defer to church fathers. Johnson observed that men and women resolved conflicts differently: "Brethren could almost fight in the church meeting and when they went out they would shake hands and laugh and talk. But the sisters would talk about it going up Broad St. and everybody would know what they had done."[28]

Mitchell made several requests for a new trial at First Church, but the dea-cons rejected his appeals. He was reluctant to leave the church of his child-hood but in April 1902 applied for membership at Fifth Street Baptist Church. The pastor at Fifth Street, W. F. Graham, was a separatist whose discontent with white Baptists dated back to his seminary days. Graham had been a stu-dent at Wayland Seminary in 1882 when the white principal, G. M. P. King, lost his temper and shoved a female student. The incident led to the resigna-tion of twenty students and demands for King's removal. Graham was a long-time trustee of Virginia Seminary and an ardent defender of Gregory Hayes. Although he often showed an accommodationist face to whites, he could speak with much more militancy to a black audience.[29]

According to the rules of Baptist governance, a member who was expelled from one church could not be admitted to another church unless that church determined that he had been unjustly excluded. On May 13, 1902, a special council was held at Fifth Street to consider Mitchell's request for membership. More than three hundred delegates from seventy-six churches in Virginia, Maryland, Pennsylvania, and the District of Columbia came to the council, giving a clear indication of the importance of this issue in Baptist circles. Mitchell's church membership had become the touchstone of a much larger quarrel. The council concluded that First Church had been wrong to expel him and that Fifth Street could lawfully welcome him as a member.[30]

First Church held its own council on July 8, 1902, to consider Mitchell's status within the church. Only twenty congregations sent representatives, and all were part of the newly founded General Association. To demonstrate their commitment to cooperation, the black clergy invited white Baptists to participate, and four downtown white churches sent delegates. Anthony Binga Jr. presided. At one point Rev. Z. D. Lewis of Second Church was quoted as saying that Mitchell "thought he was something great and wanted people to bow to him." The meeting was contentious and lasted eight hours, but in the end the council resolved that Fifth Street had been wrong to add Mitchell's name to its rolls. Unless the deacons agreed to remove his name, which was unlikely, First Baptist would sever its ties to its sister church.[31]

The church quarrel entered a secular phase in January 1903 when Mitchell's trial was held in Richmond's law and equity court. Interest in the litigation was intense among Baptist clergy, many of whom traveled great distances to view the proceedings. Both sides hired white attorneys to make presentations to the all-white jury, while black attorneys did much of the legwork. Williams was represented by the white firm of Smith, Moncure & Gordon and by black attorney Joseph R. Pollard. Mitchell's white attorneys, Wise and Meredith, were joined by J. Thomas Hewin, a black graduate of the Boston University Law School. Williams's lawyers called nineteen witnesses and in a fifty-four-page declaration demonstrated that the *Planet* had relentlessly identified Williams as " 'Hindquarters' Williams, who forged the names to the application for the meeting." They contended that their client, an honest, well-meaning schoolteacher, had been subjected to "false, scandalous, malicious, defamatory and insulting words."[32]

Mitchell's attorneys conceded that their client had utilized the "shafts of ridicule" but claimed it was an "innocent burlesque" and that Williams had in fact forged the names. They also pointed out that Johnson's private letter was addressed to the First Baptist Church of Richmond, which made it not so private in nature. During final arguments Williams's white attorneys distributed copies of the *Planet* to jurors and reminded them that the newspaper had "made Mitchell a dictator in this community, colored people placing it next to their Bibles." They pleaded with the jury to fine Mitchell a sufficient sum to force him to sell the paper. Anticipating this argument, the *Planet* editor behaved throughout the trial with impeccable courtesy, displaying his famous courtly manners and stressing his conservatism. "I was born at Laburnum," he told jurors at one point. His best defense, of course, was the presence at his side of Wise and Meredith, two of Richmond's most popular Democrats.[33]

After deliberating for more than an hour, the jury returned with a decision in favor of Williams but awarded him damages of one penny, thus giving Mitchell the real victory. An award of less than ten dollars meant that Williams paid court costs. Mitchell had cause to rejoice, but his victory was not without price. He owed substantial fees to his lawyers and had been distracted for months by the lawsuit.[34]

Once the court case was over, the quarrel among black Baptists continued, but both sides appeared weary of the conflict and ready to move on to other matters. Peace came in November 1903, three years after Holmes's death, when W. T. Johnson called a meeting at First Church to discuss the problems that had beset the congregation since his installation. Reading from a carefully prepared paper, he declared that the church conflict had caused him untold personal anguish and hampered all his attempts at ministry. He proposed that First Church end the quarrel unilaterally and restore the right hand of fellowship to Mitchell. The congregation gave its assent by voice vote, and a committee of five departed for Fifth Street, where by prearrangement Graham and his deacons were waiting. Johnson informed Graham that "for the good of the Baptist denomination," they were ending the fight. With hands joined, pastors and deacons sang the familiar hymn, "Blest Be the Tie That Binds."[35]

A more public celebration took place on the evening of December 4, 1903, when a large delegation from Fifth Street, led by Mitchell, walked as a group to First Church. Every light in the building was turned on to welcome them, and the *Planet* editor was greeted at the front door by the pastor and escorted to the pulpit by the deacons. After accepting the right hand of fellowship, he made a speech in which he promised to harbor no ill will toward any member of the church. According to the *Planet*, "There were many responses from the congregation and many an eye filled with tears." Other addresses followed, interspersed by prayers, testimonials, and hymns. One participant said that no one would ever forget the emotional intensity of the evening. Women had been accused of starting the quarrel, and they were asked to end it. The final speeches were given by Rosa Bowser and Maggie Walker, two community leaders who placed their stamp of approval on the settlement.[36]

In the afterglow of the truce, some Baptists speculated that the accord would have far-reaching consequences and that divisions within the state church would also heal. This did not occur. Neither side was able to forget the harsh words that had been said or resolve misgivings about the other's position. The Virginia Baptist State Convention and the General Association of Colored Baptists have maintained separate identities, and the American Baptist Home Mission Society continued to funnel its resources to Virginia Union University in Richmond.[37]

Virginia Seminary in Lynchburg remained independent of white control, and Gregory Hayes, who died in 1906, became something of a folk hero among black Baptists. Although contributions from black congregations increased after independence, the school remained inadequately funded just as Mitchell had feared. The main building was not completed until 1911, more than twenty years after construction began. Entirely ignored by whites and chronically short of money, the school survived as a symbol of black pride and a place where Pan-Africanism was taken seriously. Among later presidents were Dr. J. R. L. Diggs, formerly of Virginia Union, who became a follower of Marcus Garvey in the 1920s, and Dr. Vernon Johns, the brilliant, iconoclastic race leader who served as Martin Luther King's predecessor at Dexter Avenue Baptist Church in Montgomery, Alabama. Sociologist St. Clair Drake's parents were both graduates of Virginia Seminary, and he tried to explain the school's appeal: "Union University was the white Baptists' gift to the Negroes. Seminary was *theirs*."[38]

As for Mitchell, he remained a member of Fifth Street Baptist Church but became an indifferent churchgoer. He never again allowed himself to be drawn into church politics, or if he did, he kept his views out of the *Planet*. Probably the experience had been too depleting, too taxing psychically. On some level he must have understood how little was achieved by his relentless hounding of Nelson Williams and how misdirected his rage had been. Frustrated by his inability to prevent disfranchisement, he had turned against a fellow church member. "When saints quarrel and fight," he said, "the Devil opens wide the gates of hell."[39] He also must have noticed that an important change had occurred in the wake of disfranchisement. As long as community conflicts were settled in the polling booths of Jackson Ward, he understood the rules and knew the principal players, who were males like himself. When the churches became the battleground, women entered the fray, and he had to contend with new and shrewd opponents whose tactics baffled and disoriented him.

CHAPTER TEN

Jim Crow and Race Pride

The early years of the twentieth century would have been a difficult period for Mitchell even had he not been contending with church fights and assertive women. Setbacks had come in such quick succession. The loss of his council seat in 1896 was followed by the fiasco of the Spanish-American War in 1898, the closing of the armory and the disbanding of the militia in 1899, his defeat in the council elections of 1900, disfranchisement and the four-months school provision in 1902, and the redrawing of the political map and the disappearance of Jackson Ward in 1904. Amid the turmoil he tried to keep his footing and maintain some perspective on what was happening. "Some of these white folks down here may be our best friends," he noted, "but they have a very poor way of showing their friendship."[1]

The early 1900s also brought new laws dedicated to the separation of the races in public transportation. Railway cars were segregated in Virginia in 1900, passenger steamboats in 1901, and Richmond streetcars in 1904. No matter how fervently Mitchell defended the right of black Baptists to separate themselves voluntarily, he never acquiesced in proscriptive segregation laws. Under the most difficult of circumstances, he tried to find some way to counter the spread of Jim Crow without provoking more repression. He was also eager to restore his standing in the community as an effective and resourceful leader and to repair the damage done to his reputation by the church conflict.

The first Jim Crow law arrived in Virginia with surprising suddenness. On Christmas Eve, 1899, a "dirty, intoxicated negro" allegedly took a seat beside a white woman on a train traveling between Richmond and Petersburg and then refused to move. The *Richmond Times* publicized the incident and drew far-reaching conclusions that seemed strangely at variance with its earlier more moderate stance on the race issue. "God Almighty drew the color line," said the *Times,* "and it cannot be obliterated." The newspaper argued that segregation had to be applied in "every relation of Southern life." John E. Epps, a white lawyer from Richmond, introduced a bill in the General Assembly requiring separate railroad cars for whites and blacks. As a concession to the railroad companies, he stipulated that in those cases where the traffic failed to warrant a separate car, a partition could be built within the car to divide the races.[2]

In the weeks that followed, tensions rose as whites debated the merits of the bill and reported case after case of black rowdiness on the trains. Mitchell's editorials took on new urgency: "Let us make friends with as many white people as we can, colored men. The time is now at hand that we need their friendship. Yes, we need it badly." He pleaded with male readers to keep their wounded feelings in their pockets and be polite to white passengers, no matter how much they were provoked. He ended his editorials with the refrain, "Let us have no 'Jim Crow car' law in Virginia!" Other than write editorials, however, there was little he could do. Giles B. Jackson led a delegation to the law office of John E. Epps, but even he seemed dispirited. "The colored people are generally submissive and are easily controlled by the white people," he told Epps. "Why be scared of a Negro?" On January 25, 1900, a month after the incident on the Petersburg train, the Virginia Senate unanimously passed the separate-car bill, scheduled to take effect on July 1.[3]

Throughout Virginia blacks responded to the act with anguish and bitterness. One group living in a small settlement in eastern Virginia even began making plans to leave the state. "Some are disposing of their personal effects and real estate," said the *Times,* and others are "visiting the members of their family to bid them a last farewell." Closer to Richmond, in neighboring Chesterfield County, a white reporter discovered that in the small community of Dry Bridge, blacks were "a good deal excited over the passage of the separate-car bill." They were "incensed" that they would have to ride in separate cars: "They declare that they will organize and band themselves together against the whites of their neighborhood. The men say they have their own stores and shops. They will not hire themselves out to the white people anymore, but will live of and by themselves, and let the whites do the same." According to the reporter black women were even more outspoken than the men: "They say they will not cook and do the washing for the white people any more, nor will they allow any of their color to do so."[4]

In the *Planet,* Mitchell wrote tormented editorials in which he warned the General Assembly of the retribution that would follow: "God's hand is everywhere manifest and the oppression of today upon a helpless but confiding people will return to plague your children of tomorrow." He was certain the next generation would reap the whirlwind. He drew a cartoon that showed black passengers hanging defiantly to the sides of a locomotive: "The Negro will ride upon the cowcatcher of the engine or cling to the smoke-stack of your boilers, but his prayers and his efforts will result in your downfall and death just as surely as was wrought the destruction of Sodom and Gomorrah."[5]

Once the railroads were segregated, attention turned to other forms of public transportation. The General Assembly next ruled that separate compartments be set aside on steamboats. This measure affected more blacks than one might imagine as steamboats were a popular form of transportation along the coast. The steamboat companies were unhappy with the new law and threatened to challenge it in the courts but apparently never did.[6]

Attention next turned to electric trolleys. During Reconstruction black Richmonders had been excluded from some horse-drawn streetcars, but by the mid-1870s black and white passengers apparently sat where they pleased. The transit companies did not want the expense of providing separate accommodations. Talk of segregated streetcars came to the fore again in 1891, after the introduction of electric cars, but the proposal faltered in the face of practical difficulties. Whites might prefer separate cars, but they wished to board the nearest car, and the two desires appeared incompatible. "It is a difficult matter to deal with," admitted the *Dispatch* in 1891. "White men . . . would not like to be forced to await the arrival of a car intended for white men only when a car intended for negroes only was hurrying along right before their eyes." During the 1890s scores of editorials appeared in the daily press about Richmond's electric transit system, but only a fraction made any mention of race. Complaints were instead voiced about poor scheduling, crowded cars, rude conductors, and the poor hygiene of passengers.[7]

In September 1900 talk of separate cars came to the fore again when John J. Peters, a councilman from Monroe Ward, presented to the council a resolution in favor of segregated trolleys. Mitchell was discouraged by the revival of this issue, and he proposed that Peters, a housepainter by trade, be doused with black paint so he could wander the streets "pariah-like" and feel the effects of Jim Crow. The *Planet* editor knew that cities to the South were beginning to require segregation, and he worried that the contagion would spread to Virginia. Giles Jackson made one of his customary pilgrimages to the council chamber, this time on behalf of the Constitutional Rights Association. In an unusually forthright statement, he warned that separate cars would cripple the streetcar system and lead to litigation. Although a majority of councilmen professed to favor the measure, they were stymied by the problems it would cause.[8]

In March 1902 John E. Epps introduced a similar measure before the General Assembly. Mitchell's patience was now wearing thin, and he insisted that black people no longer "care[d] a fig" what white people did. "They have oppressed us in every conceivable fashion until they are well nigh ready to order us off the face of the earth." But he continued: "We shall protest and protest. We shall agitate and agitate. We shall never willingly submit." The transit companies mobilized against the measure, which would have required them to send two trolleys along every route. Primarily because of their lobbying, the measure was voted down. In the *Planet,* Mitchell urged black men to yield their seats to women—white and black—and to practice courtesy. "God knows these are trying times," he said, "but the bragging, bullying, insulting colored men can make them no better." He saw nothing to gain—and much to lose—if black men jostled white passengers and competed for public space.[9]

The demand for separate cars seemed to be losing ground when the General Assembly in January 1904 passed a twenty-page "Act concerning Public Transportation." The act was a detailed compilation of the various provisions that had been legislated over the years regarding railroads and other public utilities. Buried within the law were new provisions regarding streetcars. Transit companies were "authorized and empowered . . . to separate the white and colored passengers." They could "set apart and designate in each car or coach a portion thereof, or certain seats therein, to be occupied by white passengers, and a portion thereof, or certain seats therein, to be occupied by colored passengers." This act differed in two important ways from earlier proposals. First, the act authorized but did not require Jim Crow; and second, no provisions were made for separate cars. Instead blacks and whites were to be separated within cars. Transit officials later admitted that they sponsored the measure in an effort to forestall any move toward separate cars, which they believed would be prohibitively expensive.[10]

The act provoked no public debate, and Mitchell probably knew nothing of its passage until April 1, 1904, when the Virginia Passenger and Power Company made a surprise announcement. Beginning on April 15 (the date was later postponed to April 20), the company would segregate passengers on its lines in Richmond, Manchester, and Petersburg: "White passengers will occupy seats in the forward portion of the car, and colored passengers will occupy seats in the rear." The reasons for the company's announcement were never made clear. There had been no flurry of editorials, although some whites may have lobbied company officials privately. Mitchell speculated that

S. W. Huff, the manager, imagined white Richmonders more offended by mixed cars than they actually were. The company was northern owned and operated, and Huff himself was new to Richmond.[11]

Huff probably assumed that black passengers would shrug off this latest affront or perhaps grumble a bit before submitting. If so, he miscalculated. According to Mitchell no act since the Civil War had caused such heartache in black Richmond. From the black perspective Jim Crow streetcars were much more degrading and humiliating than segregated trains. Passengers were on the trolleys for only a brief time, sometimes for no more than a few blocks; fares were low; domestics and laborers rode them daily; and no one expected "parlor car accommodations."[12]

A closer examination of the act reveals other reasons for Mitchell's concern. Particularly troublesome were provisions describing how passengers would be separated. No partitions would be built as was done on the trains. The reason was simple: as a streetcar made its way through different neighborhoods, its population was likely to change dramatically from block to block. Some southern cities required that a portable sign be erected between the seats and then shifted, which meant that the conductor spent much of his time adjusting the sign. In Richmond conductors instead were given the authority to assign seats. As the car's racial makeup changed, they were "to increase or decrease the amount of space or room set apart for either race." Because the invisible line dividing the races would always be moving back and forth, conductors were further empowered to "require any passenger to change his seat or her seat when and as often has he may deem necessary." It was this last provision that worried Mitchell. He could imagine a white conductor playing a bizarre game of musical chairs with passengers. At least on the trains black passengers could relax and visit among themselves, and black seats remained black seats and did not become white seats midway through the journey.[13]

To complicate matters further, relations between the white conductors of Richmond and black passengers were already strained. The conductors were poorly paid working-class men, many of them quite young, and they tended to lord it over black riders. In 1902 a lynching was narrowly averted in the neighborhood of Church Hill after a black passenger shot and wounded a conductor. In the aftermath conductors routinely referred to passengers as "d . . . niggers."[14] Now conductors were to be given special police powers (including the right to carry a gun), and anyone who failed to obey the instructions of the conductor would be guilty of a misdemeanor.

The company made its announcement on Friday, April 1, 1904, and the following Monday the general secretary of the True Reformers, W. P. Burrell, decided to take action. Burrell, the son of a hotel waiter and a graduate of Richmond Theological Seminary, was president of the Baptist State Sunday School Union. He paid a visit to S. W. Huff of the transit company, ostensibly on behalf of the Sunday School Union. After making the usual disclaimers about "social equality and such bugbears," Burrell expressed concern about the way the regulations would be enforced. He admitted a preference for separate cars—if segregation was unavoidable—and predicted trouble between black passengers and white conductors. Huff assured him that the rules would be enforced fairly without discrimination. Burrell warned that if blacks were denied the "right to ride in public conveyances as other law-abiding citizens," they would have no choice but to find other means of transportation. Hinting at a boycott, he urged Huff to reconsider and save "34,000 patrons the trouble and inconvenience of walking."[15]

The next afternoon the all-black Richmond Ministers' Conference met to discuss the trouble that was brewing over the streetcars. After a long closed session that began in mid-afternoon and lasted well beyond the dinner hour, the pastors agreed to draw up a series of resolutions and present them to company officials. Diplomacy by resolution had become a standard feature of Richmond race relations, and Giles B. Jackson, the race's best-known ambassador, was called in for consultation. The ministers decided to visit Huff the next day. Jackson would accompany them and make the introductions.[16]

When the group reached Huff's office, the pastors presented a paper endorsed by the Negro Business League and the Sunday School Union that expressed concerns about the new policy. "The fear of improper treatment," they said, "has created such a strong feeling that there is much talk of walking and providing other means of conveyance." Huff was again conciliatory: "We want all to ride and we regard your people's money as good as anyone else's." A. B. Guigon, who had defended the Lunenburg women in 1896, was present as counsel for the transit company, and he made every effort to be accommodating. "We shall expect the assistance of you colored preachers," he said.[17]

The day after the preachers met with Guigon, the weekly edition of the *Planet* appeared on newsstands. Mitchell had followed closely streetcar boycotts in other southern cities, and he proposed something similar for Richmond. "Walking is good now," he wrote. "Let us walk." Maggie Walker's *St. Luke Herald* was just as vehement. "Let us walk!" was the theme of her editorial page. Mitchell and Walker both urged blacks not to board streetcars and attempt to take white seats. Instead they should "avoid trouble" and walk.

They doubtless remembered the death in 1898 of Elijah Turner at the hands of a streetcar conductor in Macon, Georgia.[18]

As it turned out, the streetcar boycott captured the imagination of black Richmonders in a way no other protest had in years. Partly this was a matter of timing. Ordinary folk who had held their tongues as they boarded Jim Crow railway cars on the trains were beginning to lose patience. Disfranchisement had not ushered in the era of good feeling that whites had promised, and no matter how many resolutions Jackson took to the white community, the results were the same. The daily papers meanwhile kept up a barrage of insulting, inflammatory, racist articles. As the *St. Luke Herald* explained, "Our self-respect demands that we walk." In much the same mood, Mitchell worried that this latest affliction "follows too closely our elimination as a political factor." Even the white press noticed that the "indignation has been pent up among the negroes for some time."[19]

There also seemed a fair chance the boycott might work. Because the General Assembly had only authorized segregation, not required it, no legislation had to be repealed. The Virginia Passenger and Power Company merely had to rescind its new rules. Furthermore, the transit company was known to be in serious financial trouble. Created in 1901 by the merger of ten competing companies, the consolidated company was plagued by labor unrest. During the summer of 1903, conductors and motormen went out on strike in a dispute over wages and nearly shut down business in the downtown area. When rioting broke out, Governor Andrew J. Montague mobilized the militia, two men were killed, and striking conductors called for a boycott. Supported by the mayor and the city's labor unions, the 1903 boycott by the Amalgamated Association of Street Railway Employees was known to have cost the company dearly.[20]

There was a final reason for the black boycott's popularity. It was a protest that could be couched in conservative language. Since the time of the constitutional convention, whites had heralded each new oppression as a move toward more harmonious race relations. "One by one our rights are to be taken away to produce the alleged harmony between the races," wrote Mitchell in disbelief. Now whites would find their language used against them. Mitchell insisted that walking would reduce racial friction and restore tranquillity. At times he wrote with tongue in cheek about racial harmony, but the conservative trappings helped make the boycott palatable to blacks who might have been reluctant to participate in a more confrontational protest. Rather than challenging segregation head-on by sitting in white seats, passengers would simply stay off the cars.[21]

The black commitment to the boycott was revealed on April 14, 1904, when community leaders gathered to discuss strategy at A. D. Price's Hall, a popular meeting place for fraternal orders. Mitchell had issued invitations to sixty men and women, and over two hundred appeared. They formed a permanent organization with Mitchell as chairman and pledged to stay off the cars. W. P. Burrell was converted to the cause, and though Giles Jackson remained on the sidelines, the Negro Business League endorsed the movement. Dr. Robert E. Jones, who headed the Richmond branch of the Business League, made a "red-hot speech" against Jim Crow. Few clergymen attended, but the turn of events was making them uneasy, and they knew that business leaders had seized the initiative. The pastors issued a statement that stopped short of endorsing the boycott but protested the misrepresentation of their views in the white press: "While we strongly advocate peace and conservatism, this is not to be construed to mean that we are in any way in accord with this change in our streetcar service."[22]

The same evening officers of Richmond's four black banks met as a subcommittee. Mitchell attended as president of the Mechanics' Savings Bank, which he had founded in 1902; Maggie Walker was there for the St. Luke Penny Savings Bank; R. T. Hill for the True Reformers Bank; and Dr. R. F. Tancil for the Nickel Savings Bank. Together they represented the combined financial resources of black Richmond. They endorsed walking and explored the possibility of providing alternate means of transportation. Using language that was beginning to sound familiar, they concluded that "some mode of locomotion should be provided in order to minimize friction and avoid trouble."[23]

On the night before the new rules were to go into effect, another rally was held, this time in True Reformer Hall. The auditorium was crowded, and the meeting lasted for more than three hours. Mitchell was elected chairman by acclamation and made the opening speech: "I beg you in the name of the God that sits on high to be conservative and law abiding, but to walk." He explained the meaning of the new rules and warned that passengers would change seats so often that they would arrive at their destinations exhausted. It would be more restful just to walk. He joked about the problems facing conductors who were required to separate "white Negroes" from whites. Should "white Negroes" wear tags when they boarded the cars? His theme, which he repeated time and again in his booming voice, was that this was yet "another invasion of the rights of the black man." Other speeches followed, including one by Patsie K. Anderson of the Independent Order of St. Luke that nearly brought down the house. Anderson said: "Negroes usually talk too much. Don't argue the question; don't get into controversy; don't say anything, but walk."[24]

Although the white press generally gave short shrift to black concerns, the reporter who covered the rally for the *Times-Dispatch* took the boycott seriously. "With the dawn of today," he wrote, ". . . begins the long, weary, footsore tramp of thousands of Richmond colored men and women, determined to bear silently whatever hardship may follow rather than submit to what they consider a wanton discrimination against them on the streetcars of the city." He said there was "no turbulence, no fierce denunciation, and no fire-eating, as many had feared," but the speakers declared, "one after another, that the black man shall desert the street cars of Richmond."[25]

The idea of "walking" fared less well on the editorial pages. The editor of the *Richmond News-Leader* made clear just how sharply the color line was to be drawn. He said that no white woman objected to sitting next to a poverty-stricken, uneducated white man, but she would never share a seat with "the best-dressed, best-behaved and most intelligent negro man in the city." Conceding that the color line worked a hardship on middle-class blacks, he countered that it was natural and necessary: "It is one of the safeguards against the breaking down of the barrier between the races and the amalgamation and mixing, which is the worst horror Southern white people can imagine." Obviously irked, Mitchell answered that the "white men who mixed the races and gave us our crop of white Negroes didn't do it on the street cars."[26]

On the Sunday before the new rules went into effect, the transit company published a set of guidelines that described how the "revolutionary new laws" would operate. Customs that a later generation would take for granted had to be spelled out in meticulous detail. The company explained that white passengers would take seats in the forward portion of the car while black passengers took seats in the rear. The number of seats occupied by white or black passengers would depend entirely on the number of passengers of each race who boarded the car. The two races would gradually fill the car, reserving any vacant seats in the center. No part of the car would be set aside for either race, not even the back seat or front seat. White and black passengers would never share the same bench, unless it had the only unoccupied seat, in which case the two individuals would separate once another seat was vacated. Black servants could sit among whites but only if tending white children.[27]

Although the rules seemed clear enough, on the first day there was widespread confusion, much shifting of seats, and considerable ill will. A white businessman was arrested after he failed to change seats, while another white rider refused to move when ordered and left the car. "If the whites do not obey the law," cautioned the *Times-Dispatch*, "we cannot reasonably expect the blacks to do so." During the early months the only black passenger arrested was a woman from New York, who, when told to move, responded, "To hell with the Jim Crow car!"[28]

From the beginning the transit company took no official notice of the boycott, and the white press downplayed its significance. "No great percentage of Negroes walked," said the *News-Leader* the first day, while the *Times-Dispatch* thought "quite a number of Negroes rode," although it conceded that the number was "nothing like as many as usual." The testimony of the white press was unreliable, however, and back-page articles occasionally belied front-page news. The *News-Leader* published this account of a Baptist Sunday School Union meeting on May 1, 1904: "The colored people of Richmond emphasized their ability to walk yesterday afternoon when young and old, little and big, marched from every section of the city . . . to the old African Baptist Church." When the meeting was over, "not a single man, woman or child boarded a car for either Church Hill or uptown."[29]

Mitchell maintained that during the opening months the boycott was from 80 to 90 percent effective, and the truth probably lay somewhere between his optimistic assessment and that of the white press. He said that from observing the Clay Street line, which ran north of Broad Street, one would believe that black people had deserted the city. He told stories that had a ring of authenticity. One white woman complained to him that her maid, who weighed over two hundred pounds, arrived at work exhausted from walking and "unfit for service." An elderly white widower protested that when his maid brought his food from her kitchen across town, it arrived cold. When he told her she must deliver his dinner by streetcar, she replied, "Yes sir, I'll bring it, but I'll walk." Many black passengers gave the boycott at least partial support. They rode only in emergencies, or when the weather was bad, or when they had packages to carry. Some rode the trolleys to work on weekdays but walked to church on Sunday mornings. Fraternal lodges showed their support by canceling streetcar excursions.[30]

Mitchell did all he could to promote the boycott in the *Planet*. He printed a series of poems by O. M. Steward, his former teacher at Navy Hill who was a veteran of the civil rights struggles of the Reconstruction era. Steward extolled the virtues of walking:

> All those who choose are free to go
> And ride in the "Jim Crow" car,
> But rain may fall and wind may blow,
> I'll not take the "Jim Crow" car.

For months scarcely an issue of the *Planet* appeared without a front-page appeal to stay off the cars. Mitchell composed little homilies that described the health benefits of walking and suggested remedies such as witch hazel and fish salts for aching feet.[31]

Although business leaders talked of forming an alternative transit system, no such system appeared, making it unlikely that the boycott could be sustained for more than a few months. A new streetcar line would have required an enormous outlay of capital as well as a franchise from the city council, neither of which was apt to be forthcoming. A more practical solution would have been a carpool service such as made possible the bus boycott in Montgomery, Alabama, in 1955–56. Mitchell explored the use of horse-drawn lorries to ferry workers and even considered purchasing automobiles, but a carpool was an ambitious undertaking at the opening of the century. In 1905 blacks in Nashville, Tennessee, purchased a fleet of steam-driven automobiles to support their boycott, but the machines lacked the power to climb steep hills and had to be returned. In Richmond boycotters simply improvised. Some refurbished old bicycles, while others hitched rides on horse-drawn delivery wagons. "It is a common thing," said Mitchell, "to see wagons on their way down town carrying three to six laboring men free of charge."[32]

Mitchell hoped the company would rescind the rules quickly before the black community lost its resolve. Victory seemed at hand in July 1904 when stockholders of the Virginia Passenger and Power Company asked for a receivership and initiated court proceedings against the company. "The streetcar company is busted," headlined the *Planet*. "Three cheers for the Richmond Negroes!" But victory proved illusive. Steadfastly ignoring the boycott, the company blamed its financial woes on the 1903 conductors' strike, and new managers persisted in segregating passengers.[33] By summer the weather was undermining the effort. A stroll through Richmond in April can ennoble the human spirit, but the same trek on a muggy July day is enervating.

Mitchell conceded that the boycott lost effectiveness during the hottest summer months but noticed an upsurge of interest once the weather cooled in the fall. "Car after car may be seen with the three rear seats empty," he wrote in October 1904. In January 1905 the Richmond *Reformer* noted that "it is now nine months since the jim-crow streetcar rules went into effect, and there are thousands of the best class of our citizens who are walking yet." Many blacks did continue to walk, but as months wore on hopes faded that Jim Crow could be reversed. In 1906 the Virginia General Assembly wrote a new law requiring rather than permitting segregation, and the Richmond boycott petered out. That same year Kelly Miller, a member of the faculty at Howard University, surveyed streetcar boycotts throughout the South and came to the conclusion that boycotts failed because black passengers, having so few resources, simply could not hold out in the long run.[34]

Mitchell had worried that blacks would protest Jim Crow by occupying white seats and violence would result, but in the early years, at least, more whites than blacks were arrested. In 1906 an editorial writer for the *Times-Dispatch* complained that Jim Crow streetcars had proved a particular burden to white people. He described how he himself had been ordered to change seats for frivolous, unexplained reasons. Segregation was important, he said, "but the enforcement of it has been left to young men who sometimes have either arbitrarily, ignorantly, or carelessly discharged their duties so as to make themselves officiously disagreeable." Perhaps it never occurred to him that black passengers might also resent this shifting of seats, find conductors officious, or consider the new rules an insult.[35]

In 1907 James R. Gordon, the president of the all-white Richmond Chamber of Commerce and the brother-in-law of Lieutenant Colonel Croxton, was arrested for refusing a conductor's order to move to the front. The *Evening Journal* responded to his arrest with an editorial that defended segregation in theory but admitted that the streetcar regulations were clumsy and difficult to enforce. How had it happened, asked the editor, that a seat could be occupied by a white passenger one minute and belong to a black passenger the next? Arguing against an overly scrupulous adherence to the law, the editor went on to say that "the Jim Crow law is presumed, like all laws, to be executed by men with gray matter in their heads and not with skulls full of lubber." An observation made about Atlanta probably held true for Richmond as well. Once the streetcars (and the gasoline-powered buses that followed) converted to one-operator vehicles, some of the tension eased. With no conductor on hand to assign seats, passengers sorted themselves out as best they could. Eventually the sign "Colored to the Rear" became Jim Crow's best-understood—and most resented—injunction.[36]

For at least a few black Richmonders, however, the boycott never really ended. In 1906 Mitchell wrote in the *Planet* that it had been so long since he had ridden on a streetcar that he had "well nigh forgotten the feeling of electric traveling." The next year he joked about his reluctance to board the trolleys and said he felt healthier as a result: "God blessed us with big feet and we are walking." In 1913 he arrived at the Main Street train station after a trip out of town. He was sixteen blocks from home, burdened with luggage, and his ride failed to appear. But he set out on foot. "I make it a practice," he said curtly, "not to ride on the streetcars in Richmond."[37]

CHAPTER ELEVEN

The Lure of Fraternalism

The collapse of the streetcar boycott failed to undermine Mitchell's faith in the ultimate triumph of right and justice. The "veil of prejudice" would one day be lifted, he promised his readers. "It may take twenty-five years. It may take fifty years; or it may take a hundred years, but it will come." He warned that "no seeming submission on our part should be construed to mean that we have . . . yielded up one iota of the rights which are guaranteed to us in the Declaration of Independence." Southern blacks bowed down before discriminatory legislation simply because they had no choice: "The position of Southern Negroes is that while they submit to these persistent and continuing exhibitions of race prejudice . . . they do so under protest. Like a rubber ball, they yield to continuing pressure but whenever that pressure is removed, whether it be this year or next year or the year after or [in] a hundred years, they will return to their normal state." [1] He was foresighted enough to know, however, that the veil of prejudice might not be lifted during his lifetime.

At a time when the race's prospects appeared bleakest, Mitchell embraced a philosophy of self-help that black Americans have traditionally resorted to when other avenues have been closed. He believed that despite Jim Crow and disfranchisement, blacks could still prosper if they focused their attention on economic advance and supported black-run enterprises. Through hard work and self-sacrifice, they could pull themselves up from poverty, better their lives, provide jobs for their children, and ensure the survival of the black community during a time of crisis. In the *Planet* he applauded every sign of entrepreneurial spirit and exulted whenever new businesses were formed. He might easily have lost heart in the early years of the century had it not been for so many signs of activity behind the veil of segregation.

By the time of disfranchisement, three organizations dominated the economic and social life of black Richmond: the Knights of Pythias, led by Mitchell; the Independent Order of St. Luke, led by Maggie Walker, and the Grand

Fountain of the United Order of True Reformers, dominated by W. W. Browne until his death in 1897. The largest by far was the True Reformers, an organization that is little remembered today but pervaded nearly every aspect of community life in black Richmond for three decades. In white Richmond the entrepreneurial ideal put a premium on individual achievement, with business success tied to hard work and lonely struggle. In black Richmond the ideal was much more cooperative, with economic success dependent upon service to others, religious commitment, and race progress.[2] Nowhere was this more evident than in the True Reformers, an organization that influenced both Mitchell and Walker and set the standard for business success in the black community.

The early history of the True Reformers is somewhat murky, but the order was apparently founded in Kentucky in the 1870s as an affiliate of an all-white temperance group, the Independent Order of Good Templars. The True Reformers retained this emphasis on temperance after breaking away from the white group. The lodges were called Fountains, symbolizing pure and clean water, while the governing body was the Grand Fountain. During initiation rites True Reformers sang this hymn:

> Welcome, stranger, to our Fountain
>   To its waters now advance
> Standing firmly on the mountain,
>   Pledged for right and temperance.
> Welcome stranger, still we're singing,
>   Hearts united cheer you on —
> To its waters ever clinging,
>   Health and honor will be won.

Initiates then took a temperance pledge and drank from the pure waters of the Fountain.[3]

As early as 1877 there were five Fountains of True Reformers in Richmond, but the organization was only one of many that flourished in the black community and connected families and neighborhoods. Many of these groups had church affiliations. There were Daughters of Elijah, Rising Sons and Daughters of the New Testament, Children of Emanuel, Sons and Daughters of Noah, and Loving Sons of Galilee. The Independent Order of St. Luke, founded in 1867 in Baltimore by Mary Prout and later led by Maggie Walker, was by 1877 the largest of these organizations, with sixteen councils. The next largest was the Independent Order of Good Samaritans, which had eight lodges and maintained close ties to First Church. Some of these groups were all male; some, such as the St. Lukes and True Reformers, welcomed men and women into the same lodge; and some were open only to women.[4]

Although few of these organizations left written records, it is probable that nearly all provided some form of insurance. When a member died, the lodge presented the family with a small purse to help with burial expenses. Lodges also paid weekly sick benefits to those unable to work. Most black families lived so close to the edge that an extended illness or a serious accident could lead to destitution. Disbursements were financed through the monthly dues, which were usually fifty cents, and through special assessments made when a member died. The rivalry among societies tended to be friendly. Obituaries printed in the *Planet* indicate that black Richmonders commonly belonged to more than one society. When James H. Holmes died in 1900, for example, he belonged to three national fraternal orders with insurance features, the Odd Fellows, Masons, and Knights of Pythias, as well as three benevolent societies with headquarters in Richmond, the St. Lukes, Good Samaritans, and True Reformers.[5]

Black Richmonders also purchased commercial life insurance, but the New York–based companies inspired resentment. In 1881 two industry giants, Prudential and Metropolitan Life, began to discriminate openly against blacks. Because mortality tables indicated that black life expectancy was lower, separate rates were worked out for the two races. A twenty-year-old white man who paid ten cents a week on an industrial life-insurance policy received $206 at the time of his death; a black man of the same age who paid the same rate received $136. "Colored men are often discriminated against by white insurance companies," wrote Mitchell in 1894. "They are [founding] insurance companies of their own." Led by Rev. Z. D. Lewis, black Richmonders in 1893 organized the Southern Aid Society, the first black-owned insurance company in the United States. The Richmond Beneficial Insurance Company, which listed Mitchell among its stockholders, was formed the next year by Rev. W. F. Graham.[6]

Although these companies grew and prospered, the most dramatic success story was that of the True Reformers. Building on traditions already strong in the black community, W. W. Browne transformed fraternalism into big business and in the process left his imprint on a generation of black Richmonders. He was born a slave in rural Georgia in 1849, the son of field hands. His skin was dark, and like Marcus Garvey in the twentieth century, he boasted of having no white blood. After the Civil War he traveled through the Midwest and attended school in Wisconsin but by the 1870s was back in the South working as a Methodist preacher and temperance advocate. He organized Fountains of True Reformers in Alabama but often clashed with white religious leaders. His experiences in Alabama left him with an enduring distrust of white people. "From any set of people that will treat me this way," he said, "I am gone." By the time he came to Richmond in 1881, he prided himself on never mingling with whites and openly espoused separatism. "Negroes and white people do not associate together in this country," he said. "By the provisions in their schools, and the training around their firesides, they are separate."[7]

Browne was a charismatic figure who wore a black clerical cloak and carried around sheets of paper covered with numbers. He boasted that his plan for the order was more ambitious than that which had been given him by the Good Templars. "I thought my brain might conceive something better," he said. Browne's famous "plan" was actually several plans, and until the end of his life, he was tinkering with various financial schemes. Essentially what he set out to do was to convert the True Reformers into a bona fide insurance company while retaining all the advantages of a mutual-aid society. As a first step he centralized the financial affairs of the order under the Grand Fountain. "When a brother dies in Washington," he said, "I feel his death as much as does his own Fountain." By the mid-1880s disbursements for death claims were being paid through the grand worthy master and not through local lodges.[8]

Browne also introduced a system of graded assessments, which meant that those who joined the True Reformers late in life paid more for their insurance than those who joined when young. This would seem an obvious reform, but most fraternal organizations—white and black—charged a uniform premium. Browne created a separate Class Department, consisting of Classes B, C, D, and E, which paid $200, $300, $400, and $500, respectively, at the time of death. Members could elect to remain only in a Fountain, where they received sick benefits and enough to pay for a funeral, or they could join one of the classes for an additional premium. The amount one received depended upon one's age at entry and also upon the number of participants in that particular class. Class B, for example, did not pay its full face value of $200 until 1894, when it had eight hundred members.[9]

Browne's plan was complicated, and it is impossible to know from this distance whether he was charging a sufficient premium, but his system gave the True Reformers a competitive edge. Death claims in other societies were dispensed in a much more haphazard way, with special assessments levied when members died. In the True Reformers benefits accrued as the organization grew, thus giving members an incentive to proselytize. In emotional speeches Browne reminded ex-slaves that no matter how meager their accomplishments, they at least could leave something to those who survived them. He also took advantage of the unpopularity of white insurance agents who each week toured black communities in the South to collect premiums on small industrial life-insurance policies. "You are not bothered by weekly collectors, who care nothing for you but to get our money," said Browne. "You are supporting an association for yourselves." He preached moral reformation, temperance, and race pride, and his employees began each day with a worship service.[10]

Under Browne's leadership the True Reformers expanded rapidly, spreading through the Virginia countryside and into neighboring states and finally as far west as California. There were 29 Fountains in 1884, 192 by 1888, and 765 by 1892. Members of struggling little lodges were known to succumb to Browne's preaching and simply reconstitute themselves as Fountains. Mitchell became a True Reformer around 1885, joining King Solomon's Fountain. Browne designated the *Planet* the official newspaper of the order and urged all members to subscribe. He also relied on the Planet Publishing Company for at least some of his job printing. Browne's endorsement was a key factor in the *Planet*'s early success, and on several occasions in the 1880s, when Mitchell was in financial trouble, Browne stood behind him and offered to loan him money.[11]

Mitchell was also named to the board of directors of the True Reformers' bank, the first black bank chartered in the United States, although the Capitol Savings Bank of Washington, D.C., actually opened several months earlier. The Savings Bank of the Grand Fountain was founded in the aftermath of the 1886 lynching of Richard Walker at Drake's Branch in Charlotte County, the lynching Mitchell investigated while wearing Smith & Wesson revolvers. The True Reformers in Charlotte County had entrusted their treasury to a white storekeeper, and after the lynching it appeared the money was lost. This experience convinced Browne that the Grand Fountain needed its own bank to serve as a depository for funds. Giles B. Jackson drew up a charter, and Edmund Waddill Jr., a white Republican, guided the bill through the General Assembly. According to D. Webster Davis, several white bankers were impressed by Browne's vision of a separate black economy and worked closely with him, "taking pains to enlighten him on . . . methods of finance."[12]

The bank opened for business in the parlor of Browne's home on Jackson Street on April 3, 1889, on the twenty-fourth anniversary of the fall of Richmond, with R. T. Hill serving as cashier. Construction began the next year on True Reformer Hall, a three-story brick building on Second Street. Designed by a black architect from Washington, D.C., the building became a showcase for black-run enterprises. Within True Reformer Hall were meeting rooms, offices, a bank vault, and an auditorium that seated six hundred. The bank's motto was, "1865, slaves; 1890, bankers." Mitchell boosted the bank in editorials and did all he could to persuade readers to entrust their savings to the True Reformers. "Colored men, the dawn is breaking for the race," he wrote in 1891. "If you don't believe it, go and look in the Savings Bank of the True Reformers of this city." He said that black Richmonders had aspired to be cashiers and bookkeepers in white banks, but "the white man laughed at his pretensions and told him it couldn't be." Now blacks had their own bank and the positions that went with it.[13]

In 1894 Mitchell resigned from the True Reformers, saying nothing publicly about his reasons, but it was soon apparent that he and Browne had quarreled. Elected grand worthy master for life in 1887, Browne tended to be dictatorial, and even his supporters admitted he ran the order with a heavy hand. "The Grand Worthy Master gave his personal attention to all matters pertaining to the Order, whether great or small," explained one officer. Conflict between Mitchell and Browne was probably inevitable. Browne was ambitious and suspicious of rivals, while Mitchell, often prickly and self-absorbed, preferred to be in charge.[14]

Their feud became public in March 1895 when Browne attacked Mitchell for his meal with O'Ferrall at the Executive Mansion. In a letter addressed to the city's white newspapers, Browne apologized for Mitchell's indiscretion and assured whites that the "well-bred Virginia negro does not seek the association of the rich white man, nor the poor white man, the official white man, nor the unofficial white man." Mitchell was furious about the "toadying" letter: "For ten years we have stood at his side ignoring all condemnation of his methods." Then in September 1895 Browne made a proposal that shook the order to its core and gave credence to Mitchell's charges of high-handedness. Browne offered to sell his famous "plan," which he had copyrighted, to the True Reformers for $50,000.[15]

The True Reformers eventually agreed to give Browne the money, although the order almost split in the process and the payments were stretched out over a ten-year period. Mitchell described the settlement as a monumental blunder and probably would have sympathized with the later commissioner of insurance in Virginia who marveled at how this "shrewd old negro preacher" managed to talk his followers out of so much money. After the "$50,000 Grab," the feud between Mitchell and Browne grew increasingly bitter. Browne founded his own newspaper, the *Reformer,* and urged True Reformers to boycott the *Planet* and buy the *Reformer* instead. At one meeting he marched up and down the platform and according to the *Planet* "amused his hearers by . . . saying 'Little Johnnie wants everybody to look up to him. I, little Johnnie, member of the Board of Aldermen. I, little Johnnie, one of the new Negroes." Friends tried to mend the riff, but when a delegation led by R. T. Hill called at the *Planet* office to ask for a truce, Mitchell turned them away. Even the avuncular Giles B. Jackson failed in his efforts to mediate the quarrel.[16]

Browne died of cancer in 1897, and his death led to a power struggle within the organization. By the turn of the century, R. T. Hill, who headed the bank, W. P. Burrell, the grand worthy secretary, and W. L. Taylor, the grand worthy master, had worked out an uneasy alliance. Taylor was a preacher who inspired the devotion of the rank and file. Burrell was educated and articulate, a skilled publicist who communicated well with white Richmonders. Hill, probably the wiliest of the lot, managed the True Reformer bank. Working closely with the triumvirate was Giles B. Jackson, the True Reformers' attorney. The order continued to prosper after Browne's death, expanding its operations to include a department store, a hotel, and an old folks' home. When white journalist Ray Stannard Baker came to Richmond in 1906, he discovered eighty clerks at work in the insurance division, which was doing half a million dollars' worth of business a year. The next year W. E. B. Du Bois described the Grand Fountain as the most remarkable black organization in the United States.[17]

The success of the True Reformers was almost bound to spawn imitations. In 1898 in Durham, North Carolina, ex–True Reformer agents founded the North Carolina Mutual Life Insurance Company, and a study of that company suggests that nearly every black insurance association founded in the region during this period can be traced back to the True Reformers.[18] Maggie Walker took over the Independent Order of St. Luke in 1899 and transformed it into a similar organization, although her approach was different in that she made appeals directly to women.

Walker was the daughter of a laundress, and she always emphasized her solidarity with those who worked in the most menial positions, even though she herself was light-skinned and educated. "I was not born with a silver spoon in [my] mouth," she told her followers, but "with a clothes basket almost upon my head." After graduating from Richmond Normal in 1883, she taught at Valley School until her marriage in 1886 to Armstead Walker, a brick contractor. She then went to work as a clerk for the Independent Order of St. Luke, an organization she had joined at the age of fourteen. She established a children's division, studied accounting in the evenings, and in 1899 took over leadership from W. M. T. Forrester. Although men were welcome in the St. Lukes, Walker appealed specifically to women, who had few employment opportunities other than domestic service and were particularly vulnerable to exploitation. "Who is so helpless as the Negro woman?" she asked. "Who is so circumscribed and hemmed in?" Like Browne, she couched her appeals in religious language and expanded the mission of the order beyond insurance to include other enterprises, such as a bank, newspaper, and department store.[19]

By the time Walker assumed leadership of the St. Lukes, Mitchell was spending much of his time promoting the Knights of Pythias. Unlike the True Reformers and St. Lukes, the Knights of Pythias was a secret fraternal order (similar to the Masons and Odd Fellows) and not a mutual-aid society founded within the black community. The distinction is worth making, although all operated in much the same fashion when it came to selling insurance. The first Pythian lodge was founded by whites in Washington, D.C., in 1864. As the order spread into the South, blacks sought admittance and were rebuffed. In 1880 in Vicksburg, Mississippi, several light-skinned men "who appeared to be of the other race" managed to join and acquired "the grips, signs, ranks, passwords and mottoes of the several ranks." They formed their own lodge in Vicksburg, and soon black Pythians were marching in regalia through the streets of nearly every southern town. The signifying difference was in their names: the white Knights belonged to the Knights of Pythias of the World, while the black Knights were Knights of Pythias of North America, South America, Europe, Asia, Africa, and Australia.[20]

When the first national meeting of the black Knights was held in Vicksburg in 1883, five lodges reported from Virginia, among them Richmond Lodge No. 1, which had been founded the year before by R. A. Paul. Mitchell became a Pythian in 1892, but the order did not make major inroads in Virginia until he left the True Reformers and became grand chancellor of the Virginia Pythians. When he assumed leadership in 1894, there were five hundred members in the state, but the treasury was nearly empty and death claims were not being paid on time. His first proposal was that fifty dollars be set aside so that after speaking in a town, he could leave a deputy behind for several days to "work up the field." His earliest converts were not far from home. Planet Lodge No. 23 was organized in January 1895. Thomas M. Crump, the *Planet* bookkeeper, was named chancellor commander, while Tom Mitchell became keeper of records and seals. Other lodge members included John R. Chiles and Benjamin A. Graves.[21]

Mitchell was soon traveling throughout Virginia to recruit new members, institute lodges, and install officers. He was savvy enough to trade on his reputation as a "Fighting Editor." At an 1895 meeting in Suffolk, for example, he spoke on the history of the Knights of Pythias but also on the trials of the Lunenburg women. In 1898 he addressed a gathering of Pythians on the subject "The National Government, Lynchings, and Citizens of Color."[22] He was already well known in the state—as editor, politician, and antilynching crusader—and his reputation served him well. Although the order remained small in comparison to the True Reformers, by 1902 there were nearly five thousand members in the state.

The insurance features of the Knights of Pythias are difficult to unravel, but Mitchell appears to have borrowed freely from Browne's plan, albeit without as many layers of complexity. Pythians paid dues of fifty cents a month to the subordinate lodge, in return for which they received $3 a week when sick and enough for funeral expenses when they died. Additional fees brought larger death benefits—or endowments—paid by the Grand Lodge. In public ceremonies Mitchell distributed the endowments that gave the order credibility in the eyes of its members. At a 1900 meeting, for example, he counted out $1,000 in cash that was paid to Pythian widows. Like other fraternal leaders he was tempted to reduce premiums as a way of attracting new members. In 1905 he boasted that the order "paid more benefits and charged less than any other." Because the membership was young and the order was growing rapidly, the Grand Lodge usually showed a profit. Reliable records are not available for the early years, but in 1908 the Grand Lodge collected $20,000 and paid out less than $5,000 in death claims; the next year the order broke even; in 1910 profits reached $35,000.[23]

Under Mitchell's leadership the Pythians placed greater stress on regalia and rituals than did the True Reformers, and the atmosphere was more secular. Only males could become Pythians, and the emphasis was on masculine virtue rather than Christian piety. A persistent theme in the rituals was the classical friendship between Damon and Pythias, a bonding that Knights were expected to emulate within the lodge. On lodge night black Pythians participated in the same sorts of rituals as white fraternalists: they knocked on doors, exchanged secret handshakes, draped themselves in collars, and whispered passwords. One lodge member later tried to explain why this experience was so satisfying: "To belong to one or several of those organizations and move up through the ranks, you have no idea of how much reward there was in that." After the rituals were completed, the members relaxed, caught up on gossip, and discussed matters "central to the existence of Blacks in the city." For many Pythians the camaraderie was as important as the insurance protection.[24]

The Knights of Pythias was never really an exclusive organization as was Prince Hall Masonry—Mitchell was too eager to sell insurance—but men of like minds and compatible backgrounds tended to congregate within the same subordinate lodge. The lodges met twice a month and were required to have at least thirty members on the roster, although only seven were necessary for a quorum. A relief committee dispensed sick benefits, but brotherhood meant more than fulfilling monetary obligations. Members were expected to come to the aid of Knights in trouble and treat each other with respect. A Pythian who refused to "sit up" with a sick Knight could be fined. A Pythian who used bad language or excessive sarcasm or repeatedly interrupted a Knight during a meeting was fined a dollar. A member who missed a Knight's funeral was fined a dollar, unless he lived more than five miles from the church, in which case his fine was remitted. As one Richmonder explained, belonging to a lodge made one "a better person, a more reliable person, a more friendly person, a person more inclined to benevolence."[25]

Although the only required regalia was a badge costing seventy-five cents, a popular Pythian feature was the Uniform Rank, which was made up of men who marched in uniforms similar to those worn in the U.S. Army. Captain Benjamin A. Graves and other veterans of the Spanish-American War trained the soldiers and judged competitions. The Pythian officers rode on horseback, and their "rich, gold trimmed uniforms and glittering swords presented a magnificent display." A photograph of a 1907 encampment in Danville shows dozens of men in uniform standing among tents beneath a U.S. flag. Pythian parades became a popular feature of life in Jackson Ward in the early twentieth century. Years later one resident recalled how families gathered on front porches on Sunday afternoons and waited for the sound of drums and bugles. "I can see him now," she said of Mitchell, "wearing that plumed hat and marching at the front of the parade."[26]

Often the Pythian soldiers marched directly past the First Battalion Armory, a reminder of a time when black men enlisted in the state militia. Much of the energy that had once gone into the military was now channeled into fraternalism, and though the Pythian army had no legal standing, the show of force probably served important functions. Stories were told in Richmond of how Mitchell would parade the Uniform Rank in front of a rural courthouse when whites threatened to lynch a prisoner, or how Pythian soldiers patrolled Jackson Ward during the 1920s when the Klan was active. These stories may be apocryphal (perhaps there was only talk of preventing a lynching or battling the Klan), but the sight of so many soldiers in uniform no doubt inspired admiration on several levels. Sometimes the Knights made excursions into white neighborhoods as well. In 1902, for example, while the constitutional convention was in session, Pythian soldiers paraded around the Capitol to the sound of beating drums.[27]

Unlike the True Reformers or St. Lukes, the Knights of Pythias was a three-tiered organization, an arrangement that eventually caused Mitchell considerable difficulty. At the bottom were subordinate lodges, such as Planet Lodge No. 23. Over them on the state level were Grand Lodges, which after 1893 took responsibility for endowments and insurance. The Supreme Lodge, which met every two years, was composed of representatives from the various states. As head of a Grand Lodge, Mitchell was not permitted to recruit members beyond Virginia, and he was bound by the rules and regulations promulgated at the biennial meetings. As one would expect, he soon became embroiled in Pythian politics at the national level. He feuded with other grand chancellors, participated in parliamentary maneuverings, and on several occasions campaigned—unsuccessfully as it turned out—for supreme chancellor. At the national meetings he also acquired a network of new friends, men who were his peers in every respect and with whom he forged long-lasting relationships. In the twentieth century he rarely traveled out of town without stopping somewhere to visit a fellow Pythian.[28]

One of Mitchell's goals at the biennial meetings was to share with the Supreme Lodge his experiences with the True Reformers. Although the Knights of Pythias was an all-male fraternity, a female association, the Independent Order of Calanthe, was affiliated with it. According to Calanthian bylaws, only women with relatives in the Knights of Pythias were eligible for membership. In this respect Pythians were conforming to the white model of fraternalism, where men resisted female encroachments on lodge life. Mitchell knew that limiting women's influence restricted the order's growth, and he had seen how Maggie Walker revitalized the St. Lukes by encouraging women to participate. In 1904 he persuaded the Supreme Lodge to permit Calanthians in Virginia to admit any woman "of good moral character." The women's branch expanded rapidly in Virginia and finally grew larger than the Knights of Pythias. The subordinate lodges were called courts, and the state governing body was the Grand Court. Josie Graham, the wife of W. F. Graham, was especially active in the Grand Court, as were Marietta Chiles and Sylvia Mitchell, Tom Mitchell's wife. The top position was reserved for the *Planet* editor, who held the title grand counsellor. By 1908 there were twenty-five lodges and forty-three courts in Richmond alone. Mitchell also persuaded the Supreme Lodge to introduce a Juvenile Rank, which offered burial policies on children. The girls belonged to Bands of Calanthe, while the boys, who dressed as Zouaves, wore red knee pants, white stockings, and red fezzes.[29]

The annual meetings of the Grand Lodge and Grand Court, usually held in May or June, were festive three-day affairs. Families gathered to watch the parades, children frolicked, and the lodges challenged each other to baseball games. In the evenings there were fireworks and covered-dish suppers. Nearly every Richmond family had relatives in the countryside, and the statewide meetings became family as well as fraternal reunions. Mitchell presided over the sessions of both the Grand Lodge and Grand Court, and he shuttled hurriedly between the two. He memorized the rituals, which were long and complicated, and orchestrated the whole affair in much the same way Browne oversaw meetings of the Grand Fountain. The annual meetings were usually held in churches. The *Planet* described Richmond's Fifth Street Baptist Church during one meeting: "The background of the rostrum was decorated with a large Knights of Pythias flag and a large United States flag, and in the center was a large-sized portrait of the Grand Chancellor surrounded by Pythian colors."[30]

Although Mitchell enjoyed the rituals and regalia, he always intended for the organization to do more than entertain. In 1900 he applied to the chancery court for a charter for the Pythian-Calanthe Industrial Association, a joint-stock company authorized to engage in industrial pursuits and invest in real estate. The Grand Lodge and Grand Court bought stock in the company, and the company in turn purchased an Odd Fellows Hall on Third Street, which was refurbished and christened Pythian Castle Hall. Pythians and Calanthians celebrated the opening of their building in 1903 with a Carnival of Nations, to which the public was invited. Eleven nations had booths, and there were sack races, games of chance, musical performances, skits, and a greased-pig contest. Forty-five electric lights illuminated the outside of the building, and over the roof hung an enormous Pythian banner. During the festivities Pythians and Calanthians recruited new members.[31]

Once the Grand Lodge and Grand Court began to show a profit, Mitchell was almost bound to consider opening a bank. His connection with the world of finance had not ended when he left the True Reformers. In 1896 Dr. R. F. Tancil, a physician with extensive real estate holdings in Richmond, organized the Nickel Savings Bank, the city's second black bank. The headquarters were on Thirtieth Street in the midst of a black community that had grown up east of Jackson Ward. When Mitchell moved the *Planet* office to Fourth Street in 1897, the bank temporarily opened a branch office in his building. The bank received its name from the nickel-plated "home banks" that were distributed to depositors to encourage thrift.[32]

On November 19, 1901, Mitchell and fifteen friends combined their resources to form the community's third bank, the Mechanics' Savings Bank of Richmond. Each founder contributed $100 toward the venture, and all served on the board of directors. Mitchell was elected president, and Captain William A.

Hankins of the Sixth Virginia Volunteers was vice-president; George W. Lewis, who had once worked for the True Reformers, was cashier. Printed on the bank's checks was a picture of a mechanic, a worker whose rolled-up sleeves and muscular arms reinforced the theme of the *Planet's* masthead. When the bank first opened, its headquarters were in Pythian Castle Hall, but the ties between the bank and fraternal order were never as close as in the True Reformers and St. Lukes. The bank was chartered by the circuit court to do a general banking business, and the founders had affiliations outside the Knights of Pythias that proved to the bank's advantage.[33]

At least nine of the sixteen bank founders were participants in insurance schemes of various sorts. During a time of racial turmoil, no business was more likely to succeed than one that offered financial protection to families. Mitchell was head of the Knights of Pythias; W. F. Graham, John T. Carter, and John T. Taylor held top positions in the Richmond Beneficial Insurance Company; Thomas M. Crump, a former *Planet* employee, was manager of Southern Aid; William Custalo served as treasurer of the Galilean Fishermen's Relief Association; Benjamin P. Vandervall and D. J. Chavers were organizers of the Security Industrial Mutual Aid Society; and E. A. Washington was manager of the People's Relief Association. All these men had been caught up in the rush to sell insurance. Other stockholders in the bank included John R. Chiles, a postal worker; the photographer J. C. Farley; and Dr. E. R. Jefferson, the medical examiner for the Knights of Pythias. Although not among the original founders, A. D. Price, the city's leading black funeral director, was soon asked to join the board. In this respect as in so many others Mitchell's outlook was conventional: no women were invited to participate.[34]

The Mechanics' Savings Bank opened for business on January 1, 1902, while the state constitutional convention was in session. During the first week over $5,000 was registered to accounts, and in June the bank made its first large loan, a grant of $2,000 to Farley to expand his photography business. Mitchell's preoccupation with the bank took some of the sting out of disfranchisement. "When we are strong enough financially," he promised, "we will go back and win all we lost politically." He believed (or at least hoped) that in the world of finance, he could operate without white interference and that the constraints that limited his advance in the Jim Crow South would somehow fall away. In 1905 he made his first major real estate investment: he purchased for $17,500 a furniture store on the north side of Broad Street with an eye to converting it into the bank headquarters.[35]

Browne once said that he intended to "hatch out banks as a hen hatches chickens," and in a sense he did. Maggie Walker opened the St. Luke Penny

Savings Bank in 1903, and the cashier there was Emmet Burke, a former True Reformer clerk. Another True Reformer, Thomas M. Wyatt, was lured away by Mitchell to oversee the bookkeeping at the Mechanics' Bank. Reports submitted to the State Corporation Commission in 1905 reveal the relative size of the city's four black banks. The True Reformers' bank remained the giant with deposits of $541,557. Until its collapse in 1910, it was the city's premier black bank. The Mechanics' Bank was next in size with deposits of $95,195, the St. Lukes' bank had $53,348, and the Nickel Savings Bank $16,976.[36]

There was competition among these black banks but also common pride and determination. In speech after speech Maggie Walker urged black Virginians to deposit their money in a black bank—any black bank—and not entrust their hard-earned dollars to those who Jim Crowed and disfranchised them. To skeptics who replied they had no faith in black banks, she answered, "Well, what has the white man done for you, to give you much great faith and confidence in him?" Mitchell likewise extolled the virtues of black businesses and boosted black-run enterprises in nearly every *Planet* issue. To his mind every dollar saved, every home purchased, and every business started was a victory for the race. Everyone seemed to understand that more was at stake than making money. During the 1904 streetcar boycott, a Pythian rose to address the Grand Lodge and promised that the day would come when the black man would own "his own railroads, steamboats, and streetcars, and earn the respect of the world regardless of color." Subjected to the indignities of Jim Crow and stripped of all political power, Mitchell and other black Richmonders resolved to build financial institutions that would protect the black community during a time of trouble and provide the opening wedge for a future assault on race prejudice.[37]

CHAPTER TWELVE

"A Sane and Sensible Businessman"

The central paradox of Mitchell's business career was that activities designed to make his race independent of white control entangled him more and more deeply in white affairs. Financial success brought freedom but left him open to a different sort of white scrutiny than he had ever experienced as a journalist. As a banker he was required to make periodic reports to city and state officials—white men, usually Democrats—who had the power to help him or undermine all he was trying to accomplish. He also found himself communicating on a regular basis with business leaders from the private sector. Some of these interactions took place behind closed doors as he sought the advice and support of whites whose influence could benefit the race. Other interactions were played out on the public stage and attracted the attention of the national press. Determined to protect the financial institutions of Jackson Ward, he set out to convince white Richmonders that it was in their self-interest that his bank and fraternal order prosper.

Mitchell's caution as a businessman was partly a by-product of the reforms of the Progressive Era. When he founded the Mechanics' Savings Bank in 1901, there was practically no state supervision of banking in Virginia. Banks were chartered by the General Assembly or a local court, and bankers had only to submit annual financial reports to the auditor of public accounts. There were no requirements regarding loan policy or maintenance of reserves, and no bank could be closed unless it defaulted. All this changed in the new century. The Virginia constitution of 1902 called for the creation of a State Corporation Commission, and government regulation of banking gradually grew more restrictive. By 1908 officials in Richmond were analyzing the quarterly statements of the Mechanics' Savings Bank and the annual reports of the Knights of Pythias. By 1910 auditors on the staff of the banking division were making unannounced on-site inspections. Black leaders were suspicious of these reforms that were ostensibly designed to protect the consumer. As Maggie

Walker confessed, it was sobering to remember that a white official had "the power to enter your bank, inspect your books, papers, notes and bonds, and to declare whether you are properly conducting your business."[1]

Whites also oversaw Mitchell's business operations in more mundane ways. City officials assessed the value of his real estate, issued building permits, inspected his property for fire and safety hazards, recorded his deeds at the courthouse, and granted charters to his various enterprises. Because his bank was too small to afford membership in the Richmond clearing house, white bankers sponsored his checks. In short, the more he sought to insulate himself from white interference, the more he found himself at the mercy of the white establishment.[2]

Mitchell would have violated the etiquette of southern race relations had he traded too openly on white friendships, but he mentioned three bankers often enough to suggest that they were sympathetic to his efforts. One was John P. Branch, born in 1830, a civic-minded Virginian of the old school who for twenty-five years headed the Merchants National Bank. Branch was a generous contributor to local charities and served as a trustee of the Negro Reformatory Association. He was little bothered by newer notions about race relations. When an old family servant died in 1900, he went into mourning, and the black woman lay in state in the parlor of the Branch mansion. After a funeral conducted by a white Episcopal clergyman, she was buried in the Branch family plot in Hollywood Cemetery. This sort of paternalism had some unhappy connotations, but Mitchell overlooked them. He was heartened that one of Richmond's most prominent white families openly expressed their devotion to a black woman. He insisted that despite decades of political and racial turmoil, the ties between individuals remained strong: "There are some colored men who would give up life itself in behalf of certain white people, and there are certain white people who would make almost any sacrifice in behalf of some colored ones."[3]

Another member of the Branch family, James R. Branch, also worked for the Merchants National Bank. Branch and Mitchell became friends during the 1890s when both served on the board of aldermen. They may have known each other much earlier. The white banker once lived in a house on Grace Street almost directly across the street from James Lyons. James Branch and John Mitchell were the same age—both were born in 1863—and they perhaps played together as children, although neither was likely to have mentioned that fact in public. In 1898 Branch left Richmond for New York, where he became executive secretary of the American Bankers Association.[4] Mitchell also gave favorable notices in the *Planet* to Oliver Jackson Sands, the president of the American National Bank of Richmond, who was probably his closest white confidant and who shepherded his checks through the clearing house.[5]

The encouragement Mitchell received from wealthy whites effectively undermined his earlier conviction that the poor whites of the South and poor blacks were natural allies. "It is evident that there are two classes of white men in Virginia," he wrote as early as 1891. "While it is a sad condition of affairs . . . yet it remains a fact that the Negro has far less to fear from the aristocratic element of Virginia white men . . . than from those who were dead poor . . . in slave times." During the 1890s he sometimes expressed contempt for "poor white trash," calling attention to the lower-class origins of prejudiced whites in the same way white editors cast aspersions on lower-class, "shiftless" Negroes.[6]

He also praised "quality white folks," but this did not become a persistent theme in the *Planet* until he lost his council seat. Almost perversely, as race relations deteriorated, he talked more and more about the bond of union that drew Virginia aristocrats and ex-slaves together. "We always find a friend in the offspring of the old slave owners," he wrote in 1900 at a time when many old slave owners were clamoring for disfranchisement. His insistence on this reservoir of good feeling in the face of so much evidence to the contrary reflected in part the desperately precarious position that black Richmonders found themselves in at the opening of the century. As historian C. Vann Woodward has observed, it was no fondness for "Old Marster" that caused southern blacks to appeal to the upper classes. It was the "hot breath of cracker fanaticism they felt on the back of their necks." Increasingly Mitchell reminded whites that he was "born at Laburnum." It was a way of connecting himself to the antebellum aristocracy and by implication to the estate's new owner, Joseph Bryan, a railroad entrepreneur and the powerful editor of the *Richmond Times-Dispatch*.[7]

Mitchell's overtures to upper-class whites involved him in a host of contradictions and led to disappointment. The "better sort" failed to stem the tide of racial oppression, and after 1910 he became increasingly skeptical about white professions of goodwill. For a period, however, especially in the years immediately after founding the Mechanics' Bank, he courted upper-class whites with all the enthusiasm he had once expended on saving Simon Walker or freeing Pokey Barnes. A man of abundant energy, he was seldom halfhearted in his approach to anything, and he set out to persuade wealthy whites that they had a stake in his success.

Mitchell's overtures to business leaders received public expression in September 1904 when he attended the annual meeting of the American Bankers Association in New York City. He went to the bankers' convention as a member of the Virginia delegation, along with Oliver Sands, John P. Branch, and other Richmond bankers, and at the express invitation of James R. Branch, the executive secretary. He was the only black banker at the meeting. While in New York he made a controversial speech that confounded his admirers and signaled a retreat from his youthful militancy.[8]

Although much about Mitchell's 1904 speech remains surprising, a close reading of the *Planet* helps explain the development of his ideas. In editorial exchanges with white journalists that took place shortly before the meeting, he discussed familiar subjects—lynching, crime, race, and class—but gave them new interpretations.

The editorial series began in August 1904 when the *Richmond Times-Dispatch* ran a piece entitled "The Bad Negro." After describing some heinous crimes, the white editor puzzled over the failure of black leaders to speak out against criminals. "It is amazing to me," he wrote, "that the great body of good negroes do not join heart and hand with the great body of white men in an endeavor to suppress the bad negro, who is making trouble between the races." Mitchell responded by saying that of course blacks hid suspects from the police when a lynching was in the offing. He was encouraged, however, by the decline in lynchings in Virginia and the willingness of business leaders to condemn lawlessness: "The liberal, business white element of the South are now waging an intelligent, persistent warfare against the bad white elements, as is evidenced by the ringing protests against lynching and the lynchers." He said black leaders were waging a similar war against crime within their own communities. "There is no enmity between the better class of white people and the better class of colored ones," he wrote. "It is the hoodlum, irresponsible elements of both races which cause trouble and stir up race prejudice."[9]

The *Washington Post* picked up the discussion several days later with an editorial commending the antilynching editor for at last having the courage to speak out against criminals. Mitchell responded with a fuller description of his views. He insisted that the "hoodlum element of both races" caused all the difficulty and asked that discrimination "be based upon condition and not upon race or color." Hoping to make room at the top for well-to-do blacks like himself, he promised to do his part to encourage better race relations. Although he was careful to castigate the lawless of both races, his contempt for the "Negro loafer" was acquiring a hard edge: "Our curse is the ill-mannered, ill-bred, disreputable, crap-shooting loafer."[10]

Not long after writing that editorial, he set out for New York. The bankers' meeting was held at the Waldorf-Astoria Hotel, a building erected in 1897 that was hailed as the finest hotel in the world, the "largest and most sumptuous structure of its kind in either hemisphere." The grand ballroom had a forty-foot ceiling and was decorated in the style of Louis XIV with elaborate crimson hangings and gold trim. There were two tiers of box seats and a balcony. Mitchell took a seat in the back row on the main floor and listened quietly to the speeches.[11]

On the second day of the convention, a white banker from Atlanta made several comments about the race issue in a speech devoted primarily to boosting Georgia and the New South. Arguing that white southerners needed to find some middle ground between mob violence and social equality, he said that both lynching and social equality served to "elevate the negro above his sphere and place him beyond the protection of his friends."[12] Mitchell must have pondered this rather macabre analogy because the next day he approached the podium and asked permission to address the audience. It was a daring move given the time and place, and he doubtless remembered how another native-born Virginian, Booker T. Washington, captured the attention of the nation with his 1895 Atlanta Exposition address.

Various accounts of Mitchell's speech survive, but he never challenged the lengthy version that appeared in the *New York Times*. He began by saying he would never have come to the meeting had he not been invited by white friends: "I love the white man. There is no quarrel between me and him. . . . I am proud of the South." He then softened his audience by telling a joke, which, if not nearly so egregious as those told by Giles B. Jackson, served a similar self-deprecating purpose. He said that when he first entered the ballroom, he assumed he had gone to heaven but then he remembered that in heaven the streets were made of gold "while here the chairs seem to be." The bankers laughed appreciatively. He next expounded on themes that had appeared in recent editorials. Avoiding any reference to lynching or social equality, he said that after he "retired" from politics, white Richmonders encouraged his entry into the world of banking: "We have found that the way for us to reach success is through finance. . . . Nowhere in the domain of business have I found the white man other than ready to help us upward."[13]

He also tried to educate his audience about the realties of black life. "There are classes among negroes, just as there are classes among white people," he said. "The negro loafers are the only block to our advance. We'd like to run them out, to throw them in a trash heap." After reviewing statistics that revealed the race's recent economic progress, he referred to remarks made by the Atlanta banker. "When you hear white men get up here and talk about the negro, they mean the loafing negro—they do not mean our kind." He continued: "Now, our friend from Georgia . . . " He then paused, as if he understood that he was treading on dangerous ground, and made a hasty retreat: "Ah, I like to hear a white man talk. No matter what he is talking about, there's something musical in his voice, even when he's abusing us. How I do like to hear the white man talk! Look at our beautiful Secretary, Mr. Branch—" With this, the white audience burst into loud applause. When the clapping subsided, he ended with a conclusion as majestic as the ballroom: "In the coming years, when our last days shall come, and the chirp of the birds are heard for the last time, . . . to those who have said unkind things of our class of negroes, while meaning the other kind, we shall say to the great God in the language of the Saviour, 'Father, forgive them, for they know not what they do!' " [14] He then returned to his seat on the back row.

According to the *New York Times*, the speech was the sensation of the convention: "The bankers rose and cheered, the women in the balconies clapped their hands and waved handkerchiefs, and dozens of the delegates rushed back toward the negro banker, crowding around him, shaking his hand, and complimenting him on his address." The *Times* thought it significant that southern bankers applauded as loudly as those from the North.[15]

The next morning T. Thomas Fortune of the *New York Age* read the account in the *Times* and noted that the speech was "incompatible with the manly position always assumed by the *Planet*." Suspecting that his former columnist had been misquoted, he sent a reporter to interview Mitchell and ask if he cared to comment about the role of white loafers in provoking racial unrest. Mitchell responded that of course white loafers were at fault, but the bankers' meeting had been the wrong venue for such a discussion. Fortune assured readers that "John Mitchell stands up as firmly for manhood rights as he ever did." [16]

Other black journalists were not so convinced. After reading various accounts of the address, J. Max Barber of the *Voice of the Negro* in Atlanta said he could not help but register a protest: "It is all right to inveigh against loafers and to counsel industry, but it will not do to think that by reducing the world to a corn and potato patch we can usher in the millennium." W. Calvin Chase of the *Washington Bee* was likewise critical. After noting a recent decision in Richmond to replace black Western Union messengers with white employees, he asked if Mitchell would explain precisely "in what respect the Southern whites are the friends of the colored people." Harry C. Smith of the *Cleveland Gazette*, a longtime admirer, noted sadly that Mitchell told only a small part of a much larger story.[17]

Mitchell's closest friends were more inclined to give him the benefit of the doubt. He returned to Richmond to find that the directors of the Mechanics' Bank had arranged a reception and dinner in his honor. During the course of the evening, he shared his experiences and described "the beauty of the palatial hotel, the courtesies extended on all sides." At one point his long-time friend Thomas Crump read aloud—verbatim—the entire text of the *New York Times* article. One can only imagine the response of the all-black audience to lines such as "How I do like to hear the white man talk!" or "Nowhere in the domain of business have I found the white man other than ready to help us upward." Probably there was laughter. In the *Planet* he sought to justify his speech, explaining that in the highest realms of business, a black man did not confront the same prejudices as one would in ordinary life.[18]

Mitchell's speech failed to catapult him onto the national scene; in later years when he reminisced about his accomplishments, he seldom mentioned the address and instead talked of the prisoners whose lives he had saved. The speech was important, however, because it contributed to the erosion of his reputation for bravery that began when he failed to support Hayes's 1902 challenge to disfranchisement. In 1905 a journalist classifying black newspapers in the United States as either conservative or radical placed the *Planet* in the former group. In 1907 Booker T. Washington paid tribute to Mitchell using words that would have seemed out of place a decade before. The *Planet* editor was among "the sane and sensible businessmen of our race who are doing much to win for us as a race the respect of our white neighbors."[19]

Mitchell attended every national gathering of the American Bankers Association for the next seventeen years, and the annual meetings helped define his new image as a race leader. Accounts of his trips, published in fulsome installments, appeared in the *Planet* every fall. He described the interiors of luxurious hotels that his readers would never see and told of train journeys to distant cities. Often he linked convention trips with personal sightseeing ventures, as in 1915 when he made a train excursion through the Canadian Rockies on his way to California. Although he did not trumpet the fact, he seldom booked a room in the convention hotel, where his presence might provoke controversy, but stayed in black-run hotels or with friends. He was rarely forthcoming about meals and dining-room experiences, probably because he remembered too well the uproar that followed his lunch in the Executive Mansion in 1895.[20]

Mitchell conceded that his annual trips took their toll, both financially and mentally. He was always the only black banker in attendance. Although some whites grew accustomed to his presence, there were invariably newcomers who pointed and stared. "It is embarrassing even to a person of our nerve and caliber," he admitted. Whites speculated within his hearing about his paternity and wondered if his success was due to the trace of white blood that ran through his veins. Occasionally he overheard the most offensive of racial epithets. He responded by assuming a mask and pretended not to notice any rudeness. At the meetings he affected the jaunty "nonchalance of a millionaire." As he explained in the *Planet,* "There was no sign from us that we noticed a stare, or observed a comment of surprise as we passed in and out. . . . Yes, we had become an actor. We moved among these white gentlemen and ladies with that studied courtesy for which we have always been noted." Or again, "No one could read our thoughts, thank God, for we had for years learned to conceal our thoughts." [21]

Often he suffered at the meetings not from vulgar insults but from a surfeit of attention. At the 1910 meeting in Los Angeles, he was met at the hotel door by a white woman eager to pin a carnation on his lapel. He tried to evade her but was intercepted, and the carnation was attached to his coat: "This was a somewhat new experience." White bankers could be solicitous, even fawning in their attention, inquiring too assiduously about his welfare. When the convention met in New Orleans in 1911, "the query was constantly made as to whether I was enjoying myself." He responded positively but admitted in the *Planet* that his sojourn in the southern city was stressful. Richmond bankers were especially doting, for reasons he understood and at times resented. His role at the convention was to serve as a "walking argument for the white South." Bankers from Virginia exhibited him to their northern friends as a "ringing testimonial of their kindness, forbearance, and ability to make something out of nothing, so to speak." [22]

The most awkward moments came in 1914 when the organization held its national convention at the Jefferson Hotel in Richmond, about half a mile from the *Planet* office. Mitchell's heart no doubt sank when he learned that the bankers were coming to Richmond, as it was by no means certain how he would be treated in his hometown or how his peculiar relationship with the city's white bankers would play out in a local setting. When he arrived at the hotel to register, he was turned away, but a white officer of the ABA intervened and procured a badge for him. He attended the daytime sessions but returned home every evening. He was not asked to speak or serve on any of the welcoming committees, nor did he volunteer to take the podium. He seemed to breathe easier the next year when the organization met in San Francisco. [23]

One wonders why he subjected himself to these ordeals, especially when Maggie Walker, R. T. Hill, and other black bankers failed to join him. Clearly he believed on some level that he was breaking down racial barriers, and he described his adventures at ABA meetings with the same dramatic flair that he had once used when investigating a lynching or visiting a rural courthouse. Presumably his attendance at the meetings added to his stature within the black community, and he clearly enjoyed seeing how the other half lived. In 1909 he attended an elaborate dress ball in Chicago sponsored by the ABA to honor President William Howard Taft. He said that as an individual he shrank from the ordeal of entering the ballroom alone, but "as a journalist we braved it all and determined to see what probably had never been seen before by a colored person in a similar position." By the time he attended his last session in Los Angeles in 1921, his accounts of mental turmoil had become a bit predictable, as if he had told the story a few times too many: "I had made the change, and I was ready . . . to appear wealthy, cultured and a man of the business world. The strain was telling on me. How should I get through it? . . . I was troubled and no one knew it."[24]

One casualty of Mitchell's preoccupation with banking was the *Planet.* Caught up in his new role as entrepreneur, he had less time for journalism. Rather than being the focus of his energies, the *Planet* became part of an expanding financial empire that included the Mechanics' Savings Bank, the Knights of Pythias, his job-printing business, and his real estate investments. He continued to write his weekly editorials and composed travelogues about his journeys, but he delegated much of the routine work to staff. After the Nelson Williams libel suit in 1903, his editorials lost much of their verve, and the general tone of the paper grew more restrained. In editorials he preached thrift, industry, and the advantages of opening a bank account, while front-page stories featured the latest Pythian news. Circulation slipped after reaching an all-time high during the Lunenburg trials.[25]

One of Mitchell's difficulties with the *Planet* was that he had made his reputation as an antilynching editor, and yet this issue lost saliency in the early years of the century, at least in Virginia. After Governor O'Ferrall left office in 1897, there was a brief upsurge of racial violence, but a lynching in Emporia in 1900 led to renewed white demands for law and order. In March 1900 Walter Cotton, a black murder suspect, and his accomplice, Brandt O'Grady, a white drifter, were lynched after a mob stormed the Emporia jail. One aspect of the lynching was unexpected. After hanging Cotton, the white mob invited a group of blacks to lynch O'Grady, in what appears to have been a spontaneous nod toward racial symmetry or perhaps a way of sharing the blame. "Another bad, bad thing," said the *Dispatch,* "was the invitation that certain of the whites gave the negroes to come and lynch the white prisoner." Mitchell felt certain that most whites failed to "see the evil of lynch-law until they heard that O'Grady, the white man, had been lynched."[26]

The incidence of lynching decreased dramatically in Virginia in the years after O'Grady's death. Indeed, fewer blacks were lynched during the period 1894–1917 than during Philip W. McKinney's single term of office, 1890–94. To Mitchell's relief, Virginia governors took strong stands against mob violence. When whites threatened to lynch a black prisoner in Roanoke in 1904, Governor Andrew J. Montague called out almost the entire state militia to protect the suspect. Eight hundred troops converged on the city, and armed with rifles they escorted the prisoner by special train to Richmond for trial.[27]

Mitchell was gratified that state officials showed such a strong commitment to law and order, but in the process they nearly preempted his issue or at least diminished its urgency. He might have focused instead on the subtler problems involving courtroom justice, a subject that had absorbed his attention since founding the *Planet,* but after the drama of Lunenburg, no other case seemed to capture his attention. Perhaps the real problem was that after years of crusading for legal justice, he was ready to move on to other issues. Certainly he had little new to say on the subject, and he understood that merely reporting outrages in the *Planet* was far less effective than personally championing the cause of a prisoner. He no longer had the time for such crusades and failed to anticipate the advantages of an institutional response such as marked the work of the NAACP. Besides, it became increasingly difficult to reconcile the stridency of his attacks on lynch law with the more subdued overall tone of the *Planet.*[28]

Mitchell was certainly not the only black journalist to grow cautious during the Jim Crow era. Throughout the South black editors found themselves buffeted by the tides of racism and fearful for their lives. After the Atlanta riot of 1906, J. Max Barber, the editor of the *Voice of the Negro* and a graduate of Virginia Union, was forced to flee the region. Mitchell was deeply disturbed by the violence in Atlanta, which led to at least twenty-five deaths and devastating property damage in a city that symbolized the New South. He acknowledged that liberal-minded white men were of little use when the "mob is assailing us." Returning to themes as old as the *Planet* itself, he urged black southerners to defend themselves against aggression and not expect others to come to their aid: "We insist that colored leaders must stand ready to make the sacrifice and die if need be in behalf of their people."[29]

Troubles came closer to home in 1907 when James D. Uzzle, a school principal and the editor of the *Peninsula Times* of Onancock, Virginia, was chased out of town during an outbreak of violence on the Eastern Shore reminiscent of the Wilmington riot of 1898. During a night of terror, white Virginians destroyed Uzzle's printing plant, invaded black neighborhoods, burned a black-owned store, fired rifles into houses, and forced more than fifty families to flee. As Mitchell noticed, those who were ordered to vacate their homes were not ne'er-do-wells but the town's leading citizens of color. Writing from the safety of Richmond, he speculated that Uzzle might have been better advised to remain in his newspaper office, firing his rifle into the approaching mob and offering himself as a sacrifice. Even as Mitchell advocated politeness and hard work, he urged readers to purchase pistols and repeating rifles, saying it would be suicidal to live in the South without them.[30]

In the eyes of many black journalists, the real ideological test during this period was not what one said about mob violence, which everyone deplored, but how one viewed Booker T. Washington, the principal of Tuskegee Institute whose influence so permeated black America. Here Mitchell's response was in most respects equivocal. Although never among Washington's vociferous critics, he always kept him at arm's length. He failed to join the National Negro Business League, which was dominated by Washington, and rarely attended the annual meetings of the National Negro Press Association, another Tuskegee subsidiary. When pressed by Washington to attend Business League meetings, he usually responded with weak excuses about being too busy. He never liked to play a supporting role and rarely joined organizations that others controlled. He also took public exception to Washington's views on major issues. He wrote eloquently in the *Planet* about the need for strong academic education in black colleges, defended the right of blacks to vote and hold public office, and protested the way Washington made patronage decisions while claiming to have nothing to do with politics.[31]

On balance, however, Mitchell's assessment was usually favorable. He conceded that Washington's accommodationist stance served some useful purposes, and he obviously had no quarrel with the way Washington made overtures to wealthy whites. He was also put off by the vehemence with which a few black journalists, such as Monroe Trotter of the *Boston Guardian,* attacked Washington, thinking it neither "wise or prudent to unmercifully assail him." As he explained in a letter to Emmett Scott, Washington's private secretary, he decided early on that the race needed to "accept the leadership of somebody and we were content to give him the right of way."[32]

Mitchell probably tolerated Washington's compromises so well because he knew he was making compromises of his own. "We find as we grow older that nothing speaks so loud as money," he wrote. He attributed his growing conservatism to age and maturity, his ambition to accumulate his share of the world's wealth, and the necessity of appealing to the better sort. Having long ago given up hope that northern whites would come to the race's aid, he reasoned that black leaders had to make friends in the South: "We recognize the difficulties which the justice-loving, liberal-minded southerner has to contend." At times he wrote with nostalgia of his youthful excesses when he did "foolhardy" things on behalf of the race and "cried aloud and spared not." [33]

Now and then there were glimpses of the old "Fighting Editor." In August 1906 W. E. B. Du Bois and other black leaders gathered in Harpers Ferry, West Virginia, for the second annual meeting of the Niagara movement, a gathering of northern activists many of whom later joined the NAACP. Mitchell did not attend the meeting, but in the *Planet* he wrote that he was profoundly moved by events that took place there. He liked Du Bois's "Address to the Country," which he printed in boldface on the front page of the *Planet*. In his address Du Bois tried to rekindle the fervor of the abolitionist movement: "We will not be satisfied to take one jot or tittle less than our manhood rights." Mitchell observed that his address rang true and pledged that thousands of southern blacks would pray silently for the success of their northern brethren. Forsaking his usual caution, he promised to do his part in Virginia regardless of the consequences: "The boldness has won our admiration and we shall dare say in Virginia all that you have uttered at Harpers Ferry, for John Brown's soul is marching on." [34]

The ordinary pressures of daily life in the Jim Crow South made such promises hard to keep, however, and a month later he acknowledged "the risk being taken . . . in speaking for the rights of a progressive but . . . oppressed people." He continued to protest vehemently against some injustices, such as Theodore Roosevelt's dishonorable discharge of black soldiers in Brownsville, Texas, but the overall tone of the *Planet* changed. He became increasingly preoccupied with the manner in which one protested, as if polite language and courtly manners might in themselves soften white prejudices. When the Niagara movement met in Oberlin, Ohio, in 1908, he questioned whether intemperate statements ever brought practical results. Priggishly he noted that "the language used would hardly pass current in polite society." [35]

That an editor of Mitchell's courage and fortitude could be so effectively silenced was a telling indictment of race relations in the early twentieth-century South. Throughout the region black journalists refused to risk their lives (and livelihoods) to register a protest that seemed unlikely to have any positive impact. Mitchell was not alone in lowering his voice, but he was not forced to take the exact tack that he did, nor did he have to make his compromises in such a grand, flamboyant, and self-serving fashion. It is thus easy to compile an indictment against him. For a time he seemed to confuse his own progress with that of the race, assuming that as his net worth increased, the race also advanced. He cast aspersions on black loafers, forgetting that he had once risked his life to save defendants who were themselves poor, illiterate, and outcast. He promised to fire on lynch mobs but hesitated to take the smallest risk if it meant endangering his relationship with "quality white folks." He condemned cringing and obsequiousness and yet pandered to white prejudices in the ballroom of the Waldorf-Astoria.

Mitchell never regained the militancy of his youth when he "cried aloud and spared not," but events that took place in Richmond after 1910 forced him to reconsider his assumptions about the benign intentions of upper-class whites. In the New York hotel, he proclaimed that "nowhere in the domain of business have I found the white man other than ready to help us upward." When he set out to erect a new bank building in 1909, he discovered that his own financial success aroused white fury and many of the better class, rather than coming to his aid, looked the other way. "We have lots of good white folks in Virginia," he observed sadly. "The only trouble is that they speak . . . in whispers while the race-haters are ranting." [36]

CHAPTER THIRTEEN

The Perils of Prosperity

Mitchell's conflicts with white Richmonders during the 1910s came about largely as a result of his efforts to make his bank profitable. Like most black financial institutions, the Mechanics' Bank was small and undercapitalized, a depressing reality that no amount of cheerful rhetoric about business success or annual visits to ABA conventions could camouflage. As late as 1910 the bank's assets (paid-in-capital, surplus, and undivided profits) were still under $35,000. Total deposits did not reach $100,000 until 1907, and another decade passed before they reached $200,000. As Mitchell realized, a bank with so little money could not pay employees' salaries, maintain a bank building, pay interest on deposits, and at the same time issue regular dividends to stockholders. The black community also lacked the commercial and industrial enterprises that form the basis of most banking business. Banks make money on loans, not deposits, and he had to find some way to invest the money that was accumulating in his vault.[1]

Mitchell concluded early on that the Mechanics' Bank could not operate profitably until deposits reached half a million dollars, and he set out to build confidence in his institution. He knew it imperative that the bank appear solid, substantial, and secure. The bank at first operated out of Pythian Castle Hall, but he was convinced that a more impressive building would increase deposits. His original plan was to renovate the furniture store on Broad Street that he bought in 1905, but in 1908 he purchased property on the northwest corner of Third and Clay Streets and resolved to tear down the existing building, which was in poor condition, and erect a new banking house. A white architect drew up the plans, and D. J. Farrar, a black contractor, agreed to oversee the construction. The four-story brick building would have offices on the upper floors available for lease to doctors, lawyers, and business leaders, making it a center of black commerce.[2]

By 1908 he had also settled on an investment strategy. As he later conceded, he knew little about stocks, bonds, and securities and was reluctant to entrust the bank's assets to New York financiers. Ordinary loans generated little income. He began instead to invest in real estate. Making use of the mapping skills he had acquired as a high school student, he drew diagrams of various neighborhoods and charted the prices of houses and commercial property. Richmond was experiencing a real estate boom, and property changed hands rapidly. Although the race had been systematically shut out of the world of finance, he felt certain he understood the real estate market and that his instincts were sound.[3]

Mitchell had a good grasp of the real estate market, but his very success got him into trouble. His problems came about in large part because of demographic changes that were taking place in Richmond in the early years of the century. The city's black population had remained stable during the 1890s but between 1900 and 1910 increased by 45 percent as rural blacks migrated to urban areas in search of jobs. Women found work in tobacco factories, took in laundry, and worked as domestics, while men did much of the city's hard labor. As the black population of Richmond grew, the neighborhoods of Jackson Ward became increasingly crowded. Single-family homes were subdivided into apartments, families took in boarders, and jerry-built houses appeared on back streets. "There is hardly an alley in what is now old Jackson Ward, which has not been dignified into a so-called street by the erection of houses, and rented at good prices," complained one resident. By the 1890s white Richmonders had begun their move to the suburbs, but blacks found themselves trapped. Hemmed in to the north by Shockoe ravine and to the east by the white business district, they began to push south and west along Clay and Leigh Streets—only to find themselves in conflict with white property owners.[4]

To make matters more difficult, the area of Jackson Ward lacked basic municipal services. "If you wish to understand the effect of colored folks retiring from politics," said Mitchell, "walk around in old Jackson Ward and then walk over [to] . . . the western sections of the city. You will be astounded to see the difference." Health officials warned of the dangers of disease, while in the *Planet*, Mitchell described dusty alleys, cesspools of filth, and crowded houses without running water. Even the most affluent blacks were compelled to live on unpaved streets.[5]

The area of Clay Street where Mitchell planned to build his bank was an attractive white neighborhood of older homes with sidewalks and other urban amenities. The typical dwelling was a brick house of two to three stories with a front porch and a small front yard with a wrought-iron fence. Many of the houses were attached, but some stood alone. The character of the street had changed over time. Before the Civil War middle-class whites, many of them immigrants from Germany, occupied the front houses while domestics lived in cottages to the rear. During the 1880s the rear houses were vacated as blacks sought independent housing, and the street became entirely white. Mitchell began purchasing property along Clay Street in 1908, but at first he rented his houses to white tenants "out of consideration for white property owners."[6]

When Mitchell announced his intention to build his bank at the corner of Third and Clay, whites protested vociferously, arguing that the construction of a black bank would reduce property values and destroy the character of the neighborhood. They pleaded with city officials to deny his request for a building permit. On July 11, 1909, he spoke at a public hearing called to consider the issue. According to the *Times-Dispatch*, he "made quite an eloquent appeal for fairness to the negroes." He reminded the councilmen that he himself had once served on the council and made important decisions: "He told of his retirement from politics and of his engaging in business and he entreated the liberal-minded white men not to block the progress of the better class of color." The council agreed to the permit, but only after he lobbied councilmen privately. "We are doing our best to get on well with some of these white folks down here," he said afterward, "but some of them make us mighty tired."[7]

The Mechanics' Savings Bank opened for business in June 1910. The four-story white and yellow brick building was designed in the Renaissance Revival style and towered over neighboring houses. "Colored People Have Skyscraper," proclaimed the white press. The bank had a roof garden reached by an elevator that could be used at night, and the bank lobby was luxuriously appointed with fixtures of green and white Italian marble. Just off the lobby was a separate "ladies room" where women could do their banking business. He furnished the room with delicate chairs and a screen to protect privacy. The most striking interior feature was a laminated-steel, round-door vault that weighed thirty-five tons, cost $10,000, and was intended to inspire confidence among depositors. A reception for "whites only" was held at the bank on the evening of June 27, 1910. Mitchell gave tours of the building and publicly thanked government and business leaders for their assistance.[8]

The opening of the bank failed to quell white fears, and controversy over the fate of Clay Street continued. After one house was placed on the market, a placard appeared on the front, which read: "The white residents of West Clay Street are determined that no negroes shall live in this neighborhood. We advise you to take warning." According to the *Times-Dispatch*, the Mechanics' Bank was making "tony investments" and had purchased twenty-five to thirty houses in the area, nearly all of which were rented to whites. The reporter acknowledged that Mitchell was "a pretty shrewd businessman" but observed that renters were seldom happy to learn the identity of their new landlord. Among his tenants was a prominent city official.[9]

In 1910 the city of Baltimore enacted a residential segregation ordinance, the first in the nation, which divided the city into separate black and white districts. Mitchell promised that such a development would never occur in Richmond where race relations were more harmonious. He continued to invest in real estate and in January 1911 purchased a three-story brick building on the south side of Broad, where blacks seldom ventured.[10]

Mitchell's assumption that his real estate dealings would be tolerated proved to be wishful thinking. On February 9, 1911, A. L. Vonderlehr, a member of the city council from Henry Ward, which included much of old Jackson Ward, introduced a residential segregation ordinance that was said to avoid some of the legal shortcomings of the Baltimore law. Like most segregation ordinances, this one appeared evenhanded in its official language but had pernicious implications. It was designed to freeze existing housing patterns and stop the movement of blacks into white neighborhoods. According to Vonderlehr's proposal, no person of color could move into a house on a city block "on which a greater number of houses are occupied as residences by white people than are occupied as residences by colored people." In other words, no black person could move onto a predominantly white block. Similarly, no white person could move onto a predominantly black block. The ordinance said nothing about home ownership, thus allowing one race to own houses that the other occupied, and the law was not retroactive; no one could be forced to vacate a house he or she already occupied.[11]

After reading the ordinance, Mitchell concluded that it was obviously unconstitutional. How could the city deny a homeowner the right to live in his own house simply on the basis of race? "If then, I own a house and lot on Clay Street in this city, can I be debarred from exercising authority over the house which I own?" White defenders answered that the ordinance was a valid exercise of police power "because the residence of a negro in a white block offends the general sense of the community."[12]

To Mitchell's dismay the *Richmond News-Leader* came out in support of Vonderlehr's proposal, arguing that the ordinance would reduce tensions in the Clay Street area. Mitchell wrote a long letter to the *News-Leader* in protest. Although he made occasional nods in the direction of "the friendly relationship now existing in this community," he was unusually frank. He pointed out that black Richmonders were not trying to "colonize or locate colored families in Franklin or Grace Streets or on Monument Avenue" but rather were occupying houses in the vicinity of Jackson Ward that had been vacated by whites. He challenged the notion that black occupancy reduced property values. On the contrary, the housing shortage in Jackson Ward had led to spiraling rents and greatly inflated prices. Almost as an afterthought he noted that black Richmonders would regret having to invest large sums of money in a legal contest or being forced to inquire in the North "for information and plans and methods upon this all-important question."[13]

The committee on ordinances, charter, and reform was scheduled to debate the ordinance on February 21, 1911, but postponed consideration after Mitchell requested permission to speak in opposition. A public hearing was held on February 27. From Mitchell's perspective the evening went poorly. He had asked to speak last but was placed first on the agenda, which put him at a disadvantage and caught him off guard. Mustering all his diplomatic skills, he did his best to sway the councilmen in the time allotted him. He insisted that black Richmonders had no desire to intrude upon whites or live in white neighborhoods but merely wanted decent housing, paved streets, and city services. He pleaded for fairness. At first his speech seemed to make a good impression, but later in the evening a white resident from Clay Street read aloud excerpts from *Planet* editorials that were of a "different tone and served to a large extent to counteract the effect of his remarks." Whites were visibly angered by his elated response in the *Planet* to prizefighter Jack Johnson's 1910 victory over Jim Jeffries. Mitchell must have realized that no matter how accommodating his editorials, they were never accommodating enough.[14]

The committee approved the segregation ordinance, and the common council unanimously concurred and forwarded the measure to the board of aldermen. Mitchell was heartsick and urged *Planet* readers to lobby the aldermen "in plain sorrow-laden language." Many white realtors had misgivings about the ordinance, but the most effective white opposition came from Mary-Cooke Branch Munford, the younger sister of James R. Branch, the executive secretary of the American Bankers Association. Munford, who was active in every phase of the Progressive movement, campaigned against the ordinance, both publicly and privately, and gathered census data to demonstrate the desperate need for better housing in Jackson Ward.[15]

The behind-the-scene lobbying appeared at first to have some impact. When the ordinance came before the board of aldermen on March 14, the aldermen tabled the measure to await a report from an ad hoc committee that would investigate ways to relieve congestion in black neighborhoods. The next month, however, the aldermen caved in to pressure and passed the ordinance without waiting for the committee's report. Mitchell's response was immediate and anguished. The adoption of the measure had shaken "the confidence of the colored people of this city. . . . It was a brutal exercise of power, and it will leave a scar that 'time will not effect or eternity wash away.'" He was particularly upset with the *News-Leader*, which "turned upon us at the critical moment," and with certain white officials whose promises of support proved worthless. After the mayor signed the ordinance, an unnamed black leader was heard to say, "We will spend a million dollars to kill this law." [16]

The difficulties in enforcing the new ordinance quickly became apparent. A week after the mayor signed the measure, a black Richmonder who owned a house on Clay Street discovered that his white tenants were moving and asked permission to live in the house temporarily while he looked for white renters. He was warned that he would be arrested if he tried to take occupancy. The next month a Jewish shopkeeper was arrested after he moved his family into an apartment above a store he owned on all-black Baker Street. He pleaded for an exception to the ordinance, saying his wife was ill and they had nowhere to go. The council turned down his request but remitted the fine on condition that he vacate the apartment immediately. In the months that followed, other arrests were made, and several defendants hired attorneys and filed appeals. "Can a citizen be arrested and punished for living in his own house?" asked Mitchell. In the *Planet* he wrote that he had had his fill of segregation: "We have been denied the right to vote, the right to hold office, the right to live on the same block with the white man, the right to ride in the same railway car, the right to occupy a seat in a streetcar beside a white man, the right to worship in the same church, the right to drink at the same bar, the right to be buried in the same cemetery, and still the cry against us continues." [17]

Mitchell formed a committee to raise funds and hire legal counsel, and by 1912 several cases were making their way slowly through the courts, with lawyers Joseph R. Pollard (black) and Alfred E. Cohen (white) arguing that the ordinance denied homeowners their constitutional rights to property. NAACP officials in New York considered taking the case but decided instead to challenge a similar law in Louisville, Kentucky. [18]

The perversity of the Richmond ordinance was best revealed in 1914 when members of the white Immanuel Baptist Church, who were departing for the suburbs, decided to sell their old church at the corner of Fifth and Leigh Streets to black Methodists. Whites in the neighborhood protested the sale of the church and argued that the block on which the building rested was a white block. The white congregation conceded that the church fronted on a white block but explained that the black congregation had agreed to cut a new side door and enter by way of Fifth Street. The racial character of Fifth Street was not entirely clear, however, and in the months that followed city officials found themselves debating mind-numbing technicalities. Fifth Street was predominantly white between Leigh and Jackson Streets (where the church sat) and predominantly black between Jackson and Duval Streets, yet Jackson Street did not actually cross Fifth Street but dead-ended there. Whether the block was black or white depended on how one defined its northern boundary.[19]

To resolve the matter and prevent the sale of the church, a councilman offered a clarifying amendment that seemed more abstruse than the original. While the amendment was still being discussed, attorney George W. Lewis purchased a house on the disputed section of Fifth Street. When he moved in, he was arrested and brought before the police court but was acquitted after city attorney H. R. Pollard conceded that the existing ordinance was unclear. Five hundred whites then petitioned the circuit court to block the sale of the church pending council action on the amendment. The judge declined to act, pointing out that nothing in the ordinance could be construed to prevent the sale of property, although blacks might indeed be prevented from occupying the building.[20]

Mitchell found these negotiations tiresome and confessed his fatigue with the continuing agitation: "Personally, all of our manhood and race pride seem to have 'petered out.'" Increasingly he recognized that appeals to the better sort were not working, and he urged black Richmonders to begin the difficult, time-consuming task of grassroots political organizing. He found it galling to appear before councilmen as a beggar, pleading with elected officials who had once been colleagues. In October 1914 the city council unanimously passed the amendment to the ordinance, but by then the black congregation had already purchased the building. It thus appeared that black Methodists held the deed to a church they could not occupy. "What is the indirect cause of all this?" asked Mitchell. "Every representative in the City Council was elected by white men's votes."[21]

In January 1915 the city attorney suggested a new interpretation that opened the way for the black congregation to occupy the church after all. If one defined *residence* as house, then Fifth Street between Leigh and Jackson was white, but many of the larger houses had been subdivided into apartments. If each family unit was considered a residence, then even this short section of Fifth Street might be black. Police were sent into houses to make a racial tally, and they reported that the majority of residents appeared to be black, although it was not certain that they occupied a majority of the apartments. Assuming they could safely occupy the church, the black congregation spent $500 on remodeling and cut a new side door. They held their first service on Wednesday evening, March 24, 1915. After the service police arrested the pastor and deacons on grounds that some members entered through the forbidden front door. Each defendant was fined $25 plus court costs. "White people of Richmond, this will not do," exclaimed Mitchell. "Colored people of Richmond, this is carrying the iron heel of oppression too far."[22]

The church matter remained unresolved while appeals made their way toward the Supreme Court. The Virginia Supreme Court of Appeals upheld the Richmond ordinance in *Hopkins v. City of Richmond* (1915), but on November 5, 1917, the U.S. Supreme Court in *Buchanan v. Warley* ruled the Louisville ordinance unconstitutional. The justices decided the case on fairly narrow legal grounds and did not specifically overturn the "separate but equal" ruling in *Plessy v. Ferguson* (1896), but the decision was a major victory for the NAACP, the first favorable Supreme Court ruling regarding segregation in nearly forty years. "God bless the Supreme Court of the United States," wrote Mitchell. "We have always believed that God in his own time would make the crooked ways straight." In the aftermath of the court decision, the city attorney dropped charges in some thirty cases that had been tied up in the Richmond courts, and Leigh Street Methodist publicly opened its front doors.[23]

Mitchell's real estate investments helped provoke the controversy over residential segregation and demonstrated the ways in which issues of race, politics, and economics became intertwined. In an unusually candid editorial written not long before Booker T. Washington's death in 1915, the *Planet* editor acknowledged that the famous Atlanta Compromise would not work: "It is absolutely essential to have political rights and to exercise them in order to protect property."[24]

By the 1910s other whites were expressing displeasure about Mitchell's real estate investments, although for different reasons. In 1910 the General Assembly created a separate banking division within the State Corporation Commission, and state officials tightened oversight and began on-site examinations. The head of the banking division from 1910 until 1919 was Charles C. Barksdale, the son of a judge from Halifax County. Only twenty-eight when he took the position, Barksdale was filled with reforming zeal and quickly determined that several Virginia banks were in precarious financial condition. Within six months he had closed four of the state's eleven black banks: the Galilean Fishermen's bank in Hampton, the Knights of Gideon Bank in Norfolk, the Nickel Savings Bank in Richmond, and most importantly, the Savings Bank of the True Reformers.[25]

The closing of the True Reformers' bank stunned black Richmonders and caused hardship throughout Virginia and the upper South. Hundreds of families, churches, and fraternal organizations lost their savings, and the collapse became known as "the downfall of Africa." According to receivers the bank's troubles began in the mid-1890s when the order agreed to buy Browne's famous "plan" for $50,000. After his death in 1897, the bank invested in a series of overly ambitious projects—a hotel, an old folks' home, and a department store— that drained the order's treasury and led to the bank's failure. Receivers also accused bank officers of incompetence and fraud. W. L. Taylor, the grand worthy master, was forced to resign, and R. T. Hill disappeared in the wake of the bank's failure and was never seen again, although there were rumors he fled to Canada. W. P. Burrell was indicted on criminal charges but was acquitted; he left Richmond and eventually settled in New Jersey.[26]

After the failure of the True Reformers' bank, the State Corporation Commission placed the Mechanics' Bank under closer scrutiny. Barksdale pleaded with Mitchell to adhere to conservative banking principles and counseled him about dozens of problems, large and small. He corrected minor bookkeeping errors, rebuked him when he overdrew his personal account, and proposed more efficient accounting systems. His chief complaint, simply put, was that the bank was losing money. Each year expenditures for operating expenses, employees' salaries, and stock dividends exceeded the income generated by loans. "Your bank has never made a dollar in profits since it was organized," he warned. As Barksdale readily admitted, however, Mitchell had disguised the bank's problems by making handsome profits in the real estate market. Unfortunately, real estate investments on the part of a bank were in direct violation of the Virginia banking code. Real property could become a liability in a weak market and was not easily liquidated. To make matters worse, the bookkeeping system at the Mechanics' Bank was "so poor that it is almost impossible to analyze the bank's earnings."[27]

Barksdale wrote Mitchell numerous letters but never convinced him that the bank's problems were serious. His tone was occasionally brusque and hectoring as he ordered Mitchell to come to his office or prepare reports. "I say I want this list Saturday, and mean that I want it Saturday, February 17th," he wrote, after Mitchell ignored repeated requests for a list of overdrafts. At other times he adopted a patronizing manner, perhaps because he suspected that Mitchell and his staff feigned not to understand unwelcome suggestions. When the cashier at the Mechanics' Bank seemed confused as to what was meant by a secured overdraft, Barksdale resorted to childlike language: "We will try to make it plainer now, so that you can understand it. . . . You must have something you can touch with your hand." In general, however, even when expressing concerns about the bank's solvency, his letters were polite. Staff members who made on-site examinations, on the other hand, were less civil and seldom prepared color-blind reports. "This bank is managed entirely by negroes, and I fear there is no remedy to overcome their falsecomings," began one examiner. Occasionally there were more revealing slips: "While these darkies are ignorant regarding book-keeping . . . they are anxious to learn." [28]

Barksdale implored Mitchell to end his real estate speculation, but Mitchell reasoned that he had to make money where he could. In 1910 he founded the Bonded Realty Company with himself as president. To comply with Virginia law, he gradually transferred the bank's property to the real estate company and paid for the property with notes drawn on the bank. Houses began to move back and forth—between himself, the bank, and the realty company—invariably increasing in value with each transaction. Barksdale was not mollified by these arrangements: "We can not see how this strengthens the bank in any way." He also ordered Mitchell to devalue the cost of his bank building to comply with new laws that prohibited a bank from impairing its capital by constructing an overly lavish banking house. Many of the upper-floor offices in the Mechanics' building remained empty, and as one examiner noticed, it was highly unusual for a bank with so little capital to have invested $10,000 in a vault. [29]

Mitchell's dependence on white support became obvious in October 1912 when there was a run on the bank. After the collapse of the True Reformers' bank, no black-managed enterprise seemed entirely secure, and on Monday afternoon, October 29, 1912, rumors spread that the Mechanics' Bank had failed. Customers lined up the next morning to withdraw their money, and within an hour the bank had lost more than 5 percent of its deposits. Mitchell telephoned Oliver J. Sands, who arranged for an immediate delivery of cash, while Barksdale made a public statement attesting to the bank's stability. "The building which this bank has here is a credit to the Negroes of this city," he told the press. "The vault is a particularly strong and handsome one." After confidence was restored, Mitchell wrote a warm letter to Barksdale thanking him for his help, and Barksdale replied in kind, "I assure you, if I was of any assistance to you in your recent flurry, I am very glad indeed. . . . I stand ready to help you whenever I can." [30]

Mitchell could not have weathered the storm without Barksdale's support, but at least one observer eventually viewed their relationship skeptically. Abram L. Harris, who grew up in Jackson Ward and graduated from Virginia Union in 1922, earned a Ph.D. in economics from Columbia University and for many years taught at the University of Chicago. In 1936 he published a monograph, *The Negro as Capitalist,* that focused on Virginia's black banks, many of which by then had failed. Harris concluded that state officials in Virginia, rather than being too severe with black bankers, were too indulgent.

Convinced that black-run enterprises contributed to racial harmony, they overlooked the errors of the "child race" and encouraged the development of parallel institutions. In return black leaders were expected to mute their protests. In Mitchell's case the banking division was too lax "either because the officials respected Mitchell and therefore gave him as much latitude as they could under the law, or because they felt it did not matter what a Negro banker did."[31]

In 1916 Mitchell was involved in an incident unrelated to banking that demonstrated that friends in high places could not protect him from everyday humiliations. On the afternoon of April 16, 1916, he was standing at the corner of Broad and Fifth Streets when an automobile struck and killed a pedestrian. He was interviewing the chauffeur for a possible *Planet* story when police ordered him to move. He tried to show his press card but was hustled into a patrol wagon and transported to the Second Street police station. The wagon took a long, circuitous route through black neighborhoods, stopping several times to pick up suspects in unrelated incidents, and Mitchell was mortified at the prospect of being seen in the wagon. At the station police frisked him and confiscated his watch and other valuables. He was charged with disorderly conduct but was released several hours later on his own recognizance. According to the white press, at the police station he appeared incensed and "upbraided the officers for taking him to the station in the patrol wagon."[32]

His trial took place in police court the following Wednesday. By then he had retained legal counsel and had persuaded powerful whites to speak on his behalf. One white friend told the judge that Mitchell "had been somewhat rampant when in politics, but since that time, he had calmed down." The prosecutor conceded that a mistake had been made and asked that the case be dismissed. Mitchell later filed charges against the white policemen but withdrew them after white "friends of a lifetime" persuaded him to let the matter rest.[33]

The next year he found himself in conflict with public officials again, this time over matters of national policy. When the United States declared war on Germany in April 1917, he expressed support for the war effort and assured whites that they could count on his patriotism. His motto was, "My country, may she always be right, but, right or wrong, my country." Hundreds of black Richmonders registered for the draft on June 5, 1917, and the next week Mitchell spoke at a rally at Sharon Baptist Church, where over $17,000 was subscribed to Liberty Bonds. "We have proven our fidelity to the government," he said afterward. "What will the government and its officials prove to us?"[34]

The depressing answer came the next month in East St. Louis, Illinois, when white mobs, worried about losing jobs to black migrants from the South, killed at least two hundred blacks in an unprecedented orgy of violence. More than six thousand men, women, and children were left homeless. Mitchell was dismayed by the news from East St. Louis and pleaded with black men "to sell their lives as dearly as possible." He seemed close to despair as he contemplated the meaning of the outrage in a country fighting to make the world safe for democracy: "We have stood many things but this latest manifestation of heathenism, savagery and fiendishness is without a parallel in the history of this country." President Woodrow Wilson refused to condemn the rioters or order an investigation, while local authorities blamed blacks for provoking the massacre.[35]

Although Mitchell publicly expressed his grief about East St. Louis, he knew he had to be careful in his criticisms of the federal government. In June 1917 Congress passed the Espionage Act, which proscribed severe penalties for anyone aiding the enemy or in any way obstructing the war effort. Black Americans were placed under special scrutiny, and federal officials tended to interpret protests against racial injustice as evidence of German propaganda. In Jackson Ward undercover agents from the Justice Department followed up rumors of pro-German activity, although without much success. "This is a densely populated colored district and the chances of finding a negro, without a protracted search, are unfavorable," complained one agent, who was investigating a report about disloyalty among hospital orderlies. In the *Planet,* Mitchell warned of the consequences of loose talk and advised his readers to exercise caution in their casual conversations: "There is no law against your thinking what you please about the government at Washington, but there is a law against your putting your thoughts in a word form." He advised his readers to "tell your troubles to God, but go into your closet and shut the door . . . else some one [other] than God may hear you and arrest you when you come out."[36]

The Espionage Act empowered the postmaster general to exclude from the mails any newspapers or magazines he deemed treasonous, and on Saturday, August 4, 1917, Mitchell discovered that the weekly *Planet* had not been delivered to subscribers. When he arrived at the post office to inquire, Postmaster Hay T. Thornton said he was holding eighteen mail sacks containing the latest *Planet* issue. Thornton was concerned about a letter from Uzziah Miner, a student at Howard University, that Mitchell printed on the front page. In his letter Miner expressed anger about East St. Louis and pledged never to volunteer for the armed services: "We are beginning to fear Germany less and to fear white Americans more." The postmaster explained that Mitchell's editorials were probably not seditious, but Minor's letter was, and he had forwarded a copy of the *Planet* to federal officials in Washington.[37]

After talking to Thornton, Mitchell returned to the *Planet* office "not in the best humor." He printed two hundred circulars that he took to the post office and defiantly mailed to fellow editors. "Right of Free Speech Denied," said the headline: "The Richmond, Va., *Planet* Barred from the United States Mails—Must Not Condemn East St. Louis Riots in Conjunction with United States Officials." Thornton mailed the circulars but as a precaution sent a copy to the Post Office Department in Washington. On Monday morning Mitchell himself traveled to Washington and obtained legal counsel. As he explained in a formal letter of complaint to Postmaster General A. S. Burleson, his patriotism could not be questioned. He had supported the war in public speeches and was chairman of the local committee for the purchase of Liberty Bonds. Striking a familiar note, he said he was "writing this letter with the hope that the southern spirit of fair play in the upper classes of the people down here may assert itself." He returned to Richmond with the matter unresolved, but on Thursday, August 8, Burleson agreed to release the August 4 issue.[38]

The following week Mitchell led off his editorial page with a one-line admonition: "Everyone must speak in favor of the national government." For months afterward he made a protest that no federal authority could easily challenge. Each week he printed in bold face—without editorial comment—the First Amendment to the Constitution, which guaranteed freedom of the press.[39] His editorials remained guarded, however, and he must have recalled the time of the Spanish-American War when his hard-hitting editorials helped inspire the "mutiny" of the Sixth Virginia Volunteers. Such dissent would not have been tolerated during World War I.

If the war exacerbated racial tensions, it also meant new prosperity in black Richmond. Jobs were plentiful and wages high, which led to more money in circulation and increased profits for black-run enterprises. In 1916 deposits at the Mechanics' Savings Bank passed the $200,000 mark for the first time, and the next year Mitchell embarked on a new project, the building of Woodland Cemetery. He purchased forty acres of land on the northern outskirts of Richmond and designed the layout of roads and burial plots. In 1918 deposits at the Mechanics' Savings Bank reached $388,824 and in 1919 hit an all-time high of $554,447. At the annual stockholders meeting in January 1919, he thanked the stockholders for their patience and "told of the long lines of depositors that now crowded the doors of the institution."[40]

By the end of World War I, Mitchell even looked more prosperous. He had put on weight as he aged, which gave him a more imposing appearance. He had grown "fat as a corn-fed shoat," joked his old friend John E. Bruce. Always something of a dandy, he typically wore a finely tailored long black coat and hickory-striped trousers.[41] In 1919 he succumbed to "automobile fever" and purchased a seven-passenger Stanley Steamer touring car, an impressive vehicle that was fired by kerosene but required periodic stops to replenish the water supply. According to the *Planet*, "Every owner of [a] gas car wanted to see the one that had no spark plugs, no gears, no clutches, but simply climbed hills with a movement of the throttle."[42]

For years Mitchell had filled the *Planet* with stories of his travels, and after he acquired the Stanley Steamer, his travelogues took on a new theme—the condition of the car. Like other automobiles of the period, the Stanley Steamer was subject to mechanical breakdowns, and he described in detail his efforts to get the car moving again. He seldom drove the car himself but relied on chauffeur and friend Robertson Davis. He outfitted the car like a camper, with cooking utensils, cots, and a tent stored in the rear. He and his friends often set up camp alongside the road and cooked meals over an open fire rather than take their chances with public accommodations. Usually his excursions were within a day's drive of Richmond, but he once drove to New York City. He enjoyed taking out-of-town visitors on tours of the city. When Howard University professor Kelly Miller visited Richmond, for example, "Dr. Miller went for an automobile ride with Editor Mitchell and Miss M. L. Chiles."[43]

Thomas L. Dabney, a student at Virginia Union, recalled another story from this period involving Mitchell and a famous visitor, although this one took place before the purchase of the Stanley Steamer. In 1916 W. E. B. Du Bois spoke at Virginia Union and after his address expressed a desire to see Richmond's historic sites. The next morning Dabney and Du Bois procured an automobile and drove to the Mechanics' Savings Bank, where they picked up Mitchell, and then motored to St. John's Church. According to Dabney, Mitchell and Du Bois stood quietly in the church while a white attendant recited the words of Patrick Henry's "Give Me Liberty or Give Me Death" speech. After the reenactment the two men entered the pew where Patrick Henry had spoken and "stood there for a while in silence."[44]

Like Du Bois, Mitchell was deeply troubled by the contrast between American ideals and the treatment accorded black citizens. As the war ended evidence mounted that black Americans were going to be poorly rewarded for their patriotism. More than seventy blacks were lynched nationwide in 1919, and race riots broke out in twenty-five cities. In 1920 members of a revitalized Ku Klux Klan, wearing white sheets and hoods, marched down Broad Street in Richmond.[45]

Mitchell had shared in the accommodationist spirit of an earlier age and had argued that black southerners had little choice but to bide their time and wait for the right opportunity to initiate fresh assaults on discrimination. He had cautioned *Planet* readers to keep their wounded feelings in their pockets and cultivate friendly relations with their white neighbors. He promised that business success and hard work would lead to the dismantling of the Jim Crow system and the restoration of political rights. None of these predictions seemed to be coming true, and after World War I his editorials reflected some of the impatience and frustration of the postwar period.

CHAPTER FOURTEEN

Collapse

As a black business leader in the Jim Crow South, Mitchell faced challenges that at times must have seemed nearly insurmountable. Committed to racial progress and inspired by entrepreneurial zeal, he had to accommodate himself to an ideology that limited his advance and constrained his every move. He had to give the appearance of propping up the region's racial customs while his very success undermined them. For years he balanced these forces skillfully, making the requisite overtures to powerful whites while always pushing against boundaries and testing limits. After World War I, however, he seemed to lose his balance. On three separate occasions between 1919 and the bank's failure in 1922, he acted in ways that were almost bound to offend white sensibilities.

Mitchell's first transgression occurred in 1919 when he purchased the Strand Theater at 118 West Broad Street. Built in 1911, the Strand was an opulent white theater, lavishly appointed in the Edwardian fashion and seating over a thousand theatergoers, that was located on the north side of Broad between Jefferson and Adams Streets. The theater was intended for live productions and had superb acoustics but by 1919 was used primarily for motion pictures. Black Richmonders could see movies at the Strand, but they entered through a separate entrance and sat in the gallery. The Hippodrome Theater on Second Street, which opened in 1915, served an all-black clientele.[1]

In a commercial sense Mitchell's purchase of the Strand was probably an astute transaction. He bought the theater for $113,000, which was below the original asking price, and he foresaw the growth of the entertainment industry in the 1920s and the money to be made from "movie palaces." He also knew that blacks were almost bound to occupy the north side of Broad Street. Events after his death proved him right. In 1934 investors from Washington, D.C., purchased the Strand and renamed it the Booker T. Until desegregation undermined its appeal in the 1970s, the theater was something of a city landmark.[2]

Mitchell's purchase of the Strand was also dangerous, however, as he was again ignoring the injunctions of the banking division. Only days before he made the purchase, state examiners made an unannounced inspection and reported the same dismal findings as before: officers and directors were ignorant of the basic principles of finance; the bank camouflaged its real estate investments by creating bogus holding companies; the bank's condition was "entirely unsatisfactory." Mitchell had heard these complaints so often that they no longer had much impact. Three days after receiving their report, he and four bank officers applied for a charter for the Unique Amusement Corporation, which had as its purpose "to establish and conduct theatres, pleasure parks, concert halls, merry-go-rounds and things of like character to entertain or amuse the public." The bank purchased stock in the Unique Amusement Corporation, and the company in turn purchased the Strand Theater. Once again Mitchell was circumventing the banking division.[3]

Mitchell's acquisition of the Strand also flouted the city's racial mores. The theater was only a few blocks south of the all-black Hippodrome, but racially it was worlds apart. According to one story wealthy whites were so upset about his purchase that they offered to buy him out at a good price, but he turned them down because of race pride. The story may be untrue, but both races understood that financial transactions were seldom color-blind and there was something potentially subversive about black ownership of a large and luxurious white theater. When Mitchell acquired the Strand, it was leased for $8,000 a year to Jake Wells, a white entrepreneur. Wells's lease would not expire until 1922, but in April 1920 Mitchell persuaded him to offer a special showing of Mary Pickford in *Pollyanna* for black children. For the first time in the theater's history, black moviegoers entered through the front door.[4]

If Mitchell's purchase of the Strand was his first offense against white sensibilities, his second was his decision to reenter politics. In July 1921 a black Richmonder attending Columbia University in New York wrote home to a friend with a surprised but cheery question. "I understand that John Mitchell has been nominated for Governor and Maggie Walker for a big position," he stated. "Is this true?" The rumors were indeed true. Mitchell was running for governor, Theodore Nash of Portsmouth for lieutenant governor, J. Thomas Newsome of Newport News for attorney general, and Maggie Walker for superintendent of public instruction.[5]

Mitchell's decision to run for governor in 1921 was the result of a number of developments, some national, others local. For years he had taken no part in politics, and he had grown disillusioned with both major parties. Woodrow Wilson's 1912 election confirmed his worst suspicions about the Democrats.

The Virginia-born president told "darkey" stories at cabinet meetings, sanctioned the segregation of government offices in Washington, D.C., and ignored black protests about East St. Louis. When a Republican president returned to the White House in 1921, Mitchell assumed better times were in store only to discover that Warren G. Harding pandered to the worst fears of white southerners and seemed intent on building a lily-white party in the South. Although Mitchell urged readers to keep the "voting habit," he knew he was a Republican only by default.[6]

Mitchell's new interest in politics was also a by-product, albeit indirectly, of the woman suffrage movement. He said little about woman suffrage in the *Planet* because he understand that antisuffragists used race as a reason for limiting the franchise. "White folks down here are opposing woman suffrage because colored women will have the right to vote," he explained. He thought the argument foolish because corrupt officials could steal the votes of women as easily as those of men, but the antisuffragists were perhaps half-right when they said that reopening the suffrage question would on some level disturb the racial status quo. After the ratification of the Nineteenth Amendment in 1920, Mitchell confessed that seeing Maggie Walker and other black women standing in line to register at city hall reminded him of the old days in Jackson Ward when "long lines of men . . . vainly attempted to vote."[7]

Finally, Mitchell's political stirrings coincided with changes taking place within the state Republican organization. C. Bascom Slemp of Big Stone Gap in southwest Virginia was the state's most powerful Republican and Harding's chief adviser on southern matters. Slemp was convinced that the Republican Party could never compete in Virginia unless it shed its image as the "party of the Negro" and adopted a lily-white policy. In 1920 blacks were excluded from the state convention in Roanoke, and in 1921 white policemen were stationed at the doors of the Norfolk convention and told not to admit blacks as either spectators or contesting delegates. The party's nominee for governor in 1921 was Henry W. Anderson, a popular Richmond lawyer who stressed the Republican Party's commitment to prosperity and sought to project a new, forward-looking, lily-white image.[8]

In the wake of Anderson's nomination, Mitchell maintained that black Virginians had three choices: they could boycott the election and stay home; they could support the Democratic nominee for governor, E. Lee Trinkle; or they could nominate their own candidate. Initially he was dubious about launching a separate campaign, citing the heavy cost and the futility of attaching a "Jim Crow coach" to the Republican train, but when black political leaders offered him the top position, he found it hard to say no. He was formally nominated for governor on September 6, 1921, at a convention in Richmond attended by six hundred black delegates. P. B. Young, the editor of the *Norfolk Journal and Guide,* was asked to run for lieutenant governor but declined and announced his support for Trinkle, which led to speculation that he was offended at being asked to play second fiddle to a rival journalist. At the convention Mitchell rejected the "lily-black" label, which whites used, and welcomed the support of all Virginians, black and white. He insisted that he was the true Republican candidate, not Anderson. "I am the nominee of the Republican Party of Virginia and desire that the official records show that fact," he explained to the State Board of Elections. He urged black Virginians to "support your own ticket and let the world know that you have self-respect."⁹

Despite early signs of vigor, Mitchell's campaign for governor turned out to be halfhearted. In the midst of the campaign, he left by train for the ABA convention in California. He remained away almost three weeks, causing P. B. Young to make disparaging remarks about his absence. The *Planet* editor was "rusticating" on the West Coast while other candidates canvassed the state. Even after his return, he was only marginally involved. He spoke at rallies in several cities but sounded at times almost apologetic about his candidacy: he was sorry he had so little time to campaign, sorry he had so little money, sorry he had no chance to win. He wished that whites who found his candidacy so irritating would see its "humorous aspect." Though proof is lacking, it seems likely that among those who were irritated was F. B. Richardson, who replaced Barksdale as head of the banking division in 1919. During the fall of 1921, Richardson increased the regulatory pressure on Mitchell, reminding him day after day that his bank's real estate investments were illegal.¹⁰

As election day drew near, Mitchell showed renewed interest in the contest. He spoke in Danville, Staunton, Newport News, and at a large rally in Richmond, and on election eve he and Maggie Walker rode in automobiles in a parade through Jackson Ward. A roving reporter for the *News-Leader* interviewed black voters across Virginia and speculated that Mitchell might make a strong showing. He quoted an "intelligent negro" from Louisa County who said, "I intend to vote the Mitchell ticket, and all of my friends will vote the same way."¹¹

The results on election day proved disappointing. As expected, the Democratic nominee Trinkle won easily, outpolling Anderson by more than two to one. Trinkle finished with 139,416 votes, Anderson with 65,933, while Mitchell was a very distant third with 5,036. The lily-black share was far below what many had predicted. Mitchell was delighted to see Anderson lose but was hard-pressed to pretend that his own candidacy had much impact. He showed some strength in Lynchburg, Newport News, Roanoke, and Staunton, and even outpolled Anderson in Danville, but did poorly in Norfolk, where P. B. Young campaigned for Trinkle. More than a fourth of his votes came from Richmond. In the rural counties of Southside Virginia, his totals were so low as to suggest wholesale disfranchisement. In Lunenburg County, where he had once fought to save Pokey Barnes, he received only two votes.[12]

Once the election was over, Mitchell sent Trinkle a telegram congratulating him on his victory, and Trinkle responded with a predictable pledge "to deal fairly and justly with your race." The Democratic governor remained true to his promise, at least within the context of the 1920s South. He made symbolic overtures to the black community and refrained from gratuitous race-baiting. In particular, Trinkle worked well with Maggie Walker, whose grandson later described how the two cooperated: "If he had a situation that came up that he thought she was aware of, he'd contact her; and if she had a problem, it would reverse, [and] she'd get in touch with him."[13]

After Trinkle left office rumors spread that the lily-black ticket had been a Democratic invention in the first place, that party officials, worried about signs of Republican renewal, persuaded Mitchell and Walker to mount a campaign to draw support from Anderson. The rumor was at best a partial truth. Mitchell had said all along that a vote for him was a vote for Trinkle, but there is no evidence that he was manipulated into running or in the hire of white Democrats. On the contrary, most whites at the time seemed to view his candidacy as presumptuous. A white woman active in the interracial movement worried that his campaign for governor would set back the cause of racial progress fifty years. "It is a great pity!" she wrote in August 1921. "I feel that if a sufficient number of white friends had taken the trouble to advise these colored people, *in time,* they would not have made this mistake."[14]

Mitchell's third "mistake," his third breach of racial etiquette, was his dalliance with Marcus Garvey, the Pan-Africanist whose appeals to race pride captivated black Americans in the 1920s. A native of Jamaica, Garvey came to the United States in 1916, founded the Universal Negro Improvement Association (UNIA), and launched the Black Star Shipping Line. His bold plans for a return to Africa and his brilliant oratory won him a national following.

Like most black Americans Mitchell put little stock in the back-to-Africa movement as such. "We do not claim Africa as our home," he said, "and we do not expect to return." He also regretted Garvey's habit of lashing out at mulattoes, a ploy that he thought divided the race. But much about Garvey's platform appealed to him. He admired Garvey's strong and manly demeanor, his calls for economic independence, and his utter disregard for what whites thought.[15]

Mitchell first met Garvey in September 1921 when he visited UNIA head-quarters in New York. He told *Planet* readers that the stocky, dark-skinned man had "an amused expression on his countenance, while his small eyes tend to make you wonder . . . what [he] is thinking about." Mitchell returned to New York the next April and visited Liberty Hall in Harlem, the "spiritual cradle" of the UNIA. Garvey was out of town that evening, but John E. Bruce, an old friend and editor of the UNIA's newspaper, the *Negro World,* made him feel welcome. Mitchell spoke for about ten minutes to an enthusiastic audience. He reported in the *Planet* that Liberty Hall was not nearly so grand as he had expected, but other aspects of the UNIA intrigued him. He liked the parades, titles, regalia, and other fraternal accoutrements that were so reminiscent of the Knights of Pythias. He admired the military might of the African Legion and was stirred by the vibrancy of life in Harlem.[16]

Mitchell's interest in Garvey intensified in June 1922 when the Jamaican came to Richmond to speak. Garvey arrived in the city on the afternoon of June 20, and he and Mitchell set out in the Stanley Steamer for a tour of the city. Unlike Du Bois, Garvey was interested in the city's black landmarks—the Mechanics' Savings Bank, Pythian Castle Hall, True Reformer Hall, the St. Lukes' Building, and the churches, hotels, restaurants, and stores that lined the streets of Jackson Ward. They drove past the Strand Theater and toured Woodland Cemetery. That evening Garvey addressed an overflow crowd at True Reformer Hall. "If . . . you Negroes are tired of being abused, misrepresented, Jim Crowed, lynched, burned at the stake and persecuted," said Garvey, "then get up and do something for yourselves." Mitchell made the introduction, and though he backed away from a formal endorsement, he was obviously a bit smitten. He said afterward that Garvey was "one of the shrewdest and ablest men we have ever met." [17]

Once the Mechanics' Bank failed, it was easy enough for black Richmonders to remember Garvey's visit and make a connection between the two events. There is no evidence that state officials knew—or cared—that Garvey came to Richmond, but worries of this sort were not entirely irrational. By 1922 federal agents were monitoring Garvey's every move, gathering information that would lead to his conviction on charges of mail fraud and his subsequent deportation. Mitchell was also under federal scrutiny, probably to a greater extent than he suspected.

The FBI first established a file on Mitchell after he attended the annual meeting of the National Negro Press Association in Nashville in 1920, even though he said nothing of consequence while there. The next year State Department officials began an investigation after reports surfaced that he had connections to Liberia. An agent from the State Department asked Richmond postmaster Hay Thornton for his assessment of the *Planet* editor. Thornton replied that Mitchell was "the leader of his race in this city" but had "incurred the very severe criticism of the white people by things he said in his public speeches and in his paper." Two months later investigators from the State Department were asking more questions, this time about his relationship with Dusé Mahomad Ali, a Sudanese-born actor, journalist, and business leader, who had known Garvey in London. When he applied for a visa, Dusé listed Mitchell as a reference and also mentioned him in a letter to the American ambassador to Great Britain. Meanwhile from UNIA headquarters in New York, Secret Agent 800 reported to J. Edgar Hoover that Mitchell had spoken at Liberty Hall. Shortly after Garvey's visit to Richmond, another undercover agent reported more sensational information. He said that "Garvey was trying to get one John Mitchell Jr., Banker of Virginia, to take charge of all business transactions for the Black Star Line and U.N.I.A., and that he, Garvey, would only carry on Propaganda." [18]

Whether Garvey truly tried to persuade Mitchell to take over financial management of the UNIA is unclear. Undercover agents often reported rumors as fact and misinterpreted what they heard, and certainly it seems unlikely that Mitchell would have left Richmond to promote Garvey's interests in New York. These investigations probably reveal more about the Justice Department's paranoia during this period than about any misdeeds, real or imagined, on Mitchell's part. "Persecuting Negro leaders under the guise of prosecuting them has become a popular past-time," he said later, in reference to Garvey's troubles and his own. [19]

Mitchell's ties to Garvey, his campaign for governor, his purchase of the Strand Theater, his rides about town in the Stanley Steamer, were all reminders that the age of Booker T. Washington was over. For nearly two decades there had been an overlay of paternalism in the banking division's dealings with him. White officials encouraged the growth of black financial institutions, seeing in them proof of the city's harmonious race relations. They applauded every sign of industry and thrift—so long as it took place north of Broad Street. By 1919, however, there were signs that some who worked in the banking division regarded the Mechanics' Bank with much less sympathy, while Mitchell was proving less tractable.

Mitchell said his troubles began when "another King arose who knew not Joseph." The unnamed "King" was probably Barksdale's successor as head of the banking division, F. B. Richardson. A lawyer from eastern Virginia and a graduate of the Washington and Lee Law School, Richardson headed the banking division from 1919 until 1923. From the outset he sought to bring the Mechanics' Bank into compliance with state regulations and refused to countenance the various subterfuges that enabled the bank to deal in real estate. Furthermore, the two men clearly rubbed each other the wrong way. Mitchell's habit of ignoring requests for information exasperated the white official, who also resented the tone he detected in some correspondence. For example, Richardson complained that one letter was "not at all courteous." When rebuked for impertinence, Mitchell tended to respond obsequiously, pouring on his southern charm, which probably made matters worse. He closed one letter with the phrase, "awaiting your further commands," a show of deference that hinted of mockery. State examiners meanwhile reported that no improvements were likely at the Mechanics' Bank as long as he remained president. "Directors & employees seem afraid of him & none seem willing to oppose him," wrote one auditor. Or again, "He absolutely controls the bank & nobody dares to oppose him or make a move without his consent." Mitchell, on the other hand, was convinced that some of the poorly paid state employees in the banking division were less than gentlemen, describing them as "fourth-rate white men" and not of the better sort.[20]

Mitchell had other problems besides his relations with the banking division. Although deposits reached half a million dollars in 1919, they leveled off not long after his purchase of the Strand Theater and then began to fall. By 1920 the ratio of cash to deposits had declined to 6 percent, nearly as low as in 1912 when there was a run on the bank; the industry norm was 22 percent. To some extent the bank's difficulties were beyond his control. The sharp downturn in the national economy that followed World War I led to unemployment in Richmond, while the real estate boom collapsed. Mitchell also faced new competition from black Richmonders. In 1920 two rival banks opened on Second Street, the first black banks chartered in the city in almost two decades. The president of the Second Street Savings Bank was insurance executive John T. Taylor, a former vice-president of the Mechanics' Bank; the president of the Commercial Bank and Trust Company was T. C. Irwin.[21]

In December 1920 Maggie Walker summoned Irwin, Taylor, and Mitchell to her office, probably hoping to establish ground rules for friendly competition. She thought the meeting brought good results. By this time some of Mitchell's closest friends had grown uneasy, and there were rumors that the Mechanics' Bank was in trouble. Mitchell's longtime associate John R. Chiles withdrew his money and joined the board at Second Street Savings Bank. George W. Lewis kept his distance because he suspected that both Mitchell and his cashier Albert V. Norrell Jr. were living beyond their means. Lewis detected a whiff of "True Reformerism" about the venture.[22]

Mitchell's problems intensified in 1921, the year he ran for governor. During the spring of 1921, Richardson made vigorous demands that Mitchell unload the bank's real estate holdings and in May threatened a receivership unless the bank increased reserves. Mitchell responded by selling for $60,000 a three-story brick building at 310 East Broad, which was technically owned by the Bonded Realty Company. The bank had purchased the property in 1905 for $17,750, and he reminded *Planet* readers that he always made nice profits on real estate transactions, although in this case much of the gain was encumbered by mortgages. By September reserves were again low, and Richardson ordered the directors to make no new loans and issue no dividends. The regular October inspection took place while Mitchell was in California at the ABA meeting. It revealed that his personal account was substantially overdrawn, which helps explain why he spent so little money on his campaign for governor.[23]

Once the election was over, Richardson met with bank officers and expressed serious concerns about the bank's solvency. He ordered cashier Norrell to submit daily reports about the status of past-due notes and asked for another audit. The new audit revealed that $83,500 worth of loans to the Bonded Realty Company were unsecured and would prove an absolute loss to the bank. This news alarmed the directors, who seemed dumbfounded at the news. At Richardson's insistence Mitchell and the directors signed an indemnity bond pledging not to dispose of their personal real estate, and they promised to establish the bank on a sounder footing.[24]

Negotiations continued into the spring of 1922. Mitchell hired legal counsel but dismissed his white attorneys in May and resumed direct conversations with Richardson. On May 19, 1922, the bank examiner pronounced the bank's condition as "very grave" and gave the directors thirty days in which to formulate a specific plan to save the bank. The directors subscribed $14,000 in additional stock, and Mitchell offered as surety thirteen pieces of real estate that he personally owned, including his home and the *Planet* office. He said he felt a special responsibility for the bank's troubles and being unmarried was willing to assume the financial burden. Lawyers drew up a deed of trust on his property, but at the last moment Richardson inserted a requirement that he pay 6 percent interest on any shortfall. Mitchell signed the papers but crossed out the provision regarding interest.[25]

Richardson found this amendment unacceptable, and he and Mitchell had a tense meeting on Wednesday, July 12, 1922. Mitchell protested that the interest requirement would ensure his bankruptcy and was intended not to save the bank but to ruin him personally. He reminded Richardson that he always made money on real estate transactions and that there had been no run on the bank. On Saturday, July 15, Richardson called Mitchell on the telephone, but he still refused to accept the interest provision. Instead he offered to drive Richardson around the city in the Stanley Steamer so he could see for himself the value of the bank's property holdings. Richardson declined the tour, and Mitchell hung up the telephone. He said afterward he hung up because he believed the conversation was over. The bank examiner thought he hung up in a fit of temper. Within hours state officials had cleared the bank of customers, and Richardson had posted notices on the front of the building announcing that the Mechanics' Savings Bank was no longer open for business.[26]

The news spread quickly through Jackson Ward, and that afternoon worried depositors gathered on the sidewalks of Third and Clay Streets. Many no doubt recalled the collapse of the True Reformers Bank and the Nickel Savings Bank in 1910. The mood turned ugly as the afternoon wore on, and the city eventually dispatched half a dozen white policemen to ensure order. Mitchell was away from his office when the news broke, but a friend summoned him to the bank by telephone. As he approached the building, he saw white policemen, milling crowds, and roped-off sidewalks, and he assumed there had been a robbery. The truth was of course much worse. On Monday morning court-appointed receivers ordered a full and complete audit.[27]

In the weeks that followed, Mitchell made frantic, desperate efforts to save his bank. He tried to adopt a suitably deferential manner toward Richardson, without the fawning that seemed to annoy him. "When you know me," he promised the bank examiner, "you will have a different opinion of me." He also reached out to powerful whites. Although it surely galled him, he crossed Broad Street with hat in hand to intercede with bankers, accountants, government officials, and his own white attorneys. He pleaded with white editors for sympathetic coverage, which he generally received. He appealed directly to Mayor George Ainslie and Governor Trinkle. Perhaps most importantly, he worked to quiet his depositors' fears. He conferred with those in the black community whose views were known to carry weight, such as Maggie Walker, and published daily special editions of the *Planet:* "The Mechanics Savings' Bank Will Meet All Requirements . . . Banking Division Friendly . . . Accountants to Make Full Report . . . The Rock of Gibraltar Yet."[28]

During this time of trouble, black leaders in Richmond closed ranks. A week after Richardson suspended operations, a mass meeting was held at the city auditorium. Rev. W. T. Johnson of First Church presided, and men and women from all segments of the community rose to express confidence in the *Planet* editor. Maggie Walker spoke with her usual eloquence and asked every black Richmonder to join her in making a deposit on "Money Day"—the day the bank reopened. Black pastors promised to reassure church members during Sunday services. Everyone spoke confidently of the time when the bank would again be open for business. "The last days have been strenuous," said Mitchell, but he was "cheered by the evidences of friendship from every quarter." He also received expressions of support from afar. Marcus Garvey wrote an upbeat letter, and on August 10 the UNIA conferred upon Mitchell the title of knight commander, Order of the Nile.[29]

Despite Mitchell's many assurances that the bank would reopen soon, days went by and then weeks with no report from the auditors. In the evenings he could see lights burning in his private office, sometimes until 10:00 P.M., as white officials sorted through his personal papers. When pressed by Mitchell's attorneys to finish their work, the accountants responded that they faced unprecedented challenges. The ledgers were misfiled and in disarray, Mitchell's own passbook was missing, no records of any kind could be found for the Bonded Realty Company, and the relationship between the bank and its many subsidiaries was "very intricate and confused." To make matters more complicated, some depositors refused to surrender their passbooks, making completion of the audit difficult. The auditors also noted that the directors had been "grossly negligent." They had allowed Mitchell "from time to time to largely overdraw his account . . . and to borrow . . . large sums of money which were unsecured . . . and that they practically turned over the entire management and control of said Bank with all its assets to the said John Mitchell Jr. to run and do with as he pleased."[30]

In August the auditors uncovered evidence that led to Mitchell's indictment on criminal charges. At the time of the bank's closing on July 15, his personal account was slightly overdrawn, but on June 29 he owed the bank $28,481. On June 30 he made a deposit of $29,000 to cover the deficit. That same day $19,000 was withdrawn from the account of the Pythian Grand Lodge and $10,000 from the account of the Grand Court. When asked by the receivers if there was any connection between these transactions, he answered that he often paid death claims out of pocket and he had "five clerks working on the matter." On Friday evening, August 25, city detectives arrived at his home with an arrest warrant, charging him with embezzlement, falsification of records, and theft of bank funds. He was released on a $10,000 bond. Also arrested that evening were his cashier Albert V. Norrell Jr. and three bank clerks, all of whom were accused of lying to protect him.[31]

In the aftermath of the arrests, the various parties hired lawyers and scrambled to protect their interests. Norrell and the bank clerks protested that they were mere functionaries who did as they were told. The bank directors protested that they had signed the indemnity bond in December 1921 only because Mitchell had promised to make good any shortfall. They would require "strict proof" of their responsibility for the bank's difficulties. For his part Mitchell denied fraud and said he had long suffered from a lack of competent commercial help. He acknowledged negligence in overseeing the bookkeeping but insisted there had been no malfeasance or theft. He promised to fight the charges, protect the assets of the depositors, and have the bank reopened. "Making charges is easy," he said. "Proving them is difficult."[32]

Although he pledged he would soon be vindicated, Mitchell's arrest demoralized his supporters, many of whom had assumed that the Mechanics' Bank was one of the race's strongest and best-managed financial institutions. Black leaders were embarrassed as stories circulated of ineptitude, fraud, and criminal activity. Depositors felt betrayed. In the *Planet,* Mitchell continued to express confidence but was obviously under enormous strain. He lost weight and seemed distracted.[33]

The harshest criticism appeared in the November 1922 issue of the *Messenger,* which was published in New York by A. Philip Randolph. In an article entitled "The Passing of John Mitchell, Jr.," an anonymous writer (probably George S. Schuyler, a graduate of Virginia Union) blamed Mitchell's downfall on greed and his unctuous pandering to the best white people. Recalling that the *Planet* editor had once been known for personal courage, he said that in recent years Mitchell had "been steadily veering towards a *hat-in-hand* Negro." He also ridiculed the travelogues that appeared in the *Planet:* "What reader does not remember seeing something in the *Planet* about 'Editor Mitchell's Travels' or 'Mitchell's Long Journeys'?" The writer suggested that Richmond needed an infusion of manhood: "John Mitchell's day is done. Negroes need shed no tears over it. When one loses his courage and devotes most of his time [to] urging the victims of oppression to be polite to the persecutors, it is time for him to go."[34]

On December 4, 1922, Mitchell was indicted by the grand jury of the hustings court on eighteen counts of fraud and theft. The next day he signed a deed of trust conveying all his real estate to the receivers, an action that would haunt him until his death. His trial was postponed to await the auditors' report, which finally appeared on February 28, 1923, seven months after the bank closed. The densely argued 153-page document revealed that the bank's shortage was larger than anticipated, probably more than $200,000. The auditors blamed Mitchell for the bank's failure.[35]

His trial opened in the hustings court on Thursday morning, April 26, 1923. He was represented by J. Thomas Hewin and four prominent white lawyers.

Before the trial began his lawyers managed to have all the counts quashed except one, which accused him of "false entry" for the purpose of defrauding the institution. Most of the first day was spent in jury selection. Twelve white men were chosen, among them a laborer, a passenger agent for a railroad, a clerk at a clothing store, three machinists, a salesman, a foreman, and the president of a manufacturing company.[36]

Once testimony began, Mitchell's lawyers tried to shift the blame for "false entry" to Norrell by insisting that their client had never been involved in routine bookkeeping. The commonwealth's attorney, David E. Satterfield, on the other hand, portrayed Norrell as a cipher who slavishly obeyed Mitchell's orders. According to newspaper accounts Norrell acquitted himself well on the witness stand, and his testimony was damaging to Mitchell's case. During final arguments Satterfield reminded the jury that the *Planet* editor had lived in high style and had campaigned for governor of Virginia wearing "a high hat and a long-tailed coat." Mitchell bleakly observed that having once been a candidate for governor, he was now a candidate for the penitentiary.[37]

The jury began its deliberations on Saturday afternoon and remained sequestered until past midnight. The jury reconvened on Monday morning, April 30, 1923, and that afternoon announced its verdict: "We the jury find the accused guilty as charged in the indictment and fix his penalty at three (3) years in the Penitentiary."[38]

Mitchell was vague in the *Planet* about what happened next, but according to court records he was remanded to jail. While behind bars he published a full-page *Planet* advertisement proclaiming his innocence. He highlighted the quotation from Shakespeare that he had used at the age of twenty-two while investigating the Charlotte County lynching: "There is no terror, Cassius, in your threats, for I am armed so strong in honesty that they pass me by like the idle wind, which I respect not." He said he would forsake life itself to see his good name restored and the bank reopened. Over the masthead he placed a new line: "This may be our last battle. We believe that it is the beginning of our final triumph."[39]

His attorneys asked for a new trial, but after a three-hour hearing on May 15, their request was denied. They then appealed the case to the Virginia Supreme Court, and Mitchell was released on bail. His two-week stay in jail was bound to have been humiliating, but he emerged with what seemed to be new confidence. Having experienced the worst, he perhaps felt emboldened, or maybe the long hours of inactivity gave him a chance to pull himself together and take stock. Henceforth he portrayed himself as the "Fighting Editor" who would vanquish his foes as in olden days. Not long after leaving jail, he traveled to Norfolk, and an observer noted that he "was in fine spirits and showed no signs of depression on account of his recent experiences. The will to fight to the bitter end was evident in his demeanor as he philosophically remarked, 'I've got a hard fight, but I'll beat 'em.' " [40]

He was also buoyed by expressions of support from friends. Even depositors who had lost money when the bank failed seemed offended at the thought of John Mitchell going to jail, while his supporters saw race prejudice behind the prosecution. John E. Bruce wrote a warm letter, saying he had known and loved the *Planet* editor for forty years and was sure his troubles began when he "had the audacity, the effrontery, to be a candidate for Governor in the State in which his father had once been a slave." A newspaper editor from Petersburg remembered his crusade against lynching: "Hon. John Mitchell is an old man now but the fighting blood in him runs as red as it did when he faced the howling mob of lynchers and defied them to take him." Ordinary folk were deeply suspicious of the judicial system and drew their own conclusions. A subscriber from Philadelphia contributed three dollars to his defense fund, along with a note saying, "The white people of the south are the meanest people in the world." [41]

After nearly two years of legal maneuverings, the Supreme Court of Appeals on March 19, 1925, overturned his conviction on technicalities. Mitchell was at the home of a depositor when the news broke and of course was jubilant. The court's decision meant he would receive a new trial, but the commonwealth's attorney evidently had lost interest in the case. He dropped all charges against Mitchell, and against Norrell and the bank clerks as well. [42]

In the aftermath of the court's decision, Mitchell expressed gratitude to those who had contributed to his defense fund. He said his enemies had assumed he would not have enough money to hire competent lawyers, but old friends proved loyal and rescued him from the penitentiary just as he had once saved Pokey Barnes. He paid special tribute to his physician, Dr. A. A. Tennant, and others who posted bail and paid his lawyers' fees. He thought it significant that no depositor or member of the Knights of Pythias was willing to testify against him. [43]

Pythian officers were especially loyal, but the collapse of the bank was devastating to the order. With all its assets frozen in the bank, there was no way to pay death claims, and members began to fall away. Mitchell watched helplessly as lodges disbanded and control slipped from his hands. In October 1922, only three months after the bank failed, the judge of the circuit court appointed Joseph S. Button, the commissioner of insurance and a longtime Democratic Party stalwart, as receiver. Button in turn hired a white lawyer, Charles J. Churchman, to oversee day-to-day operations. For two years both the Grand Lodge and Grand Court were administered out of Churchman's law office in downtown Richmond. According to auditors' reports the financial affairs of the order were "in very chaotic condition," and "such records as were on hand were scattered all around the office." They concluded that Mitchell had "mixed the money received by him . . . with his personal account, using the money for his personal needs."[44]

When the Grand Lodge held its annual meeting in Petersburg in June 1923, Mitchell attended as grand chancellor, but Button presided. Mitchell dryly noted that the white official's "unfamiliarity with Pythian law" led to procedural complications. Realizing that Button would never tolerate his continued involvement, he did not stand for reelection, and William M. Reid, a lawyer from Portsmouth, was elected in his place. The receivership ended in November 1924 when Button formally transferred all the Pythian records to Reid and bequeathed to him a more efficient accounting system. Without Mitchell at the helm, however, the organization foundered, and by 1926 membership had fallen by half and the Grand Lodge was insolvent. In the 1930s both the Grand Lodge and Grand Court gave up their insurance functions and became purely social organizations.[45]

Although he had little to gain except his pride, Mitchell continued to work at various schemes to have the bank reopened. The most promising plan required the depositors to relinquish legal claims to half their money while an advisory committee of six white bankers, including Oliver J. Sands, temporarily took over management. Once the bank was on sound financial footing, a new set of officers from the black community would resume oversight. Mitchell spent the better part of two years negotiating with receivers and trying to persuade depositors to sign the necessary papers.[46] He was quietly heartened in May 1923 when Richardson resigned from the banking division, only to discover that the bank's files had been transferred to John G. Luce, who had served as Anderson's campaign manager during the 1921 gubernatorial campaign. None of his plans for reopening the bank came to fruition, and the receivers began to sell off its assets, over his anguished objections. In January 1924 they sold the Strand Theater for $120,050 to Jake Wells, who continued to operate it as a white movie theater.[47]

In October 1924 Mitchell made one last desperate plea for help. In a letter to Governor Trinkle, he begged for an end to the receivership. After outlining his latest plan for reopening the bank, he concluded with a medley of supplications that had worked well in the past but now seemed to fall on deaf ears: "We need help. We need help now. We need it badly. In my addresses extending from Massachusetts to California, I have often proclaimed that I have never made a direct appeal in vain to the better class of white people. I have given up all that I have. I was born at Laburnum." Trinkle did not respond to this letter, and in August 1926 Mitchell quietly dropped from the masthead his defiant statement: "This may be our last battle. We believe that it is the beginning of our final triumph." He seemed to console himself that he had given it his best fight, which was all he could do.[48]

Once it was clear the bank would never reopen, he became again a full-time journalist. He published articles in the *Planet* under his own byline ("Special by John Mitchell Jr."), wrote editorials, and tried to build up the paper's circulation. He had the help of his nephew, Roscoe C. Mitchell, and his secretary of thirty years, Eva Davis. The results were not impressive. Without the capital to invest in new machinery, he had to rely on old and outmoded equipment, and much of the four-page paper was puffery. He headlined crimes, automobile accidents, and other calamities and wrote many of the articles himself, just as he had forty years before. By the mid-1920s everything about the *Planet* appeared old-fashioned—the typography, the ads, the news coverage, and the editorials.

With legal difficulties hanging over his head, he was constrained as to what he could say. "The white folks have their eyes wide open, even on the columns of Negro newspapers," he observed. Although there were occasional hints that he might resurrect himself as the old-time "Fighting Editor," his editorials were usually bland and inoffensive. "Some people eat too much and some people eat too little," he noted. Familiar themes were rehashed without the old sparkle: "Do not kindle in your children a hatred of white people. We have to live here. Teach them self-defense and urge them to be kindly disposed to every one." He often flattered the best white people but occasionally backed into controversy, as when he praised Virginia's 1924 "racial integrity" law that defined a white person as one who has "no trace whatsoever of any blood other than Caucasian." He said he had always opposed racial mixing and thought the state should define a black person as someone who "has no perceptible trace of white blood in his or her veins." W. A. Plecker, the humorless, racist registrar in the Bureau of Vital Statistics, missed the irony and wrote him a note thanking him for his support. Mitchell, in turn, printed Plecker's letter on the front page of the *Planet*.[49]

Mitchell did not release circulation figures for the *Planet* after 1918, when he reported 2,400 subscribers, but his influence as a journalist declined rapidly after the bank failed. A survey of black families in Richmond in 1929 revealed that 82 percent subscribed to a white daily, 30 percent took the *St. Luke Herald*, 25 percent took an out-of-town paper such as the *Chicago Defender, Pitts-*

burgh Courier, or *Norfolk Journal and Guide,* and 14 percent took the *Planet.* P. B. Young's *Journal and Guide* was by then the state's leading black paper and a more substantial undertaking than either the *Planet* or *St. Luke Herald.* Fewer black newspapers were being published nationwide, but some of the newer journals had mass appeal and were giants compared to the old week- lies. By 1930 the *Chicago Defender* had a circulation of 280,000, while the *Planet's* circulation was probably closer to 2,000. Even in its heyday Mitchell had never printed more than about 7,000 copies.[50]

Mitchell no longer had the money to make out-of-town trips, and so old friends came to see him. W. E. B. Du Bois and Kelly Miller made visits, and Walter White of the NAACP wrote occasional gracious letters asking his ad- vice about lynching and Republican Party politics. Marcus Garvey mailed Christmas cards from the Atlanta penitentiary. Mitchell was deeply moved by Garvey's plight, for reasons that were obvious. Maggie Walker remembered to include Mitchell when leaders met to discuss community problems. He seemed to enjoy most the visits of friends from the countryside, many of them Pythians, who stopped by the *Planet* office while in Richmond to reminisce about old times. In the summer they brought produce from their gardens, and at Christmas they slipped him a little money. A friend from the coast ar- rived regularly with a pail of oysters. "We have friends of forty years standing," he wrote, "and we are bound to them with 'hooks of steel.'" Visitors invari- ably reported that he seemed cheerful and contented, all things considered.[51]

He outlived many of his friends and foes. Among those who died before him were D. Webster Davis (1913), James H. Hayes (1917), and Giles B. Jack- son (1924). Some of his closest associates moved north. Dr. Robert E. Jones and Rev. W. F. Graham retired to Philadelphia. He considered leaving Rich- mond but reasoned that he was too old to move and would "fall into the arms of Jesus" with less of a jolt if he stayed close to home. His greatest personal loss was surely the death of Marietta Chiles in 1921. As one might imagine, his eulogy in the *Planet* revealed nothing about their private relationship, though he did say he would visit Woodland Cemetery often to place flowers on her grave.[52]

He never sold the Stanley Steamer, but for years it sat on blocks in the garage at the rear of his house at 515 North Third Street. He shared the house with his nephew Roscoe, Roscoe's wife Lilian, and their nine children. Lilian Mitchell, a fair-skinned woman with hair that reached to her waist, managed the crowded household on a tight budget. Some of the older children were sent to New Jersey to attend school and live with their grandmother Sylvia

Mitchell Scott, Tom Mitchell's widow, who had remarried. Mitchell enjoyed the children but in the fashion of grandparents often retreated to his upstairs bedroom. He was strict with the girls and indulgent with the boys. When he handed out treats, the girls got pennies, the boys nickels. What the children later remembered best about him was his fondness for dogs. Unable to turn away a stray, he fed every animal that turned up at his back door until finally, by the time he died, twenty-two dogs of various descriptions had affiliated themselves with the household. When he set out for work in the mornings, he was followed by more than a dozen dogs, adding to his reputation for eccentricity. He walked proudly and dressed with great formality. Neighborhood children called him the "Mighty Mitchell." [53]

Criminal charges against him were dropped in 1925, but his legal difficulties continued. The bank's affairs were not finally settled until 1944, twenty-two years after the bank failed and fifteen years after his death. Just as he predicted, much of the bank's money found its way into the pockets of white lawyers, although depositors eventually received about sixty cents on the dollar. In 1927 a group of impatient depositors pushed the court to end the receivership and distribute the remaining assets. They reminded the judge that Mitchell had signed over to the receivers thirteen pieces of real estate and yet was still occupying—rent-free—his house at 515 North Third and the *Planet* office at 311 North Fourth Street. They asked that all the bank's assets be sold at public auction and the proceeds distributed. [54]

The receivers responded that they had sold eight of the thirteen tracts, but mortgages and legal fees had eaten up most of the profits. They preferred to sell the remaining assets privately rather than sacrifice them at auction. Mitchell's house on Third Street was in good condition and was assessed at $4,250. The *Planet* office was assessed at $17,500, but the value was almost entirely in the lot, which was only a block off Broad Street. The building itself, an "old detached brick residence," was in a "bad state of repair, and if it became vacant would rent for not more than $25.00 a month." Lawyers asked the receivers why they were collecting no rent on these buildings. They gave no answer, but clearly it was because Mitchell had no money to pay them. [55]

Like everything else regarding the bank's collapse, this episode generated reams of paper and much controversy. On December 3, 1927, Mitchell gave a deposition. He was cautioned to keep his remarks brief but grew garrulous and for the first time seemed to be breaking under the strain. He said he would rather live in an institution of charity than have depositors lose money on his account, but his defense took some new and unconvincing twists: "I have abundant facts to establish . . . that I have been a victim of a conspiracy and that this new day young colored folks have caused me the embarrassment from which I now suffer by their love of whisky, women, gambling devices and all kinds of disreputable things." He said he was trying to work out a settlement "by which this costly litigation may be ended and that I may close my eyes in death with the reputation and character unsullied that I have built up in Richmond during a period of more than sixty years."[56]

When the judge ordered that the property be sold, Mitchell threw himself on the court's mercy. He said he had signed away his home and business only because he believed the bank would reopen. He had consented to the transaction under duress without his attorney being present. Selling the property on Fourth Street "would wreck and destroy the *Planet,* a newspaper published for the colored people of the City of Richmond, and which has been in existence for 45 years." It would "financially ruin and impoverish your petitioner." Although he lost every court battle, the receivers never got around to selling his house or the *Planet* office while he was alive, probably because they did not have the heart to put him out on the street.[57]

In November 1929 his health began to fail. He was suffering from nephritis, a kidney disease that caused his feet and legs to swell and left him sick and without energy. Few but his closest friends knew he was ill, and he blamed his fatigue on money worries. On Thanksgiving Day, 1929, he walked to work as usual but had to be carried home that afternoon. On Sunday he wrote a new will, leaving all his assets to his family. The wording of the will was vintage Mitchell. According to the courts, he owed the receivers money; according to his will, the receivers were in debt to him. He died early on Tuesday morning, December 3, 1929, around daybreak. He was sixty-six years old. According to family tradition he was sitting in a chair in his upstairs bedroom, wearing his old Knights of Pythias uniform, when he rose to his feet and said, "I am ready for you death." Lilian and Roscoe Mitchell were with him when he died. His physician and longtime friend and business associate, Dr. A. A. Tennant, signed the death certificate.[58]

His funeral took place on Thursday afternoon, December 5, at Fifth Street Baptist Church. Rev. W. T. Johnson of First Church conducted the service. Mitchell had once expended considerable energy to block Johnson's call to First Church, but the two men had become close friends and confidants. A deacon lined out the words to the familiar hymn "Abide with Me" and the congregation recited Psalm 116: "The Lord preserveth the simple: I was brought low, and he helped me." A series of speakers rose to pay their respects to the "Fighting Editor." Although there were occasional references to his "dented armor" and his trials and tribulations, this was not the time for faultfinding or recriminations. Speakers instead praised "his great intellect, his indomitable will, his unconquerable spirit." He was buried at Evergreen Cemetery next to his mother. His own grave was marked by an inexpensive flat stone, leaving his mother's much grander monument the focal point of the plot. The obituaries in the black press were brief and at best nostalgic. In truth, he had departed the national scene in 1922 when his bank failed. The white press in Richmond reported his death without editorial comment. As a friend noticed, the deaths of old house servants and black mammies generally received more attention.[59]

Epilogue

Mitchell's last years were difficult, and the collapse of his bank and the felony conviction meant that his real accomplishments were obscured. His story was too complex to lend itself well to presentations during Negro History Week, and even his most solid achievements—his editing of the *Planet,* his crusade against lynching, his work on the city council, his fight for black officers during the Spanish-American War, his leadership of the streetcar boycott—did not fit in well with a celebratory view of Virginia's past. Although never entirely forgotten in Richmond, he was seldom honored or recognized, at least until recently. In 1978 the National Park Service acquired Maggie Walker's house on Leigh Street and opened it to visitors, while Mitchell's nearby residence on Third Street remained unmarked and ignored. A modern office building was named for Giles B. Jackson, but no building was named for Mitchell.

Mitchell's difficulties as a banker were partly of his own making. Possessing a combative temperament, he never worked well with others, and there are hints of hubris in his dealings with the banking division. A more cautious businessman, who kept better records, stayed out of the limelight, kept his ambitions in check, and played the game more skillfully, might possibly have kept the bank afloat. But the challenges he faced were enormous. Committed to building a strong financial institution, he had to use as capital the petty savings of laborers and domestic workers. Never having enough money, he turned to real estate speculation as a way of breaking out of the circle of poverty and establishing his bank on a sure foundation. Because the rules imposed by whites were so often unfair, he learned to ignore them and brushed aside the repeated warnings of state officials that his bank was in trouble.

The failure of the Mechanics' Bank in 1922 also revealed in dramatic fashion the shortcomings of Booker T. Washington's accommodationist philosophy. During the Jim Crow era, there were no easy answers, but as long as black southerners were relegated to the most menial positions in the economy and lacked political influence, it was nearly impossible to build strong and independent financial institutions. As Mitchell himself observed in 1915, it was "absolutely essential to have political rights and to exercise them in order to protect property."[1] Furthermore, despite all his efforts, he never quite mastered the art of being an accommodationist. Given to extravagance and grandstanding, he found it hard to be deferential. When he tried to be accommodating, as in his New York speech at the Waldorf-Astoria in 1904, he overplayed his hand and came across as obsequious and fawning, almost a parody of the "cringing Negro" he so often derided. Given to excess, he was never modest or self-effacing. He built too large a bank building, drove too fine a car, purchased an expensive white movie theater, and ran for governor of Virginia. Qualities that had served him well as a "Fighting Editor" proved his undoing as a business leader in the Jim Crow South.

Mitchell's difficulties also serve as a reminder of the importance of electoral politics. In recent years historians have taken a new look at the ways in which those outside the corridors of power influence public policy and have opened up fresh avenues of inquiry. During the Jim Crow era, African Americans resisted white supremacy on the sidewalks, in city buses, in white kitchens, in factories, tobacco fields, churches, lodge meetings, and jazz halls.[2] It is important, however, not to forget the importance of what transpired on election day. Disfranchisement of black voters made the Jim Crow South possible. As Mitchell understood, once the race lost all political influence, the rules of the game changed, and he had little choice but to make overtures to the "better sort" who controlled the political process in Virginia. When negotiating with whites in the early twentieth century, he almost always began with a reference to his "retirement" from politics. It was a euphemism designed to save his face and theirs and to give him space to maneuver, but everyone must have known that the words were false. At the first convenient opportunity, in 1921, he came out of political retirement and campaigned for governor of Virginia.

If disfranchisement provided the foundation for white supremacy, it also altered the dynamics within the black community. Once black men lost the vote, they found their prestige and authority diminished in the eyes of black women, as the difficulties at First Church so aptly demonstrated. Men could no longer assume that they were the race's most obvious ambassadors or that they could assume positions of leadership by default. This is not to suggest that disfranchisement was in any way a boon to black women. On the contrary, it left them even more vulnerable to white exploitation. As Maggie Walker so famously exclaimed in 1901, "Who is so helpless as the Negro woman? Who is so circumscribed and hemmed in?"[3] But during the early decades of the twentieth century, as southern women advocated progressive reforms, black and white women found themselves in fundamentally different positions. As Glenda Gilmore has observed, "White middle-class women lobbied to obtain services *from* their husbands, brothers, and sons; black women lobbied to obtain services *for* their husbands, brothers, and sons."[4]

Given how often Mitchell stressed the importance of a manly protest, it is thus ironic that the most effective protest in Richmond turned out to be a womanly one. Maggie Walker often succeeded where he failed, and a comparison of the two is instructive. Certainly they were very different in physical appearance. He walked with a "sort of free arrogance and independence," reminding everyone by his dress and demeanor that he could not be pushed around. She, on the other hand, was a heavyset, matronly woman who never threatened or worried white men as he did. Physically handicapped, she barely walked at all; she spent her last years in a wheelchair. When affronted, he was inclined to scowl and frown, but her first instinct was always to smile, smooth away differences, and moderate conflicts. She was fair-skinned; he was several shades darker.

Walker was by no means a weak person, and it is important not to underestimate her. Even a brief summary suggests how much she accomplished. She revived the Richmond branch of the NAACP in 1917, ran for statewide office with Mitchell in 1921 on the "lily-black" ticket, negotiated with mayors and governors, and kept her bank in operation when dozens of similar institutions throughout the South failed. Mitchell always marveled that she got away with saying the things she did to white people; she was never sycophantic like Giles B. Jackson. If black women played such an important role in the Jim Crow South, it was partly because the necessary diplomatic skills had been honed in home and community. Black women, like white women, learned early on to negotiate from a position of weakness, to accommodate, and to make decisions while appearing to give deference to men.

Mitchell probably would be puzzled by the preoccupation of today's historians with gender. For him the paramount issue was always race, and he envisioned his bank as a fortress, protecting the black community during a time of white oppression. In pictures he stands beside his $10,000 vault, promising to keep the race's resources safe.

Mitchell's greatest legacy, however, was not his bank but his newspaper. He published the *Planet* for forty-five years without missing a single issue. He wrote hundreds of editorials denouncing racial prejudice and reported the everyday events that gave meaning to the lives of his readers. He died before the civil rights movement began to break across the South, but during that long bleak interlude between the end of Reconstruction and World War II, he and other black journalists kept alive the dream of full citizenship. What was said about the *Chicago Defender* was true of the *Planet* as well. Subscribers "could read the things they wanted to hear most, expressed in a manner in which they would not dare express them."[5]

Against all odds his newspaper survived him. After his death his nephew, Roscoe C. Mitchell, took over as editor, and in 1938 Carl Murphy of the *Baltimore Afro-American* purchased the *Planet* and renamed it the *Richmond Afro-American and Planet*. On February 10, 1996, the last issue appeared, 113 years after its founding.[6]

The sudden and unexpected demise of the *Afro-American* in 1996 brought Mitchell's name to the fore again in Richmond, and there was renewed interest in his story. In June 1996 journalists awarded him the George Mason Award for his contributions to freedom of the press. At the Library of Virginia, the staff of the Virginia Newspaper Project rescued early issues of the *Planet* and posted a website to describe what they had found: "Born in the Wake of Freedom: John Mitchell Jr. and the *Richmond Planet*." When the expanding civic center threatened to engulf his house in 2000, community leaders resolved that this building was worth saving, for both its architectural merits and its historical associations. His house was put up on blocks and transported to a new, protected location. The Mechanics' Bank building in the meantime was renovated and began to fill up with tenants. Even his gravesite received attention. In the summer of 2000, a corps of volunteers armed with chain saws and weed-eaters worked to clean up Evergreen Cemetery. They discovered a larger-than-life marble statue of an angel that had toppled over on its side. With the help of a backhoe, they righted the monument—the fallen angel—that Mitchell had erected in 1913 to the memory of his mother.[7]

Mitchell was an avid reader of history, and he was keenly aware of the importance of monuments and what historians today call "memory." When the equestrian statue of Robert E. Lee was unveiled in the Richmond suburbs in 1890, he worried about the implications: "What does this display of Confederate emblems mean? What does it serve to teach the rising generations of the South?"[8] He was afraid that some future historian might miss the fact that African Americans served on the Richmond city council in the 1890s and that the sons and daughters of slaves operated banks, insurance companies, hotels, and stores in Jackson Ward. He thought it essential to rescue black history and set the record straight.

Although copies of many black newspapers have been lost to historians, long runs of the *Planet* somehow found their way to the state library in Richmond and were preserved. Mitchell sent the *Planet* to the Executive Mansion each week, and perhaps he was the one who made certain the library got a copy. However it happened, the *Planet* survives today on microfilm in libraries across the United States as an essential resource for those who wish to understand the black experience in the postemancipation South. Mitchell reported the news but also placed his imprint on all that was happening around him. Decades after his death historians still respond to an advertisement he composed as a young man. "Have you seen the *Planet*? It is a journal published in the interests of Colored People every Saturday at Richmond, Va."

> Do you want to see what the Colored People are doing? Read the *Planet*. Do you want to know what Colored People think? Read the *Planet*. Do you want to know how many Colored People are hung to trees without due process of law? Read the *Planet*. Do you want to know how Colored People are progressing? Read the *Planet*. Do you want to know what Colored People are demanding? Read the *Planet*.[9]

To Mitchell's credit, he made a brave and manly protest when nearly all the odds were against him.

Notes

ABBREVIATIONS AND SHORT TITLES

Newspapers, Magazines, and Journals

AHR	*American Historical Review*
BHMM	*Baptist Home Mission Monthly*
JAH	*Journal of American History*
JNH	*Journal of Negro History*
JSH	*Journal of Southern History*
NJ&G	*Norfolk Journal and Guide*
RD	*Richmond Dispatch*
RNL	*Richmond News-Leader*
RP	*Richmond Planet*
RT	*Richmond Times*
RTD	*Richmond Times-Dispatch*
VMHB	*Virginia Magazine of History and Biography*

Short Titles of Published Works

BTW Papers — Louis R. Harlan and Raymond Smock, eds. *Booker T. Washington Papers.* 14 vols. Urbana, Ill., 1976–89.

BWA — Darlene Clark Hine, Elsa Barkley Brown, and Rosalyn Terborg-Penn, eds. *Black Women in America.* 2 vols. Brooklyn, N.Y., 1993.

DAB — *Dictionary of American Biography.* 20 vols. New York: 1928–37.

DANB — Rayford W. Logan and Michael R. Winston, eds. *Dictionary of American Negro Biography.* New York, 1982.

DVB — John T. Kneebone et al., eds. *Dictionary of Virginia Biography.* Richmond, 1998–.

Garvey Papers — Robert A. Hill, ed. *Marcus Garvey and the Universal Negro Improvement Association Papers.* 9 vols. Berkeley, Calif., 1983–90.

Libraries and Depositories

Duke   Rare Book, Manuscript, and Special Collections, Duke University Libraries, Durham, N.C.

JMCB   John Marshall Courts Building, Richmond

LC   Library of Congress, Washington, D.C.

LVA   Library of Virginia, Richmond

MWHS   Maggie Walker National Historic Site, Richmond

NA   National Archives, Washington, D.C.

NSU   Norfolk State University, Norfolk, Va.

RPL   Richmond Public Library, Richmond

VHS   Virginia Historical Society, Richmond

VM   Valentine Richmond History Center, Richmond

VSU   Special Collections/University Archives, Johnston Memorial Library, Virginia State University, Petersburg

VT   Special Collections, University Libraries, Virginia Polytechnic Institute and State University, Blacksburg

UNC   Southern Historical Collection, Wilson Library, University of North Carolina, Chapel Hill

UVA   Special Collections, University of Virginia Library, Charlottesville

Note: In the early 1970s I did research in the old city hall on Broad Street in Richmond. This building has since been closed, and the documents have been distributed to various depositories. Some documents may have been discarded. When possible I have given the current location, but some records were difficult to find, in which case I have given the location as RCH.

1. THE MAKING OF A "COLORED GENTLEMAN"

1. William J. Simmons, *Men of Mark: Eminent, Progressive, and Rising* (Cleveland, 1887), 201–3; Mary Wingfield Scott, *Houses of Old Richmond* (Richmond, 1940), 198–201.

2. Accounts of Mitchell's childhood rely heavily on an early sketch that appeared in Simmons, *Men of Mark*, 201–5. Although it was ostensibly written by Simmons, Mitchell almost surely provided the information. See also Cyrus Field Adams, "John Mitchell Jr.," *Colored American Magazine* 4 (Jan.–Feb., 1902): 295–98; I. Garland Penn, *The Afro-American Press and Its Editors* (Springfield, Mass., 1891), 184–87; *RP*, Feb. 16, 1895. Slave schedules normally did not include slave names, but for some reason Lyons appended a list of his slaves, written in his own hand, to the slave schedule for Henrico County, Western Division, 1860. He gave surnames for six slaves but not for John and Rebecca. Rebecca Mitchell's death certificate (Dec. 12, 1913) gives her age as "about 78," which would mean she was born around 1835. This is in accord with other census data. The 1900 and 1910 censuses indicate that she had seven children but only two lived.

3. John S. Wise, *The Lion's Skin: A Historical Novel and a Novel History* (New York, 1905), 18–59; Varina Davis, *Jefferson Davis: A Memoir* (New York, 1890), 2:205–6. A rough map of Lyons's estate is in the Lyons Family Papers, Henry E. Huntington Library and Art Gallery, San Marino, Calif. (microfilm, VHS). John S. Wise's stepmother (Mary Elizabeth Lyons Wise) was James Lyons's sister, which explains why he was so familiar with the estate (Craig M. Simpson, *A Good Southerner: The Life of Henry A. Wise of Virginia* [Chapel Hill, N.C., 1985], 95).

4. "James Lyons," *Encyclopedia of Virginia Biography*, ed. Lyon G. Tyler (New York, 1915), 3:41–2; "Peter Lyons," *DAB* (New York, 1933), 2:536–37; obituary, James Lyons, *RD*, Dec. 19, 1882; Joseph Christian, quoted in *RD*, May 13, 1883; John Stewart Bryan, *Joseph Bryan: His Times, His Family, His Friends* (Richmond, 1935), 231; W. Asbury Christian, *Richmond: Her Past and Present* (Richmond, 1912), 381; John S. Wise, *The End of an Era* (New York, 1899), 70. Wise modeled a central character on James Lyons in his 1905 novel, *The Lion's Skin*.

5. Lyons, quoting Edmund Burke, in *Four Essays on the Right and Propriety of Secession by Southern States* (Richmond, 1861), 45. On Lyons's financial woes, see Bryan, *Joseph Bryan*, 231. On Lyons's slaves, see the 1860 slave schedule for Henrico County; for other property, Personal Property Tax Book, 1861, LVA; on the use of Laburnum as a farm, Agricultural Census, 1860, Henrico County, Western Division.

6. Thomas H. Ellis to Rev. D. G. C. Butts, undated typescript, James Lyons Papers, VM; Hudson Strode, *Jefferson Davis* (New York, 1959), 2:378; *Journal of the Congress of the Confederate States of America, 1861–1865* (Washington, D.C., 1904), 5:469.

7. James H. Bailey, ed., *Henrico Home Front, 1861–1865* (Richmond, 1963), 96, 172, 226; John Beauchamp Jones, *A Rebel War Clerk's Diary*, ed. Earl Schenk Miers (New York, 1958), 343; *RD*, July 8, 1863, March 8, 1864; Hamilton J. Eckenrode, "Negroes in Richmond in 1864," *VMHB* 64 (July 1938): 199; Gurney Holland Reid, "The Negro in Richmond on the Eve of and during the Civil War" (M.A. thesis, College of William and Mary, 1936), 34.

8. *RD*, Feb. 19, 20, March 16, 1864. Lyons's 1860 list of slaves included a seven-year-old boy named Wilson, probably the son of the defendant. For references to William Mitchell, see Leslie Winston Smith, "Richmond during Presidential Reconstruction, 1865–1867" (Ph.D. diss., University of Virginia, 1974), 315.

9. *RD*, Feb. 29, March 16, 1864. According to the *Dispatch*, Wilson belonged to Joseph Angle, who had him released on $500 bail after his appearance in the mayor's court (*RD*, Feb. 25, 1864).

10. *RD*, March 17, 1864; *Richmond Daily Enquirer*, March 17, 1864.

11. Mary Chesnut, *Mary Chesnut's Civil War*, ed. C. Vann Woodward (New Haven, 1981), 587.

12. Imogene Lyons to Mary Elizabeth Wise, April 28, 1864, Mary Elizabeth Lyons Wise Correspondence, box 4, Wise Family Papers, VHS.

13. Leon Litwack, *Been in the Storm So Long: The Aftermath of Slavery* (New York, 1981), 167–70; Simmons, *Men of Mark*, 201–5; Wise, *Lion's Skin*, 39; Smith, "Richmond during Presidential Reconstruction," 176.

14. Scott, *Houses of Old Richmond*, 198–201; James Grant Wilson, *Thackeray in the United States* (New York, 1904), 1:255; John A. Cutchins, *Memories of Old Richmond, 1881–1944* (White Marsh, Va., 1973), 169–70; *RP*, Jan. 17, 1903. The house was torn down in 1937.

15. Simmons, *Men of Mark*, 202–3; *RP*, Jan. 20, 1900, July 9, 1921.

16. *RP*, Aug. 7, 1915; Wise, *Lion's Skin*, 40–1; Simmons, *Men of Mark*, 201; Bryan, *Joseph Bryan*, 231.

17. Register of Signatures of Depositors in Branches of the Freedman's Savings and Trust Company, 1869–1874, Richmond Branch, 5587, NA (microfilm, UVA); Carl R. Osthaus, *Freedmen, Philanthropy, and Fraud: A History of the Freedman's Savings Bank* (Urbana, Ill., 1976).

18. *RP*, April 1, 1893. Mitchell was identified as "black" in the 1870, 1880, and 1900 censuses and "mulatto" in 1910 and 1920, after he had accumulated considerable wealth.

19. *RP*, July 4, 1891.

20. Simmons, *Men of Mark*, 201; *RP*, Dec. 17, 1904.

21. *RP*, Dec. 20, 1913, Feb. 3, 1923; *Richmond Virginia Citizen*, cited in *RP*, Jan. 10, 1914; Cheryl Thurber, "The Development of the Mammy Image and Mythology," in *Southern Women: Histories and Identities*, ed. by Virginia Bernhard et al. (Columbia, Mo., 1992), 87–108. Rebecca Mitchell's grave is in Evergreen Cemetery in Richmond.

22. *RD*, Dec. 11, 14, 1865.

23. *RD*, Dec. 18, 28, 1865.

24. O. Brown to Lt. H. S. Merrell, Jan. 23, 1866, Letters and Telegrams Sent, John and William Mitchell, Jan. 24, 1866, Register of Letters and Telegrams Received, Records of the U.S. Bureau of Refugees, Freedmen, and Abandoned Lands, Virginia, NA (microfilm, UVA); Smith, "Richmond during Presidential Reconstruction," 315.

25. Dr. W. W. Parker, quoted in *RD*, July 27, 1893.

26. *RP*, March 28, 1891, Oct. 28, 1893. In a 1908 bond application, Mitchell said his father was a railroad porter. He gave his mother's Richmond address but no address for his father (bond application, 1908, in Commonwealth v. Mechanics Savings Bank, 1944, RCH). Rebecca Mitchell's death certificate (Dec. 12, 1913) describes her as widowed. See also Mitchell's conversation with Jesse Binga of Chicago as reported in *RP*, Sept. 25, 1915.

27. On Richmond during Reconstruction, see John Thomas O'Brien, *From Bondage to Citizenship: The Richmond Black Community, 1865–1867* (New York, 1990); Michael B. Chesson, *Richmond after the War, 1865–1890* (Richmond, 1981); Peter Rachleff, *Black Labor in Richmond, 1865–1890* (Urbana, Ill., 1989); Elsa Barkley Brown, "Uncle Ned's Children: Negotiating Community and Freedom in Postemancipation Richmond" (Ph.D. diss., Kent State University, 1994).

28. Charles F. Irons, "And All These Things Shall Be Added unto You: The First African Baptist Church, Richmond, 1841–1865," *Virginia Cavalcade* 47 (Winter 1998): 26–35; W. Harrison Daniel, "Virginia Baptists and the Negro in the Antebellum Era," *JNH* 56 (Jan. 1971): 1–4; W. T. Johnson, *Historical Reminiscences of the First Baptist Church* (Richmond, 1903), 9–16; Robert Ryland, "Origin and History of the First African Church," in *The First Century of the First Baptist Church of Richmond, Virginia, 1780–1880* (Richmond, 1880), 255, 258–59; Blanche Sydnor White, *First Baptist Church, Richmond, 1780–1955: One Hundred and Seventy-Five Years of Service to God and Man* (Richmond, 1955), 44, 96–97.

29. Ryland, "Origin and History of the First African Church," 255, 258–60; Ryland, *The Scripture Catechism for Colored People* (Richmond, 1848); O'Brien, *From Bondage to Citizenship*, 54–55; White, *First Baptist Church*, 83.

30. "Rev. Jas. H. Holmes Once a Student at Richmond Theological Seminary," *BHMM* 20 (Jan. 1898): 8; Lewis G. Jordan, *Negro Baptist History U.S.A.* (Nashville, 1930), 14; Simmons, *Men of Mark*, 460–62.

31. A. A. Taylor, *The Negro in the Reconstruction of Virginia* (Washington, D.C., 1926), 198; Edward King, *The Great South* (New York, 1969), 2:630; Charles H. Corey, *A History of the Richmond Theological Seminary with Reminiscences of Thirty Years' Work among the Colored People of the South* (Richmond, 1895), 209–11.

32. *RP*, March 14, June 20, 1891, May 17, 1902, Nov. 26, 1910; Wendell P. Dabney, *Maggie L. Walker and the Independent Order of St. Luke* (Cincinnati, 1927), 30; Johnson, *Historical Reminiscences*, 14. Mitchell's name appears in the list of those baptized during the period June 4–9, 1878, First African Baptist Church, Minute Books, Church Records Collection, LVA (microfilm).

33. James Brummell Earnest, *Religious Development of the Negro in Virginia* (Charlottesville, Va., 1914), 162, 271; Anthony Binga Jr., "The Social Conditions of the Freedmen," *BHMM* 2 (March 1880): 41–42; Binga, *Sermons on Several Occasions*, intro. J. E. Jones

(Richmond, 1889), ix–xi; Binga, *Sermons and Addresses Delivered by A. Binga, Jr.,* (Richmond, 1887), 12; Binga, "Autobiography of Anthony Binga Jr.," Richmond, 1917?, LVA; *RP,* Dec. 29, 1894. On the importance of black-run private schools, see Chesson, *Richmond after the War,* 100; O'Brien, *From Bondage to Citizenship,* 403–7; James D. Anderson, *The Education of Blacks in the South, 1860–1935* (Chapel Hill, N.C., 1988), 5–31.

34. *Virginia School Report, 1872,* 40, 196; *RD,* June 12, 1876, Feb. 6, 1877; *Richmond Afro-American,* Oct. 22, 1938. Much detailed information about the schools can be found in city and state school reports, school board minutes, and Martha Warren Owens, "The Development of Public Schools for Negroes in Richmond, Virginia, 1865–1900" (M.S. thesis, Virginia State College, 1947), and Rebekah Roberts Sharp, "A History of the Richmond Public School System, 1869–1958" (M.S. thesis, University of Richmond, 1958).

35. Samuel L. Horst, *Education for Manhood: The Education of Blacks in Virginia during the Civil War* (Lanham, Md., 1987), 224; William T. Alderson, "The Freedmen's Bureau and Negro Education in Virginia," *North Carolina Historical Review* 24 (Jan. 1952): 76; Owens, "Public Schools for Negroes," 55–56; Mary Patterson Manly (daughter-in-law of R. M. Manly) to Virginius Douglass Johnston, May 12, 1933, photocopy, VHS.

36. Alderson, "The Freedmen's Bureau and Negro Education in Virginia," 75–76; Betty Mansfield, "That Fateful Class: Black Teachers of Virginia's Freedmen, 1861–1882" (Ph.D. diss., Catholic University of America, 1980), 262–63; Wendell Phillips Dabney, "Rough Autobiographical Sketch of His Boyhood Years," 32, Cincinnati Public Library, Cincinnati; *Virginia School Report, 1871,* 205; John W. Alvord, *Fourth Semi-Annual Report on Schools and Finances for Freedmen* (Washington, D.C., 1867), 17; James M. McPherson, *The Abolitionist Legacy: From Reconstruction to the NAACP* (Princeton, N.J., 1975), 191–92.

37. *RD,* June 21, 1873, June 8, 9, 1876. On the school's declining reputation, see L. W. Betts, "Richmond of Today," *Outlook* 65 (Aug. 25, 1900): 972–73; Thomas J. Woofter, *Negro Problems in Cities* (Garden City, N.Y., 1928), 208–9.

38. Simmons, *Men of Mark,* 203–4; *RD,* June 13, 1877, June 11, 1878, June 11, 1879, June 15, 1880, June 15, 1881.

39. D. Webster Davis, *Idle Moments* (Baltimore, 1895), 73; Davis, "Negro Ideals: A Series of Lectures for the Hampton Summer Normal Institute Held at Hampton Normal School, July 1–26, 1902," D. Webster Davis Papers, VHS.

40. Dabney, *Maggie L. Walker,* 23; Dabney, "Rough Autobiographical Sketch," 32.

41. Simmons, *Men of Mark,* 202; W. E. B. Du Bois, *Mansart Builds a School* (New York, 1959), 169; James H. Brewer, "The Ghosts of Jackson Ward," *Negro History Bulletin* 24 (Nov. 1958): 27.

42. *RD,* June 15, 1881; *Twelfth Annual Report of the [Richmond] School Board . . . for the Scholastic Year Ending 1880–81* (Richmond, 1882), 69.

2. "COLORED TEACHERS FOR COLORED SCHOOLS"

1. *Virginia School Report, 1882–83,* 50–51. The average white male teacher in Richmond earned $106 a month, black males made $43, white females $43, and black females $41. These figures were skewed, however, because the salaries of Head teachers—or principals—were included in the averages. Payroll ledgers indicate that classroom teachers received the same salaries regardless of race or gender, but only white males were promoted to principal; a slight bonus was given for experience (Richmond City, School Board, Payroll Records, 1871–75, LVA).

2. George Washington Cable, *The Negro Question*, ed. Arlin Turner (Garden City, N.Y., 1958), 129; Taylor, *Negro in the Reconstruction of Virginia*, 151; *Virginia School Report, 1880–81*, 14, 20.

3. *RP*, Aug. 6, 20, 1892; *RD*, April 2, 1891; Richmond *Virginia Star*, July 24, 1880, quoted in Taylor, *Negro in the Reconstruction of Virginia*, 160; H. G. Charlton, "The Evolution of the Richmond Public School System with Reminiscences," a paper read at the Principals' Conference, June 3, 1925, box 3, Mary-Cooke Branch Munford Papers, 1881–1935, LVA; Sutton Griggs, *Imperium in Imperio* (1899; rept. New York, 1969), 4–15.

4. Biographical information is widely scattered, but see *Washington Bee*, May 30, 1885; August Meier, *Negro Thought in America, 1880–1915: Racial Ideologies in the Age of Booker T. Washington* (Ann Arbor, Mich., 1963), 174–76; *BTW Papers* 7:30; Daniel Barclay Williams, *Freedom and Progress and Other Choice Addresses*, intro. John Mitchell Jr. (Petersburg, Va., 1890), 7–18; Joan R. Sherman, "Daniel Webster Davis: A Black Virginia Poet in the Age of Accommodation," *VMHB* 81 (Oct. 1973): 457–78; obituary, James Hugo Johnston Sr., *RP*, April 18, 1914; Owens, "Public Schools for Negroes," 57–60; Veronica Alease Davis, "Rosa L. Dixon Bowser," *DVB* 2:160–62.

5. *RD*, May 21, 1879; *Petersburg Lancet*, Sept. 2, 23, Oct. 28, 1882; Minutes of School Board Trustees, Fredericksburg, Va., Aug. 1, 1879, Oct. 8, 1880, LVA; Howard N. Rabinowitz, "Half a Loaf: The Shift from White to Black Teachers in the Negro Schools of the Urban South, 1865–1890," *JSH* 40 (Nov. 1974): 565–94; Jane Dailey, *Before Jim Crow: The Politics of Race in Postemancipation Virginia* (Chapel Hill, N.C., 2000), 69–76. For a defense of integrated schools by a black Richmonder, see Walter H. Brooks, "Non-Proscriptive Schools," Washington, D.C., *People's Advocate*, May 26, 1883.

6. *RD*, July 10, 1880; Richmond *Virginia Star*, July 24, 1880; Mansfield, "That Fateful Class: Black Teachers of Virginia's Freedmen," 342–44.

7. *RD*, July 10, 1880, Sept. 1, 1892; *Thirteenth Annual Report of the [Richmond] School Board . . . for the Scholastic Year Ending 1881–82* (Richmond, 1883), 45.

8. Adams, "John Mitchell Jr.," 296; *Compendium of the Tenth Census (June 1, 1880)* (Washington, D.C., 1883), 1:425; *Virginia School Report, 1881–82*, 11, 14, 21; School Board Minutes, Fredericksburg, Oct. 8, 1880, Oct. 5, 1881, Jan. 18, 1882.

9. School Board Minutes, Fredericksburg, Oct. 8, 1880; Population Schedules of the Tenth Census of the United States, 1880, Fredericksburg, Virginia (microfilm), NA.

10. School Board Minutes, Fredericksburg, Sept. 15, 1881; *RP*, April 23, 1921; "Men of the Month," *Crisis* 22 (Aug. 1921): 166; Monroe Nathan Work, ed., *Negro Year Book, 1931–32*, 1.

11. *RP*, June 15, 1915.

12. School Board Minutes, Fredericksburg, Dec. 14, 1881.

13. Ibid., Dec. 15, 1881.

14. Ibid., Jan. 11, 1882.

15. Ibid., Jan. 11, 18, 1882, Aug. 14, 16, 1883.

16. Ibid., Sept. 1, Oct. 29, 1882.

17. Ibid., Sept. 13, 1882.

18. Important secondary accounts of the Readjuster movement include: Dailey, *Before Jim Crow*; Carl Degler, *The Other South* (New York, 1974); James Tice Moore, *Two Paths to the New South: The Virginia Debt Controversy, 1870–1883* (Lexington, Ky., 1974); Charles Clinton Pearson, *The Readjuster Movement in Virginia* (New Haven, 1917); Nelson Morehouse Blake, *William Mahone of Virginia: Soldier and Political Insurgent* (Richmond, 1935); Charles E. Wynes, *Race Relations in Virginia, 1870–1902* (Charlottesville, Va., 1961); Ray-

mond H. Pulley, *Old Virginia Restored: An Interpretation of the Progressive Impulse, 1870–1930* (Charlottesville, Va., 1968).

19. *Virginia School Report, 1883–84*, 106; James T. Moore, "Black Militancy in Readjuster Virginia, 1879–1883," *JSH* 41 (May 1975): 179.

20. Joseph E. Jones, quoted in *RD*, March 22, 1883; Wise, *Lion's Skin*, 334–35; *RD*, Feb. 23, May 13, 1883; *Richmond State*, May 12, 14, 1883; *Mahone's Game*, handbill in Scrapbook 31 (1883), William Mahone Papers, Duke; *New York Globe*, May 26, 1883.

21. Theresa M. Guzman-Stokes, "A Flag and a Family," *Virginia Cavalcade* 47 (Spring 1998): 52–63; *Richmond State*, June 1, 1883; *RD*, Feb. 20, 1883; Dabney, *Maggie L. Walker*, 20; Michael B. Chesson, "Richmond's Black Councilmen, 1871–1896," in *Southern Black Leaders of the Reconstruction Era*, ed. Howard N. Rabinowitz (Urbana, Ill., 1982), 201.

22. *Richmond State*, June 1, 1883; Daniel Barclay Williams, *A Sketch of the Life and Times of Captain R. A. Paul* (Richmond, 1885); C. A. Bryce, quoted in *RTD*, May 8, 1921.

23. *RD*, May 24, June 28, 1883; *Richmond State*, Jan. 29, May 25, 1883; *Petersburg Lancet*, July 28, 1883; *New York Globe*, June 2, 1883.

24. *Virginia School Report, 1883–84*, 21; Owens, "Public Schools for Negroes," 50–51; W. B. T. Williams, "Colored Public Schools in Southern Cities," Hampton Negro Conference, *Ninth Annual Report* (1905), 37; Rabinowitz, "Half a Loaf," 592; *New York Globe*, Oct. 20, 1883, May 17, 1884; Dabney, "Rough Autobiographical Sketch," 8.

25. Richmond *Virginia Star*, Nov. 18, 1882; *New York Globe*, July 28, 1883, Sept. 8, 1887; *Petersburg Lancet*, Aug. 4, 1883; W. P. Burrell and E. D. Johnson, *Twenty-Five Years History of the Grand Fountain of the United Order of True Reformers* (Richmond, 1900), 391–95.

26. Emma Lou Thornbrough, *T. Thomas Fortune: Militant Journalist* (Chicago, 1972), 35–67; Fortune, *Black and White: Land, Labor, and Politics in the South*, preface by James M. McPherson (1884; rept. New York, 1968), 6; *New York Globe*, April 28, 1883. (The *Globe* was later renamed the *Freeman* and then the *Age*.)

27. *New York Freeman*, Nov. 20, 1886; David Levering Lewis, *W. E. B. Du Bois: Biography of a Race* (New York, 1993), 38–39. R. T. Hill served as correspondent from May through Sept. 1883; Mitchell held the position from Sept. 22, 1883, through Dec. 1884; his successor was Marietta Chiles's brother R. J. Chiles.

28. *New York Globe*, Sept. 22, 1883; *RD*, Sept. 14, 15, 1883.

29. *New York Globe*, Nov. 3, 1883, Jan. 26, Feb. 16, 1884.

30. Ibid., Jan. 5, 19, 26, Feb. 2, 16, 23, March 8, April 5, 1884; James T. Haley, *Afro-American Encyclopedia* (Nashville, 1895), 206.

31. *New York Globe*, June 23, July 7, Sept. 29, Dec. 1, 1883, Feb. 16, 1884; *New York Freeman*, Dec. 6, 1884, Feb. 28, 1885; *RP*, Feb. 21, 1885; Rachleff, *Black Labor in Richmond*, 112–13.

32. *New York Globe*, June 30, Aug. 11, Dec. 8, 1883, Jan. 12, Feb. 9, March 1, 15, May 24, June 14, 28, 1884, July 5, 1884; *RD*, May 27, 1884; *RP*, Feb. 21, 1885.

33. Information about the Chiles-Mitchell affair is based on conversations with elderly black Richmonders and members of the Mitchell and Chiles families. For a rare explicit reference, see typescript of interview, March 13, 1981, Anthony J. Binga and Bernetta Young Plummer, 79–80, Maggie L. Walker Oral History Project, MWHS.

34. Howard P. Chudacoff, *The Age of the Bachelor: Creating an American Subculture* (Princeton, N.J., 1999), chap. 2; *RP*, March 16, June 15, 1895.

35. City directories indicate that two men named William Mitchell lived in Richmond during this period, making it impossible to know for certain which was the *Planet* editor's uncle. Naming patterns support the connection: John Mitchell Sr. named his second son

Thomas William Mitchell; William Mitchell and Elizabeth Draper named their only child John Mitchell. On Walker's childhood, see Dabney, *Maggie L. Walker;* Muriel Miller Branch and Dorothy Marie Rice, *Pennies to Dollars: The Story of Maggie Lena Walker* (North Haven, Conn., 1997); and unpublished materials at the MWHS.

36. *New York Globe,* April 28, 1883.

3. FOUNDING THE *PLANET*

1. *New York Globe,* Nov. 24, Dec. 15, 1883, Jan. 19, 1884; Washington, D.C., *People's Advocate,* Dec. 29, 1883.

2. *New York Globe,* Dec. 15, 1883; Harrisburg, Pa., *State Journal,* Dec. 13, 1883; Luther Porter Jackson, *Negro Office-Holders in Virginia, 1865–1895* (Norfolk, Va., 1945), 57; Etta Rebecca Williams, "Edwin Archer Randolph, LL.B., Rediscovered," *Richmond Quarterly* 3 (Spring 1981): 46–48; Register of Signatures of Depositors in Branches of the Freedman's Savings and Trust Company, 1869–1874, Richmond Branch, 2755, 2939, NA (microfilm, UVA).

3. *New York Globe,* Nov. 24, 1883. Much information about the founding of the *Planet* can be found in affidavits filed throughout 1891 with the judge of the chancery court in R. A. Paul et al. v. John Mitchell Jr. et al., CD28 EF468, Chancery Court, RCH.

4. Emma Lou Thornbrough, "American Negro Newspapers, 1880–1914," *Business History Review* 40 (Winter 1966): 467–90; Penn, *Afro-American Press;* Betty Lou K. Rathbun, "Rise of the Modern American Negro Press, 1880–1914" (Ph.D. diss., State University of New York at Buffalo, 1978); S. N. D. North, "History and Present Condition of the Newspaper and Periodical Press of the United States," *Tenth Census of the United States* (Washington, D.C., 1884), 8:79–177; Frank Luther Mott, *American Journalism: A History of Newspapers in the United States through 250 Years, 1690 to 1940* (New York, 1941), 411, 478–98, 508, 601; Thomas D. Clark, *The Southern Country Editor* (New York, 1948), 22–81.

5. John W. Cromwell quoted in Simmons, *Men of Mark,* 642; *New York Globe,* May 10, 1884; Richmond *Virginia Star,* Nov. 18, 1882; Henry Lewis Suggs, ed., *The Black Press in the South, 1865–1979* (Westport, Conn., 1983), 15; Thornbrough, "American Negro Newspapers," 472.

6. *New York Globe,* Dec. 15, 1883; depositions of plaintiffs, in Paul v. Mitchell, 1891.

7. *New York Globe,* Nov. 24, Dec. 1, 1883.

8. *Acts of the General Assembly, 1883–1884* (Richmond, 1884), 344; *New York Globe,* March 29, 1884; Dailey, *Before Jim Crow,* chap. 3.

9. *RD,* June 17, 27, 28, 1884; *New York Globe,* July 5, 1884; *RP,* Oct. 16, 1915; *RNL,* Aug. 25, 1953; *RTD,* May 20, 1959; *Washington Grit,* July 12, 1884. Not until 1915 were blacks allowed to teach at Richmond Normal, where salaries were higher and the curriculum was more challenging. For a fictionalized account of the *Planet* founding, see Griggs, *Imperium in Imperio,* 38–47, 112–13, 125–27.

10. Deposition of D. B. Williams, March 3, 1891, in Paul v. Mitchell, 1891; *New York Globe,* Aug. 16, 1884; *Petersburg Lancet,* Sept. 20, 1884.

11. Simmons, *Men of Mark,* 317–18; *New York Globe,* July 19, 1884.

12. *Indianapolis Freeman* quoted in *RP,* Aug. 30, 1890.

13. *New York Globe,* Sept. 20, 1884; *New York Freeman,* Dec. 6, 1884; demurrer of John Mitchell Jr., Feb. 3, 1891, in Paul v. Mitchell, 1891.

14. *Petersburg Lancet,* Dec. 13, 1884; Mitchell to Magnus L. Robinson, March 12, 1892,

Magnus L. Robinson Papers, UVA; Burrell and Johnson, *Twenty-Five Years History of the True Reformers,* 436–37; Clark, *Southern Country Editor,* 35, 44.

15. *RP,* Jan. 31, 1885, clipping in First African Baptist Church, Minute Books, Jan. 1885, Church Records Collection, LVA (microfilm).

16. *RP* quoted in *New York Freeman,* April 4, 1885; *RP* clipping in *Planet* to Mahone, April 28, 1888, William Mahone Papers, Duke; *RP* quoted in *New York Freeman,* Sept. 17, 1887.

17. *RP* quoted in *New York Freeman,* July 23, 1887; *New York World* quoted in Penn, *Afro-American Press,* 183; Simmons, *Men of Mark,* 318–21; *New York Freeman,* March 26, Aug. 6, 1887.

18. Cromwell quoted in Simmons, *Men of Mark,* 642; John Mitchell Jr. et al. to O'Ferrall, Sept. 12, 1894, Charles T. O'Ferrall Executive Papers, LVA.

19. *RP,* April 11, 1891; demurrer of John Mitchell Jr., Feb. 3, 1891, in Paul v. Mitchell, 1891.

20. The location of the *Planet* office and occupants of the Swan Tavern can be found in city directories. See also Adams, "John Mitchell Jr.," 298; Mary Wingfield Scott, *Old Richmond Neighborhoods* (Richmond, 1950), 93, 97.

21. Editor, *Baltimore Home Protector,* quoted in *RP,* Sept. 13, 1890; *RP,* June 18, 1892, March 5, 1895. For an early depiction of the *Planet* logo, see receipt, Aug. 13, 1889, Papers of John Adams, box 1, UVA.

22. W. N. Hartshorn, ed., *An Era of Progress and Promise, 1863–1910* (Boston, 1910), 437; Penn, *Afro-American Press,* 184; *RP,* June 18, 1892.

23. William S. Rossiter, "Printing and Publishing," *Twelfth Census of the United States* (Washington, D.C., 1902), vol. 9, pt. 3, pp. 1039–40; *New York Age,* March 28, 1891.

24. *RP,* Feb. 21, 1885, March 5, 1895, June 26, 1900.

25. O. M. Steward to Mahone, April 7, 1883, W. C. Chase and C. C. Stewart to Mahone, March ?, 1883, William Mahone Papers.

26. *New York Freeman,* Feb. 4, 1888; *New York Age,* March 16, 1889; *RP,* Dec. 4, 1897.

27. Rathbun, "Rise of the Modern American Negro Press," 182.

28. The circulation of the *Planet* was reported in annual newspaper directories published by Geo. P. Rowell and N. W. Ayer and Sons.

29. *RP,* Sept. 12, 1891, March 31, May 5, Nov. 17, 1894, Aug. 17, 1895. Mitchell's property holdings can be traced in the real property tax books for Richmond, 1885–1929, LVA. Chancery Court records, RCH, document the terms under which he purchased presses: Planet Publishing Company to John Dunlap, Deed of Trust, 135C382, July 28, 1888, and John Mitchell Jr. to Campbell Print Press and Manufacturing Company, Mortgage, 146A215, June 11, 1892. Court records also reveal creditors' suits against him, to which he sometimes responded that he was entirely without funds. See Robert Patterson v. John Mitchell Jr., Law Order Book 19 (March 10, 1892): 133, Circuit Court, RCH.

30. *RP,* Jan. 17, April 11, Dec. 5, 1891.

31. Albion W. Tourgée to Mitchell, Aug. 30, 1891, Albion Winegar Tourgée Papers, 1801–1924, Chautauqua County Historical Society, Westfield, N.Y. (microfilm, UNC); Otto H. Olsen, *Carpetbagger's Crusade: The Life of Albion Winigar Tourgée* (Baltimore, 1965), 310–11; Edward W. Blyden to John E. Bruce, Sept. 20, 1896, in *Calendar of the Manuscripts in the Schomburg Collection of Negro Literature* (New York, 1942), 212; Magnus L. Robinson to William E. Chandler, May 2, 1892, William E. Chandler Papers, LC; U.S., Congress, 50th Cong., 1st sess., Aug. 23, 1888, *Congressional Record* 19:7876; Stanley P. Hirshon, *Farewell to the Bloody Shirt: Northern Republicans and the Southern Negro, 1877–1893* (Bloomington, Ind., 1962), 237. A copy of Mitchell's list of lynchings, published in pamphlet form, can be found in the John Mercer Langston Personal Papers, Fisk University (microfilm, LC).

32. Rathbun, "Rise of the Modern American Negro Press," 104–16; *Washington Bee,* May 1, Aug. 7, 1886, June 18, Aug. 20, 1887, March 9, 1889; *New York Freeman,* Aug. 10, Sept. 17, 1887.

33. *Washington Bee,* Oct. 8, 1892, Sept. 30, 1893, Sept. 22, 1894; *New York Age,* March 28, 1891; *RP,* Jan. 10, 1891, Oct. 8, l892; Rayford W. Logan, *The Betrayal of the Negro: From Rutherford B. Hayes to Woodrow Wilson* (New York, 1965), 333. On Mitchell's involvement in the founding of T. Thomas Fortune's Afro-American League, see *New York Freeman,* June 18, July 2, 1887.

34. *RP,* Feb. 14, 1891; deposition of plaintiffs, Paul v. Mitchell, 1891.

35. *RP,* July 18, 1891, April 2, 1892. On earlier lawsuits, see *New York Age,* Dec. 1, 1888.

36. *RP,* May 31, Oct. 18, 1890, Feb. 15, 1913; *Washington Bee,* Oct. 18, 1890; *RD,* Oct. 14, 16–18, 1890; "The Confederate Flag Was Conspicuously Displayed," in *A Richmond Reader,* ed. Maurice Duke and Daniel P. Jordan (Chapel Hill, N.C., 1883), 165–68.

37. Gunnar Myrdal, *An American Dilemma: The Negro Problem and Modern Democracy* (New York, 1969), 2:910; *RP,* Jan. 3, 1891; editor, *Indianapolis Freeman,* quoted in *RP,* Aug. 30, 1890.

4. "LYNCH LAW MUST GO!"

1. *RP,* Feb. 14, 1891.

2. Cable, *The Negro Question,* 67.

3. *RP* quoted in *New York Freeman,* July 23, 1887; *RP,* Feb. 8, 1890. Mitchell drew a cartoon to illustrate lynching but replaced it in 1891 with a photograph from a Clifton Forge lynching.

4. *Planet* issues do not survive for 1886, but this story is told by a number of writers. See Simmons, *Men of Mark,* 205; Adams, "John Mitchell Jr.," 296–97. Contemporary accounts appear in *New York Freeman,* May 19, 1886, and *RD,* May 7, 1886. See also Mitchell's later reminiscences in *RP,* May 15, 1915. (Mitchell slightly paraphrased the Shakespeare quotation.)

5. W. Fitzhugh Brundage, *Lynching in the New South: Georgia and Virginia, 1880–1930* (Urbana, Ill., 1993), 165; Brundage, "'To Howl Loudly': John Mitchell Jr. and His Campaign against Lynching in Virginia," *Canadian Review of American Studies* 3 (Winter 1991): 325–41.

6. Petersburg *Daily Index Appeal,* May 4, 1889.

7. Commonwealth v. Simon Walker, May 14–15, 1889, County Court Order Book, Chesterfield County Courthouse. See also *Petersburg Daily Index Appeal,* May 4, 15, 16, 1889; *RT,* May 16, 1889; *RD,* Sept. 18, 1889. The jurors' names appear in the county court order book, but they were not identified by race. The 1889 personal property tax books for Chesterfield County (LVA) indicate that at least ten of the twelve jurors were white. The remaining two were not listed in the tax books, and their race is unknown.

8. The fullest account of Mitchell's involvement in the case appears in *RP,* Nov. 16, 1889, LVA. (Thanks to James B. Walthall of Richmond who alerted me to the survival of this issue and John T. Kneebone who located it at the LVA.) Mitchell published a pamphlet about the case that has not been found but probably was the basis for the account in Adams, "John Mitchell Jr.," 297. There is a broadside at Duke University: Emergence of Advertising in America: Broadsides, Simon Walker (*Planet,* 1889). The other major source about the case is a collection of letters and documents in Walker Papers, Nov. 1889, Executive Papers of the Secretary of the Commonwealth, LVA.

9. *RD,* Sept. 27, 1889; *RP,* Nov. 16, 1889.

10. *RP,* Jan. 5, 1895.

11. *RP,* Nov. 16, 1889.

12. Mitchell et al. to Lee, n.d., S. J. Sutton et al. to Lee, n.d., C. B. W. Gordon (pastor, First Baptist Church, Petersburg) to Lee, Sept. 23, 1889, Richard Spiller (pastor, First Baptist Church, Hampton), to Clopton, Oct. 15, 1889, Yorke Jones (pastor, Central Presbyterian Church, Petersburg) to Lee, Oct. 2, 1889, P. F. Morris (pastor, Court St. Baptist Church, Lynchburg) to Clopton, Oct. 15, 1889, W. F. Graham (pastor, Loyal St. Baptist Church, Danville) to Clopton, Oct. 16, 1889, E. F. Eggleston (pastor, Holbrook St. Presbyterian Church, Danville) to Clopton, Oct. 13, 1889, Henry Williams Jr. (pastor, Gilfield Baptist Church, Petersburg) to Lee, n.d., J. H. Johnston (president, Virginia Normal and Collegiate Institute) et al. to Lee, Oct. 2, 1889, Walker Papers; *RP,* Nov. 16, 1889.

13. Jurors et al. to Lee, Oct. 1, 1889, Philip V. Cogbill, Commonwealth's Attorney, to Lee, Sept. 21, 1889, Ellyson S. Robinson to Lee, Sept. 25, Oct. 7, 1889, Clopton to Lee, Sept. 21, 1889, Walker Papers.

14. *RP,* Nov. 16, 1889.

15. *RD,* Nov. 8, 1889; Allen W. Moger, *Virginia: Bourbonism to Byrd, 1870–1925* (Charlottesville, Va., 1968), 65; Lee to Clopton, Sept. 19, 1889, "Citizens" to Lee, Oct. 7, 1889, "Citizen" to Lee, Oct. 3, 1889, John W. Morris to Lee, Oct. 6, 1889, Frank G. Ruffin to Clopton, Oct. 18, 1889, Walker Papers.

16. *RP,* Nov. 16, 1889. The only mention of Mitchell's carrying weapons to Chesterfield Courthouse appears in Adams, "John Mitchell Jr.," 297.

17. *RP,* June 13, 1891, Jan. 30, 1892.

18. Penn, *Afro-American Press,* 186. Penn identified Wells by her pen name "Iola." On lynchings and gender issues, see Gail Bederman, "'Civilization,' the Decline of Middle-Class Manliness, and Ida B. Wells's Antilynching Campaign (1892–94)," *Radical History Review* 52 (Winter 1992): 4–30; Linda O. McMurry, *To Keep the Waters Troubled: The Life of Ida B. Wells* (New York, 1998); Jacquelyn Dowd Hall, *Revolt against Chivalry: Jessie Daniel Ames and the Women's Campaign against Lynching* (New York, 1993).

19. *RP,* Jan. 4, 1890, May 21, 1892, Sept. 7, 1895, Feb. 1, 1896. Mitchell was certainly not alone in urging blacks to defend themselves, though few editors became so personally involved in antilynching campaigns. White liberals from the North were ambivalent at best about black retaliation against lynchers (McPherson, *Abolitionist Legacy,* 306–7). Mitchell always distinguished between self-defense, which he advocated, and retaliation, which he did not (*RP,* Feb. 29, 1896, describing a speech in Hartford, Conn.).

20. Jacqueline Goggin, *Carter G. Woodson: A Life in Black History* (Baton Rouge, La., 1993), 10. Some of the most cogent observations about respectability appear in Evelyn Brooks Higginbotham, *Righteous Discontent: The Women's Movement in the Black Baptist Church, 1880–1920* (Cambridge, Mass., 1993), 13–14, 185–229.

21. *RP,* July 22, 1893.

22. *RP,* July 29, Aug. 5, 16, Sept. 30, Oct. 7, 21, Nov. 25, 1893, April 7, June 21, 1894; Brundage, *Lynching,* 165; Adams, "John Mitchell Jr.," 297. Jenkins was first acquitted on the principal charges but was fined $300 for distributing liquor without a license, more than he could possibly pay. He was released after Mitchell threatened to appeal to the governor for a pardon and further embarrass Suffolk officials.

23. *RP,* July 22, 1893.

24. *RP,* July 1, 1892, July 22, 1893. Brundage has demonstrated that the surge of lynchings in Virginia during McKinney's administration was caused by a "spasm of violence" in the rapidly industrializing mountains of the southwest, but Mitchell failed to detect this

pattern (*Lynching*, chap. 5, 140–41, 281–83.) Brundage has produced by far the most accurate list of Virginia lynchings, although even he omits the 1886 lynching of Richard Walker in Charlotte County.

25. Brundage, *Lynching*, 169–78; Minor T. Weisiger, "Charles T. O'Ferrall: 'Gray Eagle' from the Valley," *The Governors of Virginia, 1860–1978*, ed. Edward Younger and James Tice Moore (Charlottesville, Va., 1982), 135–46; Charles T. O'Ferrall, *Forty Years of Active Service* (New York, 1904); O'Ferrall obituary, *RTD*, Sept. 23, 1905; "Charles T. O'Ferrall," *DAB* 13:633–34.

26. Secondary accounts of the Roanoke riot rely heavily on the initial reports of the *Roanoke Times*. For more on the riot, see Ann Field Alexander, "'Like an Evil Wind': The Roanoke Riot and the Lynching of Thomas Smith," *VMHB* 100 (April 1992): 173–206.

27. *RP*, Sept. 30, 1893. For evidence of Smith's innocence, see *RP*, Aug. 11, 1894, and "The Horizon," *Crisis* 12 (Oct. 1916): 300.

28. *House Journal, 1893–94*, 52–54; *RP*, Sept. 30, Oct. 7, 1893.

29. *RP*, Sept. 30, Oct. 7, 1893; *RD*, Jan. 2, May 1, 1894; O'Ferrall to Sheriff, Clarke County, Berryville, Va., July 8, 1895, Thomas S. Keller to O'Ferrall, May 2, 1894, Charles T. O'Ferrall Executive Papers, LVA.

30. *RP*, July 20, 1895; O'Ferrall to J. K. M. Norton, Alexandria, April 23, 1897, O'Ferrall Papers; *House Journal, 1894–95*, 36–37. O'Ferrall ordered an investigation of the Alexandria lynching that led to a forty-one-page report. See also Edward Leigh Pell, "The Prevention of Lynch-Law Epidemics," *Review of Reviews* 17 (March 1898): 321–25.

31. *RP*, Feb. 23, 1895.

32. *RP*, Feb. 9, March 23, 1895, Aug. 15, 1896, June 12, 1897.

33. Samuel N. Pincus, *The Virginia Supreme Court, Blacks, and the Law, 1870–1902* (New York, 1990), 213; *RP*, July 13, 27, 1895. Mitchell interceded with O'Ferrall on behalf of Benjamin White and James Robinson of Manassas, who were convicted of rape (*RP*, April 21, 18, 1894). Both men were legally executed, although the NAACP reported this as a lynching (NAACP, *Thirty Years of Lynching in the United States, 1889–1918* [New York, 1919], 100). O'Ferrall could not call out the militia without the permission of local authorities. On limits to executive power during this period, see Brundage, *Lynching*, chap. 6.

34. "List of Pardons," House Document No. 2, *House Journal 1895–96*, 10, 20; "List of Pardons," House Document No. 3, *House Journal 1896–97*, 18, 21, 30; Governor's Message, Dec. 4, 1895, *House Journal 1895–96*, 21. Supporting documentation for pardons, commutations, and reprieves can be found in the Executive Papers of the Secretary of the Commonwealth. See also Paul W. Keve, *The History of Corrections in Virginia* (Charlottesville, Va., 1986), 95, 239–41.

35. Pincus, *Virginia Supreme Court*, 122; *Annual Report of the Board of Directors of the Virginia Penitentiary, 1896*, 31; *RP*, Jan. 19, Feb. 16, 1895, Sept. 16, 1899.

36. *RP*, Jan. 19, 26, Feb. 9, 1895; Richard Brown to O'Ferrall, Feb. 1, 1895, Richard Brown Papers (case ending April 25, 1895), Executive Papers of the Secretary of the Commonwealth.

37. *RP*, Dec. 22, 1894, Jan. 19, 1895.

38. *RP*, Feb. 9, 1895; Mitchell et al. to O'Ferrall, Feb. 1, 1895, H. M. Smith Jr. to O'Ferrall, Feb. 4, 1895, Richard Brown Papers.

39. Brown to O'Ferrall, April 5, 1895, Chas. H. Page to O'Ferrall, April 24, 1895, H. M. Smith Jr. to O'Ferrall, April 24, 1895, "Pardon of Richard Brown, presented by John Mitchell Jr.," Richard Brown Papers; *RP*, May 4, 1895; "List of Pardons," Document 2, *House Journal, 1895–96*, 17.

40. *RP*, Feb. 2, April 13, Aug. 4, 1895; Sharp, "History of the Richmond Public School System," 61; Blair, *A Southern Prophecy: The Prosperity of the South Dependent upon the Elevation of the Negro (1889)*, ed. C. Vann Woodward (Boston, 1964); Blair, "Lynching as a Fine Art," *Our Day* 13 (1894): 307–14; Charles E. Wynes, "Lewis Harvie Blair, Virginia Reformer: The Uplift of the Negro and Southern Prosperity," *VMHB* 72 (1964): 3–18.

41. *RD*, June 16, 1895. On the Lunenburg trials, see Pincus, *Virginia Supreme Court*, chap. 11; Brundage, *Lynching*, 173–77. The *Planet, Dispatch,* and *Times* all gave the trials exhaustive coverage during the period June 1895 to Dec. 1896.

42. *RD*, July 18, 21, 23, 1895.

43. *RP*, July 27, Aug. 3, 17, 1895, Nov. 14, 1914; Brundage, *Lynching*, 173–75; Davis, "Rosa L. Dixon Bowser," *DVB* 2:161.

44. *RP*, Aug. 10, 1895; *RD*, Nov. 13, 1895. For a thorough treatment of the complicated legal issues, see Pincus, *Virginia Supreme Court*, 224–45.

45. Flournoy quoted in Pincus, *Virginia Supreme Court*, 231; *RP*, Aug. 10, 1895.

46. *RD*, Feb. 11, 12, March 17, 1896. Public fascination in Virginia with the Lunenburg trials was similar to the national preoccupation with the Lizzie Borden trial in Fall River, Mass., in 1893. On the significance of these "show trials," see Lawrence Friedman, *Crime and Punishment in American History* (New York, 1993), 254.

47. *RD*, May 6, 1896; *Petersburg Daily Index Appeal,* May 10, 1896; *Farmville Herald,* May 8, 1896; *RP,* May 9, 16, 1896.

48. *RD*, July 4–5, Sept. 3, 22–23, Dec. 25, 1896; "List of Pardons," *House Journal, 1897–98,* 44–45; Pardon, Mary Barnes, Dec. 24, 1896, Executive Papers of the Secretary of the Commonwealth.

49. *Washington Bee,* June 6, 1896; *RP,* Jan. 14, 1928.

5. A MANLY PROTEST

1. *RP*, July 12, 1890.

2. Thomas C. Holt, "The Lonely Warrior: Ida B. Wells-Barnett and the Struggle for Black Leadership," in *Black Leaders of the Twentieth Century,* ed. John Hope Franklin and August Meier (Urbana, Ill., 1982), 39–61; McMurray, *To Keep the Waters Troubled,* 130–49.

3. *RP*, Nov. 26, 1898, June 4, 1927. On the Wilmington riot and Alexander Manly, see Charles W. Chesnutt, *The Marrow of Tradition* (1901), ed. Eric J. Sundquist (New York, 1993); H. Leon Prather Sr., *We Have Taken a City: Wilmington Racial Massacre and Coup of 1898* (Cranbury, N.J., 1984); Joel Williamson, *The Crucible of Race: Black-White Relations in the American South since Emancipation* (New York, 1984), 195–200; Glenda Elizabeth Gilmore, *Gender and Jim Crow: Women and the Politics of White Supremacy in North Carolina, 1896–1920* (Chapel Hill, N.C., 1996), 105–17; David S. Cecelski and Timothy B. Tyson, eds., *Democracy Betrayed: The Wilmington Riot of 1898 and Its Legacy* (Chapel Hill, N.C., 1998).

4. *RP*, Nov. 19, 26, 1898. In a letter to Mitchell in 1891, white civil rights advocate Albion W. Tourgée warned that the lynching epidemic was causing the white North to have "a great contempt for the negro *as a man;* they think he will stand everything." Tourgée surmised that some black leaders had forgotten how to be "*true men*" (Tourgée to Mitchell, Aug. 30, 1891, Albion Winegar Tourgée Papers, 1801–1924, Chautauqua County Historical Society, Westfield, N.Y. [microfilm, UNC]).

5. *The Century Dictionary* (1890), quoted in Gail Bederman, *Manliness and Civilization:*

A Cultural History of Gender and Race in the United States, 1880–1917 (Chicago, 1995), 18. During the Victorian era whites in both the United States and Great Britain took for granted that gender distinctions blurred among the darker races and only in the highest Anglo-Saxon civilization did a man (or woman) reach full potential. On manliness, see Michael Kimmel, *Manhood in America: A Cultural History* (New York, 1996); E. Anthony Rotundo, *American Manhood: Transformation in Masculinity from the Revolution to the Present Era* (New York, 1993); Mark C. Carnes and Clyde Griffen, eds., *Meanings for Manhood: Constructions of Masculinity in Victorian America* (Chicago, 1990); J. A. Mangan and James Walvin, eds., *Manliness and Morality: Middle-Class Masculinity in Britain and America, 1800–1940* (New York, 1987). Mitchell's notion of manliness also borrowed from southern ideas about honor as described in Bertram Wyatt-Brown, *Southern Honor: Ethics and Behavior in the Old South* (Oxford, 1982).

6. *RP*, Dec. 7, April 13, July 6, 1895, May 23, 1891.

7. *RP*, Feb. 15, 1896.

8. *RD*, Sept. 11–12, 1894; Holt, "The Lonely Warrior"; Ida B. Wells-Barnett, *Crusade for Justice: The Autobiography of Ida B. Wells*, ed. Alfreda M. Duster (Chicago, 1970); McMurray, *To Keep the Waters Troubled*, 149, 226–27.

9. *RD*, Sept. 11, 1894.

10. *RD*, Sept. 13, 1894.

11. Mitchell et al. to O'Ferrall, Sept. 12, 1894, Charles T. O'Ferrall Executive Papers, LVA.

12. *RP*, Oct. 10, 1896, Oct. 18, 1890.

13. Brundage, "To Howl Loudly," 325–41; Rathbun, "Rise of the Modern American Negro Press," 108–9.

14. *RD*, March 20, 1895; *New York Times*, March 21, 1895. On Teamoh, see Rathbun, "Rise of the Modern American Negro Press," 94; Penn, *Afro-American Press*, 361–64.

15. *RP*, March 23, 1895. Teamoh returned to Richmond in 1902 for the annual meeting of the National Negro Business League and made these comments to the white press (*RD*, Aug. 27, 28, 1902).

16. *RD*, March 22, 23, 1895; *New York Times*, March 21, 1895; O'Ferrall to Francis W. Darling, March 21, 1895, O'Ferrall Papers. On white prejudice against "eating with Negroes," see Orra Langhorne, *Southern Sketches from Virginia, 1881–1901*, ed. Charles E. Wynes (Charlottesville, Va., 1964), 8.

17. Raleigh, N.C., *Progressive Farmer*, March 26, 1895; *New York Times*, March 20, 23, 1895; Robert Saunders, "Southern Populists and the Negro, 1893–1895," *JNH* 54 (July 1969): 252; Willard B. Gatewood Jr., "The Roosevelt-Washington Dinner: The Accretion of Folklore," in *Theodore Roosevelt and the Art of Controversy: Episodes of the White House Years* (Baton Rouge, La., 1970), 32–61.

18. *Wilmington Record*, quoted by Sundquist in Chestnutt, *The Marrow of Tradition*, xvii.

19. *RP*, July 27, 1895.

20. *RP*, Feb. 9, Jan. 19, 1895.

21. *RP*, July 13, 1895, Feb. 22, 1896. For equally candid descriptions of interracial liaisons in Richmond, see Dabney, "Autobiographical Sketch," 69.

22. *RP*, May 22, June 29, 1895.

23. *RP*, May 18, 1895.

24. *RP*, Jan. 16, 1897. On humor, see Lawrence W. Levine, *Black Culture and Black Consciousness: Afro-American Thought from Slavery to Freedom* (Oxford, 1877), 298–366.

25. James Weldon Johnson, *The Autobiography of an Ex-Colored Man* (1912), ed.

William L. Andrews (New York, 1990), 133–34; *RP,* Jan. 20, 1900.

26. *RP,* July 20, July 27, 1895, Jan. 25, 1896, Oct. 29, 1900, Feb. 16, 1901.

27. J. B. Harrison, "Studies in the South," *Atlantic Monthly* 50 (Nov. 1882): 626. On segregation see also Wynes, *Race Relations in Virginia,* 68–88; Williamson, *Crucible of Race;* Howard N. Rabinowitz, *Race Relations in the Urban South, 1865–1890* (Urbana, Ill., 1980); Grace Hale, *Making Whiteness: The Culture of Segregation in the South* (New York, 1998).

28. *RP,* June 21, 1890; Penn, *Afro-American Press,* 169.

29. *RP,* Feb. 9, July 13, 1895, May 23, 1896.

30. *RP,* June 29, 1895.

31. *RP,* Jan. 18, 1896.

32. *RP,* Nov. 4, 1893, Sept. 23, 1899, May 31, 1913.

33. *RP,* June 4, 1898.

6. THE POLITICS OF JACKSON WARD

1. *RD,* May 18, 1888; *Richmond Whig,* April 24, 1888; *New York Freeman,* Sept. 17, 1887.

2. R. D. Wortham to Mahone, April 24, 1888, William Mahone Papers, Duke.

3. *RP* quoted in the *New York Age,* Jan. 14, 1888; William L. Royall, *Some Reminiscences* (New York, 1909), 201–2.

4. Journal of the Common Council, Aug. 6, 1888, RPL; Chesson, "Richmond's Black Councilmen," 202.

5. *RP,* May 24, 1890, Jan. 3, 1891; Journal of the Board of Aldermen, RPL; Aldermen Papers, 1874–1907, LVA.

6. Rabinowitz, *Race Relations in the Urban South,* 272; Chesson, "Richmond's Black Councilmen," 192.

7. *Richmond State,* May 30, 1883; Chesson, *Richmond after the War,* 158; Chesson, "Richmond's Black Councilmen," 191–222.

8. Chesson, "Richmond's Black Councilmen," 198–99; Jackson, *Black Office-Holders in Virginia,* 57–58; *Report on Population of the United States at the Eleventh Census: 1890* (Washington, D.C., 1895), pt. 1, 557.

9. O'Ferrall, *Forty Years of Active Service,* 277. According to Rabinowitz the practice of separating voters by race at the polls was begun by military authorities during Reconstruction (*Race Relations in the Urban South,* 275).

10. "Edmund Waddill Jr. vs. George D. Wise," in Chester H. Rowell, *Digest of Contested Election Cases in the Fifty-first Congress* (Washington, D.C., 1901), 221, 242; *Congressional Record,* 51st Cong., 1st sess., 21:3294–3314, 3348–63; William Cheek and Aimee Lee Cheek, "John Mercer Langston: Principles and Politics," in *Black Leaders of the Nineteenth Century,* ed. Leon Litwack and August Meier (Urbana, Ill., 1988), 103–26.

11. *RD,* Nov. 6, 1889; *RP,* Nov. 7, 1892.

12. *RD,* Nov. 6, 1889; *RP,* June 4, 1892.

13. Chesson, "Richmond's Black Councilmen," 210; Carter, quoted in *RTD,* June 9, 1948; Aldermen Journal, Dec. 8, 1890, May 8, 1893. See also the council's tribute to Josiah Crump, Common Council Journal, Feb. 17, 1890.

14. *RD,* Jan. 18, 1891; Chesson, "Richmond's Black Councilmen," 211. Demands for municipal reform appeared often in the daily press throughout the 1890s. See *RD,* July 20, Sept. 6, Oct. 20, 1892.

15. *RP,* June 1, 1895. On the Knights of Labor, see Rachleff, *Black Labor in Richmond,*

143–91; Leon Fink, *Workingmen's Democracy: The Knights of Labor and American Politics* (Urbana, Ill., 1983), chap. 6.

16. *RD,* May 12, 1891; Superintendent's Monthly Report, April 26, 1886, Richmond School Board Minutes, LVA; Aldermen Journal, Feb. 9, 1891, April 10, May 8, 1893, Jan. 9, Aug. 14, Sept. 11, Oct. 6, 1894; *RP,* Jan. 27, Oct. 13, 1894, Dec. 21, 1895; Chesson, *Richmond after the War,* 193; Paul S. Dulaney, *The Architecture of Historic Richmond* (Charlottesville, Va., 1968).

17. Aldermen Journal, July 14, Oct. 13, Nov. 10, 1890, Jan. 9, 1893, Dec. 11, 1894, Oct. 15, 1895; Rabinowitz, *Race Relations in the Urban South,* 278–79; *RP,* Oct. 11, 1890, Jan. 4, 1896; *RD,* Oct. 14, 1890, Dec. 15, 1891, Jan. 10, 1893, Oct. 16, 1895.

18. Common Council Journal, Jan. 7, Feb. 4, 1889; *RP,* Nov. 15, 1890, March 7, 1891, July 30, 1892, Nov. 17, Dec. 15, 1894, March 9, 1895; *RD,* Feb. 28, 1892, April 22, 1893, April 6, Nov. 10, 1894. On the importance of the city hall as a rallying point for the Knights of Labor, see Rachleff, *Black Labor in Richmond,* 141.

19. *RP,* March 9, 16, 1895; Dabney, *Maggie L. Walker,* 34.

20. The story of the crematory is pieced together from a variety of sources: *Dispatch* and *Planet;* Council and Aldermen Journals; published *Annual Reports of the Department of Health* (bound with the annual reports of the mayor and available at RPL); Minutes of the Committee on Health, 1888–1905, 3 vols., LVA; and miscellaneous materials in Aldermen Papers.

21. Aldermen Journal, April 13, July 23, 31, Aug. 4, 1891; Committee on Health Minutes, April 22, 1891; *RD,* July 14, 15, 18, 23–25, Aug. 5, 1891.

22. *RP,* Aug. 22, 1891; *RT,* Aug. 15, 1891; *RD,* Aug. 13, 15, 20, 27, Sept. 16, 19, 1891; Aldermen Journal, July 24, Aug. 14, 26, Sept. 14, 16, 17, 1891.

23. *RD,* Feb. 14, 1892; *Annual Report of the Health Department* (Richmond, 1892), 15.

24. W. P. Moore to committee on health, Sept. 15, 1892, in Committee on Health Minutes; Aldermen Journal, April 11, May 9, June 13, Aug. 8, Sept. 12, 1892; report of committee on health, June 9, 1892, in Aldermen Papers; petition presented to board of aldermen, Aug. 8, 1892, by William Howard Jones, in Aldermen Papers; *RD,* June 14, July 30, Aug. 9, 24, Sept. 13, 1892.

25. Report of the committee on health, [Sept. 12, 1892?], report of the city engineer, Oct. 10, 1892, both in Aldermen Papers; Aldermen Journal, May 15, 1894, June 11, July 9, Aug. 11, 1895; Crematory Nuisance Special Committee, adopted by the board of aldermen, Aug. 13, 1895, misfiled in incoming correspondence to the clerk, 1910, Richmond City, LVA; *Annual Report of the Health Department* (Richmond, 1893), 7–9. See also Charles E. Richard to the city council, Sept. 2, 1892, Aldermen Papers.

26. Chesson, "Black Councilmen," 208–10; Christopher Silver, *Twentieth Century Richmond: Planning, Politics, and Race* (Knoxville, Tenn., 1894), 33.

27. *New York Times,* Feb. 15, 1889; *Washington Bee,* Feb. 23, 1889; John Mitchell Jr. et al. to Benjamin Harrison, Feb. 14, 1889, Benjamin Harrison Papers, LC (microfilm, UVA); *RP,* March 22, 1913.

28. *RP,* Feb. 7, 1891; *RD,* April 24–26, 1890; "U.S. v. Belvin, et al.," 46 *Federal Reporter* 381.

29. *Acts of the General Assembly, 1893–1894,* chap. 746, 862–67; J. Morgan Kousser, *The Shaping of Southern Politics: Suffrage Restriction and the Establishment of the One-Party South, 1880–1910* (New Haven, 1974), 51–56.

30. *RP,* Nov. 17, 1894. The Walton Act was discussed extensively in the white press throughout 1894. See also Herman L. Horn, "The Growth and Development of the Democratic Party in Virginia since 1890" (Ph.D. diss., Duke University, 1947), 177–89.

31. *RD*, May 28, June 1, 1895; *RP*, Jan. 11, 1896.

32. *RP*, May 31, 1890; Gregg D. Kimball, "James Bahen," *DVB* 1:282–83; Carter, quoted in *RTD*, June 8, 1948; *RD*, May 19, 1894; Rachleff, *Black Labor in Richmond*, 153; population statistics from Chesson, *Richmond after the War*, 190.

33. *RP*, May 24, 1890; *RD*, Dec. 22, 1891; *Southern News*, Oct. 15, 1892.

34. *RD*, Oct. 3, 1890; *RP*, June 11, 1892. Although Hayes himself did not work in the post office, his wife, Julia Hayes, was a postal clerk.

35. *RP*, June 2, 1894.

36. *RP*, April 25, 1896; *RT*, March 11, 1896; *Petersburg Daily Index Appeal*, March 15, 1896.

37. *RD*, May 6, 1896; *Petersburg Daily Index Appeal*, May 10, 1896; *Farmville Herald*, May 6, 1896.

38. *RP*, May 31, 1890, May 27, 1892.

39. *RT*, May 29, 1896; *RD*, May 29, 1896; *Petersburg Daily Index Appeal*, May 30, 1896; *RP*, June 6, 13, 20, 1896.

40. Aldermen Journal, June 9, 1896.

41. Ibid., July 1, 1896. Mitchell was surely unaware that official returns showed him winning the election: James I. Smith had 517 votes, John Mitchell 410, and James Bahen 401; the reform candidate, Armistead Washington, had 126. Mitchell, rather than Bahen, therefore should have won the second seat. One can only assume the clerk transposed the numbers (box 653, City Clerk's Office, RCH).

42. *RP*, Nov. 7, 14, 1896. For a description of how Republican Party workers kept their own tally, see James D. Brady, *Instructions for the Guidance of Republican County and Precinct Chairmen for the Purpose of Insuring an Honest Count and Return of the Votes Cast on Election Day, Tuesday, Nov. 3, 1896*, pamphlet in John Mercer Langston Personal Papers, Fisk University (microfilm, LC).

7. "NO OFFICERS, NO FIGHT!"

1. *RP*, March 12, May 7, June 4, 11, 1898. This chapter relies on the pioneering work of Willard B. Gatewood: *"Smoked Yankees" and the Struggle for Empire: Letters from Negro Soldiers, 1898–1902* (Urbana, Ill., 1971); "A Negro Editor on Imperialism: John Mitchell, 1898–1901," *Journalism Quarterly* 49 (Spring 1972): 43–50; "Virginia's Negro Regiment in the Spanish-American War: The Sixth Virginia Volunteers," *VMHB* 80 (April 1972): 193–217; and *Black Americans and the White Man's Burden, 1893–1903* (Urbana, Ill., 1975).

2. *RP*, March 12, April 16, 23, May 21, 28, 1898. For more of Mitchell's editorials, see George P. Marks III, ed., *The Black Press Views American Imperialism, 1898–1900* (New York, 1971).

3. *RP*, May 7, June 4, 11, 1898; *Washington Post*, May 26, 1898.

4. Otis A. Singletary, *Negro Militia and Reconstruction* (Austin, Tex., 1957), 11; Rachleff, *Black Labor in Richmond*, 40; C. A. Bryce, in *RTD*, May 8, 1921; *RT*, July 2, 1866, quoted in O'Brien, *From Bondage to Citizenship*, 367.

5. Chesson, *Richmond after the War*, 158–59; [William H. Johnson], *History of the Colored Volunteer Infantry, 1871–99* [n.p., 1923], 38–39; *RP*, Jan. 8, 1898. See also *Annual Reports of the Adjutant General of the Commonwealth of Virginia*, 1871–98.

6. Compiled Military Service Record, Major Joseph B. Johnson, 6th Virginia Infantry Colored, Records of the Adjutant General's Office, RG 94, NA; Rachleff, *Black Labor in Richmond*, 138.

7. *RP,* May 7, Aug. 20, 1898; Gatewood, *Black Americans and the White Man's Burden,* 43.

8. *RP,* May 7, 1898.

9. *RD,* June 1, 4, 7, 1898; *RT,* June 7, 1898; Jos. Button to Tyler, June 7, 1898, box 13, Thomas S. Martin to Tyler, June 17, 1898, box 17, Jas. S. Seay to Tyler, Dec. 10, 1898, H. N. Richards to Tyler, Nov. 16, 1898, box 15, J. Hoge Tyler Papers, VT. Salary scales help explain the mania for commissions. During the Spanish-American War privates made $156 a year, captains $1,500, and majors $2,500 (*Manual for the Pay Department, Revised to Include April 30, 1898* [Washington, D.C., 1898], 38).

10. Tyler to A. A. Phlegar, April 25, 1898, box 17, Tyler Papers; *RD,* June 1, 10, 1898; *RP,* June 4, 1898. Tyler apparently lobbied the War Department on behalf of black soldiers and officers, although he implied that the pressures came from the other direction. Compare, for example, the first public call for troops, R. A. Alger to Tyler, April 25, 1898, in *Adjutant General's Report, 1898–99* (Richmond, 1899), 25, with Tyler's unpublished response, Tyler to Alger, April 26, 1898, AGO File 76106, Office of the Adjutant General, NA. See also *RT,* June 17, 1898, John W. Stebbins to Tyler, May 27, 1898, box 17, John Lamb to Tyler, May 27, 1898, box 15, Edward Echols to Tyler, May 28, 1898, box 13, Tyler to William McKinley, May 30, 1898, box 17, Jo Lane Stern to Tyler, May 31, 1898, Tyler to Jo Lane Stern, June 1, 1898, and especially an undated draft of a letter to McKinley in Tyler's hand, evidently never mailed, in box 12, Tyler Papers. Because important negotiations occurred face-to-face, it is difficult to unravel the matter completely, and Tyler was intentionally vague.

11. *RD,* May 27, 1898; Tyler to Dr. E. W. Gilliam, June 18, 1898, box 17, Tyler Papers.

12. *RP,* Sept. 3, 1898; Rev. W. F. Graham to Tyler, June 14, 1898, box 14, Bernard Tyrrell, Instructor, Virginia Seminary, Lynchburg, to Tyler, June 15, 1898, box 15, H. B. Frissell, Principal, Hampton Institute, to Tyler, June 25, 1898, box 13, W. Bishop Johnson, Washington, D.C., to Tyler, July 1, 1898, box 14, Tyler Papers.

13. *RP,* Dec. 10, 1898. The officer may have overstated the high social standing of the volunteers as most of the privates were listed in muster rolls as laborers. On the other hand, occupation was a notoriously poor indicator of standing in the black community. Muster Rolls and Registers, 6th Virginia Volunteers (LVA) include occupation, date of birth, complexion, marital status, and residence. An abbreviated printed version appears in *Report of the Adjutant General, 1897/98,* 374–414.

14. Graham A. Cosmas, *An Army for Empire: The United States Army in the Spanish-American War* (Columbia, Mo., 1971), 13, 127–28, 174; Russell A. Alger, *The Spanish-American War* (New York, 1901), 26.

15. *RT,* April 29, 1898; *RD,* June 29, Nov. 5, 1898. Much of the information about Croxton comes from his Appointment, Commission, and Personal Branch Document File, RG 94, box 1029, NA. On Thomas Croxton, see *Biographical Directory of the United States Congress, 1774–1889* (Washington, D.C., 1989), 852.

16. Efficiency reports by Major E. C. Wardruff, Dec. 31, 1891, J. M. Thompson, June 30, 1902, Philip Reade, June 30, 1907, J. E. Sawyer, July 17, 1909, Charles G. Morton, Nov. 9, 1916, also Thomas Croxton, House of Representatives, to Adjutant General, Feb. 13, 1887, all in Croxton's Personal File; *RP,* Dec. 24, 1898.

17. *RD,* July 5, 1898; medical reports of Dr. Lewis G. Bosher, May 30, 1898, Dr. Allen J. Black, Jan. 8, 1899, in Croxton's Personal File; Black to Tyler, June 3, 1898, box 13, Aug. 2, 1898, box 16, Tyler Papers; *RP,* March 5, 1898.

18. *RP,* July 23, 1898; Zachary H. Fields, Camp Corbin, to Nettie Fields, Sept. 7, 1898, Zachary H. Fields Letters, NSU; Elsie Graves Lewis, "Captain Benjamin A. Graves," *Richmond Literature and History Quarterly* 2 (Spring 1980): 47–48. The letters from Ham have been reprinted in Gatewood, *"Smoked Yankees,"* 122–27, 130–34, 138–40, 144–46, 151–56.

A second correspondent, "A Black Man," wrote to the *Planet*. He may have been George St. Julien Stephens. For his letters, see Gatewood, *"Smoked Yankees,"* 140–44, 146–50.

19. *RP*, July 23, 1898; General Order No. 18, Sept. 2, 1898, 6th Virginia Volunteers, Regimental Records, 19, NA. Croxton blamed the soldiers' illiteracy for his failure to complete paperwork on time (Croxton to Adjutant General, Oct. 31, 1898, Letters Sent, 44–45, ibid.).

20. *RT*, Nov. 4, 1898; *RD*, Sept. 13, 1898. Theodore Roosevelt in 1899 disparaged the performance of black soldiers at San Juan Hill. On Mitchell's spirited response, see Gatewood, *Black Americans and the White Man's Burden*, 202–3.

21. General Order No. 21, Camp Poland, Sept. 14, 1898, 6th Virginia Volunteers, Regimental Records, 25; *RP*, Sept. 24, 1898; Zach Fields to Nettie Fields, Sept. 27, 1898, Fields Letters.

22. General Order No. 12, Lexington, Ky., Oct. 1, 1898, 6th Virginia Volunteers, Regimental Records, 56–57; Cosmas, *An Army for Empire*, 101; *Report of the [Virginia] Adjutant General, 1898/99* (Richmond, 1899), 21–22; Testimony of Lt. Col. Richard C. Croxton, Knoxville, Tenn., Oct. 31, 1898, in *Report of the Commission Appointed to Investigate the Conduct of the War Department in the War with Spain*, Senate Doc. 221, 56 Cong., 1st sess., 3:942–43; *Knoxville Journal and Tribune*, Nov. 1, 1898.

23. William H. Johnson to Mitchell, in *RP*, Nov. 19, 1898; Johnson to Croxton, Oct. 3, 1898, William H. Johnson Papers, VSU.

24. *RP*, Oct. 15, 1898; *RT*, Oct. 23, 1898; *RD*, Nov. 16, 1898; Tyler to Croxton, Nov. 17, 1898, box 17, John W. Daniel to Tyler, Nov. 17, 23, box 13, Tyler Papers. Hundreds of letters requesting appointments are scattered through the Tyler collection. See folder, "Political 1898 Requests for Army Appointments Including 6th Va. Reg.," box 12. (Other important information relating to the 6th Virginia Volunteers is in box 12 in mislabeled folders.)

25. *RP*, Oct. 29, 1898; *Knoxville Journal and Tribune*, Oct. 27, 1898; *RD*, Nov. 2, 1898; Tyler to Croxton, Nov. 7, 1898, box 17, Tyler Papers; John Addison Porter to James H. Hayes, Nov. 12, 1898, William McKinley Papers, LC (microfilm, UVA).

26. J. B. Johnson et al. to the Adjutant General, Oct. 17, 1898 [with annotations by Croxton], Letters Received, 28, 6th Virginia Volunteers, Regimental Records; Zach Fields to Nettie Fields, Oct. 24, Dec. 6, 1898, Fields Letters; *RP*, Nov. 5, 1898. Fields had clashed with Gould and had been disciplined for drunkenness (Muster Out Rolls, 6th Virginia Volunteers, LVA).

27. R. LeMasurier to Tyler, Nov. 14, 1898, box 12, Tyler Papers; *RD*, Nov. 3, 1898; *Atlanta Constitution*, Nov. 3, 1898; *Knoxville Journal and Tribune*, Nov. 3, 1898; *RP*, Nov. 5, 1898; *RT*, Nov. 3, 1898; Edward A. Johnson, *History of Negro Soldiers in the Spanish-American War and Other Items of Interest* (Raleigh, N.C., 1899), 96–107.

28. *Atlanta Constitution*, Nov. 17, 1898; *RP*, Nov. 12, 19, 1898; George H. Bentley to Adjutant General, Nov. 22, 1898, Compiled Service Record of George H. Bentley, NA; R. LeMasurier to Tyler, Nov. 14, 1898, R. C. L. Moncure to Tyler, Nov. 14, 1898, W. L. Faulkner to Tyler, Nov. 14, 1898, box 12, Tyler Papers. The private letters to Tyler are more candid than the official letters of resignation to the War Department. According to the officers Croxton suggested that they resign. What he had in mind (if anything) is unclear, and their resignations embarrassed the governor.

29. *Knoxville Journal and Tribune*, Sept. 16, 23, Oct. 10, Nov. 10, 1898; *RP*, Nov. 5, 1898.

30. Allen J. Black, Jan. 8, 1899, medical report in Croxton's Personal File; *RP*, Dec. 17, 1898; Gatewood, *Black Americans and the White Man's Burden*, 138–44.

31. *Atlanta Constitution*, Nov. 20, 1898; *Macon Telegraph*, Nov. 20, 21, 1898; Gatewood, *"Smoked Yankees,"* 157–63.

32. *RP*, Nov. 26, Dec. 3, 1898; *Atlanta Constitution*, Nov. 20, 21, 1898; *RT*, Nov. 22, 1898;

Captions and Records of Events, Nov. 1898, Regimental Records, 6th Virginia Infantry Colored; Tyler to John W. Daniel, Nov. 25, 1898, box 17, Tyler Papers.

33. *RP,* Dec. 3, 10, 1898; Zachary Fields to Nettie Fields, Dec. 19, 1898, Fields Letters.

34. *RP,* Dec. 17, 1898.

35. *RT,* Sept. 10, 1898; *RD,* Sept. 10, 1898; Harry Wooding [Mayor, Danville] to J. Hoge Tyler, Sept. 10, 1898, Ben P. Owen Jr. to J. Hoge Tyler, Sept. 10, 1898, box 16, Tyler Papers. After McClellan was killed, Tyler's office tried to offset negative publicity by feeding the press stories reflecting favorably on black troops.

36. *Macon Telegraph,* Dec. 15, 16, 22, 23, 1898; *Atlanta Constitution,* Nov. 22, Dec. 5, 23, 24, 1898. Georgia's 1891 streetcar ordinance was ambiguous about segregation (John Dittmer, *Black Georgia in the Progressive Era, 1900–1920* [Urbana, Ill., 1977], 16).

37. Report of Captain James W. Marston, Dec. 23, 1898, in Compiled Service Record, Elijah Turner, NA; Muster Rolls and Registers, 6th Virginia Volunteers, LVA; *Macon Telegraph,* Dec. 24, 1898; *RP,* Jan. 7, 1899.

38. *Macon Telegraph,* Dec. 26, 1898.

39. Croxton to Francis R. Lassiter, Jan. 2, 1899, quoted in Gatewood, *Black Americans and the White Man's Burden,* 148 n. 54; *RT,* Dec. 24, 1898.

40. *Macon Telegraph,* Jan. 6, 1899; *RP,* Jan. 21, 1899; *Atlanta Constitution,* Jan. 25, 1899; C. W. Cordin to H. C. Smith, Jan. 28, 1899, in Gatewood, *"Smoked Yankees,"* 167.

41. W. H. Anderson to Tyler, Jan. 31, 1899, box 13, Tyler Papers; *Report of the Adjutant General, 1898/99,* 61–62; *RD,* March 3, 1899; *Macon Telegraph,* Feb. 2, 1899; *RP,* Feb. 4, 1899; Montague to Tyler, Nov. 30, 1898, Office of the Governor, Letters Received, James Hoge Tyler, LVA. After their return Tyler also refused to let black militia units from other states enter Virginia for ceremonial purposes. See W. T. Thompson, Capt. Commanding Corps, Butler Zouaves, to Tyler, Sept. 9, 1899, John R. Spillerman to Tyler, Sept. 12, 1899, Tyler to C. M. White, Sept. 18, 1899, box 15, Private Secretary to Tyler to Captain W. T. Thompson, Sept. 16, 1899, box 18, Tyler Papers. The black militia in Alabama was disbanded in 1905 (Beth Taylor Muskat, "The Last March: The Demise of the Black Militia in Alabama," *Alabama Review* 43 [Jan. 1990]: 18–34).

42. Information about the officers comes from scattered sources but primarily from their compiled service records, NA. On Graves, see Lewis, "Captain Benjamin A. Graves," 47–48; *RP,* Sept. 30, 1899. Zachary and Nettie Fields appear in the 1910 census as Jack and Mettie Fields. On Joseph B. Johnson's run for Congress, see Andrew Buni, *The Negro in Virginia Politics, 1902–1965* (Charlottesville, Va., 1967), 54. William H. Johnson for decades exchanged warm and friendly letters with Jo Lane Stern, the Virginia adjutant general during the Spanish-American War. Of particular interest is Stern to Johnson, Dec. 11, 1920 (William H. Johnson Papers), in which Stern blamed the regiment's difficulties on new recruits.

43. On Mitchell's national leadership on this issue, see Gatewood, "A Negro Editor on Imperialism," 43–50.

8. DISFRANCHISEMENT

1. W. E. B. Du Bois, *Writings* (New York, 1986), 503. The term *nadir* was first used by Rayford W. Logan, *The Negro in American Life and Thought: The Nadir, 1877–1901* (New York, 1954).

2. *RP,* Jan. 30, March 20, June 19, 1897, Jan. 7, March 4, 1905; Mitchell to Edward H.

Brown, Deed of Trust (159C4533), 311 N. Fourth Street, Feb. 15, 1897, Mitchell to Brown Folding Machine Company, Deed of Trust (160B80), March 20, 1897, Mitchell to Campbell Press Manufacturing Company, Deed of Trust (183A516), Feb. 14, 1905, Chancery Court Records, RCH.

3. *RP,* June 23, 30, 1900; interview, various members of the Mitchell family, Richmond, June 6, 1996; Mitchell to L. W. McVeigh, Deed of Trust (181A369), July 18, 1904, Chancery Court Records; Robert P. Winthrop, *Jackson Ward Historic District* (Richmond, 1978), 194.

4. *RP,* Aug. 30, 1902.

5. Brewer, "The Ghosts of Jackson Ward," 28–30. J. Morgan Kousser has argued convincingly in *The Shaping of Virginia Politics* that suffrage restrictions did more than record a fait accompli. Certainly this was true in Richmond.

6. *RD,* March 8, 1900; *RP,* April 18, May 5, 12, 1900; *RT,* April 18, 1900. Bahen's move to the Democratic Party occasioned considerable controversy among whites (*RD,* May 30, 1900).

7. *RT,* May 4, 1900; *RD,* May 4, 1900.

8. *RP,* May 12, 1900; Wynes, *Race Relations in Virginia,* 51–52.

9. *RT,* May 17, 1900; *RP,* May 12, 1900.

10. *RT,* May 10, 1900; William L. Royall, *History of the Virginia Debt Controversy: The Negro's Vicious Influence in Politics* (Richmond, 1897), 36–37; Royall, *Some Reminiscences* (New York, 1909), 201–2.

11. *RD,* May 5–6, 8–9, 11–12, 13, 1900. On Benjamin Jackson, see *RP,* Feb. 16, 1895.

12. Brewer, "The Ghosts of Jackson Ward," 28.

13. *RP,* May 26, 1900; *RT,* May 25, 1900.

14. *RT,* May 25, 1900; "Official Election Returns for the City of Richmond, May 1900," drawer 653, City Clerk's Office, RCH.

15. *RP,* May 12, 26, June 9, 1900.

16. *RD,* June 1–2, 6, 12, 1900; *RP,* June 2, 1900.

17. *RT,* June 19, 1900; Brewer, "The Ghosts of Jackson Ward," 30; Hustings Court Order Book, 38 (June 18, 1900): 11–12, JMCB; *RP,* July 26, 1900.

18. *RT,* July 6, 1900; Mitchell v. Witt, *Virginia Reporter* 98 (July 5, 1900): 459–64.

19. *RD,* Feb. 6, 1900; *RP,* May 12, 1900.

20. *RP,* May 12, 1900; Ralph C. McDaniel, *The Virginia Constitutional Convention of 1901–1902* (Baltimore, 1928), 9–18; Wythe W. Holt Jr., "The Virginia Constitutional Convention of 1901–1902: A Reform Movement Which Lacked Substance," *VMHB* 76 (Jan. 1968): 67–102; Edward L. Ayers, *The Promise of the New South: Life after Reconstruction* (New York, 1992), 305–9.

21. *RP,* April 13, July 27, 1901; James H. Brewer, "Editorials from the Damned," *JSH* 28 (May 1962): 225–33.

22. Patricia Carter Ives, "James and Hulda Jackson of Goochland County, Virginia," *National Genealogical Society Quarterly* 67 (June 1979): 104–6; *RD,* March 29, 1903; W. H. Ward, "Race Exhibition at Jamestown," *Independent* 63 (Nov. 14, 1907): 1169; *RP,* June 15, 1889. On Beveridge's high opinion of Jackson, see Beveridge to Mahone, June 6, 1888, William Mahone Papers, Duke.

23. Jackson to Washington, Jan. 24, 1901, *BTW Papers* 6:14–17. Letters from Jackson appear throughout the *BTW Papers.* The anecdote about the naming of Jackson Ward, presented in its most egregious form, can be found in *RP,* Aug. 2, 1913. Jackson was only twelve when the war ended, making these stories unlikely.

24. Louis R. Harlan, "Booker T. Washington and the National Negro Business League,"

in *Seven on Black: Reflections on the Negro Experience in America,* ed. William G. Shade and Roy C. Herrenkohl (Philadelphia, 1969), 78; Harlan, "The Secret Life of Booker T. Washington," *JSH* 37 (Aug. 1971): 397; "Constitutional Rights Association of the United States," *Colored American Magazine* 1 (Oct. 1900): 309–11.

25. *RD,* Feb. 3, 12, 1901; *RT,* Feb. 12, 1901; *RP,* Feb. 16, 1901; Jackson to E. J. Scott, Dec. 1, 1915, box 799, Booker T. Washington Papers, LC.

26. *RT,* Feb. 12, 1901; *RD,* Feb. 12, 1901; Jackson to Washington, Jan. 24, Jan. 28, 1901, *BTW Papers* 6:14–17, 23–24. Governor J. Hoge Tyler decided at the last moment not to attend (W. F. Graham and Jackson to J. Hoge Tyler, Feb. 8, 1901, Jackson to Tyler, March 18, 1901, J. Hoge Tyler Papers, VT). Washington included an account of the speech in *Up from Slavery: An Autobiography* (New York, 1901), 318–19.

27. *RP,* Feb. 9, 16, 1901, Aug. 30, 1902.

28. Negro Business League of Virginia, *A Memorial Presented to the Virginia Constitutional Convention by the Negro Business League of the State* (Richmond, 1901), LVA; *RD,* June 16, 1901; *RT,* June 22, 1901.

29. *RT,* July 10, 1901; Sherman, "Daniel Webster Davis," 458; *RP,* Aug. 11, 1900.

30. *RP,* Jan. 27, July 28, 1900, June 8, 1901.

31. *RD,* Oct. 3, Aug. 31, 1902; *RP,* June 2, 1900.

32. *RT,* June 5, 1901; *RP,* April 28, 1900.

33. *Farmville Herald,* quoted in *RD,* Feb. 8, 1902; *RD,* May 13, Aug. 15, 1899, Feb. 8, June 9, 1900; *RT,* March 3, 10, Oct. 6, 10, 1901; Anderson, *Education of Blacks in the South,* 96–98; Louis R. Harlan, *Separate and Unequal: Public School Campaigns and Racism in the Southern Seaboard States, 1901–1915* (Chapel Hill, N.C., 1958), 138–44, 162–69.

34. *Journal of the Constitutional Convention of Virginia, 1901–02,* Doc. 9, 58–59; *RD,* Feb. 10, Nov. 8, 1901.

35. *RD,* Jan. 19, 1901.

36. *RT,* July 25, 1900; *RD,* July 25, 1901; *RP,* Aug. 3, 1901; *Speech of Giles B. Jackson, Secretary of the Negro Business League of Virginia, before the Committee on Education of the Constitutional Convention of Virginia, in Session, Richmond, Va., 1901,* LVA.

37. *RT,* Sept. 12, 1900, Jan. 23, April 4, 18, 1901; *Proceedings and Debates of the Constitutional Convention, 1901–1902* (Richmond, 1906), 1220.

38. *RT,* Sept. 26, 1901; *RD,* Nov. 10, 1901; *RP,* Jan. 5, 1901; Harlan, *Separate and Unequal,* 162–169; *Debates of the Constitutional Convention,* 1193–1232, 1662–94; Anderson, *Education of Blacks in the South,* 184–85.

39. *RP,* Jan. 11, 1902; Brewer, "Editorials from the Damned," 225–33.

40. *Debates of the Constitutional Convention,* 3976–77; Moger, *Virginia: Bourbonism to Byrd,* 189–92.

41. *RP,* Sept. 27, 1902; *RD,* Aug. 31, Sept. 19, 26, 1902; *Reformer,* Sept. 20, 1902; *Negro Advocate,* Sept. 27, 1902; Buni, *Negro in Virginia Politics,* 22–24. Scattered copies of the *Reformer* and *Negro Advocate* are in Black Newspapers Collection, VSU.

42. *RD,* Sept. 20–24, 1902.

43. William A. Pendleton, *Political History of Appalachian Virginia, 1776–1927* (Dayton, Va., 1927), 459; *RD,* Oct. 2, 1902; "Register of Colored Voters, 1902–1903," LVA. Nearly every male black Richmonder of prominence registered, as did scores of lesser-known laborers and domestic servants.

44. *RD,* Nov. 2, 5, 1902.

9. "DID GOD CALL THE PASTOR?"

1. *RD*, July 24, Aug. 17, 24, 1900, Aug. 21, 1902; *RT*, July 24, 1900, Aug. 25, 1901; *RP*, Aug. 18, 1900; Negro Educational and Industrial Association of Virginia, *The Constitutional Convention: Help Save Our Public Schools . . . May 3, 1901* [Charlottesville?, Va., 1901], broadside, UVA; Buni, *Negro in Virginia Politics*, 34–40.

2. *RP*, Nov. 22, 1902.

3. *RD*, June 29, July 17, Aug. 19–21, 1902; *RP*, Dec. 6, 1902; James H. Hayes to Whitfield McKinlay, Nov. 7, 1902, Carter Woodson Collection, LC; *Negro Advocate*, Sept. 27, 1902, Black Newspapers Collection, VSU.

4. *RD*, Nov. 30, 1902; *RP*, Dec. 6, 1902. Hayes became embroiled in controversies surrounding Booker T. Washington. There is much correspondence about the court challenge in the *BTW Papers*.

5. *Cleveland Gazette*, quoted in *RP*, Jan. 31, 1903; *Cleveland Gazette*, Feb. 7, 1903; *Little Rock Reporter*, quoted in *RP*, Oct. 14, 1904; *Washington Bee*, Jan. 31, Feb. 7, May 30, 1903.

6. William E. Montgomery, *Under Their Own Vine and Fig Tree: The African-American Church in the South, 1865–1900* (Baton Rouge, La., 1993), 105; American Baptist Home Mission Society, *Baptist Home Missions in North America* (New York, 1883), 70; Elsa Barkley Brown, "Hartshorn Memorial College," in *BWA*, 543–47; Corey, *History of the Richmond Theological Seminary*; Adolph H. Grundman, "Northern Baptists and the Founding of Virginia Union University: The Perils of Paternalism," *JNH* 63 (Jan. 1978): 26–41; Ralph Reavis, "Virginia Seminary: A Tangible Symbol of Opposition to White/Paternalism and Commitment to Self-Reliance" (Ph.D. diss., University of Virginia, 1989); James M. McPherson, "White Liberals and Black Power in Negro Education, 1865–1915," *AHR* 75 (June 1970): 1357–86; McPherson, *Abolitionist Legacy*. The school that became Virginia Union went through several name changes. It was Colver Institute (1868–76); Richmond Institute (1876–86); Richmond Theological Seminary (1886–99); Virginia Union University (1899–present).

7. Reavis, "Virginia Seminary," 97–102.

8. Dabney, "Rough Autobiographical Sketch," 129–31, 140.

9. *RP*, June 20, Sept. 5, 1891; Reavis, "Virginia Seminary," 138–45; Carrie Allen McCray, *Freedom's Child: The Life of a Confederate General's Black Daughter* (Chapel Hill, N.C., 1998), 63–104.

10. *RP*, Feb. 27, April 9, Nov. 26, 1892, May 13, 1893, March 17, 1894, Jan. 18, 1896; *Virginia Seminary Messenger*, March 1895, in James Hugo Johnston Sr. Papers, VSU; *Minutes of the Twenty-fifth Session of the Virginia Baptist State Convention* (1892), 40–43.

11. *RP*, Sept. 5, 1891, July 1, 22, 1893, July 6, 13, Sept. 28, 1895, May 22, 1897; "New Schools," *BHMM* 15 (Jan. 1893): 21; "Questions for Special Consideration," ibid., 16 (Aug. 1894): 322–23.

12. James H. Holmes to T. J. Morgan, Dec. 10, 1894, J. E. Jones to Morgan, Dec. 8, 1894, both quoted in Reavis, "Virginia Seminary," 178–80; *RP*, Dec. 5, 1894; E. C. Morris, *Sermons, Addresses, and Reminiscences and Important Correspondence* (1901; rept. New York, 1980), 158–66.

13. *RP*, May 22, 1897; T. J. Morgan, "A Southern Trip," *BHMM* (March 1894): 74; Reavis, "Virginia Seminary," 127.

14. Malcolm MacVicar to Z. D. Lewis, Sept. 17, 1898, quoted in Reavis, "Virginia Seminary," 213–14; Morris, "Negro Baptists: Retrospective and Prospective," Boston, Sept. 15, 1897, in *Sermons*, 69–77; *RP*, Jan. 29, 1898; Rev. A. S. Garland of Lynchburg, quoted in *RP*, May 31, 1902.

15. "Editorial," *BHMM* 21 (Jan. 1899): 3; *RP*, Feb. 4, April 1, 15, 22, 1899.

16. *RP*, May 6, 13, 20, June 3, 1899; Reavis, "Virginia Seminary," 242–48. On the process for selecting delegates, see *Minutes of the Twenty-fifth Session of the Virginia Baptist State Convention*, 6.

17. J. E. Jones et al., *A Protest: To the Baptist Brotherhood of Virginia and to Whom It May Concern* [Richmond, 1899?], in Papers of John Adams, UVA; Elbert Earnest in *RP*, April 22, 1899; *RP*, June 17, July 1, 1899.

18. *RP*, July 15, 1899; *Proceedings of the Second Annual Session of the General Association of Virginia Held with the Calvary Baptist Church, Danville, Virginia, May 9–13, 1900* (Richmond, 1900), LVA.

19. Rayford W. Logan, "Walter Henderson Brooks," *DANB*, 62–64; William I. Lee, "A Sketch of the Life of Walter Henderson Brooks," in *One Hundredth Anniversary of the Nineteenth Street Baptist Church, Washington, D.C.*, LVA; Montgomery, *Under Their Own Vine and Fig Tree*, 242–45; McPherson, *Abolitionist Legacy*, 286; James Melvin Washington, *Frustrated Fellowship: The Black Baptist Quest for Social Power* (Macon, Ga., 1986), 164–70; Lewis G. Jordan, *Negro Baptist History U.S.A.* (Nashville, 1930), 249; Morris, "The Demand for a Negro Baptist Publishing House," address delivered before the National Baptist Convention at Washington, D.C., 1893, in *Sermons*, 56–61; *RP*, May 24, 31, June 21, 1890; Higginbotham, *Righteous Discontent*, 251 n. 63.

20. *RP*, April 8, 1893; Joseph B. Earnest, *Religious Development of the Negro in Virginia* (Charlottesville, Va., 1914), 219; "William Thomas Johnson," in A. B. Caldwell, *History of the American Negro: Virginia Edition* (Atlanta, 1921), 297–300; Corey, *Richmond Theological Seminary*, 172.

21. First African Baptist Church Minute Books, March 14, April 1, May 4, 1901, Church Records Collection, LVA (microfilm). On the role of women in this conflict, see Elsa Barkley Brown, "Negotiating and Transforming the Public Sphere: African American Political Life in the Transition from Slavery to Freedom," *Public Culture* 7 (Fall 1994): 107–46.

22. First African Minute Books, June 3, 1901; *RP*, July 6, Aug. 31, 1901.

23. *RP*, July 27, Aug. 3, 1901, Aug. 2, 1902. Nineteenth Street Baptist Church was considered a "high-tone" church (Willard B. Gatewood, *Aristocrats of Color: The Black Elite, 1880–1920* [Bloomington, Ind., 1990], 274). On Brooks and the respectability issue, see also Paul Harvey, *Redeeming the South: Religious Cultures and Racial Identities among Southern Baptists, 1865–1925* (Chapel Hill, N.C., 1997), 122.

24. *RP*, July 6, 13, 1901.

25. *RP*, July 13, 20, 27, Aug. 3, 10, 17, 1901; First African Minute Books, July 15, Aug. 5, 19, Oct. 7, Nov. 4, 1901; *RD*, Aug. 8, 1901; *RT*, Aug. 9, 1901.

26. *RP*, Aug. 10, 24, 1901, Jan. 11, 18, 25, March 15, 1902; "Nelson Williams Jr.," in Caldwell, *History of the American Negro*, 403–6; *RP*, July 6, 1895; declaration of Nelson Williams Jr. in Williams v. Mitchell, Law and Equity Court, 1903 (file 40), Richmond, LVA.

27. *RP*, March 22, April 26, 1902.

28. *RP*, March 8, 1902.

29. First African Minute Books, Oct. 7, Nov. 4, 1901; *RP*, April 12, 1902. On W. F. Graham, see *RP*, April 25, 1891, June 2, 1894; A. W. Pegues, *Our Baptist Ministers and Schools* (Springfield, Mass., 1892), 225–29.

30. *RT*, May 17, 1902; *RD*, May 17, 1902; *RP*, May 17, 24, 1902; "Church Polity" in Binga, *Sermons on Several Occasions*, 94, 97; Montgomery, *Under Their Own Vine and Fig Tree*, 116.

31. *RD*, July 9, 1902; *RP*, July 12, 19, 1902; First African Minute Books, Sept. 1, 1902.

32. *RD*, Jan. 6–10, 1903; *RP*, Jan. 17, 24, 1903; Williams v. Mitchell, 1903.

33. *RP*, Jan. 17, 24, 1903.

34. Charge to the jury, Jan. 6, 1903, in Williams v. Mitchell, 1903; *RP*, Jan. 17, Feb. 21, 1903.

35. First African Minute Books, Nov. 9, 1903; *RP*, Nov. 14, 1903; Johnson, *Historical Reminiscences.*

36. First African Minute Books, Dec. 7, 1903; *RP*, Dec. 12, 1903.

37. *RP*, Dec. 12, 1903; Raymond Gavins, *The Perils and Prospects of Southern Black Leadership: Gordon Blaine Hancock, 1884–1970* (Durham, N.C., 1977), 23–24; Anderson, *Education of Blacks in the South,* 70–72, 135, 240–44, 250–53; Emma Wesley Brown, "A Study of the Influence of the Philosophies of Accommodation and Protest of Five Colleges Established in Virginia for Negroes" (Ed.D. diss., Columbia University, 1967), 92–96; Lester Franklyn Russell, "Secondary Schools Established and Supported by Black Baptists in Virginia, 1887–1957" (Ed.D. diss., Rutgers University, 1976), 66–78.

38. Drake, quoted in Higginbotham, *Righteous Discontent,* 58; Brown, "Accommodation and Protest," 92–96; Reavis, "Virginia Seminary," 257–64; George Shepperson and Thomas Price, *Independent African: John Chilembwe and the Origins, Setting, and Significance of the Nyasaland Native Rising of 1915* (Edinburgh, 1958).

39. *RP*, July 13, 1901. In 1907 W. F. Graham resigned the pastorate of the Fifth Street church, which led to a struggle for the vacant pulpit. Mitchell's account in the *Planet* was scrupulously neutral, and neither he nor his mother voted in the subsequent election ("List of Members Whether Voting Yes or No," List of Members of Fifth Street Baptist Church, 1907, Richmond, LVA).

10. JIM CROW AND RACE PRIDE

1. *RP*, Sept. 27, 1902.

2. *RT*, Jan. 12, 1900; *RP*, Dec. 30, 1899, Jan. 13, 20, 1900; June Purcell Guild, *Black Laws of Virginia* (Richmond, 1936), 74–76. Although the story may be apocryphal, some whites thought the triggering event occurred in the fall of 1899 when Governor Tyler woke in the sleeping compartment of a train and found a "negro opposite him, above him, and in front of him" (*The Negro in Virginia,* compiled by workers of the Writers Program of the Work Projects Administration [New York, 1940], 241). A similar story was told about Kentucky (*BTW Papers* 7:313).

3. *RP*, Jan. 13, 1900; *RD*, Jan. 7, 26, 1900; *RT*, Jan. 7, 1900. The only real white opposition came from the railroads. On the "progressive" appeal of Jim Crow, see Ayers, *Promise of the New South,* 136–46.

4. *RT*, June 17, 1900; *RD*, Jan. 28, 1900.

5. *RP*, Jan. 17, Feb. 3, 1900.

6. *RP*, Feb. 19, 1901; George W. Daws to J. Hoge Tyler, Feb. 16, 1901, M. B. Crowell to Tyler, Feb. 16, 1901, box 13, Jas. W. McCarrick, Feb. 16, 1901, box 14, J. Hoge Tyler Papers, VT.

7. *RD*, Aug. 6, Sept. 27, 1891; *RP*, Dec. 27, 1890. On conflicts during Reconstruction, see Rabinowitz, *Race Relations in the Urban South,* 184, 192; Chesson, *Richmond after the War,* 101–3. The Richmond Railway and Electric Company Papers, 1897–1900 (VHS), contain detailed information about streetcar operations for this period but make no mention of racial problems.

8. *RD*, Sept. 4, 30, 1900; *RP*, Sept. 8, 1900. On the Constitutional Rights Association, see *Colored American Magazine* 1 (Oct. 1900): 309–11; Giles B. Jackson to Booker T. Washington, Oct. 5, 1900, Jan. 24, 1901, *BTW Papers* 5:649–51, 6:14–17.

9. *RT*, Jan. 26, 27, 1901; *RP*, March 8, 15, 1902, Oct. 4, 1902.

10. *RNL*, May 9, 1904.

11. *RNL*, April 1, 1904; *RP*, April 16, 1904.

12. *RP*, April 16, May 7, 1904.

13. *RP*, April 16, 1904; Jerome Dowd, *The Negro in American Life* (New York, 1926), 113; *RNL*, April 1, 16, 1904.

14. *RP*, Sept. 28, 1902, July 4, 1903.

15. *RNL*, April 5, 1904. Important secondary accounts of the boycott include August Meier and Elliott Rudwick, "The Boycott Movement against Jim Crow Streetcars in the South, 1900–1906," *JAH* 55 (March 1969): 756–75; James H. Brewer, "The War against Jim Crow in the Land of Goshen," *Negro History Bulletin* 24 (Dec. 1960): 53–57; Meier and Rudwick, "Negro Boycotts of Segregated Streetcars in Virginia, 1904–1907," *VMHB* 81 (Oct. 1973): 479–87.

16. *RNL*, April 7, 1904.

17. *RTD*, April 8, 1904; *RNL*, April 8, 1904.

18. *RP*, April 9, 1904; *St. Luke Herald* reprinted in *Washington Colored American*, April 16, 1904.

19. *RP*, April 16, May 7, 1904; *St. Luke Herald* reprinted in *Washington Colored American*, April 16, 1904; *RNL*, April 5, 1904.

20. Thomas Jefferson Headlee, "The Richmond Transit Strike of 1903" (M.A thesis, University of Richmond, 1960).

21. *RP*, Nov. 18, 1899.

22. *RP*, April 16, 1904; *RTD*, April 21, 1904.

23. *RTD*, April 20, 1904.

24. *RP*, April 23, 1904; *RTD*, April 17, 20–21, 1904.

25. *RTD*, April 20, 1904.

26. *RNL*, April 20, 1904; *RP*, April 23, 1904.

27. *RTD*, April 17, 1904.

28. *RTD*, April 21, 22, 1904; *RP*, June 4, 1904.

29. *RNL*, April 21, May 2, 1904; *RTD*, April 21, 1904.

30. *RP*, April 30, May 7, 14, 28, 1904.

31. *RP*, May 28, 1904. By 1907 Steward was so discouraged that he thought blacks had no choice but to return to Africa (*RP*, March 9, April 13, 1907).

32. *RP*, July 2, 1904; Lestor C. Lamon, *Black Tennesseans, 1900–1930* (Knoxville, Tenn., 1977), 33. On attempts in other southern cities to establish transit systems, see Meier and Rudwick, "Boycott Movement against Jim Crow Streetcars," 764–66.

33. *RP*, July 23, 1904; Brewer, "War against Jim Crow," 56–57.

34. *RP*, Oct. 15, 1904, June 10, 1905; *Richmond Reformer*, Jan. 23, 1905; Meier and Rudwick, "Negro Boycotts of Segregated Streetcars in Virginia, 1904–1907," 486; Kelly Miller, in *Voice of the Negro* 3 (Sept. 1906): 664.

35. *RTD*, July 4, 1906; *RP*, July 7, 1906.

36. *Evening Journal*, quoted in *RP*, Aug. 24, 1907; *RNL*, July 6, 1907.

37. *RP*, Jan. 13, 1906, June 29, 1907, May 10, 1913. When the Jim Crow system began to be dismantled in the 1950s, white observers discovered that in nearly every southern city, there were well-to-do blacks who boasted that they had never ridden in the back of the bus

(Catherine A. Brown, *Journey from Jim Crow: The Desegregation of Southern Transit* [New York, 1983], 18).

11. THE LURE OF FRATERNALISM

1. *RP,* June 16, July 14, 1906.

2. Elsa Barkley Brown in "Uncle Ned's Children" stresses the role of cooperative ventures. For an emphasis on property owning by individuals, see Loren Schweninger, *Black Property Owners in the South, 1790–1915* (Urbana, Ill., 1990).

3. Grand Fountain, United Order of True Reformers, *Revised Ritual* (Richmond, 1887), 13; Burrell and Johnson, *Twenty-Five Years History,* 17–20; D. Webster Davis, *The Life and Public Services of Rev. William Washington Browne* (Philadelphia, 1910); David M. Fahey, *The Black Lodge in White America: "True Reformer" Browne and His Economic Strategy* (Dayton, Ohio, 1994); Fahey, *Temperance and Racism: John Bull, Johnny Reb, and the Good Templars* (Lexington, Ky., 1996); W. T. Thom, *The True Reformers,* U.S. Bureau of Labor Bulletin no. 41 (Washington, D.C., 1902); James D. Watkinson, "William Washington Browne and the True Reformers of Richmond, Virginia," *VMHB* 97 (July 1989): 376–97.

4. *Virginia Business Directory and Gazetteer and Richmond City Directory, 1877–78* (Richmond, 1878), 51–53; *New York Globe,* June 9, 1883; Rachleff, *Black Labor in Richmond,* 13–33. More than four hundred organizations of various sorts deposited money in the Freedman's Savings Bank (Register of Signatures of Depositors in Branches of the Freedman's Savings and Trust Company, 1869–1874, Richmond Branch, NA [microfilm]).

5. *RP,* Dec. 1, 1900; W. P. Burrell, "The Negro in Insurance," *Hampton Negro Conference Proceedings,* 1904; O'Brien, *From Bondage to Citizenship,* 36, 329–32. On the African origins of fraternalism, with an emphasis on the St. Lukes, see Betty M. Kuyk, "The African Derivation of Black Fraternal Orders in the United States," *Comparative Studies in Society and History* 25 (1983): 559–92.

6. John S. Haller Jr., "Race, Mortality, and Life Insurance: Negro Vital Statistics in the Late Nineteenth Century," *Journal of the History of Medicine and Allied Sciences* 25 (1970): 247; *RP,* Dec. 13, 1890, Nov. 10, 1894; Gilbert Thomas Stephenson, *Race Distinctions in American Law* (New York and London, 1910), 138–40; William J. Trent, *Development of Negro Life Insurance Enterprises* (Philadelphia, 1932); M. S. Stuart, *An Economic Detour: A History of Insurance in the Lives of American Negroes* (New York, 1940); Walter B. Weare, *Black Business in the New South: A Social History of the North Carolina Mutual Life Insurance Company* (Urbana, Ill., 1973); Robert Christian Puth, *Supreme Life: The History of a Negro Life Insurance Company* (New York, 1976); Alexa Benson Henderson, *Atlanta Life Insurance Company: Guardian of Black Economic Dignity* (Tuscaloosa, Ala., 1990). Whites also resisted commercial insurance and joined beneficial societies. See H. Roger Grant, *Insurance Reform: Consumer Action in the Progressive Era* (Ames, Iowa, 1979); Viviana A. Rotman Zelizer, *Morals and Markets: The Development of Life Insurance in the United States* (New York, 1979); Morton Keller, *The Life Insurance Enterprise, 1885–1910: A Study in the Limits of Corporate Power* (Cambridge, Mass., 1963).

7. *RP,* March 8, 1890; Burrell and Johnson, *Twenty-Five Years History,* 18, 29–30, 35; Davis, *Life and Public Services,* 11–60, 66, 68; Fahey, *Black Lodge in White America,* 14–15.

8. Burrell and Johnson, *Twenty-Five Years History,* 15, 89. On fraternal insurance, see B. H. Meyer, "Fraternal Insurance in the United States," *Annals of the American Academy of Political and Social Science* 17 (March 1901): 260–86; Miles B. Dawson, "Fraternal Life

Insurance," *Annals of the American Academy of Political and Social Sciences* 26 (1905), 308–16; Walter S. Nichol, "Fraternal Life Insurance," in *Yale Readings in Insurance: Personal Insurance, Life and Accident,* ed. Lester W. Zartman (New Haven, 1914), 361–83; S. S. Huebner, *Life Insurance,* 4th ed. (New York, 1950), 377–82; Richard DeRaismes Kip, *Fraternal Life Insurance in America* (Philadelphia, 1953); Douglass North, "Capital Accumulation in Life Insurance between the Civil War and the Investigation of 1905," in *Men in Business: Essays in the History of Entrepreneurship,* ed. William Miller (Cambridge, Mass., 1952), 239.

9. E. N. Palmer, "Negro Secret Societies," *Social Forces* 23 [Dec. 1944]: 211; Mary Ann Clawson, *Constructing Brotherhood: Class, Gender, and Fraternalism* (Princeton, N.J., 1989), 225; Burrell and Johnson, *Twenty-Five Years History,* 72–80; Grand Fountain, U.O.T.R., *1619–1907: From Slavery to Bankers* (Richmond, 1907?), reprinted in Fahey, *Black Lodge in White America,* 258.

10. Burrell and Johnson, *Twenty-Five Years History,* 78–89, 192; Stuart, *Economic Detour,* 36–37; Grand Fountain, *Revised Ritual,* 1887; Davis, *Life and Public Services,* 184; George C. Wright, *Life behind a Veil: Blacks in Louisville, Kentucky, 1865–1930* (Baton Rouge, La., 1985), 222.

11. Burrell and Johnson, *Twenty-Five Years History,* 113, 120. After Mitchell left the True Reformers in 1894, his name was practically purged from official histories, making it difficult to document his early involvement in any detail.

12. Davis, *Life and Public Services,* 109–25; Booker T. Washington, *The Story of the Negro: The Rise of the Race from Slavery* (New York, 1909), 2:215. On the contemporary white response to the True Reformers, see Hamilton J. Eckenrode, *Bottom Rail on Top: A Novel of the Old South* (New York, 1935), 213; Howard W. Odum, *Social and Mental Traits of the Negro* (New York, 1910), 128–29; J. G. de Roulhac Hamilton, "The Sons and Daughters of I Will Arise," *Scribners Magazine* 80 (Sept. 1926): 325–31; Benjamin Valentine, "The March of the Lodges," in *Ole Marster and Other Poems* (Richmond, n.d.), 98–100.

13. *RD,* Feb. 10, 1891; *RP,* May 23, Sept. 12, 1891, Aug. 27, 1892.

14. *RP,* Sept. 14, Dec. 14, 1895, May 1, 1897; Burrell and Johnston, *Twenty-Five Years History,* 152; Fahey, *Black Lodge in White America,* 24–25.

15. *RD,* March 23, 1895; *RT,* March 23, 1895; *RP,* March 30, Sept. 14, 1895.

16. *RP,* Sept. 21, Oct. 19, Nov. 2, 16, 1895, Jan. 11, 1896; *Washington Bee,* Nov. 16, 1895; *Annual Report of the Commissioner of Insurance of Virginia* (Richmond, 1910), xi; Fahey, *Black Lodge in White America,* 26–27.

17. *RP,* Dec. 25, 1897, Sept. 17, 1898, July 13, 1901; Fahey, *Black Lodge in White America,* 29–33; Ray Stannard Baker, *Following the Color Line: American Negro Citizenship in the Progressive Era* (1907; rept. New York, 1964), 162; W. E. B. Du Bois, *Economic Cooperation among Negro Americans: Report of a Social Study Made by Atlanta University* (Atlanta, 1907), 101.

18. Weare, *Black Business in the New South,* 14.

19. Elsa Barkley Brown, "Womanist Consciousness: Maggie Lena Walker and the Independent Order of Saint Luke," *Signs* 14 (Spring 1989): 610–33; Walker, "An Address to the 34th Annual Session of the Right Worthy Grand Council of Virginia, Independent Order of St. Luke, Aug. 20, 1901, Richmond, Virginia," MWHS.

20. E. A. Williams, *History and Manual of the Colored Knights of Pythias* (Nashville, 1917), 9–17, 66–67; Dittmer, *Black Georgia in the Progressive Era,* 56–57. In 1912, after a protracted and expensive court battle, the U.S. Supreme Court upheld the right of black men to call themselves Pythians.

21. *RP*, Feb. 13, 1892, Aug. 4, 1894; Knights of Pythias, *Proceedings of the 10th Annual Session* (Richmond, 1895), 7; Williams, *History and Manual*, 61.

22. *RP*, Jan. 4, 1896, Aug. 27, 1898.

23. *RP*, Aug. 4, 1900, April 1, 1905; *Constitution and Laws of the Grand Lodge Knights of Pythias, State of Virginia, and Constitution for Subordinate Lodges as Revised and Amended* (Richmond, 1907), 40, 53, in Commonwealth of Virginia v. Grand Lodge of Virginia, 1922–1924, Richmond Circuit Court, LVA; *Annual Report of the Commissioner of Insurance of Virginia, 1908–11*.

24. Typescript of interview, Anthony J. Binga, March 13, 1981, 24, 27, Maggie L. Walker Oral History Project, MWHS. Two recent studies of white fraternalism help dispel any notion that "lodge night" was uniquely black: Mark C. Carnes, *Secret Ritual and Manhood in Victorian America* (New Haven, 1989), and Clawson, *Constructing Brotherhood*.

25. *Constitution and Laws, 1907*; typescript of interview, Anthony J. Binga, 10, MWHS; William A. Muraskin, *Middle-Class Blacks in a White Society: Prince Hall Freemasonry in America* (Berkeley and Los Angeles, 1975), 40–41.

26. Interviews in Richmond: Tom Mitchell, June 8, 1993, Tessie Davidson, June 5, 1994, Virginia Leah Lewis, June 5, 1994; *RP*, Oct. 7, 1899, July 21, 1900, May 31, 1902, June 24, 1905; *Minutes of the Grand Lodge of Va., K. of P.* (Richmond, 1908), 65, 73, property of Tom Mitchell.

27. *RP*, May 31, 1902; O. Jackson Sands III, "John Mitchell, Jr.: His Life as Mirrored by the *Richmond Planet*" (undergraduate paper, Williams College, 1971), 87, RPL; Elsa Barkley Brown and Gregg D. Kimball, "Mapping the Terrain of Black Richmond," *Journal of Urban History* 21 (March 1995): 309–12. According to Sands, members of the Uniform Rank served with distinction during World War I. Another story says that Pythians prevented lynchings despite carrying ceremonial wooden rifles. When interviewed, Tom Mitchell could not remember wooden rifles but recalled as a youngster using the Pythians' Daisy rifles (ordered from Sears) to scare white boys away from their neighborhood (interview, June 8, 1993). On militarism as an aspect of fraternalism, see Clawson, *Constructing Brotherhood*, 233–39; Muraskin, *Middle-Class Blacks*, 141.

28. Detailed information about the history of the national organization can be found in Williams, *History and Manual*.

29. *RP*, May 31, 1902, Jan. 25, 1908; Williams, *History and Manual*, 755, 773; Brown, "Womanist Consciousness"; Clawson, *Constructing Brotherhood*; Carnes, *Secret Ritual and Manhood*. See also *Constitution and Laws of the Grand Court of Virginia, Order of Calanthe, State of Virginia, and Constitution for Subordinate Courts as Revised and Amended* (Richmond, 1907), in Commonwealth v. Grand Lodge. Aside from slightly reduced fees and scaled-down benefits, the constitutions of the Grand Court and Grand Lodge were similar. According to a study of Lynchburg fraternalism, societies that admitted men and women to the same lodge were usually about 70 percent female (Benjamin Guy Childs, *The Negroes of Lynchburg, Virginia* [Charlottesville, Va., 1923], 30).

30. *RP*, Dec. 1, 1900, July 21, 1906.

31. *RP*, May 16, Aug. 11, 25, Sept. 29, 1900, July 4, Oct. 17, 1903. For insight into the importance of fraternalism to one black Richmonder, see Diary, Edward McC. Drummond, 1910–1912, VM. Drummond managed to attend several fraternal functions each week.

32. Thomas M. Crump, the *Planet*'s bookkeeper, served as branch manager briefly until he left to work for Southern Aid; George W. Lewis then took the position (*RP*, Oct. 7, 1899, Jan. 6, 1900; "Thomas Morris Crump," *Colored American Magazine* 2 [Jan. 1901]: 196;

W. P. Burrell, "History of the Business of Colored Richmond," *Voice of the Negro* 1 [Aug. 1904]: 316–22; Burrell and Johnson, *Twenty-Five Years History of the True Reformers*, 365).

33. Charter of Mechanics' Savings Bank, Nov. 19, 1901, in "Record of Charters, Richmond Circuit Court," 5:285–87, JMCB. A collection of canceled checks is in the Papers of John Adams, UVA, and a number of bank artifacts are on display at the Black History Museum and Cultural Center of Virginia, Richmond.

34. Biographical information is scattered but generally comes from city directories.

35. *RP*, Jan. 4, 11, June 7, 1902, Feb. 25, 1905.

36. *RP*, Aug. 1, 1903; *Annual Report of the Bureau of Banking, Virginia State Corporation Commission* (Richmond, 1905).

37. Maggie L. Walker, "Nothing but Leaves," n.d., "If Christ Came to Washington," n.d., "Stumbling Block," Feb. 17, 1907, Maggie Walker Addresses, MWHS; *RP*, May 28, 1904.

12. "A SANE AND SENSIBLE BUSINESSMAN"

1. Allan Garfield Gruchy, *Supervision and Control of Virginia State Banks* (New York, 1937), 65–76; Maggie Walker, "Stumbling Blocks," Feb. 17, 1907, Maggie Walker Addresses, MWHS.

2. W. P. Burrell explained the clearing-house arrangement in "Savings and Loan," *Ninth Annual Report, Hampton Negro Conference, 1905*, 64.

3. *RP*, Feb. 10, 1900, Jan. 23, 1904; "John P. Branch," *Men of Mark in Virginia*, ed. Lyon G. Tyler (Washington, D.C., 1907), 2:46–50.

4. *RP*, Oct. 14, 1905; *Proceedings of the American Bankers Association*, 1904–7.

5. "Oliver Jackson Sands," *Men of Mark in Virginia* 2:344–47; *RP*, April 21, 1923; obituary, *RTD*, Nov. 25, 1964. Oliver Jackson Sands III wrote a senior thesis at Williams College on Mitchell but failed to comment on the relationship with his grandfather. See Sands, "John Mitchell Jr.," RPL.

6. *RP*, June 20, 1891, Aug. 8, 1896, Feb. 20, 1897.

7. *RP*, Jan. 6, 1900; C. Vann Woodward, *The Strange Career of Jim Crow* (New York, 1955), 33; Bryan, *Joseph Bryan*.

8. *ABA Proceedings*, Sept. 14–16, 1904 (New York, 1904), iii, vi. States were allotted one delegate for every fifty members of the state association, but it is not clear how Virginia's delegates were chosen or how Branch arranged Mitchell's attendance.

9. *RTD*, Aug. 31, 1904; *RP*, Sept. 3, 1904.

10. *Washington Post*, Sept. 4, 1904; *RP*, Sept. 17, 1904.

11. "The Astoria Hotel, New York City," *Scientific American* 77 (Oct. 30, 1897): 281–82.

12. Robert F. Maddox, in *ABA Proceedings, 1904*, 147.

13. *ABA Proceedings, 1904*, 176–78; *New York Times*, Sept. 17, 1904.

14. *ABA Proceedings, 1904*, 178.

15. Ibid., 179; *New York Times*, Sept. 17, 1904.

16. *New York Age*, Sept. 22, 1904, quoted in *RP*, Oct. 15, 1904.

17. "John Mitchell at the Banker's Convention," *Voice of the Negro* 1 (Nov. 1904): 514–16; *Washington Bee*, Oct. 1, 1904; *Cleveland Gazette*, Sept. 24, 1904.

18. *RP*, Sept. 24, Oct. 1, 1904.

19. L. M. Hershaw, "The Negro Press in America," *Charities and Commons* 15 (1905): 66–68; Booker T. Washington, *The Negro in Business* (Boston, 1907), 124–25.

20. *RP,* Oct. 27, 1906, Oct. 9, 1915.

21. *RP,* Nov. 3, 1906, Nov. 14, 1908, Sept. 25, 1909, Dec. 31, 1910, Sept. 21, 1912.

22. *RP,* Nov. 4, 1905, Dec. 10, 17, 1910, Nov. 25, Dec. 2, 9, 1911. Mitchell followed closely the controversy regarding black attorney William L. Lewis's membership in the American Bar Association (*RP,* Oct. 5, 1912, Nov. 1, 1913).

23. *RP,* Oct. 17, 1914; *RTD,* Sept. 12, 1914.

24. *RP,* Oct. 16, 1909, Oct. 22, 1921.

25. Circulation figures for the *Planet* are drawn from newspaper directories published by Edward P. Remington, George P. Rowell, and N. W. Ayer. The numbers do not always agree but indicate that the *Planet*'s circulation during the 1890s was in the neighborhood of 4,000 to 7,500; after 1900 estimates were usually between 2,250 and 4,000.

26. *RD,* March 24–25, 27, 1900; *RT,* March 25, 27, 1900; *RP,* March 31, 1900; Brundage, *Lynching,* 178–79.

27. Brundage, *Lynching,* 281–83; William E. Larsen, *Montague of Virginia: The Making of a Southern Progressive* (Baton Rouge, La., 1965), 122–23, 242.

28. On the importance of an institutional response, see Brundage, "To Howl Loudly," 334–38.

29. *RP,* Sept. 29, Oct. 20, 1906, Sept. 21, 1907; Ayers, *Promise of the New South,* 435–37; Lewis, *Du Bois: Biography of a Race,* 333–37.

30. *RTD,* Aug. 11–14, 17, 19, 21, 23–24, Sept. 6, 8, 21, 1907; *RP,* Aug. 17, 1907. The Onancock story was more complex than I have indicated, though no less horrific. For a fuller account, see Brooks Miles Barnes, "The Onancock Riot of 1907," *VMHB* 92 (July 1984): 336–51.

31. Mitchell to Washington, July 28, 1913, box 848, Booker T. Washington Papers, LC.

32. *RP,* March 5, 1904, Sept. 16, 1905, July 6, Sept. 14, 1907, July 4, 1908; Mitchell to Emmett J. Scott, May 25, 1904, *BTW Papers* 7:499.

33. *RP,* Jan. 7, 28, April 22, 1905, June 9, 1906, Dec. 28, 1907, May 8, 1909, Sept. 13, 1913.

34. *RP,* Aug. 25, Sept. 1, 1906; Lewis, *Du Bois: Biography of a Race,* 328–30.

35. *RP,* Sept. 19, 1906, Sept. 19, 1908. Brownsville dominated the front page of the *Planet* for several years beginning in Nov. 1906.

36. *RP,* May 8, 1909.

13. THE PERILS OF PROSPERITY

1. *Eighth Annual Report of the State Corporation Commission* (Richmond, 1911), 67; Abram L. Harris, *The Negro as Capitalist: A Study of Banking and Business among American Negroes* (College Park, Md., 1936), 77.

2. *RP,* June 20, 1908, July 17, 1909; *RTD,* July 18, 1909.

3. Interview, Tom Mitchell, June 8, 1993; *RP,* Jan. 13, 1912.

4. Richmond's black population increased from 32,230 to 46,733 between 1900 and 1910; the white population from 52,798 to 80,879. See also occupation statistics in *Thirteenth Census of the United Sates* (Washington, D.C., 1914), 14:595–96. On residential segregation in Richmond, see Silver, *Twentieth-Century Richmond;* Rabinowitz, *Race Relations in the Urban South,* chap. 4; Chesson, *Richmond after the War,* 121–29, 173–77; Brown and Kimball, "Mapping the Terrain of Black Richmond," 296–346. On the building and real estate boom, see *RTD,* July 25, Aug. 1, 1909, Jan. 1, 1911.

5. *RP,* May 27, 1916; Gustavus A. Weber, *Report on Housing and Living Conditions in the Neglected Sections of Richmond, Virginia* (Richmond, 1913); Charles Louis Knight, *Negro*

Housing in Certain Virginia Cities (Richmond, 1927); *The Negro in Richmond, Virginia: The Report of the Negro Welfare Survey Committee* (Richmond, 1929); Woofter, *Negro Problems in Cities;* Silver, *Twentieth-Century Richmond,* chap. 3.

6. Winthrop, *Jackson Ward Historic District,* 27–34; Dulaney, *Architecture of Historic Richmond,* 103–15. The racial makeup of Clay Street was determined by examining city directories each decade from 1850 to 1930.

7. *RP,* July 17, 24, 1909; *RTD,* July 17, 18, 1909.

8. *RTD,* June 26, 28, 1910; *RP,* July 2, 1910; *New York Age,* July 14, 1910; advertisement for the Mechanics' Savings Bank, *RNL,* March 30, 1911.

9. *RP,* Oct. 1, 29, Nov. 5, 1910; *RTD,* Aug. 14–15, 1909, Oct. 30, 1910. The white press may have exaggerated the extent of Mitchell's investments, but he clearly owned some key property.

10. *RP,* Dec. 17, 1910, Jan. 14, 21, 1911.

11. "An ordinance to secure for white and colored people, respectively, the separate location of residences for each race, April 19, 1911," in *Certain Resolutions and Ordinances of the Council of the City of Richmond* (Richmond, 1912), 166–67; *RNL,* Feb. 4, 6, 1911; *RTD,* Feb. 5, 1911. Live-in servants were specifically exempted. On residential segregation, see Roger L. Rice, "Residential Segregation by Law, 1910–1917," *JSH* 34 (May 1968): 179–99; Charles Flint Kellogg, *NAACP: A History of the National Association for the Advancement of Colored People* (Baltimore, 1967), 186 n. 11; G. T. Stephenson, "Segregation of the White and Negro Races in Cities," *South Atlantic Quarterly* 13 (Jan. 1914): 1–18; Wright, *Life behind a Veil,* 229–45.

12. *RP,* Feb. 18, 1911; S. S. Field, "Constitutionality of Segregation Ordinances, *Virginia Law Review* 5 (Nov. 1917): 90.

13. *RNL,* Feb. 6, 8, 20, 1911; *RP,* Feb. 18, 1911.

14. Mitchell to Members of the Committee on Ordinances, Charters, and Reform, Feb. 21, 1911, Minutes of Feb. 27, 1911, in Records of the Committee on Ordinances, Charters, and Reform, City Council Papers, LVA; *RTD,* Feb. 28, 1911; *RNL,* Feb. 28, 1911; *RP,* March 4, 1911. On Mitchell's response to Jack Johnson, see Al-Tony Gilmore, *Bad Nigger! The National Impact of Jack Johnson* (Port Washington, N.Y., 1975).

15. Journal of the Common Council, March 6, 1911, RPL; *RP,* March 11, 1911, Feb. 3, 1912; *RNL,* March 7, 30, 1911; Walter Russell Bowie, *Sunrise in the South: The Life of Mary-Cooke Branch Munford* (Richmond, 1942), 158.

16. Aldermen Journal, March 14, April 13, 1911, RPL; *RNL,* March 15, 30, April 3, 13, 20, 1911; *RTD,* March 15, April 8–10, 19, 20, 1911; *RP,* March 18, April 22, 1911.

17. *RNL,* April 24, 25, 1911; *RP,* April 1, June 10, 21, 1911, June 21, 1913; petition from J. Bernstein in Common Council Journal, July 7, Aug. 10, 1911; Annual Report of the City Attorney, 1911, in *Annual Message and Accompanying Documents of the Mayor of Richmond* (Richmond, 1912), 13.

18. NAACP officials were concerned about local conditions in Richmond, where appeals were already underway and where "our coming in just now might complicate matters badly" (Miss M. C. Nearney to W. N. Colson, June 12, July 2, 1914, "Richmond" [report, c. 1916], NAACP Papers, LC; *RP,* June 1, 1912, Dec. 19, 1914). Officials were also worried because black Richmonders had divided in 1913 over a proposed public park for Jackson Ward. Mitchell argued that the park was badly needed, but some black leaders viewed the city's offer as a way of distracting the community from more important issues. See *RP,* July 26, Aug. 2, 9, Oct. 25, 1913. Scattered information about the Richmond branch of the

NAACP can be found in the *Crisis;* the NAACP Papers; and the Maggie Walker Papers, MWHS. See also *RP,* Dec. 1, 1917, and especially James Weldon Johnson to Thomas L. Dabney, Nov. 9, 1923, NAACP Papers. Although Mitchell remained on good terms with NAACP leaders on the national level, there is no evidence he ever joined the Richmond branch.

19. *RTD,* Sept. 9, 14, 1914.

20. *RTD,* Sept. 9, 14, 17, Oct. 5–7, 9, Nov. 24, 1914; *RP,* Sept. 12, Nov. 28, 1914.

21. *RP,* June 21, 1913, Sept. 19, Oct. 3, 10, 1914; *RTD,* Oct. 5–7, 9, 1914.

22. *RTD,* Jan. 27, April 4, 1915; *RP,* Jan. 30, March 27, April 10, Aug. 21, 1915.

23. *RP,* Nov. 10, 1917; Rice, "Residential Segregation by Law," 192–97; Annual Report of the City Attorney, H. R. Pollard, in *Annual Message and Accompanying Documents of the Mayor of Richmond to the City Council* (Richmond, 1918), 23–28. On residential segregation in Norfolk during this period, see Earl Lewis, *In Their Own Interests: Race, Class, and Power in Twentieth-Century Norfolk, Virginia* (Berkeley, Calif., 1991), chap. 3.

24. *RP,* June 9, 1915. Washington's response to residential segregation was characteristically muted (Louis R. Harlan, *Booker T. Washington: The Wizard of Tuskegee, 1901–1915* [New York, 1983], 422–31).

25. Report of the Chief Bank Examiner in *Eighth Annual Report of the State Corporation Commission,* viii, 61, 67; "Charles C. Barksdale," *History of Virginia* (Chicago and New York, 1924), 4:198–99. Barksdale also closed one white bank.

26. Harris, *Negro as Capitalist,* 62–74; Dabney, *Maggie Walker,* 39; Arnett G. Lindsay, "The Negro in Banking," *JNH* 14 (April 1929): 176–77; John T. Kneebone, "William Patrick Burrell," *DVB* 2:420–22; *RTD,* Sept. 15, Oct. 27–28, 1910; *New York Age,* Sept. 22, 1910; *RP,* Sept. 17, Oct. 29, 1910, April 1, Aug. 12, 1911. R. T. Hill's son, T. Arnold Hill, went on to have a distinguished career with the national Urban League but evidently never revealed his father's whereabouts.

27. See especially Chief Examiner to Mechanics, July 19, 1911, July 1, 1912, May 14, 1913, April 10, 1914, March 10, July 27, 1915, March 10, 1916, in General Correspondence, 1910–1918, Bureau of Banking, State Corporation Commission, LVA. On legal restrictions on bank ownership of real estate, see *Code of Virginia, 1919,* sec. 4114.

28. Barksdale to Mitchell, Feb. 16, 19, 21, March 1, 1917, Barksdale to Walter P. Davis, cashier, March 9, 1917, in General Correspondence, 1910–1918, Bureau of Banking, SCC; Report, June 7, 1912, May 7, 1913, Mechanics' Bank, Bank Examiners Reports, 1910–1922, ibid. The examiners issued confidential reports to Barksdale, and he summarized their findings in letters to bank officers, often adding observations of his own. White bankers also speculated in real estate and often got themselves into trouble, as contemporary banking manuals reveal. See John I. Millet, *Bank Audits and Examinations* (New York, 1927); Robert G. Rodkey, *The Banking Process* (New York, 1930); Thomas Joel Anderson Jr., *Federal and State Control of Banking* (New York, 1934); Gruchy, *Supervision and Control of State Banks in Virginia;* David C. Purcell, *State Banks and the State Corporation Commission: A Historical Review* (Richmond, 1974).

29. *RP,* Dec. 24, 1910; Report, June 6, 1912, Mechanics' Bank, Bank Examiners Reports, 1910–1922, Bureau of Banking, SCC; Chief Examiner to Mechanics, Sept. 11, 1916, General Correspondence, 1910–1918, ibid. Barksdale said nothing publicly about Mitchell's most embarrassing blunder, his involvement in the founding of the Anglo-American Finance Corporation. While attending the ABA meeting in Chicago in 1909, he met John Phillips, a British lawyer who professed interest in black-run enterprises and volunteered that he had

money to invest. The two began a correspondence, and in 1912 Phillips made a highly pub-
licized trip to Richmond. Mitchell acquired a charter for the Anglo-American Finance
Corporation and purchased on the bank's behalf $10,000 worth of stock. Phillips promptly
disappeared. See *RP,* Oct. 16, 1909, Nov. 30, Dec. 7, 14, 1912, Jan. 11, 1913; "The Passing of
John Mitchell Jr.," *Messenger* 4 (Nov. 1922): 529; Report of the Chief Bank Examiner, *Tenth
Annual Report of the State Corporation Commission* (Richmond, 1913), 60.

30. *RP,* Nov. 2, 9, 1912; *RTD,* Nov. 1, 1912; Barksdale to Mitchell, Nov. 8, 1912, General
Correspondence, 1920–1918, Bureau of Banking, SCC.

31. Harris, *Negro as Capitalist,* 102–3; Roger Weiss, "Abram Lincoln Harris," *DANB,*
291–92; transcript of interview, Anthony J. Binga, March 13, 1982, Maggie L. Walker Oral
History Project, MWHS. Abram L. Harris (1899–1963) was the grandson of Cornelius Harris, who was active in Reconstruction politics.

32. *RP,* April 22, 1916; *RTD,* April 17–18, 20, 1916.

33. *RP,* April 22, July 1, 1916; *RTD,* April 20, June 29, 1916.

34. *RP,* March 31, April 14, June 9, 16, 1917.

35. *RP,* July 7, 1917; Elliott M. Rudwick, *Race Riot at East St. Louis: July 2, 1917* (New York,
1972).

36. "Alleged Propaganda among Colored Orderlies, St. Lukes Hospital, Richmond,
April 15, 1917," in *Federal Surveillance of Afro-Americans (1917–1925): The First World War,
the Red Scare, and the Garvey Movement,* ed. Theodore Kornweible Jr. (Frederick Md.,
1986), reel 8, frames 276, 454 (microfilm); *RP,* Aug. 4, 1917.

37. *RP,* Aug. 4, 11, 1917; *NJ&G,* Aug. 18, 1917. On the larger issues, see Mark Ellis, "America's Black Press, 1914–1918," *History Today* 41 (Sept. 1991): 20–27, and the Justice Department's report, "Radicalism and Sedition among the Negroes as Reflected in Their Publica-
tions," in *Investigation Activities of the Department of Justice* (Washington, D.C., 1919), 161–
87; William G. Jordan, *Black Newspapers and America's War for Democracy, 1914–1920*
(Chapel Hill, N.C., 2001), 107–9.

38. Hay T. Thornton to Solicitor for the Post Office Department, Aug. 3, 7, 1917,
Mitchell to A. S. Burleson, Postmaster General, Aug. 6, 1917, *Right of Free Speech Denied*
[Aug. 4, 1917], and wire, Solicitor to Postmaster, Richmond, Aug. 8, 1917, Records of the
Post Office Department, Office of the Solicitor, Records Relating to the Espionage Act,
World War I, 1917–1921, RB28, case file 47505, NA.

39. *RP,* Aug. 11, Sept. 15, 1917.

40. Harris, *Negro as Capitalist,* 77; *RP,* Jan. 27, June 2, 1917, Jan. 11, 1919; *NJ&G,* April 28,
May 5, 1917.

41. Bruce Grit [John E. Bruce] in the *Pioneer Press,* quoted in *RP,* May 10, 1913; Brewer,
"The Ghosts of Jackson Ward," 27.

42. *RP,* July 25, 1914; Aug. 16, 1919; James J. Flink, *America Adopts the Automobile, 1895–
1910* (Cambridge, Mass., 1970), 73; George Woodbury, *The Story of a Stanley Steamer* (New
York, 1950).

43. *RP,* March 31, 1917, Feb. 8, Aug. 2, 16, 1919, Nov. 27, 1920, July 23, 1921.

44. Dabney to Du Bois, Feb. 23, 1950, in *Correspondence of W. E. B. Du Bois,* ed. Herbert
Aptheker (Amherst, Mass., 1978), 3:279.

45. *RP,* May 3, 1919, Sept. 25, 1920; Lewis, *Du Bois: Biography of a Race,* 578; Lawrence W.
Levine, "Marcus Garvey and the Politics of Revitalization," in *Black Leaders of the Twentieth Century,* 112–14.

14. COLLAPSE

1. Miles Rudisill Jr., "From Storefronts to Palaces: The Theatres of Richmond," 1979, 1–2, and Roy Proctor, "Richmond by Stages," n.d., 8–9, typescripts in Richmond Theaters Vertical File, RPL; *Crisis*, July 1919, 154.

2. *RP*, Nov. 29, 1919, April 15, 1922; *RNL*, May 19, 1934. The Booker T has since been restored as the Empire.

3. Report, Feb. 25, 1919, Mechanics' Bank, Bank Examiners Reports, 1910–1922, Bureau of Banking, State Corporation Commission, LVA; Unique Amusement Corporation, Feb. 28, 1919, State Corporation Commission Charter Books, 10:574–75, LVA.

4. Harris, *Negro as Capitalist*, 77–79; *RP*, April 17, 24, 1920. On other efforts by blacks to open theaters, see *RP*, Nov. 29, 1919, May 29, 1920, Jan. 1, 1921. In 1926 the General Assembly passed a law requiring segregation in public halls and theaters (Richard Sherman, "The 'Teachings at Hampton Institute': Social Equality, Racial Integrity, and the Virginia Public Assemblage Act of 1926," *VMHB* 95 [July 1987]: 275–300).

5. B. F. Vaughan to Edward Drummond, July 30, 1921, Edward Drummond Papers, VM. For a helpful overview of the black independence movement, see Buni, *Negro in Virginia Politics*, 69–89.

6. Nancy J. Weiss, "The Negro and the New Freedom: Fighting Wilsonian Segregation," *Political Science Quarterly* 84 (March 1968): 61–79; Richard B. Sherman, *The Republican Party and Black America: From McKinley to Hoover, 1896–1933* (Charlottesville, Va., 1973), 148–49; Monroe Work, ed., *Negro Year Book, 1921–22*, 48–51.

7. *RP*, Oct. 2, 1920; William Pickens, "The Woman Voter Hits the Color Line," *Nation*, Oct. 6, 1920, p. 373; Suzanne Lebsock, "Woman Suffrage and White Supremacy: A Virginia Case Study," in *Visible Women: New Essays on American Activism*, ed. Nancy A. Hewitt and Suzanne Lebsock (Urbana, Ill., 1993), 62–100. According to Lebsock (p. 97 n. 57) after the ratification of the Nineteenth Amendment in 1920, 10,645 white women and 2,410 black women in Richmond registered; the black women registrants comprised 26.8 percent of the eligible white females and 12.5 percent of the black females.

8. *NJ&G*, July 16, 1921; *RTD*, July 22, 1921; Sherman, *Republican Party*, 146–56; Sara B. Bearss, "Henry Watkins Anderson," *DVB* 1:136–38.

9. *RP*, May 1, 1920, July 23, Sept. 10, Oct. 1, 8, 1921; *NJ&G*, July 30, Aug. 6, Sept. 3, 10, Oct. 8, 15, 1921; *New York Times*, Sept. 11, 1921; Mitchell to Hon. B. O. James, Secretary of the Commonwealth of Virginia, Sept. 30, 1921, Election Expense Accounts, State Board of Elections, LVA; Henry Lewis Suggs, *P. B. Young, Newspaperman: Race, Politics, and Journalism in the New South, 1910–1962* (Charlottesville, Va., 1988).

10. *RP*, Sept. 17, Oct. 1, Nov. 5, 1921; *NJ&G*, Oct. 8, 1921. See especially Richardson to Mitchell, Sept. 27, 1921, in Commonwealth v. Mechanics Savings Bank, 1944, RCH; Report, Oct. 29, 1921, Mechanics' Bank, Bank Examiners Reports, 1910–1922, Bureau of Banking, SCC-.

11. *RP*, Nov. 5, 1921; *RNL*, Nov. 1, 3, 5–6, 1921.

12. *RNL*, Nov. 8, 1921, *Roanoke Times*, Nov. 8, 1921; *Annual Report of the Secretary of the Commonwealth* (Richmond, 1922), 419–23. The candidates all put their own spin on the numbers. The *Planet* (Nov. 12, 1921) headlined that the "Colored Republicans" had polled 25,000, which was the aggregate of the lily-black vote and not the vote of any one candidate. Anderson boasted that his total was the greatest ever polled by a Virginia Republican but failed to mention that woman suffrage had expanded the electorate and that he also lost by more than any Republican. Mitchell ran nearly two thousand votes behind Maggie Walker

(6,991), which may indicate a strong showing by black women, although the returns are difficult to interpret. The ticket leader was the relatively obscure Thomas E. Jackson (7,463) of Staunton, a candidate for state treasurer who ran well in western Virginia.

13. *RP*, Nov. 19, 1921; transcript of interview, Armstead Walker, Feb. 20, 1981, Maggie Walker Oral History Project, MWHS.

14. Ann M. Schmelz to Mary Munford, Aug. 24, [1921], box 2, Mary-Cooke Branch Munford Papers, LVA. See also in this box Schmelz to [Janie Porter] Barrett, Aug. 17, 30, 1921. The lily-black movement was a halfway station for black Virginians who had been rejected by Republicans but were not yet welcome in the Democratic Party. See Buni, *Negro in Virginia Politics,* 87; Elbert Lee Tatum, *Changed Political Thought of the Negro, 1915–1940* (New York, 1951), 130–31; Glenda Elizabeth Gilmore, "False Friends and Avowed Enemies: Southern African Americans and Party Allegiances in the 1920s," in *Jumpin' Jim Crow: Southern Politics from Civil War to Civil Rights,* ed. Jane Dailey, Glenda Elizabeth Gilmore, Bryant Simon (Princeton, N.J., 2000), 219–38.

15. *RP*, Sept. 11, 1920, Jan. 15, 1921, Jan. 7, Feb. 18, 1922. When war broke out between Garvey and the NAACP in 1920, Mitchell professed neutrality and remained on good terms with Du Bois, but his heart was clearly with Garvey.

16. *RP*, Sept. 17, 1921, April 22, 29, May 6, 1922.

17. *RP*, July 8, 1922.

18. Agent WW, Report, Feb. 18, 1920, "John Mitchell," OG384671, FBI Case Files, 1908–1922, NA; *Garvey Papers* 3:340 n. 3, 4:115 n. 2; Confidential Informant 800 to George F. Ruch, New York, April 12, 1922, report by Special Agent James E. Amos, New York, July 21, 1922, ibid., 4:597–98, 729. On Dusé, see Judith Stein, *The World of Marcus Garvey: Race and Class in Modern Society* (Baton Rouge, La., 1986), 29, 186. The agent's report about Mitchell taking over the Black Star Line was made after the Mechanics' Bank was closed, but Garvey had not yet learned of the bank's troubles. See Garvey to Mitchell, July 25, 1922, in *RP*, Aug. 5, 1922.

19. *RP*, July 14, 1923. See also "The Trials of Negro Leaders," editorial, *RNL*, July 7, 1923.

20. *RP*, June 2, 1922; Report, Sept. 13, 1920, Feb. 19, Oct. 29, 1921, Mechanics' Bank, Bank Examiners Reports, 1910–1922, Bureau of Banking, SCC; Mitchell to Richardson, May 4,1921, June 5, 1922, in Commonwealth v. Mechanics Savings Bank, 1944; interview, Tom Mitchell, June 8, 1993.

21. Harris, *Negro as Capitalist,* 77; *RP*, Jan. 17, Oct. 23, 1920.

22. Maggie Walker Diary, Dec. 7, 1920, MWHS; interview, Virginia Leah Lewis (daughter of George W. Lewis), Richmond, June 5, 1994.

23. *RP*, Feb. 18, 1922; Report, Oct. 29, 1921, Mechanics' Bank, Bank Examiners Reports, 1910–1922, Bureau of Banking, SCC. See also correspondence and papers in Commonwealth v. Mechanics Savings Bank, 1944 including: Order of State Corporation Commission, March 18, 1921, Richardson to Norrell, June 8, Sept. 16, 1921, Richardson to Mitchell, May 2, May 12, May 19, Sept. 27, 1921, Mitchell to Richardson, May 3, 13, 18, June 11, Sept. 26, 1921.

24. Richardson to Norrell, Nov. 7, Dec. 15, 1921, Richardson to Mitchell, Nov. 7, 1921, Mitchell to Richardson, Dec. 2, 1921, Report on Audit of Mechanics Savings Bank, Jan. 16, 1922, all in Commonwealth v. Mechanics Savings Bank, 1944.

25. Richardson to Norrell, Feb. 20, 1922, Mitchell to Richardson, May 16, May 29, June 17, 1922, Richardson to Mitchell, May 31, June 12, 1922, Mitchell to Smith & Gordon, May 10, 1922, ibid.

26. Richardson to State Corporation Commission, July 15, 1922, ibid.; *RP,* July 22, 1922; *New York Age,* July 29, 1922; interview, Hattie Walker (daughter-in-law of Maggie Walker), Chicago, Oct. 23, 1968.

27. *RTD,* July 16, 1922; *RP,* July 15, 1922.

28. *RTD,* July 18, 1922; *RP,* July 22, 1922.

29. *RP,* July 29, 1922; *RTD,* July 22, 1922; *RNL,* July 22, 27, 1922; Garvey to Mitchell, July 25, 1922, printed in *RP,* Aug. 5, 1922; Resolution of Baptist Ministers' Conference, July 25, 1922, in E. Lee Trinkle Papers, LVA; Special Report of Joseph G. Tucker, Aug. 12, 1922, in *Federal Surveillance of Afro-Americans,* reel 5, frame 149.

30. *RP,* Nov. 11, 1922; *NJ&G,* Aug. 26, 1922; *RTD,* Aug. 18, 1922; petition of J. W. Thompson and others, Aug. 17, 1922, bill of complaint by Tucker and Gordon, Receivers, in Commonwealth v. Mechanics Savings Bank, 1944.

31. J. R. Tucker and James W. Gordon to Mitchell, Aug. 12, 1922, Exhibit 2 of bill of complaint by Tucker and Gordon, Receivers, Aug. 29, 1922, in Commonwealth v. Mechanics Savings Bank, 1944; *RTD,* Aug. 24, 26, 1922; *RNL,* Aug. 22, 24, 26, 1922.

32. "Answer of A. V. Norrell Jr.," May 18, 1923, in Commonwealth v. Mechanics Savings Bank, 1944; *RP,* Aug. 26, Sept. 2, 1922; *RTD,* Aug. 27, 1922.

33. *RP,* Sept. 16, 1922; *New York Age,* July 22, Sept. 9, 1922. In general, Mitchell's fellow journalists tended to downplay the story or adopt a wait-and-see attitude.

34. "The Passing of John Mitchell Jr.," *Messenger* 4 (Nov. 1922): 528–29.

35. *RP,* Dec. 9, 1922, March 19, June 9, 1923; *RNL,* Dec. 4, 8, 1922; *RTD,* Dec. 9, 1922; *New York Age,* Dec. 23, 1922; "Petition of John Mitchell Jr.," Dec. 6, 1922, "Report on Audit, as of July 15, 1922, prepared by A. M. Pullen, Feb. 28, 1923," in Commonwealth v. Mechanics Savings Bank, 1944.

36. *RTD,* April 27–28, 1923. The list of jurors appears in Hustings Court Order Book, 75:416, JMCB; their occupations are in city directories.

37. *RP,* May 5, 19, June 2, 1923; *RNL,* April 26–27, 1923; *RTD,* April 27–28, 1923.

38. Hustings Court Order Book, 75:420; *RTD,* April 30, May 1, 1923; *RNL,* April 30, 1923.

39. *RP,* May 5, 12, 19, 1923.

40. Hustings Court Order Book, 75–76:449; *RTD,* May 16, 1923; *RNL,* May 16, 1923; *NJ&G,* May 19, June 9, 1923.

41. Bruce to Mitchell, printed in *RP,* June 9, 1923; *Petersburg Virginia Weekly,* quoted in *RP,* July 4, 1923; W. B. Reed to Mitchell, printed in *RP,* June 9, 1923. See also *Cleveland Gazette,* May 26, 1923, and a more skeptical view in *Pittsburgh Courier,* June 2, 1923.

42. *RP,* Nov. 24, 1923; *RTD,* Nov. 18, 1923; *NJ&G,* Nov. 24, 1923; Mitchell v. Commonwealth, March 19, 1925, *Virginia Reports* 144:541–67; Hustings Court Order Book, June 11, 1925, 70:280.

43. *RP,* Sept. 9, 1922, June 16, 1923; *NJ&G,* Sept. 23, 1922.

44. *RP,* Sept. 9, 1922; *NJ&G,* Sept. 23, Oct. 21, 1922; Report of Receiver filed Nov. 20, 1924, in Commonwealth of Virginia v. Grand Lodge of the Knights of Pythias, Richmond City Circuit Court, 1922–24, LVA.

45. *RP,* June 23, 30, 1923, July 3, 1926; *NJ&G,* Sept. 23, Oct. 21, 1922; "Miscellaneous Domestic Fraternal Orders Overseen by the Insurance Division, State Corporation Commission," in Commonwealth v. Mechanics Savings Bank, 1944; *Official Proceedings of the Twenty-second Biennial Session of the Knights of Pythias* (Nashville, 1924), 30, in Commonwealth v. Grand Lodge, 1922–24.

46. *RP,* Sept. 1923-Feb. 1924, and various documents in the Trinkle Papers, including:

flyer, "You Can Get Your Money Now—Act Quick," Nov. 1, 1923, Trinkle to Col. C. R. Kei-ley, Oct. 11, 1923, Mitchell to Trinkle, Nov. 10, 1923, copy of letter, Mitchell to Tucker and Gordon, Receivers, Nov. 9, 1923.

47. *RP*, May 26, 1923; *RTD*, May 19, 1923, Feb. 16, 1924; Mitchell to Walter White, Aug. 17, 1923, box C-399, NAACP Papers, LC; "Report of Sale of Strand Theatre, as made Feb. 15, 1924," in Commonwealth v. Mechanics Savings Bank, 1944.

48. Mitchell to Trinkle, Oct. 15, 1924, Trinkle Papers; *RP*, July 31, Aug. 7, 1926.

49. *RP*, May 14, 1927, July 12, 1924, Aug. 20, 1927, Feb. 11, 25, 1928.

50. Paul K. Edwards, *The Southern Urban Negro as a Consumer* (New York, 1932), 39, 178–81; Eugene Gordon, "The Negro Press," *Annals of the American Academy of Political and Social Sciences* 120 (Nov. 1928): 248–56; Roi Ottley, *The Lonely Warrior: The Life and Times of Robert S. Abbott* (Chicago, 1955); Suggs, *P. B. Young.*

51. *RP*, May 3, 1924, Jan. 15, Feb. 5, Dec. 31, 1927.

52. *RP*, Oct. 8, 1927, April 23, 1921; *Crisis,* Aug. 1921, 166.

53. Interview, Tessie Davidson, June 5, 1994; conversations with various members of the Mitchell family, Richmond, June 6, 1996.

54. Report of William E. Crawford, Commissioner in Chancery, Feb. 27, 1928, in Com-monwealth v. Mechanics Savings Bank, 1944.

55. Leroy Brown was the white realtor handling the property, and his father had repre-sented Mitchell for years in real estate dealings. Brown had to defend himself against charges that he was protecting an old client. See depositions, ibid.

56. Deposition of John Mitchell Jr., Dec. 3, 1928, ibid.

57. Petition of John Mitchell Jr. for an injunction, May 5, 1928, in Commonwealth v. Mechanics Savings Bank, 1944.

58. *RP*, Nov. 6, 1923; will of John Mitchell Jr., Dec. 1, 1929, Will Book 27:305, Chancery Court, RCH.

59. *RP*, Dec. 7, 1929; *New York Age,* Dec. 7, 1929; *Pittsburgh Courier,* Dec. 7, 1929.

EPILOGUE

1. *RP*, June 9, 1915.

2. A few recent examples include: Earl Lewis, *In Their Own Interests: Race, Class, and Power in Twentieth-Century Norfolk, Virginia* (Berkeley, Calif., 1991); Robin D. G. Kelly, *Race Rebels: Culture, Politics, and the Black Working Class* (New York, 1994); Elsa Barkley Brown, "Negotiating and Transforming the Public Sphere: African American Political Life in the Transition from Slavery to Freedom," *Public Culture* 7 (Fall 1994): 107–46; Dailey, Gilmore, Simon, *Jumpin' Jim Crow.*

3. Walker, "An Address to the 34th Annual Session of the Right Worthy Grand Council of Virginia, Independent Order of St. Luke, Aug. 20, 1901, Richmond, Virginia," MWHS.

4. Gilmore, *Gender and Jim Crow,* 149.

5. Emmett J. Scott, *Negro Migration during the War* (1920; rept. New York, 1969), 30.

6. *Richmond Afro-American,* Feb. 10, 1996.

7. Ben Cleary, "Toppled Stones & Fallen Angels," *64* 1 (Oct. 2000): 52–56. The website address is: <www.lva.lib.va.us/pubserv/vnp/planet/ajax.htm.>

8. *RP*, May 31, 1890.

9. *RP*, Feb. 14, 1891.

Index